The International Library of Sociology

SAMPLES FROM ENGLISH CULTURES

PART ONE

Founded by KARL MANNHEIM

The International Library of Sociology

THE SOCIOLOGY OF CULTURE
In 9 Volumes

SAMPLES FROM ENGLISH CULTURES

Part One
THREE PRELIMINARY STUDIES
ASPECTS OF ADULT LIFE IN ENGLAND

by

JOSEPHINE KLEIN

ROUTLEDGE
Taylor & Francis Group

This edition first published in 1965 by
Routledge

Reprinted 1998, 2000, 2002
by Routledge
2 Park Square, Milton Park, Abingdon, Oxon, OX14 4RN
or
270 Madison Avenue, New York, NY 10016

First issued in paperback 2010

Routledge is an imprint of the Taylor & Francis Group

British Library Cataloguing in Publication Data
A CIP catalogue record for this book
is available from the British Library

Samples From English Cultures: Part One
ISBN 978-0-415-17595-1 (hbk)
ISBN 978-0-415-60565-6 (pbk)
The Sociology of Culture: 9 Volumes
ISBN 978-0-415-17824-2
The International Library of Sociology: 274 Volumes
ISBN 978-0-415-17838-9

Publisher's Note
The publisher has gone to great lengths to ensure the quality of this reprint
but points out that some imperfections in the original may be apparent

CONTENTS

Contents

Contents

Section Three (in Volume Two)
CHILD-REARING PRACTICES

                    And so each venture
Is a new beginning, a raid on the inarticulate
With shabby equipment always deteriorating
In the general mess of imprecision . . .
                    And what there is to conquer
By strength or submission, has already been discovered
Once or twice, or several times, by men whom one cannot hope
To emulate—but there is no competition—
There is only the fight to recover what has been lost
And found and lost again and again: and now, under conditions
That seem unpropitious. But perhaps neither gain nor loss.
For us, there is only the trying. The rest is not our business.

                                        EAST COKER

INTRODUCTION

I T was my purpose, when I started to write this book, to compare and contrast current patterns of living in England, in such a way that similarities and differences might offer themselves for further investigation or for incorporation into theory. At the time, it seemed to me that English urban sociology and social psychology were becoming increasingly handicapped by the lack of attention given to differences between different geographical regions and different social classes. This lack is now being supplied by a number of social scientists, and the present work is intended to further the same purpose.

In practice, I found it difficult to strike a correct balance between fact and theory, and difficult also to select, from the heap of unorganized data, those facts which would be most representative of the ways of life under consideration. In the early stages of the writing, I had the title *Patterns of English Culture* in mind, to point the resemblance of this book, in aspiration at least, to Ruth Benedict's classic *Patterns of Culture*. It soon became clear, however, that this was altogether too ambitious a project. The sub-cultures with which I was concerned shared too many culture traits and were not static enough to merit the title *Pattern* in the sense in which Benedict used the word. Moreover, in any single one of the sub-cultures under consideration, too many of the data were missing which would be needed to display a pattern convincingly, or perhaps I was too close to them to be able to perceive it.

Thus it was that I came to the present title, which stands for a work less ambitious in scope. I have taken a sample here and there from the total array of culture traits displayed by present-day English society. The *Shorter Oxford English Dictionary* defines a sample as *a relatively small quantity of material or an individual object from which the quality of the mass, group, species, etc., which it represents may be inferred.* This has been my intention exactly.

The dictionary supplied a second definition which confirmed my belief that *Samples* was the appropriate title for my work, and for the procedure I had adopted in accomplishing it. Facts must be organized by theories. This was possible for some of the facts available; more often, however, my conclusions could attain the status of theory no more than that of culture pattern, and conversely, some of the conclusions I reached or cited were not definitively proven by the facts. Fortunately, the dictionary tells us that since 1529 it has been correct usage to employ the word 'sample' in the sense of *a fact, incident, story or suppositious case which serves to illustrate, confirm or render credible some proposition or statement.* This also corresponds exactly to my intention.

The preceding apologia, propitiatory as it is, may raise in the minds of some a doubt as to whether the work was worth doing. I have no such doubt. The conscientious juxtaposition of hitherto unrelated phenomena deepens the intuitive insight into the motivation of behaviour and into the structure of present-day English culture. And there were some sets of phenomena which permitted the application of available theories, and sometimes the construction of new ones, even at a level where social policy could be affected. Indeed, the coveted status of predictability came at times in sight. Though much is yet only at the level of plausibility, the facts are beginning to fall into place in an orderly fashion.

The theoretical background is uncomplicated. I have taken for granted the basic postulates of comparative sociology and cultural anthropology. These are, very briefly, as follows. All social groups face some very similar problems of survival. For a way of life to survive over several generations, the attitudes acquired in childhood must be confirmed, or at least not contradicted, by the experiences of adult life. The experiences of adult life are affected on the one hand by the behaviour of other people (both directly in personal interaction and more remotely by the aggregate consequences of such interactions—variously called social forces, institutions, etc.). On the other hand they are affected by the personality of the adult who is living through the experience. His personality, in terms of which he now experiences his world, has itself been formed by what happened to him in the past, and so on, regressively, back to childhood, infancy and the womb. Experiences in early life have to be regarded as especially significant because they impinge on a more fluid, less rigidly formed personality structure. To round off the circle of argument, the personalities of most adults will, by virtue of their parental role, provide a part—at first an overwhelmingly important part—of the experiences of the next generation.

In describing a way of life, therefore, one must take into account the locally normal experiences of most children, the kind of people with whom most adults are likely to interact in their normal social life, and the economic and social forces which the adult experiences as impersonal, over which he has no control, with which he nevertheless has to come to terms.

In practice, it has been possible to follow such a tidy outline for description only in the first three chapters. The people there described are comparatively isolated from the social life around them. In the first case, this isolation is enforced by the attitudes of those outside the community, who regard the people living in the area with contempt. In the second case, the isolation is rather more self-imposed: these are people who regard outsiders with some mistrust and who try to avoid the contagion of attitudes they consider inferior. In the third case, the isolation is that of a mining-town set in a more rural environment. These three samples constitute the first section of Volume One.

The second section brought a more complex problem of presentation, all the more vexing because the difficulty lay both in the insufficiency of data about any particular geographical area, and in the minuteness of the details in which the areas nevertheless differed from one another. Information given about one area might not be given about another; was this because the two areas differed or because the two authors differed? I therefore organized the available material in a less localized form, three chapters dealing respectively with traditional working-class life, with changes in that way of life, and with the middle classes.

Introduction

This second section in the first volume deals mainly with adult life. Section three, published in a second volume, deals with the same adults considered in their parental role, and with the reaction of children to parental behaviour of one kind or another. This section is not divided into chapters but into a series of briefer sub-sections. The difficulties encountered in writing on these topics are discussed in the introduction to that volume.

Soon after I began the formal writing of this study, another awkwardness arose. Since I was using evidence which I had not myself collected, and the significance of which often depended both on the minutiae of the behaviour described and on the style in which the description was cast, I found myself hesitant to alter the wording of the original accounts. In any case, what would be the point? To rewrite the evidence in my own words would not avert the charge of plagiarism. My only originality lay in putting side by side some ideas and descriptions which had not yet been so juxtaposed. I saw my function to be that of compiling and commenting on the available facts from the vantage-point of one who had surveyed much of the field, and was therefore able to compare and contrast more easily than those who had done the basic work. My debt to those who provided me with my material cannot be repaid, but it is gladly acknowledged.

My procedure in the first three chapters, where only one or two sources were tapped, was therefore to write what required to be written. without distinguishing between my own notions and those of the major original investigators, to whom formal reference is made at the beginning of each chapter. In the later chapters an effort was made to keep the cited passages intact, and their attribution clear; even so, much that is not printed in quotation marks is derived from the insight of others. The work was thereupon submitted to those from whom I had gleaned my facts, for approval and, where my notions had been mistakenly based, for correction. I am grateful for the help and consideration I obtained in this way from my collaborators.

SECTION ONE
Three Preliminary Studies

Chapter One

'BRANCH STREET' 1944-49

THE first group of people to be discussed lived in a London district Marie Paneth called *'Branch Street'*. In the discussion which follows, her book of that name is one of the two main sources of information, the other being Spinley's very important account of the 'deprived' in her book *The Deprived and the Privileged*, which is about the same London district. Although changes have come about since these writers were there, there are similar areas in many large towns. Therefore, though the evidence for this chapter is drawn from one place at one particular time, the pattern there made manifest may be observable elsewhere at the present time.[1]

Branch Street is a 'residual area'. All those who can get away from it have left. That includes not only those capable of achieving respectability under their own steam, but also those who, in the opinion of housing authorities, are capable of doing better in more favourable circumstances.

Branch Street is also a 'transitional area'. Immigrants into the city come here, but they do not stay if they have any chance of going somewhere better. A large proportion of the inhabitants are Irish; Spinley quotes a social worker saying: 'The Irish

[1] The district is Paddington. In view of the accusations which have been levelled against coloured immigrants in recent years, it cannot be stressed too much that the conditions described in this chapter were conditions which existed before there was any coloured immigration. Branch Street is the by-product of a white society. The drifters were English drifters, unpalatable though this fact may be. Spinley writes, moreover, in a private communication, that the numbers of Irish in the district was much lower in her opinion than was believed by the social workers there.

land here and, while the respectable soon move away, the ignorant and the shiftless stay.'[1]

The district is notorious for vice and delinquency. A large number of prostitutes drift into Branch Street towards the end of their career. The Probation Service consider it the blackest spot in the city for juvenile delinquency. Typically the people who live here belong to a group whose education finishes earliest, whose illegitimacy rate is highest, where those who commit crimes of theft and violence are most to be found. School truancy-rates are very high, and so are absences from school for reasons of health. These are the people with the highest rate of rejection from the armed services on the grounds of health or illiteracy.

The district has also the highest incidence of the poverty diseases: tuberculosis, venereal diseases, bronchial infections, skin infections, bad teeth. Paneth noted that only three children out of 400 were in the top grade of nutritional standard when tested by the Medical Officer of Health. The borough had at that time the densest population of all the metropolitan boroughs: nearly 100 people per acre.

The men are in unskilled, ill-paid, casual employment. They are often out of work: they obtained little satisfaction from their work; they express no interest in it. Few Branch Street boys start apprenticeship training, and few of these persist in it.

Social workers of all kinds are in and out of such houses continually. The home is usually hopelessly overcrowded. Seldom, if ever, is a house occupied by one family only. Families have either two rooms or only one; occasionally a family will have two rooms and a kitchen, but this is rare. The rooms are poorly furnished, with probably two beds, one for the parents and youngest child, the other for the older children; if the family can afford another bed the children will be segregated by sex, but this does not always happen. The beds have the usual bedding and stained mattresses, probably smelling of stale urine. Apart from the beds there is a table, some wooden chairs, a cupboard and possibly another piece of furniture and a wire-

---

[1] Much of what follows is taken more or less *verbatim* from Spinley or Paneth. Quotations from other sources are always explicitly noted.

less. More recently, a television set. In one corner of the room is a stove and a washbasin, but all water has to be carried from the one tap in the building, which is half-way up the stairs. Some families, but not all, will have a small tub in the room, for there are no bathrooms in the buildings. Sometimes there is no indoors lavatory. If there is, there is only one for all who live in the house. Because of this, and because the plumbing is often out of order, a family may keep a bucket in the room.[1] On the walls and ceilings are large damp ugly marks, the paper or distemper is possibly peeling, and the floor is bare but for a small mat. Clothes are drying over the back of a chair, or from a line stretched across the room. The most noticeable characteristic is the strong and unpleasant smell, indeed on a first visit the middle-class stomach may find it impossible to stay longer than five minutes. These strong odours are partly due to the fact that the windows are not opened and so no current of air can carry away the smells of cooking, lavatory buckets, mattress wet in the night, and baby's vomit only hurriedly wiped up. Also, even when the housewife is extremely conscientious, the houses are so old and damp that they have a smell of their own which it is impossible to combat.

No wonder that contempt and disapproval from neighbouring groups is a permanent part of the social and psychological environment of Branch Street. Such feelings are perhaps a general characteristic of the British character throughout the social range, but here is a group with no one lower to despise. This disapproval is an experience each child meets at least once, upon going to school. He is told he is untidy, that he does not wash a large enough area of his skin often enough. He is told to be polite in speech. He is perhaps told that he is no good and never will be any good. He may hear his teacher talking to visitors about his 'awful' background and the difficulty of making anything of him, and he is almost certainly regarded as a potential delinquent. This is likely to be a realistic assessment, but there must be a number of marginal cases in which prejudgements of this kind are bound to have an additionally deleterious effect. The prejudice is often surprisingly obvious. Spinley relates an anecdote of a boy who wanted to go into the

[1] In Paneth's time there was neither tub nor lavatory, only an outhouse.

Air Force rather than the Army for his term of military training. He was given an intelligence test in which he did very well. Thereupon he was asked from whom he had cheated and told he must have copied someone else's answers. The test was discounted. In the same way an Employment Officer might say that any vocation was open to these young people, but Spinley noticed that he ended with the sentence: 'Of course it would be no use letting one of these girls take up such and such a job, since she would not be happy out of her class.'

The general atmosphere of contempt may help to explain the lack of ease felt by the Branch Streeter when away from home. Within the area there is at least the protection of being unnoticeable in a crowd of similar people. Here again it is the marginal person who is most affected: tempted to move away in the hope of making a better life for himself, he is discouraged when he thinks of the attitudes he will have to contend with.

On the whole, however, the Branch Street inhabitant is not tempted to move, because of the demands which would be made by the higher standards elsewhere. Instead, he is likely to reciprocate the hostility and mistrust he experiences in his dealings with outsiders and with those in authority. Almost the only benefits willingly received at the time of Spinley's study were the orange-juice and other amenities provided by the Welfare Clinics which the mothers attend during pregnancy. The strict boundaries which isolate Branch Street from the influence of other communities are thus maintained not only by the members of the other communities, but also by those who live in the area.

We turn now to the main question: how does the personality develop which survives these conditions and perpetuates this social pattern? The answer is to be found in certain peculiarities of the life-cycle made possible by the isolation just referred to. We shall break into this cycle by looking at the new life from the moment of conception.

INFANTS AND TODDLERS

The average first child will have been born when both father and mother are round about twenty. The child is not likely to

6

have been planned. He is as likely to be born out of wedlock as into it. More precisely, the mother may be unmarried without a man around the house, or she may be living with a man but not married to him, or she may be married but have conceived the child in a union with another man. Illegitimacy does not cause overmuch adverse comment in this area.

At first, the child sleeps with his mother, so that for much of the time the mother is readily available to give the warmth and contact he needs. At first, too, the child is breast-fed, and fed almost whenever he cries, so that in these very early days there is little frustration of his needs. Because he tends to be fed whether he cries from hunger or for other reasons, food comes to have attached to it a general feeling of comfort and consolation which it retains in later life. But since the mother does not always feel like feeding him when he cries, satisfaction does not come to the child at regular intervals, or on predictable occasions. Thus there is some restriction on the infant's satisfactions, but it is not a systematic restriction. If the child were fed at regular scheduled times, though he might find the rhythm imposed on him very uncongenial, he would certainly learn that satisfaction does eventually come, regularly, reliably. This would be the beginning of his training in time-perspective; the fact that the Branch Street baby lacks this training will have effects which are considered later in this chapter.

There seems to be no particular age at which most Branch Street mothers change from breast-feeding to bottle-feeding. Weaning involves the breaking or weakening of one of the ties which keep the child dependent on the mother. Though little is known for certain about this aspect of child-care, the psychological significance of such breaks seems to depend as much on the way they are brought about as on the age at which they are experienced. One such break occurs when the child is put on the bottle. This is not as sharp a break in Branch Street as it is in some environments, for breast-feeding is not normally considered an opportunity for the expression of tenderness in Branch Street. Nevertheless, it does provide some occasion for contact between mother and child, and this ceases when bottle-feeding starts. The baby is tucked up in his pram and the bottle propped into his mouth by an ingenious arrangement

7

of pillow and blanket. He is still apt to be fed whenever he cries. Food thus retains its consoling significance, but contact with the mother is removed from the general context of this gratifying experience.

The consoling significance of a full mouth is also seen in the importance of the 'pacifier' or dummy. Every Branch Street baby has one, and can keep it as long as he wishes. Younger children at school may still rely on one. Bottle or dummy, it is noteworthy that the satisfaction gained this way is, as it were, self-supplied and does not come to the child in an inter-personal or social context.

The baby is kept in the pram or cot as long as he submits quietly to such restriction. At this happy age, protest is sufficient for him to gain his freedom. Once he is out of the pram, he is allowed to go anywhere without prohibition on touching things or spoiling or soiling things. Here, as elsewhere, no systematic restrictions are imposed on his behaviour.

The absence of restriction is also noteworthy in connection with toilet-training. Briefly, there is none. Throughout childhood there is little concern with bowel-functions; the mother does not check on the regularity with which he evacuates, and no consistent attempt is made to train him to use a pot. He is wet both in the day and at night until quite late. Throughout childhood and adolescence, indeed, he has little control over his sphincters. This forms part of a characteristic and general pattern, in which the absence of restriction and the absence of training in regularity and foresight are important components.

Before turning to consider the effects of various degrees and kinds of mother love, a point may be made that really needs to be repeated before and after every paragraph in this book. Not all babies even in an isolated community go through exactly the same experiences at the hands of their parents, and in so far as parental treatment affects the child's adult personality, this means that there are going to be deep-lying differences among the adult personalities of the second generation. In addition, it seems sensible to assume, though as yet our anthropological techniques and our information on any particular community are inadequate to prove the point, that a child is affected by the behaviour of others of his age, which he is likely to imitate even though the emotional significance of such behaviour may be different for him because of his parents' effect on his developing personality. Neighbouring children will take over from one another patterns of behaviour more explicable in terms of the others' parents' personality than in terms of their own. At a gross level of analysis this increases the apparent homogeneity of behaviour-patterns in an isolated community. On the other hand, at a more detailed level, it bedevils the social psychologist engaged in relating parental treatment to personality in the second generation.

These considerations are relevant when we analyse the children's early experience of affection, for it is possible to identify among the adolescents and adults at least three well-established types of behaviour pattern: those normally attributed to an affectionless early childhood, and those attributed to a childhood in which affection was rather suddenly and permanently withheld. There is also a third variant in which affection is given, but not in a sustained way, being given unexpectedly or when not especially wanted, and withheld at times when the need for affection is strongly felt.

There are infants whose mother 'does not bother with them'. She never cuddles them, she feeds them when the whim takes her, sends them off to her sister, her mother, a neighbour or institution to be looked after, fetches them back, changes her mind about them ten times a year and generally provides a completely unstable background. These children are likely to grow up incapable of giving or receiving affection. But at least as often, the babe-in-arms in Branch Street seems to have a lovely time. The characteristic lack of restriction on the child's instinctual satisfaction is in these early days accompanied by plenty of affection (except in so far as the mother's casual ways have produced their own kind of frustration). At best, he will be petted and cuddled by the mother when she thinks of it and has time to spare, and so he learns to need affection and to enjoy it. At the same time, or alternatively (and later effects will presumably differ accordingly), brothers and sisters and neighbours and relatives play with the baby, encouraging him to smile, to stand, to walk. So, generally speaking, this period of life provides much pleasant experience. Though the attention

9

may be inconsistent and is likely to begin and end abruptly, the child does have a true taste of emotional warmth. This may make all the more painful the break with the mother when the next baby is born or she goes out to work.

There is a third variant of experience at this stage of life, which has not been discussed with reference to Western personality, which may well be relevant to Branch Street. For even at this stage, because of the personality of the adults who are loving the child, pleasure and pain may mingle in a way which has ill consequences later. Branch Street adults act on short-lived impulses; they lack persistence. They cannot concentrate. They are easily distracted and hence their behaviour changes direction rather abruptly. The effect of this on the child is such as will perpetuate inattentiveness and easy distractability over the generations. Such shallowness of emotion and motivation was noted and described by Bateson and Mead on Bali in 1942. The adult sees the child, plays with him for a while, then loses interest and stops. The adult stops when he loses interest, not when the baby does. Hence the child is stimulated and then abruptly ignored, many times a day. This is therefore a different kind of 'rejection experience' from the once-for-all-time kind noted by Spinley, Robb and others, upon the birth of the next baby. Bateson and Mead recount an extreme form of this 'broken-sequence' pattern and some of its consequences:

> The Balinese baby is subjected to a peculiarity of the mother–child relationship which is apparent when the child is only five or six months old and which becomes steadily more definite as the child grows older. This is a series of broken sequences, of unreached climaxes. The mother continually stimulates the child to show emotion—love or desire, jealousy or anger—only to turn away, to break the thread, as the child, in rising passion, makes a demand for some emotional response on her part. When the baby fails to nurse, the mother tickles his lips with her nipple, only to look away uninterested, no slightest nerve attending, as soon as the baby's lips close firmly and he begins to suck. She sets the baby in his bath and teasingly thrusts her fingers between his lips, only to look away, dissociated, as the baby bites delightedly at her hand. She hands the baby to another woman, and then threatens to leave him, 'I'm off home! You I will leave', but when

the baby bursts into tears, her attention has already wandered and she takes him without looking at him, as she comments to her sister on the price of beans in the nearest market.

For the first two or three years of their lives, children respond to these stimuli . . . Later, the child begins to withdraw . . . The withdrawal, which marks the end of early childhood for a Balinese, and which comes anywhere between the ages of three and six, is a withdrawal of all responsiveness. The mother borrows a neighbour's baby [to tease her own child] but her child looks on unmoved. He skirts any group in which he thinks there will be someone to stretch out a hand toward him . . .

Most children reach this stage by the time they are three or four, vacillating at times, falling into deep sulks or violent tempers, only to resume again their newly acquired imperviousness. (For girls this change usually coincides with their taking up the role of child nurse, and starting to carry a baby everywhere with them.)[1]

To sum up the Branch Street infant's experience so far, we see that he does not grow in a soil which allows to take root such ideas as that there is a time and place for everything, that good things arrive regularly though one may have to wait or even cry for them, that foresight and effort will please the parent and be rewarded by them. The absence of this kind of learning is to be connected with the absence of striving, the intolerance of frustration, the inability to wait for a gratification, which marks the adult personality.

The happy period of 'King Baby'—for those who experienced it—comes abruptly to an end. When he is a year or so old, another child is born, or the mother goes back to work, and the infant is no longer treated as the baby of the family. The attention which had been centred on him is now withdrawn, often to be transferred to a new baby. For those who have learned to expect affection, however irregularly, displacement by a younger child, or simply the sharing of the mother's attention with other children, is bound to create some resentment. This resentment is not necessarily directed at the new baby, because the child may not be aware of the source of his discomfort, but he is likely to be discontented and upset in a generalized,

[1] G. Bateson and M. Mead (1942), *The Balinese Character*, Special Publication of the New York Academy of Science, II.

undifferentiated way. The consequences of such a feeling would be a heightened irritability, easily aroused tension, regression in terms of accomplishments and an active tendency to seek overt affection from the mother. Because such a child is irritable it is not surprising if he sometimes displays hostility towards inoffensive objects.[1]

There are relatively few only children in the world, and so such feelings, with the easy irritability which is their concomitant, must be pretty general. But the way these feelings are expressed will depend on the general emotional context in which they are experienced at the time, and in which they are later re-activated. They may turn inward and produce an extremely inhibited personality; coupled with firm training they may be found in highly ambitious personalities who direct their abnormally strong drive to socially permissible goals; or, in this underprivileged community, they may confirm a general feeling that the world is not fair and really owes them a living, that they are entitled to get what they can grab as a sort of compensation, but that nothing will really make up to them for their loss—hence the frequent reaction of resentment and despair.

The sudden rejection convinces the child that no good comes of loving or being loved: he feels betrayed and never commits his heart again. (Even so he may be better off than the child who never learned to need affection.) Bennett, in a study of delinquent and neurotic children,[2] is reminded of a behaviour-syndrome which Healy and Bronner called the 'anti-social grudge'.[3] The characteristic anti-social grudge is very like the Branch Street pattern of blaming and accusing others, of resentment, bitterness, long-term grudges, martyr attitudes, and feelings that others are against you. Bennett quotes with approval from an article in which this grudge is considered to be

a reaction at the deepest level to frustrated and unrequited love in the earliest years, accentuated by a vicious environment that

[1] A. L. Baldwin (1955), *Behaviour and Development in Childhood*, Dryden Press, New York, page 199.

[2] I. Bennett (1960), *Delinquent and Neurotic Children*, Tavistock Publications, London.

[3] W. Healy and A. Bronner (1938), *New Light on Delinquency*, Yale University Press, New Haven.

stimulated aggression without providing satisfactory repressive or sublimating influences. The delinquent's bitterness is held to be typically related to early psychic traumata, to early deprivation of love, and to lack of normal emotional security within the family unit. Such an attitude, on which psychopathic egotism and selfishness may be based, cannot be modified by ordinary educational procedures.[1] Such a child lives entirely for himself, using others only for what he can get out of them or for what the world owes him. In contrast to other forms of delinquency, no environment, however considerate, can help him, since no ordinary environment can provide the catering and ministering to his wishes that he craves.[2]

Infancy comes to an end when the Branch Street baby leaves his mother's bed and goes to share the bed of his brothers and sisters. The parents now want him out of the way. He is sent out to play in the street, and at the earliest opportunity, to school. Spinley sums it up: 'From now on he must grow up as best he can.'

CHILDHOOD

The locale of this growing up is likely to be the street, where he finds a lot of other children in the same position. As he grows older, he will join successive playgroups, composed of the children in his street, the boys in his neighbourhood, a gang. He plays with others of roughly his age, while his brothers and sisters play around nearby with those of their own age. He spends considerable time with his brothers and sisters; the bond between them is probably the closest and firmest of the social ties which members of this deprived community experience, even in adult life. According to Spinley, if a boy or a young man is in trouble it is to his sister that he will go first to borrow money, and he will probably receive it.

If tenderness is to be found anywhere in these lives, it is between the children of a family, and this in spite of the burden imposed by the need to look after the younger ones. Paneth

---

[1] Consider, however, the methods used by Bruno Bettelheim (1950), *Love is not Enough*, Free Press, Glencoe, Ill.

[2] J. Karpman (1948), 'Conscience in the psychopath', *Amer. J. Orthopsych.*

draws a touching picture of the loyalty of these children to their young charges. They carry them about, keep an eye on them in the play-centres, see that they go to the lavatory, take them there if necessary. They are proud of them and really kind to them. All the same, Paneth notes, these too early and sometimes very burdensome responsibilities may not have an entirely good effect:

> Bill, nine years old and very good with his little brothers and sisters, came once without them. That time he was excited, wild and rough, and joined in with our toughest ones . . . I can imagine that many of our hooligans of ten and over have been in some ways like young Bill . . . There comes a time when they are relieved of the strain of incessantly looking after little ones. And then they get twice as tough as they would have been if they could have spent their time in child's play instead of being pressed into service as nursery maids.

Neither in the street nor at home has the child much opportunity to be alone and free from casual interference with his activities. There is no adult protection of the child, no supervision of the children as a group. The child grows accustomed to the pointlessness of pursuing any activity with concentration and self-involvement, since at any moment it may be abruptly brought to an end by others. He grows accustomed to being roughly treated and bullied by other children.

Freud and Burlingham describe a psychologically similar situation, as they saw it develop in a war-time residential nursery for (mainly middle-class) children:

> These children do not start to meet a world of contemporaries secure in the feeling that they are firmly attached to one 'mother-person' to whom they can revert. They live in an 'age-group', that is, in a dangerous world peopled by individuals who are as unsocial and as unrestrained as they are themselves . . . In a crowd of other toddlers they have to learn unduly early to defend themselves and their property, to stand up for their own rights and even to consider the rights of others. This means that they have to become social at an age when it is natural to be asocial . . . It is a known fact, though perhaps not sufficiently stressed, that the ability to defend oneself develops later than the ability to attack. The same infants who can be very aggressive when prompted by

their jealous or envious feelings, who bite, hit, and push . . . suddenly stand helpless, cry and run for protection when attacked by others. Often they seem amazed or surprised at the aggressive acts of another child, though they themselves have committed similar acts only a few minutes earlier.[1]

His experience in the street play-group teaches him that running away is the wisest move when he finds himself in difficulties. The lack of adult supervision on the one hand, the as yet untrammeled strength of impulse on the other, makes for a good deal of simple bullying among the children, not necessarily for the sake of the hurt it inflicts but simply because a stronger child may want what a weaker or younger is playing with. The little one learns that he will lose in the end, so he may save himself pain and effort by running away at the first hint of trouble.

One might say that the Branch Street child is conditioned against the more useful civic virtues. First there is the lack of early training in persistence, forethought and effort which many other infants experience in the form of schedule-feeding and firm and regular potting. Then in his play-group he is convinced of his own helplessness. In this sequence of experiences may be detected the roots of the behaviour which Spinley discusses under the general title 'a tendency to leave the field'. When she compares her deprived group with the privileged public-school group, the characteristic which strikes her most forcibly (and which is most irritating for outsiders when they deal with members of this group) is that of escaping any situation when it is considered unpleasant or uninteresting. Looking at a hypothetical Branch Street child from birth to maturity, Spinley sees that he never faces up to circumstances which displease him. He runs from the spasmodic punishment of the home, he truants from school, he leaves his evacuation billet, he lies, changes his work, takes unofficial leave from the army, abandons the girl he has made pregnant, leaves his wife and family. With no standards of 'duty' and no effective

---

[1] D. Burlingham and A. Freud (1943), *Infants without Families*, Allen and Unwin, London. (For a hair-raising fictional account of the child's environment when there are no adults to protect, see 'The Playground' by Ray Bradbury (A. Derleth, ed. (1954), *Portals of Tomorrow*, Cassell & Co.)

concern an individual may be expected not to deal with unpleasant or indifferent situations in a thorough fashion, but,
Spinley continues, there are ways of dealing with these situations
other than running away. One alternative, for instance, is
frontal attack. But this has not been a rewarded technique in the
streets of childhood, and it does not become a regular reaction
later in life. He will fight only when he can obviously win—that
is, he will fight 'dirty' and he will fight only those who are
patently weaker than he. To this we return later in the chapter,
as also to the related fact that he will prefer an authoritarian
leader who can save him from lawless chaos.

In the street play-group the child learns that life is now catch-
as-catch-can, look after number one for if you don't no one
will, any good thing may be taken away by others, you had
best enjoy it while you can. In this way the street confirms, and
gives detail and substance to, such earlier predispositions as
greediness for food and other enjoyments, unwillingness to defer
a present gratification, pessimism of the outcome of concentrated effort. The child has no reason to believe that a promised
good will certainly come about, and consequently he has great
difficulty in postponing an immediate response for the sake of a
later gratification.

Marie Paneth provides several illustrative anecdotes. At one
time, for instance, there was a move on the part of the local
authorities to make a better house available for club purposes. . . .

> Talking about the house became an item of our activities. It
> was astonishing how distrustful the children were. They did not
> believe it would really be for them. And consequently, after the
> first excitement was over and the first questions answered, they
> were reluctant to talk about it. They have come up against so
> many promises which were not kept . . . they were cynical to
> the core. They expected all sorts of snags. Surely only children of
> war-workers would be allowed to use it, they told me. Or, it will
> be a nursery for the small ones only, and we will have to look after
> them.

And again, when one of the very nice young voluntary
workers left, the children asked Mrs. Paneth: 'Will you leave us
too?' and seemed very relieved when she denied it.

16

On a visit to the Zoo, 'they did not stay long in any of the houses. Over and over again they were torn away by the urge to see the next one, and the fear of missing something.' (The easily distracted attention typical of these children is also noticeable here.) They are unable to wait, even for a moment, without severe distress: 'They would fling themselves on us with a rush of enthusiasm when they saw us approaching the shelter, but two minutes later they could use the most insulting language and swear at us, because we asked them to wait a moment before letting them in.'

In as unpredictable and hostile environment as the young child now experiences, it is not a rational procedure to forgo a present satisfaction for the sake of some future good; accordingly, the child does not learn to do so: he learns the opposite. The expedient attitudes are (1) worry, for it (the good) may never happen, and (2) don't worry, for it (the bad) may never happen. Hence neither hope nor fear of consequences can govern present behaviour usefully.

Yet this is the age at which the normal Western child begins to learn, from the direct consequences of his actions and from his parents' reactions, the distinctions between right and wrong, between the praiseworthy, the permitted and the prohibited, and to regulate his impulses accordingly.

Two forms of impulse-control must here be distinguished: super-ego control (the conscience) and ego-control (common sense or reason). There are many theories of the origin and operation of the super-ego but the differences between them are hardly relevant to the present account. All agree that the child comes to want to be like the beloved parent, to 'identify' with him or her, and comes to feel the discomfort we call guilt when he falls short of what he perceives to be parental standards, even when the parent is ignorant of his failure to live up to them.

Identification has been defined as the imitation of the behaviour, values and attitudes of key persons in the environment.[1] Identification with a parent normally provides an incentive for the early training in what will later be the correct

---

[1] J. K. Myers and B. H. Roberts (1959), *Family and Class Dynamics in Mental Illness*, Wiley, New York; Chapman and Hall, London.

performance of adult roles. But in Branch Street this identification may either be lacking because no affection exists to start it off, or it may be an identification with a parent who is reprehensible by normal social standards. In the latter case, in which the child does identify, he may grow up with an anti-social or even criminal super-ego, and find cause for self-approbation in the performance of anti-social or criminal acts. No identification, or very inadequate identification, results when the child cannot take his parent as a model, cannot confide in him or look on him as a friend. Few Branch Street parents encourage the child to relate in this way. Indeed, he is more likely to be involved in the parental warfare and used by each as a weapon against the other, being urged to take sides. In the cramped conditions of the home, the child is a witness to the parents' frequent quarrels. At times they come to blows. There is no companionship: they seldom go out together. At times the child witnesses their sexual intercourse and is frightened by what seems to him an act of uncontrolled aggression.

Many mothers do not hesitate to lie to their children and to mislead them. At the children's hospital it is not uncommon for a child to be greatly shocked because his mother has said he is being taken to the seaside for an outing, when in reality he is put in the children's ward to have his tonsils removed. Children are promised treats to keep them quiet and the treats do not materialize. If their position in the family is irregular they are not told the truth about their parentage. They are lied to in countless little ways.

The man is certainly regarded as the official head of the household. He is in fact seldom at home, and therefore seldom demands obedience from the child. But if, when he does issue orders, these are not immediately obeyed, he is quick to punish. When really angered, a man will beat the children severely. The son's identification with the father is also hindered by the absence of continuity in the father-figure. The men of the household may come and go. A man may refer to the children in the presence of the mother as 'your children' and he may be right—someone else may have fathered them. In any case, the men seem to believe that the time not spent at work is entirely their own; seldom do they take the children off the mother's hands.

It is therefore not surprising that these children do not develop much of a conscience. They feel unloved or betrayed; the adults in their world define no behaviour as right or wrong on general grounds; rather, the rightness and wrongness of behaviour is dependent on its coincidence with a good or a bad temper in the adults. There is little opportunity to idealize any known person, because, with living conditions as they are, they see people in their real form, which may be very sordid. These factors, plus the ability to escape punishment, mean that there is no firm figure of authority to identify with, and hence no strict super-ego.

The second form of impulse-control—ego-control—is realistic and expediential. At this level, if the child is to learn a form of behaviour which does not come natural to him, and to respond with that behaviour whenever stimuli of a certain kind are present, it is normally necessary for the right response to be rewarded whenever it occurs. Similarly, for a child to learn not to behave in a way which does come natural to it, that behaviour must be consistently punished.[1] Such learning sequences can act as mechanisms to control impulses which are considered undesirable in the society: this is the way a puppy learns not to chew slippers. But even this kind of simple learning requires a stability of environment which is lacking in Branch Street, where the learning of only one rule of behaviour is regularly reinforced: steer clear of trouble, give in to stronger force.

On the street, as in the home, there is a constant aggressively tinged excitement. Parents shout at neighbours and at their children. When they can get away with it, the children shout back. Adults cuff or thrash children, who will do the same to those who are weaker than themselves. Through it all the mother is constantly talking at the child, issuing orders and prohibitions, making threats which are not carried out. All this adds to the unreliability of the environment in which the child

---

[1] In the broadest sense of the word, punishment ranging from non-reward when reward is expected, through the tactful presentation of alternative attractions and verbal correction, to a beating. For other discussions of this point, see pages 447 ff. and 623-4.

has to learn habits of behaviour which could be useful to him in later life. Actually, the children seem to ignore their mothers' shouts except on the rare occasions when they are punished. The constant background irritation caused in this way may, however, be connected with the marked 'ego-sensitivity' of this population. The people often express their dislike of a disliked person in terms of his or her being constantly 'on at them', and they sense reproach or prohibition even where it is not intended. To this we shall return when school days are discussed. The inconsistent treatment confirms the child's general experience of life: it is no good looking ahead and taking consequences into account, anything you do is bound to be interfered with.

In spite of the constant nagging, the mother mostly has considerable difficulty in obtaining obedience. She is not likely to have rested adequately after her children are born. Her life is one continuous incompetent battle to cope with the demands made on her—she may have given up the struggle. Constantly tired and a little under the weather, she tends to be irritable and short-sighted in her treatment of the children. Much depends on how she feels, on the mood of the moment. Like the children, to whom she is teaching the same behaviour-pattern, she is impulsive, inconsistent and lacking in persistence. What the child does may at one time be smiled at indulgently or even proudly, and at another time be greeted with a shout and a blow.

The Branch Street parent does not systematically control the childish impulses which English parents normally modify. The many forms in which rage, anger, aggression may be expressed are not checked in Branch Street. On the contrary, the parents themselves act at any moment as they happen to feel. Nothing is controlled; neither food, nor sleep, nor cleanliness, nor sexual play, nor aggression. The children are not rebuked for petty thieving. Sometimes they steal for use, sometimes they simply destroy the stolen object. They are not deterred by the fear of parental displeasure. In this kind of living there is little room for experiences which encourage the use of common sense or reason to channel the impulses.

It is in a way unfortunate that this violent, unpredictable, unprotective home is in some respects indulgent to the immediate needs of the child. Such indulgence shows in a number of ways: the anger of the mother when another adult punishes her child, the expensive toys which the child is given and which are destroyed or stolen within the month, and perhaps most of all in the matter of food. The children are given something to eat whenever they feel like it. The day passes in a sort of endless meal. The dinner at school, though it is reported to be dietetically well-balanced, is both too large and too unfamiliar to be attractive to the child. The child is very fussy about food eaten away from home. Food is one of the few more or less satisfactory emotional experiences of his life, and to reject food outside the home may be a way of saying to the outsider: 'I do not want what you have to give me.' Frequently he piles large quantities on his plate, but he wastes it, not eating, taking a couple of bites off cakes which he then leaves, going for the most attractive whilst keeping an eye on what is left, generally destructive and distractible in the familiar pattern.

This kind of do-as-you-like indulgence (as well as the contempt of outsiders to which reference has already been made) gives the home a connotation of refuge, of safety from the demands of the outside world. Like any other child, the Branch Street child is homesick when he is away, and very pleased when he does not have to go to school.[1] But in this particular case the home is a refuge from demands which, if they are inescapable and must be met, shape the personality to be well-adjusted to modern civilized standards of living.

He need not learn to exercise self-control at home, for self-control is realistic—the anticipation of consequences shapes the present course of behaviour—and at home it is impossible to predict. He need not learn self-control elsewhere, because if it requires the inconvenient inhibition of a present impulse, he can always escape the situation by going off home where such demands are not made. The Rorschach test administered by Spinley, in which the subject looks at standard patterns apparently made by ink-blots and says what he can see in them, shows the same kind of reaction in a different context. If the young Branch Street subjects find a situation disturbing or unpleasant,

[1] Perhaps more homesick than most, writes Spinley in a private communication, just as any children not sure of their place at home are abnormally tied to home emotionally.

Spinley notes, they give the easy, obvious response if there is one, or they quickly reject the whole situation. (It is interesting to note that these records contain many of the original Rorschach signs of depression—the children are easily discouraged and do not believe that what they can do will amount to much.) The shallowness of emotional response is also noticeable here. They are not intrigued or challenged to do well by the puzzle. If it seems difficult they can't be bothered and give up.

The peculiarities of development just outlined affect the later emotional life of the Branch Street personality also in indirect ways, by their effect on his attitude to school and on the way he thinks at what appears at first sight an intellectual level. The Branch Street personality is intellectually handicapped because it is emotionally handicapped, and emotionally handicapped because of peculiarities in intellectual development. Before this is discussed with direct reference to Spinley and Paneth, Kate Friedlander's psycho-analytic approach to the study of the anti-social character provides a theoretical structure which will serve as a bridge to the next section.

There are, in the study of culture and personality, two mutually stimulating and correcting approaches. On the one hand, one may, as in the present volume, relate the typical experiences of childhood in a particular geographical and social region to the personality-type most often encountered in that region. On the other hand, one may, like Friedlander, consider the same set of childhood-experiences in a variety of social contexts, and relate them to the adult personality which most frequently results. Friedlander's boy-patients Billy and Peter came from social classes very different from Branch Street, but Billy was subjected to many similar experiences and showed many comparable reactions. Friedlander's theory seems mainly concerned with the super-ego—the moral regulator—but in her account of the boy's problems, the results of inadequate ego-development—to do with a realistic, expediential assessment of a situation—are also seen to be very like those of Branch Street.

Her starting point is that 'where identification with the parent has not led to the internalization of their demands, the relationship to persons in authority does not lead to identification with them'. To us this means that because the Branch

Streeter has not experienced those in authority as protective and rewarding, he has no wish to please them; because he has no wish to please them, their demands have no attraction for him and he does not feel that compliance to their demands is necessary for his own self-respect: he has not internalized them. Because compliance is not necessary to him, he feels no guilt when he has done wrong. He has no super-ego.

In Billy's case, ego-development was influenced by the mother's inability to be consistent in the ways in which she gratified or frustrated the child's instinctual urges during the first year of life. Under such conditions there is no need for a child's learning to wait for gratification. This is the necessary requisite for satisfactory development from the pleasure-principle to the reality-principle. During the latency period [more or less from the beginning of schooldays till the onset of puberty] the usual methods of education proceed on the assumption that the child *wishes* to conform—in contrast to the early years when the child's instinctual urges are opposed to the demands of the environment. In the latency period it is the educator's task to strengthen the child's super-ego formation and to help it to become successful in its fight against the instincts; the child is usually eager to get this help which will prevent him from feeling guilty. Not so with Billy. *For him, being good simply meant giving in.* He wanted what he wanted, and felt no compunction when he got it. In his case, punishment did not lead to a strengthening of the super-ego, but was felt either as instinctual gratification or as a frustration permitting the expression of further hostility against the person administering it.

Peter [a boy with a different problem] consciously wanted to learn. Though concentration on school subjects was unpleasant for him, he felt he ought to try. Billy, who felt the same displeasure when confronted with a difficulty, tried his utmost to avoid any repetition of such a disagreeable experience. [Comment on the general tendency of the Branch Streeter to withdraw from the field has been made earlier in this chapter.] He was extremely pleased when he succeeded in reading a word and was praised for it. But he was unduly displeased when confronted with a word he could not recognize: he shut the book and gave up. Whereas most children are able to bear the tension of learning provided that satisfaction follows achievement, Billy could not bear any tension whatever, nor did the prospect of future gratification attract him. One day, toward the end of his analysis, Billy said, 'I should not have been late yesterday, then I would have been allowed to go out today. Now I cannot go out today and that is worse than if I had been on time yesterday.' This was the first time that the boy was able to judge his actions not only from the stand-point of immediate pleasure, but also from the stand-point of future results. Such consideration are usually present in children very much younger than Billy and certainly by the age of nine the behaviour of normal children has already come under the control of the reality-principle.[1]

SCHOOLDAYS

Because of experiences at home, the children of Branch Street at first see the demands imposed on them by the school, or by any other authority, as meaningless. They are ignored, just as the demands made by the mother were ignored, and then fiercely resented when it becomes evident that the authorities mean their demands to be met.

The discrepancy between the behaviour expected by these 'outsider' authorities and the behaviour in which the children have been trained would be comic if the personalities were not so needlessly stunted and the social consequences so often dangerous. Put on their honour, or asked to give their word at school, they give it casually with no intention of keeping it; often they do not seem to know what 'giving your word' means. No wonder the young teacher is shocked, the old one cynical. But their opportunity to learn these forms of behaviour and to find them rewarding has been abnormally restricted. Neither the mother's fibs to keep them quiet, nor the jungle-experience of the street play-group at an age when ideas of fairness and consideration would be too difficult to grasp or pursue, are conducive to such learning.

Or consider team-games. The children are taught to play team-games at school. But they have learnt no 'team spirit'. Watching a team of these young people Spinley notices that although many of the players are more than competent, the team does not do its best, because each player wants to hold the

[1] K. Friedlander (1945), 'Formation of the anti-social character', *The Psychoanalytical Study of the Child*, Vol. I.

attention of the spectators, wants to make the brilliant run, the winning goal. Few players are content to defend, support and pass on the opportunity to those in a better position.

Some reasons for this will readily present themselves, but less obvious points of a non-emotional, cognitive nature deserve to to be stated in full. Firstly, to play a team game requires that the player keep in mind at least eleven variables (the members of his own side) and preferably the whole twenty-two. The inability to conceptualize so complex a social situation may therefore be as relevant as the oft-noted ego-centrism of the individual player.

Secondly, team-games are played according to set rules. Now these children have not encountered many general rules in their lives. The idea of rules governing a game may well be at a level of abstraction of which they have no experience. Not only have they not been taught any general rules by their parents in the sense of being told to be in at eight o'clock and being punished if they were not. The lack of training goes deeper than this. The unpredictability of the social environment makes it difficult for the intelligent Branch Street child to grasp the very concept 'general rule' at the same age as his socially more fortunate equals, simply because the social world of Branch Street presents fewer examples of conformity to such rules.[1]

Baldwin has argued that self-control is linked with the ability to foresee the consequences and the more remote abstract implications of an action.[2] The young child is more or less completely at the mercy of present sensory stimulation and reacts to stimuli without reference to time or logical implication. With maturity comes the ability to look ahead (regulating behaviour by reference to consequences) and the ability to look back (drawing on generalized past experience to analyse what is happening now). Intellectual as well as emotional training is needed for self-control.

The mood-swings and the senseless violence so characteristic of Branch Street, though they have other roots as well, may also be related to this difficulty in seeing past or future in relation to the present. The relation of self-control to time-perspective is brought out in several of Paneth's observations. She remarks,

---

[1] See also the discussion on pages 497-8.   [2] A. L. Baldwin, op. cit.

for instance, that these children, who today would steal and lie about everything under the sun, would tomorrow bring back the things which they had stolen, and because they happened to be in a different mood, would be most helpful though on a previous evening they had destroyed everything within their reach. On one occasion, after a dress-making session, she allowed them to take the left-over materials away. They came and grabbed like wild animals, while she incessantly explained that she meant them to have it all. Having ransacked the lot, they did not know what to do with it. Wastefully, ostentatiously, they destroyed it. Paneth tried explaining to the children in the play-centre that everything used there belonged to them. If they broke things or destroyed them, they spoiled their own belongings. If they took them away, their own things disappeared and they could not use them any more. She thought that this seemed to make a certain impression on them, but it did not stop them. There was no logic in their destructive actions, they did it for the sake of destroying and her reasoning bore no fruit.

Paneth found herself in a situation where her reasoning could not bear fruit, because the children's intelligence was not sufficiently trained to allow them to think of themselves now as they might think of themselves tomorrow, or to think of themselves as others might see them. Such impersonal or relativist viewpoints could therefore not affect their behaviour. This disability may have another far-reaching consequence: it weakens the power of public opinion.

Reference has already been made to impulse-control by moral considerations and by considerations of expedience. Public opinion is a third form of control. Morris has suggested that these three are not as separate as they at first appear. He attributes the lack of capacity for guilty self-reproach and the consequent lack of control over behaviour partly to an inability to cope with abstract ideas. Self-control is normally supplemented and strengthened by a fear of what the neighbours will say. Neighbourly condemnation may have been more frequent in Morris' Croydon area than in Branch Street, but Morris notes that ostracism and hostility on the part of neighbours are not effective as social controls when 'there is

scarcely any guilt on which they may operate'. When the neighbours make judgements of behaviour, these are not felt to
be 'evaluations on the basis of normative criteria', but expressions of personal hostility, characteristically to be countered by
hostility. The mother of the Approved School boy does not hang
her head in shame, but ensures that any detractors feel the sharp
end of her tongue. The ability to judge behaviour on the basis
of normative criteria, that is, in terms of general rules to which
all in the community subscribe, presupposes an ability to think
in general terms and to think in terms of abstractions, not
personalities. This type of thinking is unfamiliar and maybe
unattainable in Branch Street. Criticism is intended and interpreted at the personal level, a low level of abstraction. Criticism
is not kept separate from the speaker, who is known to be also
no better than she should be.[1]

Hence criticism or the fear of it does not arouse any of the
internal resonances of guilt. The woman will not say to herself:
'I have let myself (or someone else) down', or 'This reproach is
true of me'. Instead she has an aggressive reaction: 'She is
attacking me.'

Morris also notes that the passivity which is one way of
coping with an unpredictable environment militates against a
feeling of responsibility for one's own actions. His informants
did not seem to feel that they had exercised a choice which
might have been other than it was. Their reaction was: 'I
couldn't help it', or, of a past event: 'I can't help it now', or, at
a deeper level, they seemed to say: 'You're blaming me for
something I never *chose* to do.' 'I never envisaged this would
happen when I did that.' Here again the effects of a faulty time-
perspective are to be noted.

By school age, the absence of general rules of behaviour and
the corresponding unpredictability of life may create a level of
anxiety in the child which will make him relatively stupid in
his reactions, unenterprising, and intellectually incurious. The
level of competence the child reaches at school will not be
high. When a club-leader of Spinley's acquaintance wished to
take play-readings with boys between ten years and eighteen,

---

[1] T. Morris (1957), *The Criminal Area*, Routledge and Kegan Paul, London.
This whole matter is discussed in greater detail on pages 514–16 and 519–20.

she had to abandon the attempt because many of them could not read sufficiently well to follow the simple scripts. Girls seem to be rather better in reading, but are still below the standard met with among middle-class children of the same age. (The sex difference may be explicable in terms of a slightly greater social licence for girls to use their mental capacities.) Letters written by young men of seventeen and eighteen are neither grammatically correct nor orthodox in spelling, and the writing is laboured. There is some evidence that literacy actually declines after the children leave school. If so, concludes Spinley, then it is not the teaching which is at fault only, but also the motivating of the pupils to maintain a standard of literacy which will make it possible for them to understand printed and spoken words and to express their ideas to others.

Both Paneth and Spinley comment on the marked lack of creative imagination and aesthetic appreciation among these children. In painting they had little choice of ideas, they were rigid and thin in the way they expressed them, and far below their age in ability. One favourite theme in Paneth's time was the crinoline lady: no face but a hood, no hands but a muff, no feet because they are hidden by a long skirt. Nearly all the houses they painted were surrounded by huge fences, some of them of frightening size and weight. Very few of them had a sun in the sky. These children drew more pictures of people than the average in other groups, but the expression of the faces, the detail which was represented, made a really frightening impression on Paneth. The drawings she reproduces in her book seem, even to the layman, extraordinarily significant of the children's experience of life.

Spinley arrives at similar conclusions about their imaginative faculties as well as some other interesting findings by means of a Rorschach test. When faced with a new situation the subjects tend to react rapidly (this confirms what was said earlier in this chapter about the lack of intellectual control over the response to stimuli) and they do not alter their original impressions of the situation (that is, they do not reflect upon their experience and absorb it intellectually). The situation is seen as a crude whole with little discrimination of components. The tests indicate that these young people are making an adjustment which is orientated towards the outside world rather than one which rests on a developed acquaintance with their own impulses. They do not have a rich inner life; indeed their imaginative activity is meagre and limited.

The inability to appreciate the nature of rules and the inability to find pleasure in working within self-imposed or socially-imposed constraints may also help to account for the other aspects of these children's lack of sportsmanship. Spinley found the need to win strikingly evident, even in casual amusements like musical chairs. The children were bad losers, and would cheat rather than be fairly beaten.

Spinley sees this trait in terms of a tremendous ego-involvement. It may be argued that such involvement is to be welcomed rather than condemned, as a symptom indicating the possibility of recovery as well as present ill-health. A play-situation with some adult supervision is free from the grosser forms of bullying interference. This makes it more difficult for the bullies to win except either by genuine skill or by undetected guile, and offers those who are normally bullied an exhilarating and unusual opportunity for once to achieve their goal. Either of these situations would increase the ego-involvement of the participants. In addition, however, cognitive aspects must be taken into account. A highly sensitive ego and narcissistic trends may be connected with an intellectual inability to appreciate the reality of other people's feelings as well as with the irritability which comes from continual interference with the child's activities.

Certainly it is true that these children hate to seem foolish and are, comparatively speaking, very sensitive to slights, suspicious of anything that might smack of insult. Spinley's Rorschach tests record that, though the children are predominantly extraverted, they do not show the (expected) spontaneity in reacting to the world and the people in it. Their emotional response is limited and seems accompanied by a fear of external contacts. In general, Spinley is much struck by the Branch Street inability to form close affectionate ties. She relates this inability to the absence of good love-relations in the family, and to the general insecurity of life. These factors do partly account for the suspicion which enters into every relation with another person; the child cannot be expected to meet people with warm, open and ready friendship, for there is nothing in his experience to suggest that other people will be reliably friendly towards him. Instead, he realizes that they are likely to get the better of him by any means possible. So the child does not expect the teacher to be well-intentioned towards him. He does not expect anyone to be.

The foundations for this mistrust were laid in pre-school days. It is now confirmed by school, club or whatever other outside agency may deal with the child, not only because he overhears other people's bad opinion of himself, but also because of a kind of verbal aggression which he particularly fears. The people in authority with whom he comes in contact often engage in sarcasm, being, for one reason or another, prevented from using physical means of discipline. The child, physically violent and used to violence, is unable to retaliate verbally, because his ability to manipulate words is too limited. The powerless feeling of being unable to pay back in the same coin is fiercely resented. It is not difficult to feel that an incomprehensible sentence is being used as an aggressive weapon. Too often it is used as such. After such experiences, even a well-wisher will be resented when he says something that is not understood, the inference being that he is making fun of the other.

It is not exaggerated to argue that the early contacts with the world outside this deprived community can be a traumatic experience. Paneth, as well as many others, notes that the first appearance of an adult in a club tends to be accompanied by a bout of especially bad behaviour, even on the part of those who are not normally violent. The advent of a newcomer arouses in an acute form the hatred and fear which other outsiders have instilled by their contempt and sarcasm. This theory is confirmed by Paneth's observation that children under six do not react in this way. In general they have a more trustful attitude to the adults who deal with them. They have not yet been through the shock of meeting the 'outsider's' attitude at school. 'The younger ones under six also fight, spit, destroy, steal. But they smile at grown-ups, like being touched, come and cling occasionally and are natural (that is, not on the defensive or self-conscious) with strangers.'

The upshot is that the gentler ways of thinking and acting, which require sympathy, imagination, love of harmony (and which are normally taught in the family circle, characteristically by the mother), are first introduced to the Branch Street child by an outsider who is seen as representative of those who believe that 'these children will never be any good'. Schools and clubs and voluntary effort do make an attempt to develop this side of the personality, but the experience of contempt, and the return with interest of the same attitude, must often have the effect of associating such softer, more imaginative traits with the hostility that exists between the two groups, even when a particular outsider does not have this attitude. Softness is an outsider's trait. In this light we may interpret another anecdote of Paneth's, who had taken some girls camping and was teaching them how to dry flowers. The girls went out picking flowers. Eileen soon came back with a few in her hands, laughing and sparkling. 'We know a quicker way of pressing flowers. I'll show you,' she offered. She dropped the flowers on the dirty floor of the hut and then violently and with gusto trampled on them with her heavy boots. 'That's our way,' she said triumphantly.[1]

It has been argued that people of the Branch Street type stand to gain by attributing hostility to well-meaning outsiders. Thus Cohen uses, in his discussion of American delinquent sub-cultures, a theory of Redl's which he calls 'protective coloration'.

> Certain kinds of behaviour, to which we are strongly inclined, may encounter resistances because this behaviour would do injury to the interests or feelings of people we care about. These same kinds of behaviour would, however, be unequivocally motivated, without complicating guilt-feelings, if those people stood to us in the relation of enemies rather than friends. In such a situation we may be unconsciously motivated to act precisely in those ways

[1] In my opinion, a whole set of highly desirable values have been brought into disrepute because those who hold and seek to inculcate them are, rightly or wrongly, associated with the outsider's contempt for the less privileged. It is especially unfortunate that the mass-media give facilities to those who wish to make capital out of this. The particular values under fire at any time can be easily identified by, for instance, listening to radio comedians, or by reading the editorials and 'features' in the popular press. Fairness ('playing the game'), tenderness or aesthetic appreciation in men, intelligence in women, the intellectual or cultural interests of minority groups, seem to be among the more permanent of these targets.

calculated to stimulate others to expressions of anger and hostility, which we may then seize upon as evidences of their essential enmity, and ill-will . . . The hostility of the out-group thus engendered or aggravated may serve to protect the in-group from mixed feelings about its way of life.[1]

Paneth had a very similar intuition after a destructive outburst had followed an increase in privileges.

At the very moment when the children for the first time in our acquaintance seemed ready to do the disagreeable thing for no other reason than that of general contentment with the situation; at that same moment they grasped at the slightest chance of their being their old miserable selves. They knew very well that it had been I who had opened the door for them. They knew very well that my colleague did not like it. But they preferred to make her seem right and me seem wrong. They worked into the hands of forces which opposed their freedom. They were apparently terribly frightened of being free; of behaving well. They were not very far yet on the road to a better land.

ADOLESCENCE, COURTSHIP AND MARRIAGE

So they enter adolescence, and the now established traits ramify further. Because these personalities now inhabit larger bodies, it is at this stage that their aggression and senseless violence come to public notice. What, we may ask in summary, have been the roots of this characteristic? There is the inability to take consequences into account: the inability to perceive where an action, once begun, will lead. Certainly their ideas are rigid and uncomplicated. The lack of creative channels through which energy may be expended must be taken into account, and the present constraint in their circumstances, the lack of opportunities for socially permissible means to self-respect and self-

---

[1] A. K. Cohen (1956), *Delinquent Boys*, Free Press, Glencoe, Ill. When we look at Cohen's delinquent sub-cultures, we see that they are non-utilitarian, malicious and hedonistic. The members destroy or steal for no apparent reason or gratification, 'for the hell of it'. Cohen gives the useful label 'short-run hedonism' to other behaviour we have noted in Branch Street: the lack of interest in long-term goals, in planning activities or budgeting time, or in activities involving knowledge and skill to be acquired only through practice, deliberation and study. The two populations are therefore not dissimilar.

advancement. There must also be some simple re-directed hatred, stemming partly from the sudden childhood rejection and partly from having been bullied so much. Then again, as Spinley sums it up, the child does not in childhood or in adolescence have enough rest or sound sleep. Overcrowding, the constant impinging of other personalities on the child, the impossibility of privacy or relief from being always in an interpersonal situation, the constant noise, lead to a tension which is partly the result of never being able to relax, even in sleep, and partly due to the deliberate raising of psychological defences. In this way, the individual is in a constant state of 'easy irritability' which, with added irritants, may result in outbursts of aggression.

By adolescence the characteristic extreme touchiness and exaggerated sensitivity are also firmly established. Spinley remarks on the length of time for which resentments go on smouldering; grudges are harboured, not forgotten and finally paid off savagely and often meanly.

That is the more dangerous because the youth is a 'dirty fighter'. If he hits and runs away, or hits a smaller child or a girl, no one accuses him of cowardice. He fights to win, just as he plays to win, and neither there nor here will he stick to the rules. Since he receives as well as deals out such punishment, and has from early days been subjected to casual, almost purposeless aggression, he fears pain and physical violence more than is thought acceptable in middle-class circles.

This almost paranoid situation is of course in part created by his early social experience with his play-group, but with the economy that is to be found even in the least attractive social systems, the group or gang will at this later stage afford him the only protection he has against the real or imagined grudges of others. If he comes into the club and his gang is not there, he is ill at ease. If he has to go home through the streets alone by night, he will move quickly and quietly and look round suspiciously. He notices when any member of his gang is missing and will want to know where he is. He cannot do without a gang. He will not leave one gang until he is sure of acceptance in another. Here, also, extreme touchiness pays off for the individual. For it is not to be supposed that life inside a gang is all beer and skittles. He has to defend himself against the aggressive attacks of his fellow-members. Presumably looking foolish is a sign of weakness he cannot afford in the pecking-order characteristic of this kind of association.

Almost certainly he will join a club. Spinley, in her chronological account of the life of those in the area, says succinctly: 'He joins a club', 'He is barred from a club'. The two experiences follow one another as simply as that. Her account of behaviour in the club illustrates how the patterns of childhood are ever repeated.

Illustrating the lack of persistence, the lack of ego-involvement, the poverty of ideas:

> At the club, various classes are held by L.C.C. instructors. It is interesting to consider for a moment the response to these classes. At the beginning of the term, club-members are asked what they would like to do. They offer certain suggestions if prodded, and show enthusiasm for some of the ideas. Classes are therefore arranged. The instructors arrive on specified nights and the members have lost much of their enthusiasm. However, they attend the first meeting . . . The next evening no-one is interested in the activity and the members refuse to attend, or they will take part for a short time, and then drift out again, possibly to drift in again later when bored elsewhere.

Illustrating—from Paneth's experience when camping with some older girls—how the lack of the appropriate skills may combine with the fear of future loss and an emotional attitude to food in general:

> They over-estimated their appetites and made too much of everything. Every slice of bread they cut was too big, every pancake too thick. There was too much tea in the pot. Things were too sweet. In a word, there was plenty of waste . . . They behaved like the poor man in the fairy tale, who became rich in a minute.

Illustrating loss of control, senseless violence:

> Now and then a club will become very noisy. Usually it is the boys who make the noise, rushing up and down the stairs, letting off fireworks, throwing chairs about the room and generally getting out of hand . . . At the times when the young people become very excited, either boys or girls, they are completely

beyond control, not only of the club-authorities but also of themselves; it is almost a state of dissociation, and if the mood is ugly, can be a frightening experience for the observer.

Illustrating practically everything:

> Some boys are caught stealing from the canteen. They are told politely to give the money back and to pay for the cake strewn all over the floor. They object to being spoken to 'like that' and break a chair. They are then suspended from the club for a week or a month and come in surreptitiously and slash the green of the billiard table. When re-admitted to the club they complain that the club does not provide proper facilities and use as evidence the billiard table on which it is impossible to play. Neither they nor the other club members see the ruined table as a result of their own behaviour; it is for them evidence that the club is trying to frustate their desire to enjoy themselves.

They were 'larking about'. Larking about is a definite subcultural pattern of behaviour. Since it is a named and predictable pattern, we may speculate that this may be an institutionalized (i.e. socially recognized and tolerated) means of tension-relief. Until boys go into the forces (Spinley was writing of a time when conscription was still in operation) they are excused any form of behaviour if they claim they do it for a lark. The expression covers any kind of behaviour from pricking someone with a pin to theft and destruction of property. No one need feel guilty or apologetic, after all, it was for a lark. Whatever they do, they can deny or justify or defiantly assert to be only fun. They are quite unable to appreciate the point of view of the person who is being the victim.[1]

Aimlessness and violence characterize also the other experiences of an adolescent's life. When he leaves school he takes the first job which offers, or the one with the highest starting wage. He takes little interest in his work and gets little satisfaction from it. He takes a day off when he feels like it and changes his job for no clearly stated reason at frequent intervals. After he has left school his mother has even less control over him than before. He fears his father only until he can match his strength physically. Because he brings money into the home he has more privileges than before and more time to himself. He is no longer

---

[1] Other aspects are discussed on pages 86-7.

expected to perform any household duties. He is given, with the father, a share in the best and largest portions, and indulged in many other ways.

At work or in the army, his irresponsibility, his inability to control himself and his rebellious reaction against any form of external discipline often get him into trouble. He fears and resents the authority of the police. But this is not a soil in which revolutionaries flourish. On the contrary, Spinley notes a general anxiety when the situation is left too unstructured. He feels that a good leader should be authoritarian, and reacts badly when those in authority allow too much freedom of choice in a context where it is not expected, in a class room or in a club, for example, as Paneth found to her sorrow, in the anecdote cited on page 32. He resents the forces that impinge on him, but he cannot react against them constructively. When asked whether he likes the army, his work, any of the circumstances of his life, the reply will be 'What's the use of not liking it? You got to do it.'

Both boys and girls meet this crisis in adolescence. At this stage, girls are given considerable latitude; they are allowed to keep a large part of their earnings for extravagant dress, for cigarettes, cosmetics, paste jewellery. Indulgence of the adolescent is characteristic of large sections of the English population. The young Branch Streeters differ from others because of the extreme hopelessness of their situation which, moreover, they know to be hopeless. They know the chances of a happy life, a happy marriage, to be slim. In the youth club they will talk of wanting a job where they can keep their hands soft and clean, at the same time saying that it is not possible because they have neither money nor sufficient learning. A girl who has lived in the area all her life and who is an average girl in her group says that when she is married, she will send her daughter to a boarding school to be a lady. Spinley is impressed by the girls' efforts to buy expensive clothes copied from fashions in magazines for the upper middle classes. They are very highly prestige-suggestible, and the prestige is attached not only to the more obvious superficial attributes of class. They want very much to know things, to be able to discuss intelligently. Incapable of making the prolonged effort necessary, however, they cling to the pleasures that they have and do not attempt to obtain those out of reach.

So the young people complain of being 'browned off with everything', but cannot articulate their wants. In these depressed moods they sit or stand about, not interested in larks or dancing. They play sentimental music on the radiogram, and their eyes mist with tears. Nobody is ever amused by someone else's depression.[1]

Once married, a girl must settle down to child-bearing and domestic duties, and, when she has not a young baby on her hands, work outside the home. Spinley found it sad to look at the young unmarried girls of seventeen, with a surface smartness and sophistication, clean, although heavily painted, neat, with bright ear-rings and the latest mass-produced clothes, and then to turn to the married women of twenty-two, their hair greasy and straggling or in curlers, with untidy, unkempt clothing, grey unhealthy-looking skins, and postural slump. It is as if all

---

[1] It is during such moods, Spinley found, that the young people are most approachable, and prepared to discuss themselves, their families and their problems. Someone who listens intelligently to a boy when he is unhappy is rewarded by his greater responsiveness at many times later.

Now that the issue of help towards a better life has been broached, two other points may be added. The ease with which some of the dark impulses may be diverted to more harmless expression, even here, is sometimes striking. To give the fighting spirit of her young (pre-adolescent) rascals a more useful form, Paneth thought of having them taught boxing and wrestling. Luckily, some of the men helping in the club had had training in these sports and started teaching the boys. The boys were keen and did astonishingly well. Moreover, 'for the first time in our acquaintance the small leader (a terror some nine years old) caused no trouble and behaved like a keen and happy child'.

Secondly, there is the question of the extent to which early socialization determines unalterably the later behaviour patterns of any person. The answer, once one stops to think, is obvious. It depends on the extent to which the environment which produced the early roots continues unaltered to strengthen the later shoots. The less established the roots, the greater will be the effect of changes in the environment. Thus Hilda Lewis gives an example which might have been drawn straight from the population of the Paddington area as here described: One little boy from a very poor home, much despised by the families near by, had repeatedly played truant from school, where his ragged clothes and dirt put him to shame and the other boys would not play with him. At Mersham (the reception centre at which Lewis did her work) he at first kept entirely to himself, regarding all adults with fear and suspicion; but after a while he became more friendly and trusting. Needless to say also, it is very difficult to forecast the effects of a change in environment, much more difficult than forecasting what will happen to the majority of a population which does not experience such a change. (*Deprived Children: the Mersham Experiment* (1954), Oxford University Press.)

effort is made to attract a husband, and then inertia and apathy follow.

To understand how this change comes about one must consider the meaning of sex for the Branch Street personality. Having been accustomed to sleep in the same bed as their brothers and sisters, and parental control in general being minimal, the children tend to have engaged in sexual play with one another. All their information on sex will have come from other children. These are children who, according to Paneth, ask a pretty new worker whom they see for the first time, 'Are you Peter's tart?'; who in the painting sessions draw pictures usually to be found as anonymous scribbles on the walls of lavatories; who incessantly accuse every grown-up person of promiscuity; who sleep three or four together in the same bed; who may sleep under their parents' bed on the nights father comes home drunk; who may return from school to find that a baby has been born in the bed which they have to share the same night with the young mother—an older and unmarried sister.

Yet, in spite of language and behaviour which strikes most observers as distressingly lewd and knowing, there are large patches of ignorance in the child's knowledge of sexual and reproductive behaviour. The fact that he sleeps in the same room with his parents and has opportunities to witness their sexual intercourse does nothing to enlighten him on those aspects of which he is ignorant. Sex is considered purely in terms of an outlet for the man, an outlet moreover with a large aggressive component.

Paneth, in a terrifying episode, records a discussion with some of her girls, which shows how they confused aggression and sex: 'Does it hurt, Miss?', 'What do you say when you want to stop?' Then they reproduced overheard shouts and quarrels. 'You beast, I've had enough of it. Don't hurt me. Leave me alone.' At the end of this discussion one of the girls, thin and wizened-looking, turned shuddering away and said that she did not want a baby, ever.

In Branch Street sexual intercourse is correctly regarded as an aggressive act on the part of the man. The tenderness which has never been learned or experienced does not accompany the sexual act. If one considers the emotional training to which the Branch Streeter has been subjected, it comes as no surprise that there is also an important exploitative component in the 'love-relationship', at least on the man's side. Throughout courtship he plays the reluctant or indifferent partner. All the efforts of courtship seem to be made by the girls. There is no convention that the girl grants favours; it is the boy who bestows his company. The boy may be overtly exploitative, not only of the sexual intercourse which the girl permits, but also of what he can get out of her financially. It is the girl who takes the initiative in asking a boy along to the pictures. He will meet her inside the cinema, thus making sure that she pays for her own ticket. He expects, and receives, expensive presents from the girl(s) with whom he spends his leisure. He may become friendly with a girl some time before Christmas, get his present, and then drop her. Spinley says this is thought to be very smart and rather amusing. (On the same page Spinley notes that people use the social welfare agencies unscrupulously—their idea often being to get as much as possible.)

The sexes have not since childhood spent much of their time together. The girls and women are (possibly willy-nilly) company for one another, and the men spend their time together, except possibly in the months immediately preceding their marriage. It is not immediately obvious why the girls should go to so much trouble to acquire a husband. Spinley suggests as a reason that there is no role for the single woman in Branch Street. She knew of only one girl over twenty-one who was neither married nor attached to a man: she was in a mental hospital. And if there is no place for the single woman, the Branch Street girl is not likely to philosophize about courses of action alternative to the one she is pursuing. She does not choose, she does what appears to her to be natural. It is difficult to envisage what she might do instead. But it is not much of a life. And once she is married, the fantasies of escape, that something, somehow, will save her, that she will marry out of her class, a good man, a prince or film-star, are known by her to be forever out of reach. She knows it in her moods of depression during adolescence. Paneth puts the matter in a nutshell. 'The girls have nothing to look forward to when they grow up to be women. Their future takes the shape of what they overheard when they do not sleep deeply, and wake to witness the unwillingingly-granted intercourse of their mothers.' So the future loses its glamour and its hope. There is nothing to look forward to but brutality and pain. The girl lets herself go. She ceases to make demands upon life, or upon herself. In this state of mind she bears her children.

Chapter Two

'SHIP STREET' 1956

THE ENVIRONMENT OF SHIP STREET

THE present chapter is mainly concerned with the formation and perpetuation of one pattern of life found among others in a Liverpool area which resembles Branch Street in a number of ways. The people of Ship Street are best regarded as a selected sample, chosen for study by Kerr because their personality and way of life were of particular interest to her. 'Ship Street', in fact, is best thought of as the name of a personality type, rather than as a locality.

The people of Ship Street live in a nexus of streets within walking distance of each other in the centre of Liverpool.[1] The area, according to Kerr, is a typical slum of today, having been devastated by neglect and poverty, and more recently by bombing.

If we compared the dwellings here with those of Branch Street, we should find them somewhat better. Kerr noted that in only three cases, out of the sixty she knew best, were the rooms physically distasteful through dirt or smell. The others tended to be reasonably clean, and sometimes very clean. Moreover, though the houses might be decrepit and dirty, attempts had often been made to alleviate this by paint. Within the house, rooms might be out of use owing to the damp, or the ceiling might have collapsed and caused general disrepair. Few houses had electric light; one or two still used oil-lamps. Most, too, had only cold-water taps. (The flats, being newer, are better equipped and most of these have bathrooms.) In

[1] Much of what follows is reproduced *verbatim* or in slightly abbreviated form from *The People of Ship Street*.

some cases, a parlour was kept for ritual occasions, though often it had to be put to more mundane use to accommodate a married daughter who had come home, with her family. Little money was spent to make the home a more comfortable place to live in. Suites might be bought on the cheque system and they were appreciated, but they did not seem to have the high status-value they tend to have in a slightly higher social class.

Ship Street was a residual area. The reasonably successful, and those who had become assimilated to the English upper-working or lower-middle class patterns of behaviour, have moved away. The genuine Ship Streeter had been in the area for two or three generations. It was not a transitional area. The people we worked with, wrote Kerr, form a residual core of families for whom the life of the street is the only one they know and the only one they want to know. At the time of the study they were being gradually moved out of their generally large houses into Corporation flats. To Kerr, this seemed not to lead to a related change in their way of life. The rituals and traditions of the past were preserved in the present, in the corridors and yards of the tenement flats. At the time of writing, thirty-eight of the families lived in houses, eighteen in flats and five in lodgings.

There is a good deal of background information about Dockland, the locality in which Ship Streeters live, thanks to the writings of John Barron Mays, whose knowledge of the area derives from many years' wardenship of the University Settlement.[1] In the books used as sources for this chapter, he is drawing more specifically on information given by the boys in the clubs he ran, and by their parents. There is no doubt that Mays' Dockland may be called a 'problem area'. In one set of sixty-six families—admittedly of boys in a club recruited on the basis of recommendations by teachers, policemen, probation officers and other people of authority, who considered them to be in need of special care and attention, presenting behaviour problems, or slipping into delinquency—thirty-one had fathers

---

[1] *Growing up in the City* (1954); *On the Threshold of Delinquency* (1959), both of which are used in the present text; and more lately *Urban Redevelopment* (1961) by Vereker and Mays. All are published by the Liverpool University Press. Much of the description of Dockland life is taken *verbatim* or in abbreviated form from these books.

away at sea, or dead, or gone, or chronically ill. From another sample of sixty boys we find that thirty had been convicted at least once of some offence, and another twenty admitted to Mays that they had committed offences, though they had not been caught.

Much that Mays has to say about these boys and their families resembles closely the behaviour prevalent in Branch Street, though he insists that there are many more respectable families as well. He notes the premarital and promiscuous sexual intercourse, the illegitimacy without stigma, the mothers up too early after confinement, haphazard feeding in infancy, the abrupt loss of maternal protection when the next baby arrives, submission to the life of the streets from the time the baby can toddle, the toughness of the children towards each other, their irritability and violence, their aimless destructiveness, their cruelty to animals and lack of response to beauty, their inability to persist in any activity, the food-fads, the absence of a common family meal, the broken promises, the bad health, the adolescent gangs, and so on and so on.

In *On the Threshold of Delinquency*, Mays discusses the relation of his own findings to Spinley's. Her list runs:

A basic insecurity; a serious sexual disturbance which is associated with feminine identifications; an inability to form close affectional ties; the absence of a strong and efficient superego; an inability to postpone satisfaction and an absence of conflict over pleasures; a highly sensitive ego and marked narcissistic trends; a ready aggressiveness; a tendency to 'leave the field' when circumstances and experiences are unpleasant; a rebellious attitude to authority.

This definition (Mays continues) may be recast in non-psychological terms and filled out with the addition of some other characteristics as follows:

A general feeling of inefficiency when faced with any unfamiliar problem; close emotional attachment to the mother and a slender relationship with the father resulting in diffidence in playing the culturally prescribed male role; difficulty in forming deep personal relationships and strong friendships together with a lack of tenderness; a weak conscience; a poor resistance to temptation and acceptance of a comparatively low moral standard regarding goods and property in general; inability to look ahead or to plan for or have faith in the future, coupled with a strong desire to enjoy all pleasures immediately; general touchiness, moodiness, insensitivity to other people's feelings, irritability, quickness in anger; dislike of facing up to uncomfortable situations; poor sportsmanship; an ambivalent attitude towards all in authority and an accompanying dislike of having to be a leader and to be different from one's fellows; unreliability in keeping appointments; distrust of promises and a strong urge to become a member of a small group.

Mays' accounts show the boys as resembling Branch Street in many ways, but often—perhaps simply because there are alternative patterns available—just a little less extreme. In the matter of time-perspective, for instance:

> The train journey [from Liverpool to a Southern sea-side resort] was tedious . . . The boys were very excited and restless on the way . . . Every five minutes someone would ask the time. The train had not been travelling for more than a few minutes when they were enquiring if they were halfway there yet. The youngest members of the party had no idea of either distance or time.

And:

> An attempt was made with some of the boys to play a game called tip-it, involving the hiding of a coin in a hand and guessing its whereabouts, but this was equally unsuccessful. Neither of the Rees would play unless they had the halfpenny hidden in their hand and Ian broke all the rules by trying to peer behind people's backs and into their closed fists.

Yet later this same group of boys is found playing games with sense and gusto, even such relatively complicated games as Lotto and Monopoly, which would seem beyond the emotional and intellectual capacities of Branch Street. On the development of moral attitudes, also, Mays writes in terms which are hardly applicable to Branch Street.

> Discussion with young people suggests that there are two strands to a growing ethical awareness which interweave and reinforce one another as the child grows into an adolescent. On the one hand there is an increasing ability to appreciate the unpleasant consequences; and on the other hand a deepening fellow

feeling and sympathy for the injured party . . . Many of the boys who were interviewed said they began to see the folly of misbehaviour and, if they did not repent in the moral sense, at least acquired sufficient self-control to refrain from committing certain delinquent acts. One boy abandoned shop lifting because he realized it would grieve his mother if he were found out.

Mays' account of Dockland family structure also assumes a more stable relationship than is normal in Branch Street. The man is seen as the ultimate source of authority and discipline in the family. While the mother is the comforter, caterer, planner, the role of the father in most homes is that of wage-earner and disciplinarian. He is the economic master who decides how much of his income will go to housekeeping and how much he will keep for his own personal use. It is rare for this kind of husband to take a hand in planning the weekly budget ; few tell their wives how much they actually earn. He may keep back as much as half his income for himself. Overtime and bonus are thought of as additions to his personal spending-money rather than as accretions to the common pool.

The way in which the housekeeping money is spent is largely the woman's field, the man expecting that he will be given adequate meals and the standard of comfort he requires. His comfort is usually put first, and his meal must be ready for him by the time he gets home from work, whatever else happens. He assumes that his non-working time is his own to do with what he likes. (This pattern of masculine pre-eminence is also observed in the treatment of children—the boys are often excused household chores, while there is no more common sight than that of girls of school age taking full charge of brothers and sisters outside the home, bearing at too early an age the heavy responsibilities which the mother cannot herself discharge, however large her heart.) All too often, writes Mays, the husband sheds his responsibilities and places them on his wife's shoulders. He does not accept it as part of his duties to supervise the children's leisure or to play with them. If he is of a violent disposition the children will fear him and the more protective mothers will tend to conceal the children's misdemeanours from the father, because they dread the excessive punishment. This may go to the lengths of the father not knowing that his child

45

has come before the courts. The children, in such circumstances, may be quick to exploit their mother's sympathy to secure indulgence for their misdeeds.

Dockland fathers seem to be a varied crowd. Some show something of the violence of the 'absentee' father of Branch Street. But the effect of such behaviour is different because the women can follow the 'Ship Street' pattern and take active steps to prevent such a father from having a secure place in the household. In other important respects, the father's role resembles that of the men in many traditional working-class families (as described in a later chapter) though it is perhaps a little harsher. This harsh form of male dominance is found in a purer form in Ashton, an area described in the next chapter.

When Kerr's account of Ship Street comes to be compared with Mays' descriptions of life in Dockland as a whole, it should not be assumed that there are no problem families in the former and no stable families in the latter. Both sources provide evidence to the contrary. But it does appear as though the Ship Street mothers are normally in firm charge and control of their families, with the men normally accepting this pattern and supporting her, while the majority of Mays' people manifest alternative patterns: stable families in which the man is the indisputed authority; unstable families in which the man is violent and feared, to which the mother may react with equal violence, or with submission, or with cunning and concealment.

According to Kerr only about a quarter of the adult males of Ship Street are of the kind which predominated in Branch Street: casual, unskilled, unemployed or in gaol. About a third are dockers: a skilled and in these post-war years not a casual form of employment. About a quarter are sailors. Kerr does not describe Ship Street men's working lives in any detail. It is hoped that a description of the Manchester docker in another study issued from Liverpool University's Department of Social Science bridges this gap.[1] The occupational categories correspond. According to *The Dockworker*, many of the dockers used to go to sea, there is a close association between seafaring and dockwork, and during the inter-war years it was common for men to alternate periods of dockwork with periods at sea.

[1] *Liverpool University Social Research Series* (1954), University of Liverpool Press.

'Ship Street' 1956

It has been generally recognized for many years that the social characteristics of the docker are intimately related to the system of casual employment which has prevailed in the industry. As Charles Booth pointed out in 1896 'the character of the men matched well with the character of the work, and that of its remuneration. All alike were low and irregular.' The Shaw Inquiry conducted in 1920 was also very explicit on this point: 'So serious has the problem become that it has evolved habits of mind and body on the part of the workmen themselves which are detrimental to them, and on a wide scale deeply injurious. Many workers have got into the habit of thinking that day labour is a sign of independence and that labour secured even for a week leaves them devoid of that liberty to do nothing which they have come to prize.'

Those familiar with the organization of labour in manufacturing industry will realize that the conditions which obtain in the docks are very different from anything that can be found in a factory. When he is first employed, the factory worker is placed somewhat arbitrarily into a working group and has to adapt himself both to the personal characteristics of its members and to its routine of work. If he fails, he will ask either for a transfer to another job or to be 'given his cards'. But before he does so he will usually make a serious effort to overcome these difficulties by amending his own behaviour. He thus becomes subject to a process of social discipline and control, surrendering some of his own ideas and attitudes and accepting those of his workmates. In return he is given a satisfying sense of belonging to a group, and a feeling that he is, to some extent at least, protected against the uncertainties of the world.

This process of adaptation is almost entirely lacking on the docks. Dockworkers who are not members of permanent gangs are not subject to the social control exercised in them and do not gain security from membership of them. On the other hand, gang members who accept discipline and control voluntarily get a certain limited measure of security thereby.

But permanent gangs, composed of members of a family, of a particular religious denomination, or of supporters of a favoured football club, are less frequent than might be expected, though they do exist. The relationship thus established can be easily disrupted, because there is no formal recognition of the existence of the gangs, and because gang members can, if they wish, repudiate at will the controls that hold them together. Once formed, the continued association is entirely voluntary, for every gang member has an opportunity to leave the gang each time he goes into the call stand.

Once or twice a week the men go to the call stand, for the foreman to tell them where to report for work. A blackboard in the dock office window tells them what ships are in and they can often deduce the cargo and evaluate the attractiveness of working there from this information. They wait in 'pens' to be called. As each foreman appears on the gangway and looks down at the mass of men surging forward both he and they are well aware of the relative advantages and disadvantages of the various jobs available. The men rush forward and make strenuous efforts to get their books accepted by foremen who have attractive jobs to offer. The foreman is allowed in the first few minutes to accept books from men he is particularly anxious to employ, ignoring any others. The Liverpool Report comments that

> the calling-on procedure must be deemed to provoke excessive competition and even conflict between individual dockworkers. The struggle which arises in this way is moreover exacerbated by the physical conditions in which it takes place. These are not likely to encourage orderly or co-operative behaviour.

Because of the way the men are chosen for their work, competing against each other for the attention of the foremen, there is no real solidarity between them. One docker is quoted as saying: 'Dockers are not really solid—it's each man for himself and the devil take the hindmost', and another: 'People wouldn't say that dockers were solid if they saw us in the pen squabbling like a lot of monkeys to do ourselves a bit of good.'

Thus it is that the report sees the social life of the docker as having been, and to a large extent still being, a paradox.

> Despite the loyalty and solidarity which he displays to the outside world, the society of which he is a member is only held together by the most tenuous of bonds. It was 'the universal dislocation of the social life of East London' that impressed itself on Booth's mind, which was manifested in the docks 'not only by the absence of all ties between employer, foreman and man, but in the complete severance of the different grades of labour, and among

48

the more respectable of the working class, in the isolation in the individual family'. To which may be added that Ernest Bevin's task has been seen as the welding together into a single community of transport workers and dockers, 'who despite, indeed in part because of, their separateness from the outside world were not only suspicious of others, but were very often split into exclusive groups within the dockland community itself'.

This description of the men's working conditions completes our brief account of the wider social context within which the Ship Street personality survives. In spite of many handicaps, it is yet clearly a more favourable environment than Branch Street.

GROUP RELATIONS

Although surrounded by immigrants, near the brothel area of the town, and with their derelict houses gradually superseded by flats, Ship Streeters preserve a pattern of living of their own. Compared with Branch Streeters, they live in a somewhat better area, with a better way of life. But they too are looked down upon by the outside world, which possibly does not distinguish them from their immediate surroundings as carefully as is called for. They themselves are aware, however, of their superiority, though no great fuss is made about the difference. It is a part, though not the whole, of the reason why the women only leave their own streets accompanied by another woman.

Several factors prevent the Ship Streeter feeling his social isolation as rejection by neighbouring groups: the fact that worse districts are known to exist within walking distance, the fact that Ship Streeters are Catholics and proud of it, the closeness of the family relations.[1] They stick together more because they want to, and less because they are excluded by others. Since the children go to Catholic schools and are taught by teachers whose cultural background is more compatible with that of their charges than was the case in Branch Street, the shock of meeting a hostile environment occurs very much later, if it occurs at all. According to Mays, many of the men teaching in the Catholic

---

[1] The proportion of Catholics in Mays' samples may be smaller. In one sample, for instance, only a third of the boys went to an R.C. school.

schools, at least, derive from working-class backgrounds and have known long years of struggle and difficulty. Many of them were born and bred in the area. Reciprocally, there is not the same hostility towards the school. Kerr talked to a mother just after her child had been punished by a teacher. In spite of the fact that she was most indignant at the way the teacher had treated Moira, she made excuses for her. She said she supposed the teacher's nerves were bad through having to deal with children all the time. There is no evidence here that the teacher's attitude to the child was resented, or to be resented; only that the teacher was mistaken in picking on Moira.

In Ship Street, it is the small group that counts. It is possible to see the progressive attenuation of social ties as the groups become larger and more remote. No obligations are felt to the remotest and largest groups. This is very well brought out in Kerr's discussion on crime. Two words are used to describe taking things which belong to others: thieving and robbing. The former is permitted, the latter strongly condemned. Thieving is taking things from an employer, 'who'll never miss it', or from the large stores in the city. This calls forth no condemnation and hardly any comment. Robbing, on the other hand, is taking things from people who belong to one's own group, from friends or relatives, and this is strongly condemned. Kerr tells a story of a girl of eleven who had been looking after the club canteen and giving free cocoa to her friends, which she charged up to others. She got into trouble (with the club authorities, not the police), while the neighbourhood sympathized. Mays also tells a charming anecdote:

> One afternoon a wagon tipped a quantity of coke on to the pavement of one of the largest institutions in the district. While the driver and his mate were inside the building, an old lady appeared on the scene and commenced picking up pieces of coke and stowing them away in a large shopping-bag she was carrying. Two small boys observed her activity and took compassion on her age. They immediately offered their assistance and soon all three were busily engaged on the same task. The small boys would no doubt have been astonished if they had been told they were breaking the law or doing wrong. It was no more than a gesture of juvenile altruism, a deed worthy of Baden Powell himself.

As soon as a more personal relation is established, thieving turns into robbing and comes to an end. A boy of twelve, when asked if he and his gang stole from a main street of shops near where they lived, replied: 'No, because we're nearly all on orders now' (i.e. delivering for the shops for a few pennies' payment). The same discrimination between behaviour appropriate to members of the primary group and behaviour appropriate to those who are more remote occurs in Kerr's discussion on gambling. Playing toss in your local street, where you may do someone else down, is 'gambling', and condemned. The pools and the horses are run by large organizations and at least some Ship Streeters do not realize that this is also gambling. In any case it does not fall under condemnation. Some of Mays' boys earned a bit of pocket-money by co-operating with local street-bookies.

In looking at the concentric circles of recognized social obligations, we may start with the immediate family. Within the group of kin, there is great generosity. Anyone who has had a windfall brings home presents for all; they do not keep their money or their luck for themselves. When in luck, there is a splash which sends its spray over the whole family.

Relatives beyond the immediate family are in and out of the house all the time. Visits between kin are frequent and, indeed, form the main out-of-the-house leisure activity for most age-groups except the adolescents. Even when relatives move away, they are remembered and, where possible, visited. Occasionally there are individuals with a personal friendship for someone who is not a relative, but this is not common in adult life.

Whereas there is a great deal of visiting between kin, neighbours do not visit one another. This does not seem to be the expression of an underlying hostility. Neighbours are very good to one another in crises and emergencies. Their services may range from baby-minding, through seeing that nothing is stolen from an empty house, to carrying a bucket of coal to a poor family that is having to do without, and sitting with the bereaved.

Like the Branch Streeters, these people do not want to leave the area, though it is clear that the balance of the attraction of the familiar versus the fear of the outside is different here. Only three of the sixty families expressed what could be called a genuine desire to move, two others expressed a more half-hearted desire.

Mrs. E. told Kerr that she would not move far from this neighbourhood. She had been offered a house on a housing estate, but would not take it. She would not be happy there. Her husband would move, but then, he'd be out all day. She refused. Kerr asked Mrs. E. if she had a lot of friends in this neighbourhood. She replied: 'Not particular, I don't make friends with all. I go to Mrs. F.'s yard sometimes.' Kerr asked her what tied her, then, to the neighbourhood. Mrs. E. repeated: 'I've always lived here.'

Mrs. S. was born in a nearby street. She had always lived in this neighbourhood. She hoped that when these houses are pulled down, they would put up some flats instead, and that she would get one. She wouldn't like to leave the neighbourhood. Yet she said to Kerr that she had no friends here and was not on friendly or visiting terms with her neighbours. 'They're a rough lot; we keep ourselves to ourselves. We keep our front door shut.' On being pressed, she said she had no friends who come round to her home, and she visited no one except her brothers and sisters, and that when you are a large family you haven't the time or the need for friends. She saw her brothers and sisters frequently: 'I never go out except to see my relations.'

When relatives have not only moved out of the neighbourhood but also up in the world, relations do tend to be broken off. They are now too remote. Ship Streeters are deeply resentful of snobbery and very sensitive to it. The break may cause bitter unhappiness for a while, but seems to them the only solution.[1] Similarly, it seems a reasonable fear to them that their children may grow away from them, for instance if they accept a scholarship at school. The family as a unit must be preserved.

In general, Ship Streeters are not very status-conscious. There is no problem of keeping up with the Joneses of Ship Street. This is partly because the families are much on the same level anyway, partly because an increase in spending money does not change the pattern of consumption but only provides a little more of the same, partly because with a little more money you

[1] Cf. the Newbolts, pages 244-5.

are more able to give pleasure to your family, and most important, because emotional interest is turned inward to the family, and you don't care what outsiders think. The Ship Streeter's interest is centred on the family, and those who share this interest and are not for other reasons offensive are easily acceptable. He is not interested in the abstract aspects of status-differentiation. This is how Kerr accounts for her own easy acceptance by the parents of the children in which she took an interest. But then, Kerr was not a member of the community. If she had been, her experience might have been different. According to Mays there is a fairly wide-spread hostility towards those members of the group who are willing to shoulder responsibility and act as leaders in organizing leisure-time activities. Such people are likely to be described as big-headed and are said to like themselves too much. Even joining an association is thought of as a deviation from the normal pattern.[1]

Ship Streeters are not joiners of associations. They belong to Trade Unions, but participate little in the activities. Even though the majority are Catholics, they do not go to church (though they send the children) and they do not belong to the many clubs which the church runs in the parish. Equally in keeping with the emphasis on primary group ties are the loosely organized groups formed by the men in their favourite public house. Some of the pubs run their own football teams. Men will go to football matches as spectators, some of the younger men play.

In the evenings the men go to the pub, generally on their own during the week, while on Friday or Saturday they may take their wives. The women tend to go with another woman. Two women who would almost certainly never visit each other's homes will meet night after night at the pub for a glass of beer. It is more general for people to go to the pub with non-relatives, the only instance of this choice of company found in Ship Street. Husband and wife do not go out together much. The family is not kept together by this sort of social interaction. The children also have their own play-groups, and the social life of the adolescent is, again, segregated from that of his parents.

To sum up: Ship Streeters are comfortable and at home

[1] Cf. pages 209-12 and 242.

within their locality, where they can cope and behave well. What is outside is not desired and little resented. Within their (restricted) environment, they are well-adjusted.

THE HOUSEHOLD

Kerr defines the household as a group of people living and eating together and sharing the money earned by one or more of them. The structure of the household shows how different these people are from those in Branch Street. The household often contains three generations; in fact, in all but three cases, three generations lived together whenever there were three generations of the family alive.

It is customary in this area for at least one married daughter to live in her mother's house. When married daughters bring their husbands home to live, the custom is for them to cook their evening meal in the communal household kitchen and then to 'take it upstairs'. During the day the daughters and their children have their meal with the mother.

If the house is not large enough to have all the married daughters and their families living at home, great efforts are made to live as near to 'Mum' as possible, in the next house or flat, across the street, or 'just round the corner'. Sometimes the daughters take it in turns to live in: a girl may get married and move out with her husband. An older sister will then take the opportunity to move back. When she produces more children than the house can possibly hold, she may move away again, and the other sister move back.

The children grow up in this three-generational setting. In their lives both mother and grandmother are permanent and important figures. Kerr cites an instance in which the grandmother was regarded by the children as the more important of the two. Normally, however, she is simply always there, to mind the children, to cook the midday meal if necessary, to cope in a crisis. She will help at her daughter's confinement. Some grandmothers like always to have at least one child sleeping at their house. A child will go and sleep at its grandmother's house without any previous arrangement having been made. This is what it means in practice to live in an extended kinship group:

54

similar practices can be found in the accounts of more primitive tribes.

Kerr analyses the intricacies of some of the kin-relations created. Admittedly, the instance is extreme, but without it, it would be difficult to imagine how extreme an extreme can be in reality.

When Mrs. S. got married (the same who was quoted on page 52) she took her husband home to live with her parents. As the children came along (she had fourteen), she was forced to move. When her eldest child, Mrs. X., got married, she repeated the same pattern. She took her husband home to live with her mother, Mrs. S., who was now a widow, despite the fact that Mrs. S. had all her unmarried children still living with her. Mrs. X.'s youngest brothers, twins, were only four years old at the time. As Mrs. X.'s children came along, she again was forced to move. She moved near her mother. Eventually Mrs. S. handed her house over to her married daughter Mrs. X. who returned to it, while Mrs. S. herself went back to live with her yet older Mum, taking her only unmarried child, a son, with her. When this boy got married, he brought his wife home. Thus three generations lived together. When his first child was born it made four.

Now returning to Mrs. X.'s household, she has succeeded in doing what nearly all the women in Ship Street want to do, that is to have her married daughters bring their husbands and children back to her house. During the five years Kerr had known this family, the eldest daughter had twice taken her husband and children away because of the overcrowding and the unhealthy dampness of the house, but she had always come back on some pretext. Her second daughter went to live with her husband's family on her marriage, but in her own words, she was 'looking for an excuse' to return to her mother's home. She found it four months later. She moved back while her husband was at sea. On his return he joined her there.

Even Mrs. X.'s second son, who left home on his marriage, returned without his wife six months later, saying he was going to stay at home till he and his wife could find a house. She was an orphan, so she went to live with an aunt.

Often it is Mum, the mother of the family, who ties the junior household to the area. The attachment of the adult daughters to their mothers is very strong in Ship Street. Mr. Y. told Kerr that he did not really like the neighbourhood or the house and wanted to move. Twice this was nearly achieved but on both occasions Mrs. Y. ratted at the last moment. The first time he was offered a very nice house on a housing estate. His wife said she wanted to move and they went over the house. She liked it very much. As they were leaving the house, she burst into tears and said she could never leave her mother. On a second occasion the same thing happened. Another informant tells the following story.

When Billy and Maureen first married, Bill got her a lovely home. One day he returned from work to find a removal-van driving away from what looked like his house. He stopped the van and asked the men whose things they were moving. He learned from them that they were moving his own. His wife had ordered the van and given instructions. Billy went in and questioned his wife. She said: 'I'm going back to me mother. You can please yourself.' Billy returned with her. It's been like this throughout his married life.

Clearly the man cuts very little ice in the family. This may be partly due to the nature of his employment if he is a seaman: he may be away from home for long periods. But in any case, according to Ship Street norms a good man is quiet and leaves the authority to the women. He hands over his entire wage-packet to the woman of the house—his mother or his wife—and receives back a sum to spend for himself. Even when he does not hand over his total earnings, the woman expects at least to see the wage-packet and to know exactly how much he has earned that week, so that she is in a position to judge for herself whether she has received a 'fair wage' or not. In short, the Ship Street 'Mum' pattern works out in such a way that the man in the family has relatively little authority.

The man may be as devoted to his mother as the wife is to hers, but from Kerr's descriptions one gains the impression that whereas the daughter interacts with her mother on a footing of potential equality—being regarded as an apprentice 'Mum'—the son interacts with his mother on an unequal footing, always subordinate since he cannot, by reason of his sex, ever hope to perform her role.

Conformity, first to the wishes of his mother and then of his wife, is the established role of the man. It is how a good man behaves. It is the only respectable role open to him. There is no reasonable alternative. Rebelling, he goes to the bad, becoming violent, work-shy, a .trunk. The poverty of the number of roles available to the Ship Streeter is one of the recurrent themes of Kerr's analysis.

THE FORMATION OF THE INDIVIDUAL PERSONALITY

We are now in a position to consider the kind of personality likely to be fostered by the social environment of the Ship Street type of family. Kerr is left in no doubt that many of the mothers have more children than they would have chosen to have. The families are very large. As Catholics, mechanical devices of birth-control are forbidden them, but it is very doubtful whether non-Catholic mothers of the same educational and social level have the temperament to use contraception regularly. Safe contraception requires more foresight and patience than they can normally muster. Because of this combination of temperamental and religious peculiarities, it is not really surprising that many Ship Street mothers admit to attempts, often successful, at procuring an early abortion, either by means of medication or through strenuous physical exertion.

There is a good deal of illegitimacy in Ship Street, and no strong social stigma attaches to having an illegitimate child. But the clearly defined behaviour-pattern for men who get a girl into trouble shows how much more organized this sub-culture is than Branch Street: either the man marries the girl, or if he does not, he must accept financial responsibility for the child till it is fifteen.

Though the mothers complain bitterly when they find they are to have another baby (Mrs. H. said that when she discovered her tenth pregnancy at the age of forty-one: 'I nearly went mental during the first three months', and Mrs. P. said as soon as Mr. P. went out of the door: 'If I have any more I'll put me head in the gas oven or throw meself in the canal'), when the child is born, it is generally loved and cared for. The first baby is likely to be born in hospital, the later ones at home, with the mother's mother in attendance, and this is what the daughter would prefer.

Much affection is shown the child. Cots and prams are bought for the new baby, but whenever the mother thinks that the child is unhappy, or not thriving, she takes him into her own bed. Kerr comments that this habit persists, so that adults are often frightened to sleep in a room by themselves and children in a bed by themselves even with others in the room: the extremely close physical intimacy with a few people helps to cement the group family tie.

Toilet training, although casual and belated by middle-class standards, again seems to be just a bit more effortful than was the case in Branch Street. Kerr concludes, from the frequent remarks mothers make about the dirtiness of other people's children, that it seems that cleanliness is not acquired for several years. But we may conclude from the same evidence that these mothers do seem somewhat concerned about cleanliness, more worried about discrepancies from the norm than the Branch Street mothers.

The baby is breast-fed for a short time; he is also fed whenever he cries in spite of local hospital advice to the contrary. The age of weaning from breast to bottle varies as much here as in Branch Street. In neither area is the feeding itself regarded by the mother as a time when tenderness might be expressed. It appears to be regarded as just the preparation for another meal. Mothers have not the patience nor the time to sit with the baby while he feeds. Bottles are propped up in prams or beds and the mother gets on with coping with the other children. As families are large, the mother would in any case not often be able to sit peacefully with the newborn baby—she would only be immobilized in the midst of a clamouring throng of small children getting into every conceivable kind of trouble.

As in many large families, the older children look after the younger: washing, dressing, feeding them, taking them out, and having them to sleep in their beds. They love them as dearly and show them off as proudly as do their opposite numbers of Branch Street. They help in the house also, but apparently unlike the Branch Streeters, they get money for doing odd jobs, as well as more regular pocket-money and windfalls from relatives. They run errands for old ladies, fetch newspapers, and so on. This is of some importance, not only because it gives them money to go to the pictures but also because it gives them an experience of reward after effort: it is worth while running errands rather than going out to play, because they will get money which they can use for pleasant purposes of their own. Some time-perspective, and some training in delayed responses for the sake of later rewards, is thus inculcated.

Food has something of the consoling significance here that it has in Branch Street. In most homes, bread and marge are always on the table or in some other accessible place and the children are allowed to help themselves. As there are seldom enough chairs for the whole family to sit at once, meals can hardly be of a formal nature. Again, if more than one member of the family is at work, he or she will want food immediately on arriving home. Food is therefore often taken on a sort of running-buffet system. It is used, too, as a reward: in childhood when favourite foods are given as treats, and in adulthood when those earning are given more or better food than the others.

In a very perceptive passage Kerr notes how food may be used as an almost aggressive assertion of choice. From early childhood, individuals tend to have innumerable food fads which are catered for as a matter of course by the mother. Kerr suggests that one reason why this may be so is that there are too few areas of life which allow the pleasure of choosing between a number of rich alternatives, so that choice of food becomes over-emphasized. The practice of feeding the baby as a means of comforting it whether it cries from hunger or from some other cause may also contribute to the emotional significance of food. Finally it may be noted that faddiness about food seems to be a characteristic of all children whose mothers are over-protective.

In spite of some similarities, the emotional significance of food here is not the same as in Branch Street, consoling though it be in both areas, for these babies have many more personal sources of emotional satisfaction available to them than is the case in Branch Street, where food is almost the only pleasurable experience. Though tired and irritable from the same causes as in Branch Street, the Ship Street mother, because of a more regular home life (and the help and support of her own mother), is capable of greater and more sustained affection. Though she blames her 'nerves' on them, the Ship Street mother loves her children. Accordingly, the children also grow up with a greater capacity for love.

Love and care are closely connected. The Ship Street mother tends to interpret her powerful position protectively, and this has important consequences even at the toddler stage. Because she keeps a more careful eye on the toddler at play, he is less at the mercy of bullying companions, and is therefore less likely to feel so helpless and so helplessly aggressive as his Branch Street counterpart. Not being subjected to the same devastating experience of having to cope with attacks from equals at too young an age, there is less ambivalence in later social relationships. Affectionate ties have more opportunity to develop undisturbed. Certainly, arguing from negative evidence, there is in Ship Street much less of the senseless violence so characteristic of Branch Street, though it does occur.

Nevertheless, the fact that the mothers say that the children 'get on their nerves' also implies that the mothers' control over their children's behaviour depends on their temporary state of mind as much as on their constant underlying affection. Kerr sums up the position by commenting that 'discipline' takes the form of an attempt to secure peace for the moment and is not based on any long-term policy. The patient, persistent, self-confident training regarded as desirable by the Child Guidance Clinic is not often found here. 'I hadn't the patience' is the more typical approach. Quite often the children know that if they make a nuisance of themselves for long enough, they will get what they want. One mother said of her eight-year old: 'I give him the money to get rid of him.' This could be heard in Branch Street, too, but the context and the consequences of the remark are so different that comparison between the two streets is hardly feasible. In Ship Street, the inconsistent and indulgent treatment of children is as a rule markedly protective. From a Child Guidance point of view, the danger here is not maternal rejection, but too great a maternal possessiveness.

Maternal over-protection is the most striking psychological fact about Ship Street, in the same way as lack of impulse-control is the most striking feature of Branch Street, and in the same way as a taboo on tenderness will be shown to mark the personalities of Ashton. These are all complex patterns of behaviour which may be found anywhere on the social scale as a deviation from what is considered normal, but which may also be a normal phenomenon in a particular sub-culture.

Maternal over-protection is synonymous with excessive maternal care of children. Its manifestations in the mother–child relationship have been grouped, according to the manner in which they occur, under four headings. Three of these concern maternal activity primarily and paraphrase the common observations: (1) 'the mother is always there', (2) 'she still treats him like a baby', and (3) 'she won't let him grow up'. These expressions are rendered into the groupings: (1) excessive contact, (2) infantilization, and (3) prevention of independent behaviour.[1]

An absence or an excess of maternal control is the fourth criterion of over-protection. Levy found that over-protective mothers fell into two categories.

Mothers of dominant children are indulgent, mothers of submissive children are dominating. If a child is submissive to his mother, it is implied that he readily yields to her demands, that he keeps away from the company she forbids, that he goes to bed on time, and the like. On the other hand, if a child goes to bed when he pleases, eats only what happens to suit his fancy, the fact that his behaviour toward his mother has been consistently undisciplined implies she has been consistently indulgent.

In the descriptions of Ship Street it is not possible to distinguish two categories of mothers in this way. Indeed the evidence suggests, rather, either that the mothers are inconsistent by temperament, being sometimes indulgent and at other times domineering, or that the mothers are indulgent in some traditionally defined respects (say food choices or helping in the house) and dominating in other ways. This, at any rate, is the way we shall interpret the evidence. Such an interpretation is to some extent justified not only by the facts as Kerr gives them, but also by some findings from a later study, to the effect that a mother who shows irritation at the child's clinging while yet at the same time indulging his dependence on her, produces

---

[1] D. Levy (1943), *Maternal Over-Protection*, Columbia University Press. These forms of behaviour are discussed in a different context on pages 563–6 and 578–85.

the most dependent kind of child.[1] This is exactly the pattern of maternal behaviour in Ship Street, where dependence on the mother, even in adult life, is the norm.

The resemblances between Levy's subjects and those of Ship Street are quite striking. The mother protects the child, and her own primacy in the child's life, in a whole variety of ways. She will always get the child out of trouble and defend him in conflicts with the world outside. Whatever the child does, she will stick to him. He is never to blame, but has always been led astray, or been just mischievous and blamed for other children's faults. If a child does not like school, no strict check is kept on his attendance. If he does not like school dinners, he is encouraged to come home. If he objects to the food at a convalescent or holiday home, his mother will go and retrieve him. If he is sent to Borstal, for offences which the mother denies he committed, she will visit him and bring him (strictly forbidden) cigarettes.

Being protected from unpleasantness caused by the outside world, the child will continue to depend on his mother at an age when most children learn to be independent. She can thereby handicap his ability to do without her, and if she is possessive, she will do so. For instance, as Kerr pointed out, the mother will gain from having the child dislike the school and resenting its discipline. It means that the school is not tempting the child away from her. Nor does she have to contend with another authority which might make an impact on the child and weaken her own position. She may encourage the child to stay at home from school on occasion and reward him with her affectionate presence. Levy describes the manner of it.

> When overprotection is revealed by all four criteria, the picture presented is well portrayed by a mother who holds her child tightly with one hand, and makes the gesture of pushing away the rest of the world with the other. Her energies are directed to preserving her infant as infant for all time, preserving it from all harm and from contact with the rest of humanity. For her child she will fight hard, make every sacrifice, and aggressively prevent interference with her social monopoly.

[1] C. J. Finney (1961), 'Some maternal influences on child personality and character', *Genetic Psychol. Monog. LXIII*. For further discussion, see pages 460, 516–17 and 558–9.

This makes the father's role a very unenviable one. Quite obviously, such marked over-protection on the mother's part must affect his position in the house.

> Mrs. Z. said that Bill was a nice boy. He should never have been sent away. He did nothing wrong. His father did not want the trouble of rearing him and so he went down to the Court and asked that Bill should be put under care. He said he was unable to control him. Continuing to talk of the father with resentment (with some reason, as Mr. Z., when drunk, was in the habit of 'going for them') she said that the time would come when the sons would turn on their father and leave home.

> Mrs. W. mentioned that her husband comes home from work in the evenings, has his tea and then goes out. She never goes with him . . . He likes his beer. 'To tell you the truth I prefer it when he goes out. When he's in the children keep begging him for money for the pictures and he only shouts at them to shut up.'

From these quotations it seems as though the husband was 'driven out' by the wife. More usually, the man's position depends on whether he has accepted the role which is normal for men in this group. If he has accepted the superior standing of the women of his community he will himself be indulgent, playing the gentler of the two parental roles. The mother may bring in Dad to back her up, but most children do not worry over the threat that 'your Dad will bash you when he comes in': they know that Mum will not allow him to hit them hard. This must be one of the normal patterns, for Levy also notes that the fathers of overprotected children are in general submissive, stable husbands and providers who play little or no authoritative role in the lives of their children.[1]

When the father conforms to the Ship Street norm, the child grows up in a happy family. Mrs. G. on discovering her twelfth pregnancy told Dr. Kerr in utter exhaustion, 'Me love is turned to hate.' She went to hospital to have twins and stayed there a fortnight. On the Sunday morning of her homecoming 'we saw a procession. It consisted of Mrs. G. carrying one twin, of Margaret aged 16 carrying the other, of Robert aged 10 carrying his brother aged 1, of Maureen aged 12 leading her sisters

---

[1] See also the discussion on pages 72, 566-7, 569 ff. and 583.

Sylvia aged 4 and Eileen aged 3 by the hand. The twins were sleeping, everybody else was grinning. Mother was coming home. Mrs. G. looked well and was hurrying . . . Dad, they all reported with glee, was cooking the Sunday dinner at home.'

If on the other hand, the father has rebelled against his subordinate position, he may become a feared, unpredictable, violent figure. Then, when the father does not confine his disciplinary activities to those occasions which the mother considers appropriate, she assumes the protective posture characteristic of her role. 'When me father beats us, we hide behind our mum; when me mother beats us I run out on the street.' Kerr deliberately misinterpreted and suggested, 'So your father must beat you much harder, Vi?' 'Oh, no,' came the spontaneous reply, 'me mother will protect us but me father won't.'

If we compare Ship Street with Branch Street experience of discipline, the first and most obvious point of note is that there are here more and stronger controls. In Branch Street only two social ties were generally acknowledged and thus capable of exerting an influence: ties between sibs and ties between members of a gang. Ship Streeters are familiar with at least two other controlling forces which they respect: the Church and the stable family unit, especially the mother. In this connection it is worth noting that there are two offences for which children are consistently punished: swearing, which includes blasphemy, and an interest in sex. Children consider it daring to write swear-words on the school blackboard or chalk them on fences. They all exclaim with horror at the idea of saying them before their mothers. Characteristically, sex education is left out, or left to the school. Parents seem to feel that discussion of such matters will undermine their authority and the respect which children should show towards them. It is generally considered, in Ship Street, that mothers who let their children know they are going to have a baby are 'disgusting'. Kerr expressed surprise in one interview that a boy had not been told about the coming baby. Both Mr. and Mrs. E. said that they would not dream of that, 'though, mind you, they know: all children round here know everything'. Kerr asked the E.s if they did not think perhaps it might be better if the children first heard of such things from their parents rather than from other children. Mr. E. replied he would not dream of it: 'It might make them rude.'[1]

There seems to be an almost absolute prohibition about speaking to children on matters of sex. The older generation of Mums think the topic should never be mentioned at all, except perhaps by the teacher at school. The school stands in a different relation to the child and in any case it matters less if the children think rudely at school. The younger Mums feel that they have some responsibility but the content of their instruction is to warn the girls to keep away from the boys. They express horror at the idea of telling their daughters even about menstruation. Sex is referred to as 'dirty things' by the children, presumably under the influence of this ban. Great modesty is shown on such occasions as changing clothes. There are many jokes on these matters, generally of a lavatory character. This, Kerr comments, would agree with the general level of immaturity of this group.

As far as sex is concerned, therefore, children learn to be furtive about something it is later permissible to enjoy. Sally, aged ten, asked: 'But do you and Daddy have to do dirty things together before you can have a baby?' The mother answered that if she and Daddy do them together and love each other, it isn't dirty. Sally asserted: 'It's still dirty.' But in adolescence the attitude changes. One girl who at eleven had used that very phrase, when asked at sixteen if she still felt that the expression of love between adults is dirty, replied quite simply, 'Of course not.' All the same, when adult they teach the 'dirty things' attitude to their children.[2]

'Purity of thought' about sex is an important aspect of Catholic teaching but Ship Street is interesting because it manifests a peculiarly Irish form. The difference in culture is most

[1] Although the children do learn things from their age mates, their ignorance is still considerable. Mrs. K. went into hospital at the age of nineteen to have her first child. She asked the woman in the next bed: 'Here, where does the child come from?' The woman replied: 'Same place as it went in.' As she tells the story: I said, 'Here, I'm going home. You see, I thought it came out of your navel.'

[2] It may be permissible to comment that although one would not wish anyone to have to struggle in adult life with a conviction, however unconscious, that sex is dirty, it is a bit of a relief to see sex in the context of dirt rather than of the aggression which accompanies it in Branch Street (see pages 38-9).

tellingly illustrated in Brendan Behan's *Borstal Boy*. One Irish Borstal boy is talking to another about the English in their institution.

> The prisoners, though, though they're all right in their own way, they have as much respect for themselves or for one another, as a bloody animal. They talk about things, aye, and do things, that the lowest ruffian in Ireland, Catholic or Protestant, wouldn't put his tongue to the mention of, things you could be born, grow up, and die an old man in our country without ever hearing the mention of.[1]

The mother's power is backed not only by affectionate ties, but also by the Church, which attaches great importance to the sanctity of the family in general and idealizes the role of the mother in particular. It is a church, moreover, which makes much of the virtue of obedience. So does the mother. In so far as she exacts obedience, and thereby controls the activities of the child, we have here the necessary preconditions for the formation of a super-ego: the child loves the adult who exercises control.[2] Yet the Ship Street super-ego is a rather peculiar one, because the mother is rather peculiar. For one thing, the obedience she exacts is to her as a person and not to a consistent code of behaviour. Rather, as long as the child does as *she* bids him and has not personally offended *her*, she is reliably on his side and protects him from the effects his actions have on others. It is deviation from her ideas that is interpreted as disobedient and punishable.

Yet her social experience is very limited; she is mainly engrossed with her family. The child, especially the adolescent, who becomes aware of a discrepancy between her standards and those of the outside world finds himself therefore in a difficult position. Being not very sensible, and, one gathers from Kerr, at least on occasions a bit power-mad, the mother resents

---

[1] Brendan Behan (1958), *Borstal Boy*, Hutchinson, London.

[2] See also page 477. However perverted some of the manifestations of her affection may be, the attitude of the Ship Street Mum towards her children is normally positive and loving. Kerr notes the remarks children make on this topic, concluding, *inter alia*, that the mother will deny herself many necessities so that the child will have food and clothes. 'Me mother never buys herself any clothes. If Dad gives her money and tells her to buy something for herself, she buys clothes for the children.' See also pages 181-4.

any attempt at emancipation and has quite a repertory of techniques for frustrating any attempt at moving away from her.

Moreover, because as long as the child is obedient she will always get him out of trouble, the child learns to plan not too far ahead. (Indeed, planning ahead, in so far as it means planning further ahead than the mother, is characteristically a resented act.) The child learns to anticipate the consequence of his actions in terms of the mother's reactions, not in terms of the train of external, non-social consequences which the action may set in motion.[1] The outcome of, and the mother's reaction to, any events but those in the immediate future is difficult to predict. So the young personality finds itself rather nearer a trial-and-error form of sanction than is normal in our culture. The only consistently rewarded behaviour is that suggested or approved by the mother. Though some internal sanctions exist, therefore, there is a continued reliance on external rewards and punishment.[2]

To sum up it may be concluded, first, that though the Ship Streeter has a stronger super-ego than is found in Branch Street, it is a barely internal form of control. Secondly, we conclude that the mother plays an unusually strong role in super-ego formation and, more generally, in the development of personality. She may weaken the capacity to form other social ties to an extent which is abnormal in our culture. This negative aspect is most clearly to be seen during the adolescent phase.

ADOLESCENCE, COURTSHIP AND MARRIAGE

The children leave school at the earliest possible opportunity. The work of the school-leaver is what one would expect from an area where not much skilled work is freely available. According

[1] See also pages 516–17.

[2] This reliance on external supports or control also shows itself in a number of other ways, as for instance, in the belief in luck, chance and destiny. 'It was meant', as well as representing an adaptation to an environment which is more unpredictable and unmanageable than most, also supports the negative attitude to planning and foresight. Institutionally it is represented by the clothing clubs and savings clubs—which demand no interest on what is acquired from them—which see to it that what is acquired is paid for. Individual saving without such external support is rare in Ship Street.

Three Preliminary Studies

to Mays, the girls work in shops like Woolworth's, or for a Liverpool Pools firm. They are simply filling in time before marriage. Few of the boys appear to follow in their father's footsteps. Few of them are fitted for office work, and they are prejudiced against it. Brawn more than brain gives prestige to a job. Often they take blind-alley jobs which lead nowhere. There are many changes of work. On the one hand, the reasons for these changes may appear flimsy and demonstrate that the ability to persevere at a less pleasant task, and to tolerate frustrating discipline, was never acquired. On the other hand, it is not easy to see why a boy should not leave one blind-alley job for another if he feels like it. Often the reason given for a change has to do with a difficulty in the sphere of personal relationships: the foreman may have been unkind, for instance. Outsiders tend to criticize boys who do this, but a boy may have been sensible in leaving a social situation he disliked. After all, he is not sacrificing a later satisfaction for the sake of a present impulse.

As the young people leave school and start earning money, they have an opportunity to grow into independence. As well as the new world of work and sexual maturity, with more money and the ability to move about more freely than before, there are the cinemas and the other mass-media of communication, which give them glimpses of other ways of life. Both boys and girls become very interested in their appearance. Much money is spent on hair, clothes and general hygiene. They look and are clean, and contemptuous of those who have not made the same effort or have made it less successfully. They have as examples the practices of the somewhat better-off adolescents a couple of years older than they are.

At this stage there is a brief time of relative freedom and happiness in which the young people enjoy themselves with no thought for their later responsibilities.[1] Inevitably therefore it is the time when the girls' battle for independence from Mum is fought, and in most cases lost. When they start work, they give a portion of their earnings to their mother for their keep. This may not cover the cost of keeping them, and though many mothers are very generous about money, Kerr also gives quite

[1] Cf. page 144, 'A brief flowering period'.

68

a few examples of mothers grumbling that it is not enough. The financial aspect of the battle may however be only a surface symptom of the conflict. The money the girls keep for themselves is used to assert their independence from the mother, or at least this is how the mother may well see it. Instead of helping the mother out of her difficulties and thus showing her solidarity, the girl spends the money on herself, and thus shows her independence and difference.

(A further social distance is created by the mother's inability to discuss matters of sex, and in particular, by the embarrassment consequent upon the girl's first menstruation. As Kerr puts it, the child is unable to speak to the parents about anything other than trivial matters and has therefore a secret life of her own completely outside the parents' knowledge.)

Hence it is not surprising that the conversations Kerr had with the girls show an awareness that the mothers tend to resent them at this age, 'are jealous of them' and 'forever nagging'. The girls feel that too much is continually demanded of them: helping in the house (especially because boys cease to give such help when they hand over their first wage-packet), handing over money, staying at home in the evenings and so on. Adolescence for the girls is a time of rebellion.

As for the boys, it is Kerr's impression that in adolescence it is not the rougher and more independent who go in for delinquency, but rather the sissy, the boy who has complacently accepted his mother's indulgence, it is the spoilt boy. He takes wild risks. He feels entitled to take what he wants. He is too certain that all will be well as long as mother is not displeased.[1]

---

[1] Four of Levy's sample were considered by him to be psychopathic. He describes these as egocentric, with an exaggerated interest in the gratification of personal desires, with scholastic and occupational instability, and with an inability to modify any behaviour-difficulties through experience. On the opposite page he gives a description of 'parasitism' which adds sharper colours: selfish, dependent, demanding, irresponsible behaviour; social charm; self-indulgent and undisciplined behaviour. . . The argument then continues: 'The deviation from normal behaviour in the (psychopathic) examples cited is not usually revealed until adolescence or later. This is due probably to the fact that egocentric behaviour in children is more or less taken for granted. It becomes clearer when more responsibility is anticipated from the older child. The condition is realized the sooner the adult forms of behaviour become necessary in terms of self-maintenance or economic aid for others . . . The greater the requirements of routine and acceptance of authority, the more difficult the adjustment for the indulged over-protected.'

Three Preliminary Studies

The mother–child relation at this time is typically that created by a strong controlling mother, hampering the further development of the child because normal development would be away from her. Whereas the Branch Street child was thrown back on its own resources too early, these children have never needed to stand on their own feet. The Ship Street mother continues in adolescence to be a rock of support. If an illegitimate child is on the way, Mum will help you through. If you are in financial difficulties, she will go out to work to earn for you. Still she takes your side in your battles and gets you out of trouble. Still in return she expects implicit obedience.

For she insists on being the only support you have. Her training in earlier days did not inculcate the virtue of looking ahead, or the planning which goes with a lengthier time-perspective. She has always coped from crisis to crisis. She does not plan ahead, and if you want to, she makes trouble. This conflict comes to a head during adolescence, when the young person's wishes might begin to diverge from the mother's and when efforts to satisfy them are likely to be interpreted as acts of disobedience, mistrust and ingratitude. 'Has she not always looked after you? Do you no longer trust her to know what is best? Do you think you can do better?' If so, she will fight you. Kerr writes: 'The first steps into independence are made too difficult', and quotes Bettelheim and Sylvester:

> The parent counteracts any emancipation. In this respect the child entering adolescence becomes a particular challenge since the adolescent's assertive independence is felt as a threat by the parent, while his greater need for identification is used by the parent to cement closeness through seduction.[1]

As a consequence the child may regress to a dependent state, giving up its desire for emotional gratifications, even for those which are legitimate.

It is in connection with marriage that the Ship Streeters suffer most from their renunciation of what are normally considered legitimate sources of emotional gratification. For the love normally due to the spouse is felt as a form of disloyalty to the mother, and thus to some extent incompatible with it.

[1] B. Bettelheim and E. Sylvester (1950), 'Delinquency and morality', *The Psychoanalytic Study of the Child*, Vol. V, Imago Publishing Co., London.

Here, as elsewhere, power corrupts. When the mothers happen to be unpleasant people, they are exploitative, greedy and cruel in their relations with their sons. They can go to extraordinary lengths to keep a son at home where they will receive his wages, rather than allow him to marry and lose the income. One pulled down the blinds in her house as for a death on the day her son was married, and did not go to the wedding. Another was in such a state that her son asked his best man to stay the night before the wedding so that he would have someone to help him if, as he feared, his mother locked him into his room on his wedding-day. Thus baulked, this same Mum had her son sacked from his job, by making her husband—her son's father—pull strings on the docks. The son was out of work for two years.

When the second generation marries, conflict with the mother disappears. The outbursts against the mother seem characteristic only of adolescence. That is the one time in a Ship Streeter's life when he rebels against the power of the Mum. It is particularly interesting to note that the rebellion takes place during the period when, for girls anyway, there is maximum contact with the outside world. In adolescence, the girl generally says she wants a home of her own. Yet observation convinced Kerr that most married girls live with or near their mothers. When they have been married a short time, and babies arrive in quick succession, they find themselves unable to cope with their responsibilities on their own. They give up and, inevitably, go back to Mum. The husband becomes 'him' and the rebellion is over.

The marriages are by other standards only moderately successful. It may be that the idea that sex is 'dirty things' plays some part in the conviction prevalent in Ship Street—as elsewhere—that if the woman can block all feeling of pleasure in the sexual act she is less likely to conceive. Pregnancy was so feared that it could easily come to be thought of as a punishment for engaging in dirty things, and the dissociation of the sexual act from the rest of the personality may have been felt, in a vague magical sort of way, to avert the dreaded consequence of intercourse. Ship Street girls before they married seemed to Kerr to be quite definitely interested in sex and to take a romantic and sentimental view of marriage. But the girls' interest dies, with some exceptions, when the glamour of marriage wears off and they find that sex means babies. In every case in which a woman admitted pleasure in sexual intercourse, the number of children was small.

A second reason for the lack of depth in the marriage relationship must be the fact that the mother–daughter tie is stronger than other love-relationships. The strength of this tie leads to a lack of inner certainty, a lack of independence, an inability to take responsibility. To make decisions without consulting Mum must be almost unimaginable.

Thirdly, therefore, it must be recognized that in these marriages the conjugal pair is not the normal decision-making unit. When the daughter has returned to the home and acknowledged her mother as supreme, her husband's social role reverts to being a sort of brother or uncle to his wife's younger siblings. He is useful for taking them to the pictures or giving them pocket-money. Where the young family does not live with the wife's mother, the conjugal relationship is not necessarily closer. For the man, too, is tied to his Mum, and in disputes between his wife and his mother, he will tend to take his mother's side. When the offspring of two such families marry, neither spouse will expect to co-operate with the other in deciding for the household.[1] Instead, the two- or three-generation feminine group perpetuates itself:

> 'I couldn't get on without me mother. I could get on without me husband. I don't notice him.' And, facing down the generations: 'I knew in the first week my marriage was a mistake, so when I was pregnant I prayed that the child would be a daughter. All the time I was carrying her I kept saying to myself, "Please, dear God, let it be a girl, please dear God, let it be a girl. She'll be my companion, she'll be my companion. I'll never be lonely any more." '

Kerr asks herself how it comes about that the dependent girl, afraid of responsibility and indissolubly tied to her mother, develops into the dominant and responsible Mum. At first it appears as if on the death of Mum some complete reversal of

[1] See H. Ingersoll, quoted on pages 551 and 565, and the discussion on pages 174-7.

character structure occurs in one of the female members of the family. This, of course, is not the case. There has to be a Mum: she is the central figure in the social organization of this group. Her roles are socially approved, rigid and limited. The daughter who inherits them will not be asked to produce new behaviour-patterns but only to continue the old. She will already have helped her Mum in most of the old roles. Especially if she has lived in the same house—and it is often this daughter who will succeed to the role—she has had additional opportunities for studying the appropriate behaviour. While a daughter she played a daughter-role, now she is a Mum she plays a Mum-role, and prays for a daughter to succeed her.

Chapter Three

'ASHTON' 1956

ASHTON, with a population of nearly 14,000, lies in the centre of the Yorkshire coalfield. It is thought to be fairly typical of the area by Dennis, Henriques and Slaughter, the authors of *Coal is our Life* whence the source-material for the present chapter comes.[1] For the last hundred years, the inhabitants have depended on coal for their existence. Most of the men work in the mines; there is little opportunity for the women to work outside the home.

The dominant feature of the Ashton landscape is the spoil or slag heap: there is no point in the town from which there are none visible. Houses and mineworkings crouch under their shadow. To the observer the spoil heap is the physical symbol of life and work in Ashton.

The pollution of the air is such as to reduce clothes, houses and streets to a drab uniformity. All the same, the housing could illustrate a whole range of ideas which employers, individuals and authorities have had during the last century. One can walk in five minutes from 1870 to 1955. The agent's mansion, the suburban semi-detached, the local authority's housing estate, the squalid rows of back-to-backs with their communal privies, the terraced rows of artisans' houses all have their quota in the town. Back-to-back houses are in a minority: there are only about a hundred of them. The period 1891–1911 saw the building of about a thousand houses of the 'superior artisan' type, with three bedrooms, a kitchen/living-room, a separate yard and separate W.C. Another thousand or so were built in the last

---

[1] Much of what follows is reproduced *verbatim* or in slightly abbreviated form from their account.

fifty years on various estates, of much the same kind but with the advantage of a bathroom and good garden space.

There is a similar variation in the interior of the houses. Homes will reflect the relative prosperity or poverty of the owner. But it cannot be said that there is any necessary connection between bad housing, dirty homes and poverty. There are homes on the new housing estates which are excessively filthy but in which there seems to be plenty of money for the household, and there are back-to-back homes which are impeccably clean. In general, as far as material background is concerned, the standards vary a good deal, though at the upper limit they do not approach those of the urban middle class. Nor at the lower level are they as bad as those of the typical urban slum.

Ashton families have, on the whole, lived there for two generations at least. Thus it comes about that in a place of this size, they share to a large extent the same experiences—they know about each other's streets, places of work, schools and so on. The uniformity and stability of life is characteristically that of a community in which all do the same work, which they themselves respect and for which others in the community respect them. This is both connected with, and further reinforced by, the strong links between contemporaries which the work imposes on the miner. The fact that all follow the same occupation and have the same sort of income also produces a similarity in the way they spend the money. Consumption-patterns which are similar indicate a common way of life.

Before going more deeply into the question of the miner's way of life, it may here be acknowledged that there are a number of respects in which the Ashton community bears a strong resemblance to those whom, in the next chapter, we shall call traditional working class. The fact that it is presented in a separate chapter should not suggest that there is as great a difference between Ashton and other working-class people, as between them and the people of Ship Street or Branch Street. But there are a number of reasons justifying separate treatment:

(*a*) Ashton is in the North of England; the sources used in the next chapters are mainly Southern.

(*b*) Ashton is a relatively isolated community, the last of the three sub-cultures which are discussed on a local basis.

(*c*) Ashton is as markedly male-dominated as Ship Street is female-dominated.

(*d*) Ashton shows a very remarkable interrelation between attitudes connected with the work-situation and attitudes connected with domestic matters.

One way in which Ashton is distinguishable from Branch Street and Ship Street is in the way this group and the neighbouring groups regard one another. Ashton external relations are different. The people of Branch Street, in their contact with the outside world, were aware primarily of the contempt with which other groups regarded them, and only secondarily concerned with their own deprivation relative to other groups. Ship Street was a closed and isolated community, conscious of its superiority to neighbouring groups, though also aware, without much caring, that other more remote groups were better off. In Ashton there are no neighbouring groups worse off than the miners. On the contrary, because it is a small town and because they do not deliberately isolate themselves, the groups with reference to which the miners make comparisons are better off. In this, the Ashton miner resembles other working men. Dennis and his associates argue that the working man tends to have a concrete view of his relations with other classes, i.e. he sees and remarks in the main the outward signs of the fundamental relations.[1] He thinks of the fact that the other classes do not perform manual work rather than of specific social and economic categories. He confirms this view by a consideration of the spending and consumption patterns of the different social strata. In general his class is the class that has to work for an amount of money that will give enough to live on, with a margin for enjoyment.

There is a feeling here that the worker's efforts do not reap a commensurate reward, as well as a feeling of sturdy self-respect. His pride in being a worker, and his solidarity with other workers, is a pride in the fact that they are real men who work hard for their living and without whom nothing in society could function. It has always been a favourite point of Socialist speakers to tell their audiences how indispensable they, the workers, are in comparison with the 'parasites' of the upper

[1] By fundamental relations these writers mean economic relations.

76

classes. The 'parasites' are marked off essentially by the fact that they get a living without working; working, for reasons we shall explore later, means, essentially, working with your hands.

We shall find, on the one hand, that the Ashton man differs from the men of Branch Street and (to a lesser extent) from those of Ship Street because his skill gives him self-respect while, on the other hand, his work subjects him to routines over which he has little of the control to which he feels his skill entitles him. In this, he resembles many other skilled working men, from whom he differs, however, in the intensity with which he holds his attitudes. He also, be it said, differs from them in that he has in fact rather more freedom than they have.

SOME EFFECTS OF LIVING AT RISK

Freedom

This freedom relates in many distinct ways to the miner's peculiar occupational situation. He is highly skilled, he works in a team, in circumstances which make supervision virtually impossible. These circumstances typically lead to the kind of psychological freedom in working life which also characterizes the independent craftsman and the professional. The miner's relative freedom is however peculiarly affected by the generally accepted fact that his work is hard and perilous. Mining is a dangerous occupation, with the risk of death or incapacitating injury markedly higher than in most other kinds of work. There is furthermore the memory of insecurity of employment: the miner may cease earning because the pit has closed down or reduced production. More than in most trades there is a risk of being killed at work or laid off for a while by unemployment due to injury. Zweig reports a conversation in *Men in the Pits*.[1]

'Why do most of them look so grim, or, rather, so serious?' I asked.

'Because life in the pits and the colliery village is serious; because it is a hard struggle, with certain defeat at the end,' came the answer.

'Well, in the end all men are defeated,' I joked with them. 'We all end by being worn out and weary in body and mind.'

[1] F. Zweig (1948), *Men in the Pits*, Gollancz, London.

'Yes, but there is a difference between pit-life and work in the light, in the fresh air, and in natural surroundings which do not constantly threaten you with danger. Can't you see for yourself the number of disabled men with amputated legs or arms or fingers, or even blind, or with twisted spines or necks, or otherwise laid on their backs?'

I had to agree that nowhere else can you see the same relative numbers of disabled men as in a colliery village.

The effect of living at risk is familiar to all who have lived through a time of war. There is a socially licensed insistence on having all one can get, a greed for getting the most out of life, a lot of gambling, no thought for the morrow.

Oh let us not think of tomorrow
Lest we disappointed be.
Our joys may turn to sorrow
As we may daily see.
Today we may be strong and healthy
But soon there will be a change
As we may see from the explosion
That has been at Trindon Grange.

This attitude of living for the day has its financial implications. Because of the irregularity and insecurity of income, saving does not pay. The money saved is too likely to be spent on normal household maintenance when the man is off work or on reduced rates. Some short-term saving does go on. Dennis, Henriques and Slaughter call it saving for a sunny and not for a rainy day: for an outing, for an article of furniture, for clothing or for a treat at Christmas. But even in this respect, saving is not very important, because the miner can make a lot extra by working at full stretch for a brief period.

After such an effort, the husband will probably miss a couple of shifts when his turn for working nights comes round. One may see in this alternation of hard work and relaxation some exercise of the freedom of choice and control over everyday life.[1] Even though the men do not appreciate it as such, it is a freer life than many other workers have.

Saving is normally a family matter rather than an individual one, but not in Ashton, where the idea that saving does not pay

[1] See also pages 193–6 and 464–5.

works out to the men's advantage. Almost everything in Ashton does, for the hardship of the men's lives is considered to justify their enormously privileged position relative to the women. The distribution of income within the family is very much affected by the interrelated factors of the man's privileged position and the vicissitudes of mining life. A miner must be in the prime of condition if he is to earn top wages. This cannot last. The highly-paid age runs from twenty-five until forty-five. There is a great difference between what is earned then and what is earned before or after the peak, and, taking into account the other reasons for insecurity, the general attitude is one which counts on a wage-level well below peak earnings. The difference between peak wages and what are regarded as expected wages is thought of as 'free income', in the sense that there is no family expenditure which has a firm and regular claim on it. The miner can spend it as he wishes, and he spends it with his mates. It is not thought of as due to the family as a unit. Though the family is at this time increasing, it is an unsuccessful competitor for the pleasures which are procurable by means of the free income.

The fact that the husband's work is considered so disagreeable has another effect. The woman is considered the more fortunate member of the household because she does not go down the mine. For this reason the woman never puts pressure on her man to go to work; she never asks him directly whether he will work, but asks instead whether she ought to get his clothes ready for him, or some such circumlocution. This in spite of the fact that taking a day off lowers the amount of money available in the house. The man must feel free to go to work or not, as he pleases.

In these ways, one may argue, the Ashton miner experiences more freedom than the ordinary skilled working man. On the other hand, because our authors were in Ashton at a time when comparative material was not available, they occasionally exaggerate the extent of careless living on such evidence as this. By the standards of Branch Street or Ship Street, however, these lives are very strictly regulated. One has, additionally, to take into account that in lives of great hardship there may grow up a tradition of extreme permissiveness and indulgence in certain

79

circumstances or at certain times of life. Often, though apparently not in Ashton, infancy is such a time. Often, as in Ashton, adolescent behaviour is indulgently regarded.[1] The peculiar situation of the miner is that, outside the pit, he is regarded as entitled to self-indulgence because of that stage of life when he works in danger at the pit.

The hardships of a miner's life are in some ways balanced by the lack of pressure outside the pit. In his non-working life few demands are made on the miner's self-control or endurance. In addition, the strain of work below is eased by a number of psychological adjustments, among which a reliance on habit may be counted.

The contractual attitude

Mining is a noisy, dirty, dangerous occupation. The awareness that this is so is bound to affect other aspects of the miner's way of life. The ramifications of its effects may be traced through a number of spheres: industrial relations, leisure activity, family life. Zweig suggests that only very strongly established habits would make life tolerable to the miner.

> I had never realized until I came into contact with miners, how strong can be the force of habits and how great is their functional value . . . Habit-forming has great functional value for miners. It enables them to overcome strong resistance against carrying on their jobs. It must be realized that it is not very pleasant to go down the pit, to the dust, sweat and darkness every day, and the miner frequently asks himself, 'Must I?' But the habit helps him a lot . . . It is characteristic that holidays result not in better attendance and performance, as should be the case on *a priori* grounds; on the contrary, it takes a whole fortnight before the miner can get over a week's holiday . . . His mechanism of adaptation, the automatism of habit, has been loosened, he sees how different life can be without this drudgery; his appreciation of fresh air, light and relaxation is increased, and he has to struggle with a strong inner resistance. Even a long week-end has this effect . . . The miner can do his job properly only if he is helped by strong habits. Once his habit system is weakened he is lost.

Dennis, Henriques and Slaughter confirm this when they argue that the temptation to stay away on a Monday night

---

[1] See also pages 144 and 196 fn.

is exacerbated when the miner is not required for work until
10 p.m. on Monday, and has finished the previous week at
8–10 p.m. on Friday. This makes for a long week-end, at the
end of which he has acquired a taste for freedom. For a man
working days and nights alternately, i.e. finishing at 1.30 p.m.
on Friday, this tendency is naturally stronger.

Habit reduces the strain which might otherwise be felt on
each occasion when the work must be taken up again. We shall
have reason to note in a variety of contexts the importance of
habit, routine, tradition and other such words signifying regularity in Ashton life. Habitual behaviour reduces the number of
choices that have to be made in a given period. Choice requires
consciousness. If life is disagreeable, choices are likely to be between alternatives which are none of them especially attractive,
and consciousness, in these circumstances, is too often consciousness of danger, squalor, sadness, deprivation. Habit allows
people to take their conditions for granted.

The habits of people, if they arouse habitual expectations in
others, and if they are socially recognized as characteristic of a
category of people—'males', 'children', 'bosses'—may be called
role-performances and role-expectations respectively. One of
the very striking things about Ashton is the system of very firm
and strictly defined role-relationships which obtain there, so
much so that there is a strongly contractual and 'bargaining'
flavour in all role-definitions, even, as we shall see, in the conjugal relationship. Each performs the duties prescribed as appropriate to that role and has a right, with sanctions attached,
to expect others to perform their reciprocal role. There is, comparatively speaking, little latitude in the performance of these
roles: people 'give nothing away'. The attitude is remarkably
consistent over different aspects of life.

The Ashton miner works in a team with a clearly defined
division of labour. Not to be able to rely on fellow-workers may
have serious consequences in any industry, but in mining the
work of others, even on a different shift, affects a man's work,
making it easier or more difficult, affects his pay-packet, indeed
his very life. A man is therefore expected by his mates to be
competent at his work and to pull his full weight. If he does not,
he is ejected from the group. (So it happens that the better

workers are in teams which may persist for years, only occasionally losing or adding a member.) A man is given a fair chance to prove himself a worthy member of such a group. In the accounts which follow, the starkness with which the reciprocal rights and obligations are expressed in action shows up in all its justice and toughness.

When a new man joins an established work-team, in the first stage, i.e. before he has become recognized as a bad worker, being the slower team-mate, he is helped out by a neighbouring worker so that he does not fall behind or create danger. This will happen even though the men are on piece-rates, so that their earnings drop when they slow up. If the man makes no progress after such help, the others warn him that they are thinking of excluding him from their team. In due course, if he shows no improvement, he is excluded. In mining conditions there is no room for personalities that are feckless, lacking in self-control or perseverance, impulsive and unused to considering themselves in relation to others as part of a team.

The system of relationships is such that it is easy to maintain a stable equilibrium. On the negative side of sanctions, the fear of contempt or of being a traitor keeps the group of men solidary. Disloyal and blackleg miners are social outcasts not only in the mine but in the community, since most men work in the mines and communication spreads easily through the village. Those whose actions are most in danger of misinterpretation are particularly careful not to give offence. For instance, there are miners—'market-men'—who are employed as substitutes for an absentee; they may be sent on a different task every day or so. They themselves are quick to suspect that they might be sent to cut down the work of certain contractors and they will often say 'I'm not going to do someone else's work, am I?' A union man will also be standing near to gain assurance that the management does not get the chance of splitting the men in this way. One of the authors of *Coal is our Life* was sent one day during a short working period at Ashton Colliery to help two rippers. The men refused to start work until they had seen the deputy and made sure that their wages would not be affected.

To those who have fallen on evil days through no fault of their own, or to those who are poorly off for reasons they respect, the men are very generous. But strict reciprocity is upheld in principle. An old miner who had been permanently disabled as the result of an injury told the following story:

> When I was lamed five years ago and I came out of hospital on crutches, I. J. was the first one to buy me a drink. Since then he has given me half a crown or three shillings or whatever change he has happened to have in his pocket so that I could have a quiet drink . . . I can't pay him back straight away. But I had a pair of glasses and I. J. put them on. 'Champion! Just right!' he said. 'Put them in your pocket,' I said. 'What do you want for them,' he said. 'I want you to put them in your pocket, that's what I want. My eyes are too far gone for reading glasses.'

The taboo on tenderness

In a previous quotation, it was suggested by Zweig that the miner must to some extent do violence to his natural feelings if he is to contemplate without despair a lifetime of descents into the pit. One way in which he may adapt himself is by developing deeply ingrained habits, which do away with the necessity of forcing himself at the beginning of each shift. In addition he may learn to avert his mind from any of the feelings which would make it more painful for him to pursue his calling. This brings us to a concept evolved in psychoanalytic practice—the taboo on tenderness—which covers a set of attitudes markedly similar to those discernible in Ashton.

Just as Kate Friedlander was able to throw light on some aspects of Branch Street behaviour and Levy on Ship Street, so Ian Suttie's *Origins of Love and Hate* provides us with a background to some aspects of emotional life in Ashton.[1] He, like those others, derives his insights from his practice of psychotherapy with a mainly middle-class clientèle. Suttie had been working with a young woman who had systematized delusions of persecution. Her whole existence was a struggle for power and revenge. She loathed and despised 'sentimentality'; to her, anything except ruthless egotism was hypocrisy and weakness. When she began to get a little better, she started a counter-attack on Suttie which worried him.

[1] Published in 1935 by Kegan Paul, Trench and Trubner, London, and later in the Pelican series.

I had not loved her well enough to make her well. I had taken her on . . . because I had a scientific interest in her . . . I had, perhaps, done it as a sporting effort and kept her on because I did not like to admit defeat. I had done it out of humanity and a sense of duty, which she disliked most of all . . .

. . . It became apparent that her unloving attitude was an arte-fact of her disease and, although her love was as egoistic as a baby's, the craving for love was there, and in some way, this 'greed' still seemed to carry the beginnings of liking and consideration . . . The whole paranoid mask was, in fact, a defence against an unloving world, against the pain of isolation and the longing for tenderness and security, against the dread of the rebuff to which 'snivelling' would expose her.[1]

It became clear to me at the same time that I myself had a positive intolerance to 'mawkish' sentiment and 'babyish' tender-ness, that, in fact, my correct, practical, 'frozen' attitude had been maintaining her anxiety and rage. This intolerance of senti-mentality was no revelation to me. It appeared the most natural, rational and practical attitude possible . . . I was surprised, how-ever, that any pleas for sympathy should occasion me embarrass-ment and impatience, whereas sexual and excretory interests in the patient leave me undisturbed. Why, if tender feeling is a sublimation of sexuality, should it evoke a more active repulsion than its supposed origin? . . . The answer was clear: because it is *childish* and the adult has been compelled to put away childish things . . . I immediately began to study both the patient's and my own defences and came to the conclusion that there is a *taboo on tenderness* every bit as spontaneous and masterful as the taboo on sex itself.

Suttie then considered the childhood experiences of patients like this. It struck him that 'the exhibition of tenderness is per-mitted to the mothers of young children, but goo-goo talk is rather reprehended. It embarrasses us.' Why? he asks. 'Because there is a taboo on tenderness or anything else that savours of infantility. The state of mind here described is a reaction against the sentiments related to the mother and the nursery, from which these children have just emerged, in all probability unwillingly.'

This led Suttie to consider the effects of a strict definition of what the child's behaviour should be at each stage, so that the

[1] See, for instance, the account on page 116, where the little girl is chastised for 'moaning'.

84

stages of development are related to the child's chronological age rather than to its current needs. The more strict a society's role-definitions, the more rigidly these expectations are likely to be enforced.[1]

. . . 'One by one the attentions formerly enjoyed are withdrawn. This is appreciated by the child as a withdrawal of love itself, and, more important still, as meaning that its love and itself are not wanted or welcome by the mother. In our culture in particular, the brusqueness of the cleanliness training, the frequent and prolonged separation of mother and infant, and the mother's own intolerance of tenderness, bring about a precipitate 'psychic parturition' attended by an anxiety, acquisitiveness and aggressiveness which are reflected in our culture and economic customs and attitudes . . .

To the anger attending the thwarting of tenderness-feelings must be added the grief for the loss of the mother, and, above all, the anxiety caused by her *changing attitude* . . . The child discovers that what it has painfully and obediently learned, does not after all satisfy the parent who exacts these sacrifices, that its childish ways of pleasing are no longer acceptable, and that there is really nothing on which it can depend. The very roots of its sense of security and justice are struck at by the denial of baby caresses and by the rejection of those offered by the child . . .

The child must then either develop normal companionships and interests in lieu of the contracting love-absorption, or it must develop less desirable characteristics: fighting for its rights, and/or finding satisfaction in surreptitious regressions and substitutes, and/or avoiding the pain of privation by repression. This last places the taboo on tenderness.

Suttie thereupon proceeded to trace the effects in social life of the constraint which society imposes upon the expression of tenderness.

The most typical example (indeed, proto-typical) can be found in the gang of larger or smaller boys who idealize what is euphemistically called 'manliness' in contradistinction to 'babyishness' and 'girlishness'. The ideals of such a community are intensely anti-feminist, as indicated by the coining of such epithets as 'milk-sop', 'cry-baby', 'mummy's boy', etc. On the positive side, this ego-ideal holds up toughness, aggressiveness, hardness, as

[1] See also the discussion on pages 466 ff.

prime virtues . . . Power, violence, cunning and crime have such a fascination for these children that (when in due course they arrive at Fleet Street) every burglary is 'daring' and every swindle 'clever' . . .

These little boys when grown up and 'civilized', have no less inhibition in expressing, and embarrassment in receiving, cordial regard. Sentiment makes them 'squirm'. 'It is simply not done', 'It is wet' . . . So that expressions of liking and esteem have actually to be disguised more carefully than a smutty joke. One very common cover for expressions of warm or tender feeling is mock abuse. Quite outrageous epithets are employed as terms of endearment.

In a later section, forms of speech and their emotional significance are to be discussed in considerable detail. We may note here, however, that poverty of speech, of thought and of emotion go together.[1] Bernstein has argued that where speech is restricted, it tends to be 'tough', accompanied by 'tough' behaviour in a way which clearly supports Suttie's argument:

Tender feelings which are personal and highly individual will not only be difficult to express in this linguistic form, but it is likely that objects which arouse tender feelings will be given tough terms—particularly those referring to girl-friends, love, death and disappointments. The experience of tender feelings . . . may produce feelings of acute embarrassment, discomfort, a desire to leave the field and denial or hostility toward the object which aroused the tender feelings. To speakers of this kind of language, tender feelings are potential threats, for in this experience is also the experience of isolation—social isolation . . .

Another psychological correlate of this linguistic form is that it discourages the experience of guilt and shame in relation to particular situations. This is not to say that all feelings of guilt are minimized, but that they are minimal to certain social acts. Consider these social terms for a situation where the individual deliberately avoids an allotted task or duty: 'skive', 'scrounge', 'dodge the column', 'swing the lead', etc. These terms are by their very nature social counters which the individual can attach to a particular class of act . . . The terms take the form of a type of euphemism which disguises or blurs the implications of the intention. Certain sociological and psychological associations which

[1] See pages 173, 211–12 and 298–9.

would follow from the appropriate description of the act—avoiding work deliberately—are neutralized. Perhaps one of the most important is that experiences of guilt are minimized. This is not to say that the individual will not be aware that the act is wrong nor that punishment is unjust but that feelings of guilt are divorced from the notion of wrongness.[1]

When people feel guilty but have not the equipment to attach this feeling correctly to particular acts, they are incapacitated from dealing with their guilt rationally. This may further encourage the inhibition of emotional life, so that a vicious spiral is constructed.

Bernstein considers this kind of language—he calls it 'restricted code'—to be characteristically the language used by equals among themselves: it is the speech form of the peer-group. We find a good deal of support for the theory here outlined in the descriptions of informal social life in Ashton.

COGNITIVE POVERTY

There is a connection and mutual support between the taboo on tenderness and a related set of psychological phenomena which may be called 'cognitive poverty'. Even the most sympathetic writers on working-class ways of life remark on what appears as a stubborn determination not to develop—and not to allow others to develop—attitudes or behaviour which would make for a richer and more interior life. Hoggart, in his discussion of the tolerance of working people towards one another, relates this tolerance 'chiefly to the unexpectant, unfanatic unidealistic group sense, to the basic acceptance by most people of the larger terms of their life'.

The tradition of the group is a personal and local tradition. It seems to have its strength initially from the ever-present evidence,

---

[1] B. Bernstein (1959), 'A public language: some sociological implications of a linguistic form', *Brit. J. Sociol.*, IV. The cited passage continues: 'The social counter "lark", e.g. "I only did it for a lark", covers a dimension of behaviour from a harmless prank to a major delinquency. The term defines the situation as one of play so that if there are any unfortunate consequences these will be regarded as unintended, accidental developments, so freeing the doer from individual responsibility' (see also page 35).

in the close, huddled, intimate conditions of life, that we are, in fact, all in the same position.

As the outer world becomes more streamlined, so the family and the neighbourhood come to be regarded, even more than formerly, as something that is real and recognizable.

If we want to capture something of the essence of working-class life in a phrase, we must say that it is the 'dense and concrete life', a life whose stress is on the intimate, the sensory, the detailed and the personal.[1]

According to Dennis, Henriques and Slaughter, there is little provision for the pursuit of 'intellectual' interests in the clubs and pubs where much of the social life of Ashton takes place, if one excludes by definition the intellectual interest of conversation. The clubs have no books. There are 'reading rooms', but their sole provisions are the national daily newspapers and several copies of the papers which specialize in horse-racing.

At the club the members spend most of their time simply conversing over their beer. Conversation is notably free and easy. The men have often been life-long acquaintances; having been at the same school and played together as children, they now, as adults, work at the same place and spend their leisure together in such places as the clubs, pubs and sports grounds. The topic which surpasses all others in frequency is work—the difficulties which have been encountered in the day's shift, the way in which a particular task was accomplished, and so on. The only other subject which is regularly discussed is sport.

Most clubs have a 'best room', in which the conversation is thought to range rather more widely than it does in the other rooms and where those who 'like to talk and debate', as one man put it, can do so. Dennis, Henriques and Slaughter consider the conversation in one 'best room'. Any evening a group of between ten and twenty will be there, discussing the topics of the day. On a particular evening there were twelve, whose ages ranged from twenty-five to the late sixties. Seven were contract-men, one was a former contract-man, the others were a store-

---

[1] R. Hoggart (1957), *The Uses of Literacy*, Chatto and Windus, London. I would not wish to imply that cognitive poverty marks the working classes only; cf. pages 367-8 and 385-7.

keeper at the colliery, a colliery tradesman, a colliery crane-driver, and the manager of the local cinema. A recent Rugby League match was first discussed. This was followed by a heated argument concerning an international boxing match. The conversation at this point turned towards Government policy in regard to roads and eventually led to the topic of housing. All these matters were dealt with from the Ashton point of view, that is, from the point of view of their relationship and importance to Ashton. (In fairness, it should be added that the plight of Seretse Khama aroused great interest in Ashton.)

Even in the 'best room' there is a strong tendency to suppress by ridicule any attempt at refinement or differentiation. This may be seen in the slightest events. On one occasion, someone produced a rather more expensive brand of tobacco. The cry immediately went up, 'My, aren't we posh', and the middle-aged collier concerned put the tin away in confusion. Again, someone using a slightly unusual word, such as 'proximity', will find himself the butt of 'good-natured' banter.

Dennis, Henriques and Slaughter in a very interesting passage argue in effect that the collier's normal working conditions have had an effect which the psychologist recognizes as typically the effect of anxiety in quite other situations: a reduction in exploratory behaviour, a constricted horizon, a restriction of demands upon life. 'To become too used to a high standard of living (in the years when he is earning well) might make adjustment exceedingly painful (in the period when his earnings drop). There is a temporary sense of loss attendant upon the deprival of even the most trivial possession which is avoided if at all possible . . . By keeping his standard of living low in relation to necessities, the miner avoids the possibility of that permanent sense of loss suffered by decayed gentlemen or gentlewomen.'

From a less individual standpoint, it is a commonplace in the field of small-group studies that, when a group habitually penalizes members who do not conform very exactly to the norm, the social life of that group becomes progressively more impoverished.[1]

---

[1] A more theoretical discussion of the impoverishment of ideas in inward-looking groups will be found in J. Klein (1956), *The Study of Groups*, chaps. 5, 6, 10.

That this is so in Ashton can be illustrated from a whole variety of anecdotes, some of which have already been cited in previous pages.[1] The first which follows below demonstrates, besides the narrowness of interests which is our present concern, the inferior position of women, a topic to which we shall return.

A Labour Party General Meeting was held. Twenty-two members turned up, of whom thirteen were women and nine were men. The men knew all the fine points of procedure and made much of them. The women seemed to be ignorant of procedure and all their contributions at the meeting were treated with amused tolerance by the men.

The minutes of the previous meeting were read and passed as a true record. Among the correspondence was an invitation to the local Labour Party to send delegates to a British Asian Fellowship conference at the county town. There were no volunteers. . . .

'I've a long letter here about British Guiana,' the Secretary said. 'It's a bit of a long letter. Does anybody want me to read it?'

'Don't bother,' one of the ladies cried out. 'We've enough trouble in Ashton.' The letter was accordingly left unread . . . For the remainder of the time the meeting discussed the arrangements which the social sub-committee had made for the annual dinner and dance.

The predominance of social rather than political interest is not restricted to women members of the party. For example, while there were only 26 members at the Annual General Meeting of the local Labour Party in 1954, there were 153 at the Annual Dinner.

If the interest of the local community turns inward-looking in this manner, it encourages a way of life that is uncomplicated and clearly defined in structure, but narrow and relatively incapable of absorbing new experience. When faced with novel ideas or experiences, the urge to select those aspects which are already familiar will then be correspondingly greater.

It might be expected, and it is often stated, that the development of road transport has immensely widened the social horizon

[1] This topic will be taken up again on pages 255-7, 367 ff. and 379 ff., because social pressures to conform—though they assume different forms in different social regions—are characteristic throughout English society, and indeed, must be characteristic of any social group. The English variants seem to me distinguishable because they are always accompanied by strong anti-intellectual trends; this seems less true of Welsh or Scottish or Continental society.

for the inhabitants of the once isolated mining communities. It is interesting to observe, however, that the people who go on the trips from the Ashton clubs in fact seek out those activities in the places they visit which most closely resemble those provided in Ashton . . .
In 1953, forty-five members of the tourist club visited London. The capacity which they showed in selecting, from the London environment, traits which resembled Ashton was remarkable. And having found, for instance, the Ashton-like public houses, instead of avoiding them, they insisted on spending the evening in them . . . He [the Ashton miner] is able to withstand the influence of a new environment by selecting only those aspects of it which fit in with his established pattern of existence.[1]

Similar considerations apply to the influence which the cinema might have had. Here also there is a selection from the environment of those aspects which least disturb the Ashton pattern of life. The films that are seen resemble one another in their irrelevance to the problems of the day. When Ashton people visit the cinema, they protect themselves by attending only those films which portray events so utterly remote from any they know that their portrayal has no real impact on their lives.

Hoggart, writing about this psychologically frozen North (it is very possible that Southern regions differ in this respect), comments on the attitudes underlying this restriction of demands upon life. He makes much of the connection between a cheerful stoicism and resignation on the one hand, and, on the other, the advantages of a short time-perspective, with its stress on the here-and-now and its assumption that things cannot be changed.

When people feel that they cannot do much about the main elements in their situation, feel it not necessarily with despair or disappointment or resentment, but simply as a fact of life, they adopt attitudes towards that situation which allow them to have a liveable life under its shadow, a life without a constant and pressing sense of the larger situation. The attitudes remove the main elements in the situation to the realm of natural laws, the given

[1] See Hoggart, op. cit., pages 116–18 in the Pelican edition, for a similar observation. But though a brief outing, made in a coach where the everyday group is present to exert its influence, may not produce much change in outlook, the motor car, used for a family outing, could do so, and according to Zweig, does so (see page 265).

and the raw, the almost implacable, material from which a living has to be carved. Such attitudes, at their least-adorned a fatalism or a plain accepting, are generally below the tragic level; they have too much of the conscript's lack of choice about them. But in some of their forms they have dignity.

By and large the note that is struck seems to be that we [the traditional working-class people] are not asked to be the great doers in this world. Our kind of life offers little of splendour or of calls for the more striking heroisms, and its tragedies are not of the dramatic or rhetorical kind. At least, that is the sort of view this world seems to invite us to take: to do its heavier work, with sights fixed to short distance.[1]

It is appropriate to anticipate at this point a later discussion on Ashton parents and their children, in order to point up the relation between the attitudes and situations so strikingly described by Hoggart, and their perpetuation in Ashton, even against the wishes of those most concerned. Ninety-three Ashton people, selected at random, were asked how they felt about encouraging a son to work in the mining industry. Sixty-six said they would not or did not encourage their sons to this step, many of them expressing themselves most emphatically. But although parents deny that they encourage their sons to be miners, the great majority do in fact become miners. Again, when the same people were asked whether they thought it advantageous to have a grammar-school education, seventy-nine answered in the affirmative. Yet only very few Ashton children actually go to grammar school, and very few develop interests broader than those of their parents, whose interests can be satisfied by life in Ashton. We have, conclude our authors, given two examples of the failure to coincide of parents' expressed wishes and the actual fate of their children. In each case an important consideration is the fact that the position of the parents in the social structure unfits them for the task of (a) holding their ideas very strongly or practically and (b) carrying them out. These two disadvantages, not by any means perceived or understood by all parents, reinforce that characteristic already described by these authors as 'basic'—the approach to life on only a day-to-day footing.

[1] See also pages 87–8 and 214.

In this same paragraph our authors then proceed to link their argument to the anti-intellectualism which runs through English society. Miners, they write, like many other industrial workers, are often very cynical about 'book-learning' in anything to do directly with their own life and work. They recognize the value of book-learning for getting on in school and as a training for professions out of their experience, but for their own lives, and in contact with their own people, they are sceptical about 'theory', so that any child not showing exceptional talent with books at school is given little encouragement to study.[1]

The mistrust of anything unfamiliar, 'fancy', has implications for intellectual life which are worth considering in greater detail, particularly in relation to a general mistrust of abstract thought. We may here be dealing with a set of personality traits which are characteristic of the members of many traditional societies. Abstract thought is by definition about possibilities, not actualities. In so far as people are traditional, actualities do govern their lives. If they were to give a sufficiently strong allegiance to what they felt to be possibilities, changes would be going on. The lack of interest in possibilities is one of the things which keeps them traditional.[2]

The passages from Hoggart which we are using in this section support the theory that (traditional) 'working-class people are generally suspicious of principles before practice. In the more articulate this occasionally becomes a thrusting brass-tacks "realism" which is in fact a self-glorification, masking a disinclination to probe uncomfortably—"let's get on with the job. All this theory gets you nowhere".' This expression is exactly matched by an observation from *Coal is our Life* that there is a scarcity of conversation on the level of general principles. Any attempt to do so is dismissed as 'talk'—that is, empty argument. Credit goes to the man who 'knows a lot' of facts. Thus for instance, in conversation about work and football, general considerations or abstractions scarcely ever appear. The discussion is almost always about concrete cases, whether of actual incidents at the colliery, or actual incidents on the field of play. Dennis, Henriques and Slaughter add as a footnote here, that

[1] See also pages 300 and 590–2. [2] See also pages 269–70.

men will often go into great detail about such things as who was the deputy on No. 21 district when so-and-so broke his leg, or who it was who scored the try that won the match so many seasons ago. Spirited discussion will often take place on what the facts actually are or were.

Partly, this is a matter of socio-economic position. When living so near the unalterable unpleasant realities of life, it is very hard to believe that 'talking will do any good' for the simple reason that it really will not. Talking about what is not here-and-now will have all the features of wishful thinking, including its pointlessness. And so it is despised.

With the mistrust of ideas goes a great difficulty in handling any ideas which have not been absorbed into traditional vocabulary or phrasing. That is to say, there is a difficulty in thinking along other than traditional or stereotyped lines. Mogey, to whose studies in Oxford reference will be made in subsequent chapters, recounts an anecdote which illustrates the difficulties and distress which may accompany an attempt to get people unaccustomed to individual mental effort to think without the aid of the stereotyped reactions to which they have become accustomed. He ran an extra-mural class in Oxford and came up against the difficulty of getting members to participate in discussion.[1]

[1] J. Mogey (1956), *Family and Neighbourhood*, page 46. Zweig's general comments may also be aptly quoted here:

'When examining the workers' views on life we must distinguish between different layers. Not all of them have the same depth of conviction and the same significance. Some of the views presented are purely conventional [i.e. traditional], being a repetition of proverbs, popular sayings, and precepts from the Bible and similar sources, or repetitions of views often repeated in the popular press. Others are personal views, the generalization a man has drawn from the experience of his own individual life. Frequently they are a rationalization of what a man has actually done, or of his interests, drives and urges, if they are approved by his group . . . There is also a third category of views, thought out by the men themselves by hard thinking or study with the basis of observation in the radius of his own experience . . . The difference between the second group and this is only that in this a man shows a greater radius of experience and a deeper penetration . . . Finally, we have purely impersonal ideas derived from the study of books, reviews, lectures or broadcasts, which come nearer to the views of intellectuals . . . These four layers of thought may co-exist in any man's mind and in a course of conversation you may come across them one after another' (*The British Worker*, page 216).

A few pages later he points out that these layers are not to be related directly to intelligence or education. There is a bottom level of inferior intelligence . . . Men in this group never exercise their brains, and think only of the scraps of life

This difficulty had little reference to the intellectual content of the topic to be discussed. It arose because the students had a fixed stereotyped phrase which was believed to fit the case, so that further discussion was not considered necessary. Thus, after a talk on class-divisions in society, an ex-naval student expressed the thinking of his class like this: 'In the navy, you know where you are. There's officers, petty officers, and men. In civvy street, there's no difference. What you've been saying is all a lot of snobbery, that's what it is.' 'That's right,' said a nurse. 'I'm as good as the next person, even though I do live in a council house. It's all snobbery, that's it.' Here [Mogey continues] it was obvious that the word 'class' had a strong bias and was misunderstood. So, echoing the phrase 'It's all snobbery', the tutor proceeded to try to enlarge on the meaning attached to it. This produced evident signs of distress instead of the expected attempts to re-phrase the definition and see it in another light.

This is what cognitive poverty amounts to in practice. To restate the argument so far: Cognitive poverty describes habits of thinking rigidly, concretely, without speculation, without pleasure, over a narrow range of interests. Cognitive poverty may characterize a society, and if it does, that society will main-tain and perpetuate its traditional outlook. When people live near subsistence level, cognitive poverty is more likely because there is neither leisure nor other incentive for more abstract thought to develop. The tradition is maintained in a number of ways which inhibit innovation or originality of behaviour. There is unvarying ridicule of minor deviance (a generally very frequent form of social control). There is the interest in personal detail as contrasted with an interest in wider and more abstract issues, concern with which is felt to be incomprehensible as well as slightly ridiculous and unfitting for members of the group. There is the preference for the familiar, as contrasted with a

---

that come their way, the daily details of their lives. The process of thought in them is jumpy and trivial; they cannot concentrate on any problem. However, not all semi-literate men, especially in the older age-groups, are of inferior intelligence . . . I met some men who could hardly read a newspaper, who were very intelligent, could think for themselves, and recount vividly their own experience of life, with interesting conclusions. There are also fully literate men who read newspapers mainly for football and racing results who can be classified among this group, and who, when asked about their views of life, can hardly say more than: 'Life is just life' or 'I don't know'.

view that considers the novel as more interesting and chal-
lenging. (In so far as people are traditional they are bound to
regard novel ideas with misgiving—or, starting from the other
end of the attitude—in so far as they are traditional, whatever
exists in front of their eyes is likely to be felt as either right, or
natural, or unalterable.)[1] There is the dislike of the unfamiliar,
the abstract, the not-here-and-now-factual, as well as an inability to keep ideas at this level in mind or rehearse them intellectually. A traditional way of life is conducive to this set of
traits because by definition a traditional way of life offers few
choices to its members. The linguistic equipment needed to deal
with the unexpected is therefore correspondingly small.[2]

We have taken one aspect of Ashton society and traced some
of the connections between the characteristic culture and the
typical personality of the place. We shall now take another
aspect—the actual work situation—and go through the same
procedure. The main point of interest will be the strength of
the bond between the men who work together and their
hostility to those outside. Eventually the taboo on tenderness,
cognitive poverty, the contractual attitude and the strong peer-
group will be seen to support each other.

THE MEN AT WORK

The men work in shifts. On one shift, a team of four or five
'machine-men' operates the coal-cutter. It is their function to
make a cut some two or three inches wide into the coal seam,
to a depth of from four to six feet. Between them the members
of the team divide the jobs of driving the machine, operating
the belt and the panels which control the power, cleaning away
dust and making the roof safe. At the same time, other men, the
'drawers-off', are engaged in removing timber and steel supports from the area left empty by the previous shift working at
the coal face.

On the following shift comes the team of colliers. Their job is
to get the coal, by hand or with the aid of machines and ex-

[1] See pages 270, 464 and 517 ff.
[2] This is as far as we need take the argument here. Further implications will
become relevant later in the book, e.g. pages 500 ff.

plosives, and to shovel it on to the conveyer-belt. Each man has his own area of work adjoining that of his neighbour. The ease with which he works depends on the quality of the cut made by the machine-men on the previous shift, whose work in turn depends on the regularity with which the coal has been cleared from the face. A collier cannot leave a bit of his area uncleared at the end of his shift, because that would make the cutters' work impossible. He has to call on the help of his team mates if he gets into difficulties or is too slow to leave the face reasonably regular. Colliers also have to place pit props so that the face is safe and will not cause a fall of coal. On the third shift, the panners come to move the equipment so that it can be used by the next team of machine-men. At the same time, 'rippers' are engaged in the difficult and dangerous task of clearing the road-way, so that men, machines and coal can safely pass.

This is only a rough outline of the division of labour in a mine. There are many other kinds of worker engaged in other tasks at the same time.

Perhaps the first thing to take note of is the continual presence of danger. A careless piece of work may lead to disaster for a whole team, even for teams on a different shift. A second point concerns the extent to which the work involves machinery. Machines tend to set their own pace of work. This may well be experienced by the men who work with them as irritatingly restrictive of their freedom. We may also note that the way the machine rules the responses of the men requires in them certain personality-characteristics developed more fully here than in some other areas of English life: persistence, self-control, the ability to adjust to what cannot be altered.[1]

Thirdly each man's work is related to that of others in a complex way. Trist and Bamforth, commenting on social and psychological aspects of different coal-getting techniques, discuss a very similar division of labour in the following terms:

A primary work-organization of this type has the advantage of placing responsibility for the complete coal-getting task squarely on the shoulders of a single, small, face-to-face group which experiences the entire cycle of operations within the compass of its membership. For each participant the task has total significance

[1] For a more detailed discussion of these characteristics, see pages 467-75.

97

and dynamic closure. Though the contract may have been in the name of the hewer, it is regarded as a joint undertaking. Leadership and supervision are internal to the group, which has a quality of responsible autonomy. The capacity of these groups for self-regulation is a function of the wholeness of their work-task, this connection being represented in their contractual status.[1]

This kind of group is contrasted by Trist and Bamforth to the 'large undifferentiated collectivity' represented by modern factory personnel. The contrast poses the here basic question: Is the worker an expert (as it were, a professional) or is he a hand? In the former case, little supervision is required; in the latter case it is assumed that there must be much supervision. The underground worker of a coal-getting team such as here described is an expert. He is, and he has to be, for he is difficult to supervise, partly because he cannot be under anyone's eye in the dark, and partly because the unpredictable elements in his task require him to be a man who thinks for himself sufficiently to adapt to changing circumstances. Trist and Bamforth point out that 'it is virtually impossible to establish the kind of constant background to the task that is taken for granted in the factory'.

It may be that skilled workers at any level have reason to chafe at strict supervision from those who are not themselves engaged in the work (much as a professional man would chafe at strict supervision by administrators). Or it may be that the situation is particularly aggravating for skilled men working in a team which has divided the labour among its members, a situation in which co-operative give-and-take is normally the more congenial.[2]

There are a number of other reasons why supervision goes especially against the miner's grain. The hardship of his working life sustains his self-respect. Miners constantly say that no non-miner can appreciate the nature of pitwork, and few would challenge them. When they hear complaints of miners' high wages, they confidently offer an exchange of jobs, and this

---

[1] E. L. Trist and K. W. Bamforth (1951), 'Some social and psychological consequences of the Longwall method of coal-getting', *Human Relations*, IV, 1.

[2] For full reasoning in support of this argument see J. Klein (1961), *Working with Groups*, chap. 9: 'Structure, function and morale.'

is enough for most public-house politicians. In the pit itself, among his workmates, the miner is proud of doing his job as a good man should. He becomes identified with his particular job. Recognition that one job belongs to one man is recognition of that man's fitness and his control of that job.

Yet the plan of production does not allow much scope for initiative and creative effort. It does not depend on him: it incorporates his labour just as it incorporates raw materials, machinery, depreciation and every other constituent of the final product. Moreover, like other workers, the miner is aware that the class from which the direction and control of his work comes is marked by possession of a comparatively large supply of money, either 'in the bank' or assured at definite intervals. It is from this secure non-manual class that the regulations which govern his working day come. Pride in work is a very important part of the miner's life. He sees himself as a highly skilled, competent, independent man working in circumstances in which the exercise of these traits is inhibited or controlled by people leading softer lives.

Although Dennis, Henriques and Slaughter do not do so, it could be argued that there are, in the situation, many elements which might have encouraged the miner to feel that he had more than the normal working man's scope for initiative and independence of life. But the history of management–labour relations is against it, and so are the attitudes which have enabled both sides to survive. It is interesting to cite, for comparison, a group of miners in 'Lakeport', U.S.A. These mined gypsum for an organization which had in the same town both the underground mines and the factory for processing the material. Thus the attitudes and situation of the miners could be compared with those of factory workers in their typical form.[1]

In many ways conditions in this gypsum mine supported personality-traits which may be found among miners generally. But if one compares 'Lakeport' with Ashton, one is struck mainly by the difference between the way these personality-traits express themselves in Ashton, where there is a long history of worker–management conflict, and 'Lakeport' where worker–

[1] A. Gouldner (1954), *Patterns of Industrial Democracy*, Free Press, Glencoe, Ill.

manager relations are excellent. This difference shows in the 'Lakeport' miner's consciousness of his standing as an expert, capable of making his own decisions, and not needing a supervisor to ensure that he performs well or stays on the job till it is finished. The supervisors themselves were conscious that the miners behaved in this 'professional' manner. In the factory area, on the other hand, men and foremen were defined respectively as 'requiring to be strictly supervised' and 'strictly supervising'. The people in the town were aware of this kind of difference between the miners and the factory workers.

The Ashton miner's distrust of management is deeply rooted in history. In a community as close-knit and homogeneous as Ashton, the memory of past exploitation is kept alive by constant informal recital of past exploitation, each dispute providing the stimulus for the rehearsal of past iniquities.

This situation is aggravated by the fact that there are uncertainties blurring the outlines of the contract. Because the task is constantly changing as conditions change and the rates for the job are normally somewhat behind the change in work conditions, and because tales of past exploitation are still vividly remembered in the area, there is plenty of opportunity for the men to feel that they are getting the worst of the wages bargain. The procedure is for a 'price-list' to be agreed between a collier or a group of colliers and the management. All concerned know that all the work involved cannot be fixed at a definite rate per day. Conditions of safety and efficiency vary and allowances of all sorts are included in the price-list. It is in the claims for these allowances that the daily opposition between men and management is manifested.

The miner's view of the contract is further affected by his feeling that the other side is likely to have the advantage anyway. 'Experience shows,' he says, 'that if management suggests any change, it works eventually to the detriment of the men.' In his turn, then, if he can get away with a looser rate for the job (the nature of the work having changed and others not yet realizing it) he will obviously do so, because it balances out adjustment-lags in the opposite direction. He will do what he has agreed for, but because the contract was not an entirely fair one in his eyes, if he can extract any additional advantage, that is good luck. This pleasure in getting the better of those defined as outside the group we shall meet again in the relationship of some men to their wives.

In discussion with officials of the National Coal Board an attempt was made to discover the attitude of the administration to the large number of disputes in the Yorkshire coal-field. One principle dominated the replies: 'Every strike is a wages strike.' Men may go on strike because of bad roof conditions, because of water, because of difficulties caused by mechanical breakdowns; but in all these cases it is the effect on the pay-note that is really at stake. This should not be taken to imply that the miner is concerned solely to get the maximum amount of money for every single task he performs. The wage structure, with its differentials for skill and danger, has been built up in such a way that a man's status as a strong and skilled worker, and as a man worth his pay, is conveyed by what shows on the pay-note. His pay-note is seen as objective recognition of the miner's ability. The man's right to take a pride in his work, and hence in himself, depends to a fair extent on his pay-note. This is the more so because the typical Ashton personality is such as to prefer tangible or visible proofs to more intangible convictions. The clearly defined is preferred, and the pay-note clearly defines the worker's standing. Any factor helping to cut down the amount of his wage is an attack on the status of the contract-worker.

In the authors' description of the mutual role-expectations— the contract—of the miner and the man who represents him in his struggle with the management, we may again note the moralistic tone of the role-definition which was apparent in the description of the 'good worker', the simplicity of the social conventions by which the miner makes his life more manageable and comprehensible, the starkness of the psychological attitudes underlying them, the absence of elbow-room for give-and-take, and the strong in-group loyalties and out-group hostilities.

Firstly, the Union representative should be a good talker. By this is meant that he should be able to speak confidently, without hesitation, reservations or qualifications. He should not 'say one thing upstairs (i.e. in the manager's office) and another in the pityard'. Such expectations are part of a definition of honesty and straightforward manly behaviour. In brief, he must make it clear where his loyalties lie. This is the less difficult since he is normally a contract-worker, that is, the type of worker who is highly paid, highly skilled, most at risk, and used to arguing with the deputy over his contract. His attitude should be 'my men, right or wrong, without concessions'.

Secondly, he must never give way, because to give way is an admission of weakness, in the group or in the case. What the men demand is that when the official speaks he should speak confidently, as though he knew what he was talking about. A man who qualifies his statements is thought to be on poor ground. Our authors consider that in the circumstances this emphasis on confidence is probably sound, 'and something of an unreflective adaptation to the social environment'. The inability to give-and-take his historical roots. All remember that since 1926, when there was a depression in the coal trade, the Tunbridge colliery was willing to grant very little which was not forced upon it by the fear of the greater loss which might be incurred by a strike. But it is also firmly planted in the Ashton personality, perhaps so firmly as to make rational discussion of the issues wellnigh impossible, even in changed circumstance. This basic attitude is perhaps best described as a conviction that you must fight for what you want against powerful persons capable and sometimes eager to frustrate you, who expect you to conform to their needs without taking much account of your own. Hence when you can, you must be quick-witted to evade their demands and adamant even against your own immediate interests in the fight for independence, equality and eventual advantage. To qualify a statement is to give something away, a form of softness, a break in the habitual tough front which has proved its survival value.

If the representative plays his part as defined, the men will in return show him great loyalty: their side of the bargain. A man who has once been elected will tend to be re-elected time and again. This is due, as the authors say, not only to a belief that any given piece of work can really be done as well by one man as by another, but also to a generous objection to doing a man out of his job. The practice is also supported by the belief that elected officials may be corrupted, or at least 'softened', when they no longer work with their hands at the coal-face. Their role is sufficiently remote from the men's to be subject to the suspicion that it may be used for personal advantage. They may be getting away with something. Thus, the general feeling is, if an official has not so far been corrupted, why take the risk with someone new?

It seems difficult to overestimate the importance of past history for present-day Ashton patterns. Gouldner confirms many of the personality-traits to be observed in Ashton as characteristic of men in dangerous occupations: the insistence on independence, the overt but brief bursts of aggression which seem curiously lacking in hostility, the swearing, the pride in strength and manliness, the relation of danger and solidarity, the tough attitude to wives, the peer-solidarity. (If the 'Lakeport' surfaceman wanted to compete with and impress his neighbours by buying a new car, the 'Lakeport' miner preferred to 'set one up for the boys'. He wanted to be a *good* fellow, not a better one.) But in contrast, and this contrast seems largely due to very different management–worker relations in the past, we find a lack of insistence on proper spheres of competence, an attitude very much more easy-going than— indeed almost diametrically opposed to—contractual relationships, a feeling that the plant's rules are made in conformity with a set of ideas shared by management and worker alike. It is this historical aspect which makes the Ashton complex of attitudes so interesting for the student of culture and personality. These attitudes have survived the institutional conditions which first gave rise to them or, at the least, confirmed them as the ones most likely to pay off in the circumstances. They are now so deeply rooted that they pervade non-industrial as well as industrial relationships. In this way their survival is maintained.

We are now ready to consider the men's leisure-time groups.

THE MEN'S LEISURE-TIME GROUPS

In adolescence the young man starts work, and the pattern of manliness which is so important in this community takes on its adult form. The strong interdependence of the men at work is reflected in their out-of-work and social relations. If the woman's place is in the home, the man's place is as definitely outside it. After work, the men go home for a wash and a meal, and then go out again to meet their friends at the club, the pub, the corner, the sports-ground. The bond between the men who are accustomed to meet in this way is so strong and deep that Dennis, Henriques and Slaughter liken these groups at one point to 'secret societies'.[1] It is here that the men experience most fully the emotional satisfactions which social life affords; it is with other men that they are at their most relaxed, at ease and emotionally expansive. A man's centre of activity is outside the home. He works and plays and makes contact with others outside his home. It is outside his home that the criteria of success and social acceptance are located.

Mining is an occupation which encourages the formation of peer-groups. 'The finest lot in the country,' Zweig often heard ex-miners say about their former comrades. 'I agree,' said Zweig. 'But tell me why you think so.' To this came the reply: 'If a man is willing to die for his comrades, is that not proof enough for you? And a miner would never spare himself or hesitate for a moment to rush with help into the most dangerous spot.'[2]

Mining encourages peer-groups. Conversely, in a place where there is a tradition of strongly established peer-groups, a young man's choice of employment is affected. The interdependence of the economic and the social aspects of a way of life is not all in one direction. A boy in Ashton is typically destined to be a miner. Even if he or his parents have other ideas about his future, they are up against very strong forces. To take his place in the community, to share the continued friendship of his boyhood friends, a young man cannot long stay out of mining. The lack of shared experience would make continued membership of a peer-group difficult, for conversation at leisure is very much about what is happening in the pit. Moreover, the men are proud of their dangerous trade and a little contemp-

---

[1] 'Another feature of this kind of character development is worth noting from the social point of view, namely the tendency to form 'brotherhoods' or secret societies. We may conjecture that the social needs of these juvenile outcasts from the nursery draws them together as a band of brothers united by a common bereavement' (Suttie, op. cit.).

[2] Zweig, like other authors, relates this characteristic also to the miners' generosity, solidarity and sense of justice.

tuous of those with softer working lives. Lastly, the pay in other employment is not good enough to sustain the leisure pursuits of the young male community.

The youths in Ashton spend most of their leisure time in groups of about half a dozen. Such a group will grow naturally out of schoolday friendships, perhaps with additions from work-mates or from those with whom sporting interests are shared. After his evening meal, the youth of between fifteen or eighteen will walk down to the street corner or the cricket field or the youth club, wherever it is that his particular group is accustomed to gather. Together, they will go to Calderford to the billiard saloon, go to watch a football match or play themselves, and at the week-end visit a dance together. Round about the age of eighteen most of them will begin to drink beer, though very few of them are heavy drinkers yet. It is usual for them to spend an hour or two in the public house before a dance. On occasion one of them will become involved in a scuffle and his mates will come to his aid. Often this results in a full-scale fight.

Fighting is only the extreme of solidarity which is found in these groups of young men. The group is a community group of the most exclusive and possessive kind. For years on end the members will continue to share their leisure time. They do not take kindly to part-time members who have interests elsewhere. It is soon remarked upon if one of the members begins to mix more with another group.

The strongest competition for the attention and time of the group's members is, of course, sex-interest. When a young man begins 'courting strong', the group reacts with strongly discouraging sanctions to the possible diversion of attention. He is teased and threatened with social isolation. 'Well we'd ask thee to come for a pint,' the others say, 'but we expect tha's off to get thy feet under t' table.' To stay with a girl and enjoy her company would be a form of unmanliness. Tenderness is not thought of as part of a man's psychological equipment. The young man has to insist that he is 'getting something out of it'.[1] He will play down his emotional involvement with the girl, justifying to the group the time he spends with her by claiming that she allows him sexual intercourse. The justification is not

[1] See also page 39.

in terms of giving but in terms of taking. In the group's behaviour and the youth's relation to it at this stage, we see the beginning of what will be a continuing conflict between home ties and peer ties.

MEN AND WOMEN

The strength of the peer tie does not noticeably diminish with age. In adult life the group of men with whom the miner shares his activities will often still be the one within which he has grown up. When arrangements are made to visit a certain sporting event or when the group goes on a drinking spree, he does not like to be left out; he likes it to be thought that he is still 'one of the lads'.

The male group, over the years, develops a set of attitudes and ideas which very deliberately exclude women, children and strangers. It is at this point in the discussion that the authors refer to the resemblance to a 'secret society'. One of the exclusive mechanisms which define the limits of the group is the use of swear-words; these are directed familiarly to members of the group and offensively to those outside. Women are not supposed to hear these words from men, though they may use them in their own women's circle. Thus for instance the bookie's office is part of the men's world, where women have no place. A woman going into the office is subjected to jokes and language which in a more neutral locality would lead to a fight. The pub is somewhat less a male preserve than it was. A man in a pub swore in the hearing of a girl, was stopped and apologized. A minute or so later he repeated the offence. Her escort bristled. 'I'm sorry, old lad, but she must expect to hear what comes out if she comes into the place at all.' Nevertheless, the offender had to leave. This swearing is known as 'pit-talk', characteristically used in the pit and left behind there except in so far as the conditions are reproduced in other typically male assemblies. 'Pit-talk' not only demarcates the boundary between the women's world and the men's. It also preserves the gap between the generations.

I'm like any other miner; I can swear as well as anybody, and, of course, my son as well—after all, he's twenty-seven and he's working at the face. But we've never sworn in front of each other. In fact I don't think he's ever heard me swear. But one day I was sitting waiting to go out to the pit and a group of colliers came and sat nearby and he was one of them. They started talking and they swore just like any other lot. My lad didn't know I was there and so he swore as merrily as anybody else. Well, I've never felt so awkward in my life before. I could feel myself blushing and managed to creep away without him seeing me. I'm glad I did because we'd both have felt very awkward.

The distinction between men's conversation and women's conversation is determined not only by 'pit-talk'. Just as the men in the clubs talk mainly about their work and secondly about sport and NEVER about their homes and families, so do their wives talk first of all about *their* work, i.e. their homes and families, and secondly within the range of things with which they are all immediately familiar. The men discourage any transgressions over the line of this division of interests. When a women does express any interest in politics or other general topic, she speaks rather apologetically, and can be prepared for her husband to tell her not to interrupt intelligent conversation: 'What the hell do you know about it?'

Except at the weekend, when the men's clubs and the Miners' Welfare Institute allow women in, the women keep together much as the men do. For women as for men, the enjoyment of the company of others is a major source of leisure-time satisfaction. (The other leisure interests of the women are also as few and uncreative as those of the men.) At one or other house in the street, the women will be 'callin', taking a cup of tea, with family, neighbours or both, spending some time in the morning or the afternoon regularly in this way. At these women's gatherings there is endless gossip about the neighbours, about their own husbands and children, about the past.

With some exceptions, the women are quiet and appear somewhat depressed in mixed company. This leads the male authors of *Coal is our Life* to say: 'In the evenings when the men of the family talk about the pit, and the wife or daughter sits weariedly knitting or half-listening, one knows that the conversation is more or less meaningless to her.' But it is possible that the women's conversation is in fact livelier than that of the men, since they suffer less from the insistence on a harshly defined 'masculine' behaviour and from the taboo on tenderness that accompanies it. They may well be verbally more skilled than the men because of this, though in mixed company the consciousness of the general inferiority of women would normally inhibit them.

But, for instance, during a straightforward discussion on marital relations, one of the authors noted that the women could cope with the discussion and could contribute to it, while the men were tongue-tied and sat there with red faces. The women had a chance on this occasion because for the men the discussion of sexual matters is bound to have an embarrassing, rude and dirty connotation which seems less salient for the women. 'The only context in which they discussed sex was in a circle of jesting males.' Another anecdote recounts how girls in a cinema queue were able to tease the boys about Marilyn Monroe, keeping up a derisive commentary for minutes while the boys were unable to answer back, apparently because the only retorts they could think of were in terms of 'pit-talk' which was inappropriate to the situation.

This separation of the men's world and the women's world may be accompanied by an underlying difference in psychological reactions. It seems as though the male pattern in Ashton is such that the men's reaction to frustration or disappointment is crudely directed outward, whereas the women's is turned inwards. Swearing is part of this outward-turning pattern. It is associated both by the authors and by the men as a reaction associated with the general unpleasantness of the pit. 'No doubt pit-work provides factors of danger and nervous tension which give added incentive to swearing. In other places of male exclusiveness, such as pub or club, it is not uncommon to use the secular swear-words, but in the pit it is the *extreme* of this liberty among men.'

This more or less harmless outward re-direction of anxiety may be compared with a more unpleasant form which involves other people and, in Ashton characteristically, the women. It is a joke (*sic*) in Ashton that when the local football-team is defeated 'two thousand teas are thrown at t' back o' t' fire'. The men are said to be too distressed to eat.

The women, on the other hand, seem less noisy, more depressed and resigned. The force of public opinion not only defines the woman's role as inferior, but also keeps her in lower standing. No self-respecting young woman goes to the pub without a man, and, we have seen, not even the man can save her the unpleasantness associated with such a visit. If a wife continues to look even reasonably attractive after marriage, she is adversely commented upon, by women as well as men. Child-bearing, hard work, self-induced abortions and lack of medical care grind all into the same mould. The authors tell of two girls who, before marriage, appeared to have very different personalities and abilities. One bright and intelligent, the other dull, after some years of marriage they both came to hear of a family planning clinic in the town. The one was interested in the possibilities and decided to go, the other not. They talked and talked about it together. Finally both decided they would go. But neither actually went. The pattern of daily life simply did not allow for so important a step outside the day's routine. It would involve fixing an appointment and making the journey to a nearby town. They were unused to telephones, to keeping appointments, to discussing intimacies with strangers. They hardly knew how to behave and explain themselves in front of the other housewives they knew.

HUSBANDS AND WIVES

The recurrence of strictly contractual attitudes within the domestic sphere, and the way the bargain operates on the whole to the women's disadvantage, makes striking reading for those from another culture. Strictness of role-definition is of course not necessarily related to male dominance, but it happens to be so in Ashton. In extreme cases, the management–worker catch-as-catch-can is repeated by husband and wife, he up to cunning dodges admired by his mates to avoid giving her house-keeping money—she after him to get the money off him before he has spent it all. Dennis, Henriques and Slaughter tell a remarkable story illustrating a possibly legendary extreme in the reproduction of man/management relations within the family sphere. A young panner married a girl from neighbouring

Norwood and went to share the house of her parents. His wife's father was an old collier and before the marriage he confided in him:

> 'Now lad, tha knows we used to have to pay at t' pit if we broke a shovel or a pick. Well, I've never told Mary's mother any different, and every fortnight or so I knock a few shillings off her wages for a shovel or a pick, even though we get 'em supplied now. Mary knows I claim (*sic*) for these things so don't let on I've telled thee t' secret; anyway, tha might as well do t' same thesen because she knows no different.

The young panner maintains he still does this, and his workmates joke with him about his wages every week, making suggestions for deductions. He says that all his brothers-in-law carry on the practice, and one of them, while still living at home, once took no wages to his mother for a month after his pony had been killed in the pit.

Just as industrial conflict is endemic, so is conflict in the home. Our authors note that the many disagreements between husband and wife are essentially concerned with the question: in which sector of the community shall the money be spent— in the family and the home, or in the club? A girl of eighteen, who had been married two months, replied, when surprise had been expressed at her having a row with her husband: 'Oh, that's nowt. We have a row regularly every Saturday when I ask him for my wage and he doesn't want to take me out with him.' It is not an exaggeration to say that the row is an institution for the present-day family in Ashton. Conditions external to each individual family are responsible for tension within; those same conditions make it impossible for harmony to be achieved by revolt against the whole structure of relations in the family. Nor does friendly and rational discussion of differences seem available as a technique for smoothing out the disagreements. Instead, there will be 'a row'. The row is the conventional way of expressing the conflict. At the same time it is a release.[1]

The wife's role is defined in terms of the husband's convenience much as the husband's role of employee is defined in terms of

---

[1] See also pages 169 and 173-4.

management's convenience. (The children, similarly, are firmly kept in their place and from an early age made conscious of the social difference between the sexes.) The husband pays his wife an agreed weekly sum, called 'her wages'. She may not know how much he earns or what proportion of his earnings is given her. Indeed, the authors cite an instance in which a woman, asked whether her husband worked in town or nearer home, had to call a neighbour to ask if she knew. With her wage, the woman rules the household and makes all expenditure decisions, except for big items, such as a new cooker, for which her husband will pay out a further share from his wages. This practice is a great help to the wife, for ordinary hire-purchase items are paid out of her wages.

The pattern is established before marriage. The young single men are earning well and very generous in buying each other drinks. Once married, who is going to get the free money? The men's custom of paying the wife a regular wage ensures fairness at home (fairness here referring to the men's feeling that they have fulfilled their contractual obligations) and yet enables them to pay their proper share when drinking with the boys. The club, the pub, the bookie, have first claim on the free money. Leisure may also be bought with it, and the wife is conventionally prevented from putting pressure on the man to go to work. If money is plentiful, why not knock off work for a day? It isn't as though the work were so attractive.

The increased prosperity of the miner has not added in fair proportion to the wife's wages. Rather, because his pleasures are centred in the male group outside the home, it has added to the free spending money. By spending his money with his friends, in the way which is conventional in Ashton, the Ashton way of life is perpetuated: the miner maintains his own standing while that of the women is as low as ever.

It is by reason of processes like this that the authors are led to the conclusion that in Ashton the family as a unit is weakened by the existence of a series of institutions and practices which are the domain of the adult miners in the town and which are fundamentally opposed to the families of these men. From the age of courtship, the attraction of the 'secret society' is a challenge to the growth of a full relationship between the miner and his girl or his wife. When he marries, the group's attraction competes with the amount of time, interest and money which he is willing to devote to his family. The authors have no doubt that the conflict between married couples springs from the antagonism between family interests on the one hand and the husband's group on the other.[1]

Unlike the husband, the wives spend little on themselves without the approval of their spouse. The husband will query expenditure on items outside the normal household budget. This budget includes little for her clothes, less for her leisure, nothing for self-improvement. In this way the wife's life is restricted to her family and her neighbours.

Restricted to the home as they are, wives do not appear actively to resent it. When pressed they will acknowledge jealousy of their husband's freedom, but many of them say that they find satisfaction in the care of their children. (Indeed the confinement of the wife to the internal affairs of the family brings her much closer to her children than the father.) The husband having fulfilled his obligations when he has paid over the wife's wage, it is part of the women's side of the bargain that the home must be a comfortable place to come back to after work, with a meal prepared, a room tidy and warm, and a wife ready to wait upon him. There must be no cold meals, late meals, washing lying about, or ironing to do while he is at home. These duties should be performed while he is at work; when he is at home the wife should concentrate on his comfort. The wife agrees with these stipulations; both acknowledge that a miner's work is hard and that it is a 'poor do' if the wife cannot fulfill her part of the contract as long as the husband fulfills his. The authors cite an instance where a wife had gone to the pictures after asking her sister to prepare a meal and serve it when the husband came home. The husband so confronted threw the dinner 'to t' back of t' fire'. It was his wife's duty to look after him. He would accept no substitute.

In fairness, it must be said that the contractual relation shows in a better light when one considers what happens when the man is unable to fulfil his part of the bargain. If the man is out of work or paid very low wages, he may agree that the wife

[1] See page 222.

should go out to work. Then the bargain changes, a new contract is made: he may cook or make the beds if he comes home before she does. That this is a deviant pattern is shown by the embarrassment of the man in acknowledging that he does this. That it is a socially permitted alternative is shown later in the history of this very man who had thrown the food away. Because of deafness he was forced to change to a job with much lower pay. His wife now goes out to work at 7 a.m. and returns at 5.30 p.m. He helps her in all manner of ways in the house and has a meal ready for *her* when she returns home.

In view of all these considerations it is no surprise that the authors comment that no developing or deepening of the conjugal relationship takes place after the intensive sex-life of early marriage. Marriages in Ashton are a matter of 'carrying on' pure and simple. So long as the man works and gives his wife and family sufficient, and the woman uses the family's 'wage' wisely and gives her husband the few things he demands, the marriage will carry on.

Because of the division in activity and ideas between men and women, husband and wife tend to have little to talk about or to do together. Here, in Ashton, the family is a system of relationships torn by a major contradiction at its heart; husband and wife live separate and in a sense secret lives. Many married couples seem to have no intimate understanding of one another; the only occasions on which they really approach each other is in bed, and sexual relations are apparently rarely satisfactory to both partners. The stress on manliness defined as absence of tenderness, and the connection of sexual matters with pit-talk, are obvious components for an explanation of this. In addition, the lack of give-and-take, the contractual view of all relationships, and the unusually rigid division of labour must be taken into consideration.

THE CHILDREN

The stoicism, carrying on and putting up with things, the absence of tender feeling, the stress on a web of reciprocal duties, is bound to show itself also in the treatment of the children. As is to be expected when there is a very firm system of role-relationships, the children are very much more strenuously trained than is the case in Branch Street or Ship Street. There is more for them to be trained in. Strong habits have to be formed to relieve the strain of the stark life.

Very few parents play with their children or talk much with them. The vocabulary is not available, nor the tradition, nor the inclination. In the parents' interaction with the children there is little sharing of ideas or experiences, no notion of bringing out potentialities in them or introducing them to a new world. The general attitude towards children is that they have to be 'looked after', 'dealt with'. Such phrases, our authors suggest, imply a restriction of the children's activities, a channelling of energy into required patterns, nothing developmental or creative.

Even this channelling is largely in terms of physical wellbeing and education. It is not a concern for the individual psychological needs or characteristics of the child. In a very important sense, the mother 'puts up' with the children. A child is said to be bad-tempered or jealous in the way it might be boss-eyed or tall for its age—a matter for approving or disapproving comment without any feeling that something can be done about it. Such characteristics are thought of as unalterable. There is little psychological insight or interest.[1]

> The mother's preoccupation with the routine of her daily duties gives rise to an attitude to the children which detracts from any serious or truly helpful handling of their development. A mother may be proud of the growth of her children, she may earnestly enquire after their progress at school, but her own relations with her children consist of dealing with them, coping with them.

The authors argue that because women are denied participation in those activities whereby the men achieve success or reputation, they are led to assert their individual worth among other women by doing the job of motherhood as well as or better than their neighbours. Because of the taboo on tenderness and the general cognitive poverty this tends to a concentration on

---

[1] This is another manifestation of cognitive poverty. Cf. Hoggart (op. cit.), 'Bachelors are the exceptions, but they are viewed with tolerance. Some men, it is felt, are born bachelors.'

the outward signs—new clothes, new toys, well-fed children. It is by these standards that a mother is immediately judged. 'The child is in the dangerous position of being a status-object for the mother.'

In effect, there may be among the women a sort of rivalry over their children. At Christmas and Whitsuntide a woman buys clothes for her children not only because they need them but because she does not want to feel inferior to other mothers who do this. A woman who dresses her children shabbily is talked about. When women gossip together they describe the Christmas presents they are buying for their children. In much the same way they will say of each other that they are clean or not so clean in their household duties; and the acquisition of gas cooking-stoves or of kitchen-cabinets may spread along a street as much for prestige-value as for anything else.

Dennis and his associates describe the process of bringing up these children as characteristic of a hand-to-mouth outlook. Punishment, they note, varies not so much with the seriousness of the offence as with the state of mind of the parent. A child will repeat the same slight offence a dozen times before receiving a tap or blow at the point where the father's or mother's patience is exhausted. Or the reason for chastisement may be simply that the child's desires have conflicted with an express parental purpose. Nevertheless, looking at the matter comparatively, this kind of upbringing is worlds removed from Branch Street or Ship Street. The position of the child in the household is firmly defined and firmly maintained. It is the definition as inferior to the adult, with less important needs, which leads to parental behaviour of an apparently inconsistent kind, and in particular to the child's subjection to parental moods. In much the same way, the man feels subjected to management and pit conditions, and the wife feels subjected to the man. There is nothing inconsistent or hand-to-mouth about that. The children know they will arouse anger and be disciplined if they interfere with adult activities. Here cause and effect are consistently related: the child can count on it. Discipline may be rather erratic—the child may 'get away with it'—but the nature of the offence is usually clear to the child: failure to allow the daily routine to run smoothly. Such discipline may appear hand-to-mouth from the adult's angle, but not from the child's.

A second regularity in the child's existence arises from the emphasis on a household routine which must be kept to because of the man's demands and the shifting work hours which are part of his work. This routine is not designed for the child, but it does strongly impinge on him and affect his life. In these pages, our authors have recourse to the word 'routine' with a frequency which is unthinkable in connection with the groups previously discussed. The children are washed, dressed and given breakfast in the morning and then 'placed in their routine activities for the day'. Placed there, *nota bene*, not turned out or allowed to go their own way with casual irregular parental supervision. Children under school age are 'put out to play' and 'given something to occupy themselves with'. At a certain time the children are washed, undressed and put to bed. Regular meals, family meals, are the norm; though the man's shift-work may interfere with these, the pattern is not that of the running buffet customary in Branch Street or (for the evening meal) in Ship Street.

A third regularity is the clear differentiation between the girls' role and the boys', which fits them for their later functions in more detail and more purposefully than was the case in the other areas discussed.

From the beginning, boys are the more privileged children. Although the father does not normally spend much time with his children, there is usually on his part a strongly marked favouritism towards his sons. He will occasionally play with his baby son; with his daughters he spends no time at all. It is a common sight to see the small daughter in the family standing mournfully aside while the father and son play together, and then be chastised for 'moaning' when she tries to attract attention. Later, parents find themselves much more interested in the educational progress of their sons. For the boy who does not gain entrance to the grammar school at eleven, this interest ceases, but there will usually be some concern about what job he is going to take, some concern for his future. For the girl this is not true at all. Education for women is regarded as a waste of time, since they are destined to spend their time as mothers and housewives.

From an early age the little girl will take pleasure in sharing the household tasks with her mother. During adolescence she will be expected to help her mother in the home. A young woman knows the life of her mother; she grows up into the idea of how a good woman should behave and should go about her work. Like her mother she will know that she will be praised for 'looking after' her husband well, making a pleasant and easy-going home as a contrast to his arduous toil at the pit. The girl's acceptance of her future as a housewife with no other prospects of advancement, no notion of social participation outside the home, fits in very well with the more subtle aspects of what is in our society considered 'natural' for the feminine temperament. A woman is likely to have little initiative beyond the fulfilment of her household duties; she knows that she will work within the limits of her husband's wage standard. Within these limits she will have responsibility; she must exercise patience, restraint and passivity in the face of hardship. Like her mother, subordinated to the needs of the men in her natal household, she will develop the characteristics of submissiveness and stolidity.

When a young man marries, he has already in his own home become accustomed to seeing the women do the housework while he is at work or at play. From the beginning he grows into the sex-division of the household and looks forward to the day when, like his father, he will be working. He models himself on his father, even though he is not very often at home. He takes on the requisite personality characteristics by imitation of the men and by simply fitting into each situation as he is obviously expected to do. While the little girl continues with her mother in the home, the boy, under the influence of his father and friends, has begun to pursue the more 'male' activities. He takes an interest in sports; he is allowed to accompany his father to the football match. From adolescence on he, like his father, is not required to do any work in the house. He spends his time out of the house, with others of his own age. Adolescence sees the consolidation, from their early beginnings in the play-group of school-days, of those male peer-groups which are so cardinal in Ashton's social life. Progressively there develops in these groups a clearer knowledge of what it is to be one of the lads, and not a girl. Softness, gentleness and sentimentality are discouraged and eventually crushed permanently. And so the wheel turns full circle.

SECTION TWO

Aspects of Adult Life in England

Chapter Four

ASPECTS OF TRADITIONAL
WORKING-CLASS LIFE

THE patterns of living described in the previous chapters were either extreme types or outside the main stream of social development because of the relatively isolated position of the people concerned. This gave them a somewhat exotic air.

The three chapters of which the present is the first may prove to be less exciting, since they describe how the majority of English people live. This chapter focuses on the lives of adults in the rather more traditional working-class communities, the next on post-war developments, the third on some aspects of middle-class life.

In nearly every chapter the nature of the subject-matter has demanded different treatment. In the previous three, it was possible to describe the life-cycle of individuals, breaking into it where convenient and relating the cycle to the environment which sustained it and to the personalities of those who were carried unquestioningly along the sequence.

The patchiness of our knowledge and the effect of regional, occupational and idiosyncratic variations make it impossible always to relate modal personality, social influences and the parental perpetuation of the pattern in this way. Perhaps this is just as well, for it forces the social psychologist to mind a truth which his normal procedures tend to obscure. The pleasure of understanding the interrelation of these three components where their connection is obvious tempts him to assume that the function of any one of them must be immediately traceable to the others. More concretely and particularly, the social psychologist is tempted to look at a peculiarity in the social structure and seek for a personality-trait or attitude which 'explains' it. When he has done that for a number of such peculiarities and has found a variety of personality-traits, he will show how these traits fit a consistent personality: the modal personality. For instance, skill at work is related to self-respect; self-respect to a stable and solidary community; stability and solidarity to a past lack of encouragement for talented men to rise; and so on. This approach is at least orderly, and often exciting. But it is not always possible. Personality-traits or culture-traits which no longer serve a function of this kind may survive for want of discouragement, and this will obscure the tidy pattern for which the social psychologist hopes. It then becomes impossible to show why a personality is what it is, and one can only hope to show how some traits or attitudes make life easier in a particular situation, whereas others would make it more difficult. This is all that can be done here. Since it is impossible to present a single personality-type, aspects of traditional working-class life will be presented in convenient order. Whenever a psychological trait is clearly discernible and appears to have a fairly general function for this population, a digression will be made to discuss it in more detail.

In the second volume, child-rearing patterns will be compared. Some of the psychological traits apparent here are then related to their roots in infancy.

SOURCES

The material on which the arguments of the present chapter are based comes from a number of studies in which somewhat similar patterns of living may be observed: Bott's account of the Newbolt family; Young and Willmott's description of Bethnal Green; Mogey's work in St. Ebbe's (a central area in Oxford); Hoggart's reminiscences of his childhood in the North of England; an investigation under W.J.H. Sprott by M.Carter and Pearl Jephcott, of a Midland town, 'Radby'. We shall also draw on the less localized work of Zweig and Gorer. Zweig's research method was to accumulate information from numerous random informal discussions with working men in pubs, parks, sports-grounds or wherever the opportunity presented itself. He found, as many have found, that being obviously a foreigner, and thus quite outside the English class-structure, is a wonderful help in getting people to speak from the heart. Gorer was able to publish a lengthy questionnaire in a popular Sunday newspaper. Over a hundred questions on aspects of English social life were answered by over ten thousand people.[1]

In spite of certain differences which will become clear as these areas are described in detail, there are some common features which justify their being grouped together. The families are working-class, living in towns, traditional and self-respecting. Traditional is here a word used to highlight a feature which contrasts them with a later group of working-class families: the traditional group has relatively little social ambition and does not view a change in its way of life with optimism. The later group—consisting often of working-class families which have been moved to new housing-estates—will be seen to be more ambitious and more willing to take active steps to get still further ahead. The traditional group has seen changes in its way of life, almost all for the better, but on the whole these changes have not been brought about by their own effort; they are the fortunate recipients, rather than the active participants, of changes in the social and economic environment.

I am writing particularly of the majority who take their lives as they find them, and in that way are not different from the majority in other classes; of what some trade-union leaders, when they are regretting a lack of interest in their movement, call 'the vast apathetic mass'; of what the song-writers call, by way of compliment, 'just plain folk'; of what the working classes themselves describe, more soberly, as 'the general run of people'.

Those I have in mind still to a considerable extent retain a sense of being in a group of their own, and this without there being necessarily implied any feeling of inferiority or pride; they feel rather that they are 'working class' in the things they admire and dislike, in 'belonging' . . .

Most of the employed inhabitants of these areas work for a

[1] Unfortunately the data are not always presented in a form which makes social or regional identification easy for our purpose and the statistical methods have been much criticized. Before more reliance is placed on these findings than the present carefully-worded text allows, reference back to source should be made.

wage, and the wage is paid weekly: most have no other source of income. Some are self-employed; they may keep a small shop for members of the group to which, culturally, they belong, or supply a service to the group, for example as a 'cobbler', 'barber', 'grocer', 'bike-mender', or 'cast-off clothing dealer'. In most of the families described here a wage of about £9 or £10 for the chief wage-earner, at 1954 rates, would be regarded as roughly normal. In occupation they are usually labourers, skilled or unskilled, or craftsmen, or perhaps apprentice-trained. This loose boundary includes, therefore, men who do what used to be called 'navvying' and other outdoor manual work, commercial and public-transport workers, men and girls on routine jobs in factories, as well as skilled tradesmen, from plumbers to those who perform the more difficult tasks in heavy industry. Foremen are included, but office clerks and employees in large shops, though they may live in these areas, are on the whole better regarded as members of the lower middle classes.

This very fine summary comes from Hoggart's *The Uses of Literacy*. Because Hoggart was bound to be influenced by memories of his childhood, it has been said that the book describes the situation of the nineteen-thirties rather than that of the nineteen-fifties. Certainly very important social and economic changes took place during that time. On the other hand, Hoggart's critics may have been confused by a geographical difference. Life away from the Home Counties does seem, for a number of reasons, to be harsher and poorer. So the Ashton study would suggest; and Hoggart and the Radby study support the idea.

Radby is a mining town with marked resemblances to Ashton, though the man does not seem quite so dominant, perhaps partly because the women can go out to work if they wish. The Radby Report grades households (sometimes streets) into five groups. The core of the population investigated is of the kind with which we shall be concerned in this chapter: Grade III. These households do not stand out as presenting features which are likely to have a particularly adverse or a particularly beneficial effect on the children's conduct. Then there are the 'bad' households, which include those that public agencies would call 'problem families', as well as a number of households which, though they could not strictly be considered problem families, are yet not up to the standards governing the behaviour of the Grade III group. The former were classified as Grade I; we are not concerned with these here; they are very like the people described in 'Branch Street'. The Grade II group we shall have occasion to refer to in this chapter: they are the traditional 'roughs'. Intermingled with them are the traditional respectable Grade III households, easy-going about their neighbours, regarding them (in Radby) in the spirit of 'live and let live'. In this respect they are different from the higher grades (IV and V) as also in the allied fact that they have not their social aspirations. These last two grades belong to our next chapter.

St. Ebbe's, the Oxford area described by Mogey, is a set of some fifty streets with, all in all, nearly a thousand inhabited houses. The actual number of building lots is greater, for the region is now a zone of dilapidation, and gaps where buildings formerly stood appear here and there in the monotonous rows of houses. Over half the streets contain now less than ten houses, most of them contain less than forty. Very few of the houses have baths. The lavatory is normally out in the backyard. About a quarter of the houses have a garden to them. Shops are sprinkled around the area, about one to every fourteen houses. The inhabitants of St. Ebbe's are aware that outsiders are prone to take a superior attitude to their homes and backyards and 'are defensively on the alert to try and detect this opinion in a questioner'. But they do not cringe. One informant said, 'This is the oldest part of Oxford. There were people living here long before those upstarts came along and built the colleges.'

The majority of the men in St. Ebbe's are in unskilled, or at most semi-skilled occupations, in motor-car construction, building, distributive trades, or in service in the Colleges. In this community it is accepted that women should also work outside the home, and many of them have been earning, with short breaks for child-bearing, since they left school.

In the Bethnal Green sample nearly half the men are skilled workers, one-ninth are semi-skilled, two-ninths unskilled, another ninth are clerical workers. Bethnal Green is therefore a cut above St. Ebbe's where class position is concerned. The men are predominantly engaged in such locally important industries as furniture, clothing, transport, docking and engineering. Over half the marriages were between people who lived in the area. About 8 per cent of this sample is Jewish. Bott's 'Newbolts' lived in Bethnal Green.

The working classes here described [by Hoggart] have their own recognizable parts of the town; they have, almost city by city, their own recognizable styles of housing—back-to-backs here or tunnel-backs there . . . To isolate the working classes in this rough way is not to forget the great number of differences, the subtle shades, the class distinctions, within the working classes themselves. To the inhabitants there is a fine range of distinctions in prestige from street to street.

If East London is without class snobbery, it has snobberies of its own. The poorest people in Bethnal Green have been delighted that the eighteenth-century street-name of Satchwell's Rents, admittedly recalling long-vanished exploitation, has been changed to the dull Satchwell Road. And there is a series of geographical snobberies in East London which is an expression not of 'class' outlook but of that acute parochial isolation which is the heaviest handicap of the East London communities. Benighted Bethnal Green despises Wapping as a place of rough and drunken longshoremen who are not as respectable Bethnal Greeners that go charring in the city. Benighted Wapping despises Whitechapel as a place full of bleeding foreigners. Benighted Whitechapel despises Bethnal Green as a horde of starvelings who could not afford between them to buy one prosperous Whitechapel fruit barrow. Hackney despises all three areas as 'the East End'. And the patriots of Stepney Green despise Hackney as a mere dormitory suburb.[1]

THE SOCIAL NETWORK AND THE PERPETUATION OF TRADITION

The concept of a 'social network' was first employed systematically by Bott in order to clarify certain important differences in family behaviour. Supposing that a family X maintains relationships with friends, neighbours and relatives who may be designated as A, B, C, D, E, F . . . N. Some, but not all, of these persons know one another. B might know A and C but

[1] R Sinclair (1950), *East London*, Robert Hale, London. See also Zweig, *The British Worker* (chap. 1, 'Grades of Labour').

none of the others; D might know F without knowing A, D or E. Furthermore, all of these persons will have friends, neighbours and relatives of their own, who may or may not be known by the family X. The more of these persons outside the immediate family know and interact with one another, the more close-knit the network is said to be.

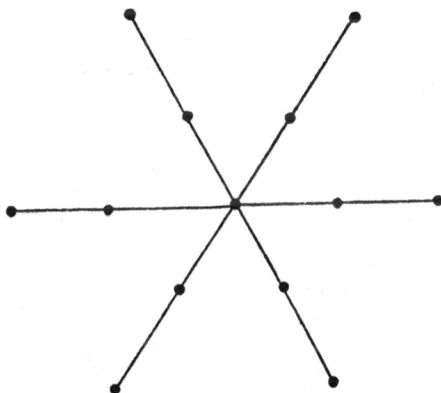

loose-knit

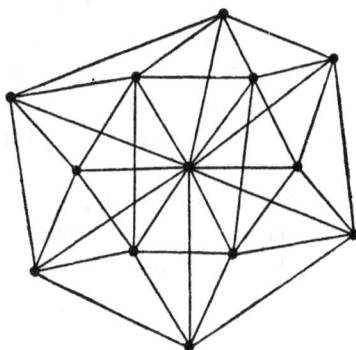

close-knit

Extreme Types: loose-knit and close-knit networks.

Bott uses the adjective 'close-knit' to describe a network in which there are many relationships among the component units, and 'loose-knit' for networks in which there are few such relationships. 'Connectedness' is the general term for the extent to which the people related to one unit also know and meet each other independently of that unit.

The relevance of this concept for the study of traditional communities is clear. In these communities, the networks of component families are often so close-knit, and the relationships within the local population group so clearly distinguished from external relationships, that the local population can almost be called an organized group. The members' activities are known to all; none can escape the sanctions of gossip and public opinion. In these conditions, people tend to reach consensus on norms and exert a consistent informal pressure on each other to conform. This is the way a tradition is perpetuated, relatively immune from change as long as the network remains intact.[1]

The communities with which this chapter is concerned are traditional and close-knit.

The Newbolts had grown up in the neighbourhood, as had many of their relatives and friends. They knew a considerable number of local people and many of these people were acquainted with one another. The local area was definitely a community for them: they had local pride. They felt their neighbours were like them. Bott adds that this is likely to lead to an overlapping of social roles: people are not sorted into separate categories—friend, neighbour, relative, colleague—the same person fills several roles simultaneously.

Robb quotes evidence for Bethnal Green that in 1944 three-quarters of the heads of families had been born within the borough. One informant, himself living in the house that had been occupied by his parents and grandparents, stated that he could not remember a new family coming into the street of seventy houses during the previous forty years. Another reported a movement of six families in twenty-five years, in a longer street.[2]

---

[1] Mogey, in a private communication, points out that one good example of this is the perpetuation of a local accent, socially disapproved by the mass of society and detrimental to the social advancement of those who speak it.

[2] J. H. Robb (1954), *Working-Class Anti-Semite: a psychological study in a London borough*, Tavistock Publications, London. The evidence is from R. Glass and M. Frenkel (1946), *Profile of Bethnal Green*. A mimeographed report for the Association for Planning and Regional Reconstruction.

Traditional Working-Class Life

According to Mogey, over half the housewives in his St. Ebbe's sample had been born and brought up there. Seventy per cent of his sample population had been married and living in their present house for ten years or longer. 'Most families have been living in their house long enough for the neighbours to become familiar shapes in the landscape. Names and characteristics are known too, carried along the gossip chain and treasured as a way of making contact with the world beyond the front door.'

Unless he gets a council house [thus Hoggart] a working-class man is likely to live in his local area, perhaps even in the house he 'got the keys for' the night before his wedding, all his life. He has little call to move if he is a general labourer, and perhaps hardly more if he is skilled, since his skill is likely to be in a trade for which several nearby works provide vacancies. He is very unlikely to be the only one doing his kind of work in the area. He is more likely to change his place of work than his place of living: he belongs to a district more than to one works. He may have a cousin who teaches, married a girl in Nottingham and settled there; he may have a brother who met a girl in Scotland during the war and brought her down here. But by and large the family live near and 'always' lived near; each Christmas-day they all go to tea at Grandma's . . . To a visitor they are understandably depressing, these massed proletarian areas; street after regular street of shoddily uniform houses intersected by a dark pattern of ginnels and snickets [alley-ways] and courts; mean, squalid, and in a permanent half-fog; a study in shades of dirty-grey, without greenness or the blueness of sky . . . The houses are fitted into the dark and lowering canyons between the giant factories and the services which attend them . . . The goods-lines pass on embankments in and around, level with many of the bed-room windows . . . But to the insider, these are small worlds, each as homogeneous and well-defined as a village. Down below, on the main road running straight into town, the bosses' cars whirr away at five o'clock to converted farm-houses ten miles out in the hills; the men stream up into their district. They know it in intimate detail—automatically slipping up a snicket here or through a shared lavatory-block there: they know it as a group of tribal areas. Pitt Street is certainly one of ours; just as certainly as Prince Consort Street next to it is not . . . Similarly, one knows practically everybody, with an intimacy of detail—that these people have a son who 'got on' or emigrated; that those have a daughter who went wrong or married away and is doing well; that this old man living alone on his pension shops at the horsemeat place in town and smokes a sixpenny mixture of herbs.

In Radby we find the household's network-connectedness neatly correlated with its respectability-rating. A quarter of the Grade III husbands and wives had relatives living within a few houses of their own residence. In the rougher Grades I and II the proportions were one-half and one-third respectively. The corresponding proportion for the top grades was one in ten. We find therefore that the lower down the social scale we go, the more close-knit the network, and, by inference, the more traditional the way of life.

From these accounts it is clear that a number of social variables are related to a close-knit type of network, all of them clearly also of a nature to discourage changes in traditional ideas or practices: the concentration of people in the same or similar occupations in the same local area, little migration into or out of the area, local inter-marriages, continuity of social relations, opportunities for relatives and friends to help one another, little demand for physical mobility, little opportunity for social mobility.[1]

Bott found that these variables were in fact interrelated in her sample. Gorer confirms this finding and, additionally, indicates that there are important regional variations in the extent to which traditional features are still to be observed. From his data it would appear that (ignoring the rural south) the further north his informants lived, the more likely they were to have lived longer at their present address, the more likely they were to have parents living in the same town, to have kin within five minutes' walking distance, and to have their best friends living near rather than far away. Gorer was also able to

---

[1] A national investigation of occupational and job mobility carried out in 1949 by the Government Social Survey found that 90 per cent of job movements by wage-earners took place within the boundaries of the communities in which they lived (G. Thomas (1950), *Labour Mobility in Great Britain*, Government Social Survey). This fact is cited by M. W. Susser and W. Watson (1962), *Sociology in Medicine*, Oxford University Press. This valuable work, which unfortunately appeared too late to affect the fundamental lines of the present book, confirms and substantiates many of the facts and arguments here presented.

relate length of residence to the proximity of brothers, sisters or married children, and found that the longer his informants had lived in the neighbourhood the more likely they were to have such kin live near them. He concludes from such data that

by practically every criterion, the break-up of the extended family (i.e. the large kinship group which includes married brothers and sisters and cousins, etc.) has proceeded much further in the South of England than in the Midlands and the North. Furthermore, the very poor, with incomes under £5 a week, and the prosperous, with incomes over £12 (in 1951), both tended to live more isolated from their kin. In the middle-income groups, in medium-sized towns (under one million inhabitants) and among the working classes, such isolation was much less common.

These are, therefore, the groups most likely to show traditional patterns of life.[1]

THE NETWORK: FRIENDS, NEIGHBOURS, KIN

A Bethnal Green inhabitant said to Young and Willmott: 'I was bred and born in Bethnal Green and my parents and their parents before them: no, I wouldn't leave Bethnal Green, I wouldn't take a threepenny bus ride outside Bethnal Green.' Another took a walk with one of the interviewers. In half an hour, they met:

I. MARY COLLINS: She's a sister of Sally who I worked with at the button place before I got married. My Mum knew her Mum, but I sort of lost touch until one day I found myself sitting next to her in Meath gardens. We both had babies with us, and so we got talking again. I see quite a lot of Mary now.

2. ARTHUR JANSEN: Yes, I knew him before I was married. He worked at our place with his sister and mother. He's married now.

3. MAVIS BOOT: That lady there, I know her. She lives down our turning. She's the daughter of one of Mum's old friends. When she died, Mum promised to keep an eye on Mavis. She pops in at Mum's every day.

---

[1] Mogey, in a private communication, comments that in London and the South-East at least, neighbours are added to the kin groups already existing in the area. 'Mobility creates neighbours in the place of kindred.' See also pages 231 and 347–8.

Aspects of Adult Life in England

4. JOAN BATES (serving behind the counter at the baker's): She used to be a Simpson. She lives in the same street as my sister. My Mum knows her better than me.

5. SYBIL COOK: That's a girl I knew at school called Sybil.

6. KATIE SIMMONS: She's from the turning. Mum nursed her Mum when she was having Katie.

7. BETTY SALMON AND HER MOTHER: They live in the next turning to ours. Betty says she's had nothing but trouble with her daughter since she went to school.

8. RICHARD FIENBURGH: That man over there at the corner. He's a sort of relative. He's a brother of my sister's husband. He lives near them.

9. PATRICK COLLINS (this was a man in an old car parked by the shops): His mother lives in the turning.

10. SADIE LITTLE (this time there was not even a nod. The two women walked straight past each other): 'She's quarrelled with my sister so we don't talk to each other.'

11. AMY JACOBS (an old bent woman who turns out to be the informant's godmother): Usually it's only when I'm with Mum that we talk.

12. ALFRED CROSLAND. (He is the father of the Katie seen a few minutes before.)

13. VIOLET BELCHER (talking to another woman at street corner). An acquaintance of Mum's. She's got trouble with her inside.

14. EMMA FRANCE: 'How's that sister of yours?' 'Lily?' 'Yes, your Mum told me. She's gone to live in Bow, hasn't she?' 'She's got a place with her mother-in-law there.' 'She don't like it? No! It never did work and I don't suppose it ever will.' (They both collapsed into laughter at this. Afterwards the informant explained that Mrs. France had been her landlady in the first rooms her Mum had got for her.)

This was just one unexceptional shopping trip.[1] 'Some days,' said this informant, 'you see so many you don't know which to talk to.' She kept a record over a week of all the people she saw in the

---

[1] On a Sheffield estate investigated by Hodges and Smith, 'the housewives are very much the creatures of their immediate environment, and, as the majority of those who do not go out to work live their life within a comparatively small circle of neighbours and relatives, their choice of acquaintance is restricted . . . Friends were often within twenty or thirty yards from the home . . . The street is indeed a most important point for social activity.' M. W. Hodges and C. S. Smith (1954), *Neighbourhood and Community*, Liverpool University Press.

132

street and whom she considered herself to 'know'. There were 63 people in all, 38 of whom were relatives of at least one other person she had seen.[1]

Young and Willmott may justly say:

> The person who says he 'knows everyone' is of course exaggerating, but pardonably so. He does, with various degrees of intimacy, know many people outside (but often through) his family, and it is this which makes it, in the view of many informants, a 'friendly place'. Bethnal Green, or at any rate the precinct, is, it appears, a community which has some sense of being one. There is a sense of community, a sense of solidarity between people who occupy the common territory, which springs from the fact that people and their families have lived there a long time.

Great store is set by such good neighbourliness, which Hoggart defines as 'not just doing fair by each other', but as 'being obliging' and 'always ready to oblige'. To call anyone neighbourly or right sociable, he continues, is to offer a high compliment; a club may be praised because it is a 'real sociable place'; they will say of a church, 'it is a nice friendly church'.

The sense of community, of solidarity, is a response easily evoked in a variety of situations. It is highly regarded in the men's world of work. Indeed, it could be argued that this is where it is felt most strongly. We shall see that the men are not all enthusiastic about community solidarity, 'neighbourliness'. But the ideal worker, as seen by other workers, is described to Zweig as a sociable man who goes about in a crowd and regards himself as part of his community, eager to give help and ready to accept it.

> The worker has more emergencies in his life than anyone, and he has to rely on the help of his family and friends. The model worker must be a 'good fellow'. He must be ready to do his mates a good turn. He must not only be friendly but generous; he must carry out in practice the principle 'live and let live'. He must be happy, that is, he must keep himself happy and make others happy.[1]

The frequency of neighbourly contact and the intimacy with which people know the details of each other's lives makes it easy in some ways for neighbours to be helpful to one another and thus create a feeling of solidarity. According to some commentators, there is a good deal of neighbourly help in these old traditional areas. The evidence is not very easily interpreted. We shall argue that kin living in the neighbourhood rather than unrelated neighbours are mainly responsible for what is loosely called 'neighbourliness'. The oft-expressed belief that women spend a lot of their time 'popping round next door' to mere neighbours receives little factual support from any of our sources. Nor is it borne out by Gorer's informants. Those who visit their neighbours, whether formally or informally, are concentrated at the top and the bottom of the economic scale. And only about a third of Gorer's informants felt they could rely on their neighbours 'in a pinch'. The smallest proportion (only one in ten) of those who felt able to rely on their neighbours 'in a pinch' came from the group at the bottom of the literate social scale—those who called themselves lower working class. Gorer comments: 'the middle class has repeated for generations the cliché that it is the poor who help the poor; the poor themselves seem to doubt it'. Poor kin may help each other, poor neighbours more rarely.

There is as much evidence that people do not get on with their neighbours as that they do. One reason is obvious. A very close-knit network has its disadvantages as well as its advantages. The more people live on top of one another, the more they know of each other's needs and can be helpful, but also the more of a nuisance they may be to each other. If we argue that much of the helpfulness observed in traditional communities is specifically helpfulness between kin who live in the neighbourhood—unrelated neighbours helping in emergencies or in those infrequent cases when there is no kin living near— it becomes less difficult to reconcile the famed 'neighbourliness' of the traditional areas with the apparently contradictory finding that neighbours are often disliked and mistrusted in a number of ways. The greater the connectedness, the greater the feeling of intrusiveness does seem to be. Gorer supports this nicely. The further north (this we assume to be associated with greater connectedness and stronger traditions), the smaller the number of complaints about 'unfriendliness', but the greater the number of complaints about neighbours' inquisitiveness and neighbours' borrowing. And taking England as a whole, the poorer the group of informants, the more often they complained about their neighbours' gossip and tendency to borrow things. Hodges and Smith relate the wish to 'keep oneself to oneself' directly to the fear of gossip.

> To talk about one's own affairs puts the individual in the position of being talked about behind his back, and so it is safer to withdraw. Lack of mutual confidence brings with it low morale. Where this is so, a vicious spiral is set up, insofar as low morale decreases communication still further.

Neighbourly strain is inherent in close-knit networks. It is not simply that living in close contact has its disadvantages as well as its advantages: the rough *is* the smooth. If people talk about you in the little shop, they will know incidentally when you are in trouble. This may not be very pleasant if you want to keep it quiet, but it is very useful if you need help. You cannot expect people to exchange only news that is useful to you. Bott sees this very clearly.

> Neighbours frequently accused one another of something—betraying a confidence, taking the wrong side in a children's quarrel, failing to return borrowed articles, gossip. One has little privacy in such a situation. But if one wants to reap the rewards of companionship and small acts of mutual aid, one must conform to local standards and one must expect to be included in the gossip. Being gossiped about is as much a sign of belonging to the neighbourly network as being gossiped with . . . no gossip, no companionship.

In addition to inherent strains of this kind, there are others induced by the fact that even in the more traditional communities some changes are taking place. When, for reasons connected with divergent rates of change or for other reasons, households of different standards live in close proximity, neighbourliness may suffer.[1]

What this means for the traditional respectable household is by no means clear. In Radby, the Grade III family seems

[1] For detailed discussion of this process, see next chapter, pages 251–64.

135

able to live and let live in the circumstances. The four families there singled out for detailed study lived in circles in which delinquency was common. To them, the delinquency record of their neighbours was not an abnormal thing. They disapproved of bad behaviour and warned their children against it, but their families and the delinquent families were mingling at a certain level all day long. Under such conditions 'juvenile delinquency is not a matter about which one takes a rigidly censorious attitude'. Broadly speaking, Grade III consists of those households which are content—or at any rate, not seriously perturbed—to live alongside the two lower grades, whilst maintaining a different set of standards with regard to behaviour and physical appearances, a set of standards which accords more with that of the higher grades. Nevertheless, Grade III homes, although they may decry the standards and codes of the lower grades, do not take great pains to ensure that their children do not mix with those of the lower households, nor are they contemptuous of them.[1]

As mobility increases, local variations in helpfulness are likely to increase too, for as the family network becomes more tenuous, a greater burden is placed on the unrelated neighbours. A process may then develop which Bott describes thus:

> In an area of low population turnover, formerly the same people lived there all their lives. Close-knit networks could develop not only because the area was homogeneous but also because there was continuity. Now, as some of the inhabitants move away, the networks even of those people who remain in the area are becoming less connected.

This idea may be carried one stage further. Might there not be a 'critical level' to network-connectedness? Below that level the number of people who can be called upon to help is too small for such calls not to become an intolerable burden—each one's turn to help comes round too soon. When such a critical level is reached in an area, there must be an abrupt drop in the total exchange of services.

In a community in which everyone is in the same boat, or where in most people's lifetime outrageous fortune visits all

---

[1] For detailed discussion of comparative material, see pages 462 and 556-7.

more or less equally, mutual help is possible because of a general feeling that it will be *mutual*. Tomorrow you may need help, today you give it. When changes take place so that some people see themselves as no longer, or never again, needing help, these people will soon begin to feel that they are permanently at the 'giving' end of what used to be a reciprocal exchange of services, and then they will begin to see the others as always begging, always cadging.

We shall see in the next chapter that a growing divergence may separate those who can do without help and those who, without help, go under. Then the former may keep away from and dislike the latter. The respectables will keep away from the roughs. This certainly seems to be so in the South and/or among the economically more secure. Mrs. Stacey, for instance, in her Banbury study, came across the generally-held notion that the bad managers and the poor are the ones who borrow most frequently. To be independent of one's neighbour, to keep a certain formality in social relations, would then be a mark of respectability, epitomized in the ubiquitous 'I keep myself to myself'. The popping-in-and-out set is one with which the respectable would not wish to be associated or confused.[1]

So it may be that one reason why the evidence concerning stand-offish or friendly and helpful neighbourhoods has been so difficult to interpret is that the issue has been confused because helpful kin lived so near that neighbours can be said to be friendly, though the kin normally provide the help. The norm is for neighbours to help in emergencies. If they do more than that, they may be resented.

The issue may also have been confused by the use of the word 'friend'. It is not irrelevant to remember that in Ireland 'kin' and 'friend' have been interchangeable terms. The fact that neighbours are 'familiar figures in the landscape' does not mean that they are 'friends' in the sense in which that word is used by middle-class people. Nor, indeed, should it be assumed that neighbours are 'not-friends'. Friendship is a category of social behaviour which does not fit easily into traditional working-class life and hence its definition presents difficulties both to the social investigator and to those whom he questions

[1] M. Stacey (1960), *Tradition and Change*, Oxford University Press.

about it. For instance, nearly two-thirds of Mogey's sample of families in St. Ebbe's reported that they had no friends, and only one in ten reported more than one friend. The same proportion seems to obtain in Bethnal Green: only about a third have friends with whom they are on visiting terms, whereas nearly everyone visits relatives. Yet the neighbourhoods are thought of as 'friendly'.

One aspect of this vagueness of the concept 'friend' is that many of the functions conventionally thought of by the middle classes as characterizing friendship—mutual help, comfort, advice, stimulus—are here the traditional prerogatives of relatives, who are not thought of as friends but as mothers, aunties, and so on. Neighbours help out in emergencies, but they do not thereby necessarily acquire the status of friend as defined in the middle classes. The mutual rendering of services produces a 'friendly neighbourhood'. So it seems that friendliness describes a communal quality, while the individual descriptive 'friend' is in less frequent usage.[1]

Where people admit to friendship, the notion of a friend often has a sound unusual to the middle-class ear.[2] Thus, according to one St. Ebbe's informant, 'A neighbour is someone you happen to live beside; a friend is someone you have known all your life.'[3] 'Mind you,' said another, 'we never go into each other's houses, people begin to chatter. You can be just as friendly meeting in the road.' In the same vein, a man in Bethnal Green tells Young and Willmott:

'I've got plenty of friends around here. I've always got on well with people, but I don't invite anyone here. I've got friends at work and friends at sport and friends I have a drink with. I know all the people around here and I'm not invited into anyone else's

[1] See also P. Willmott (1963), *Evolution of a Community*, pages 64-8.

[2] Mogey, in a private communication, suggests that the middle-class notion of friendship is an exclusive one, shutting out the rest of the community, and that this is the difference between the two definitions. If this is so, he argues, there is no essential or semantic difference between the working-class use of the phrase 'we're all friends' and their use of the phrase 'we've no friends'.

[3] 'Only after people have lived at the same address for ten years or more do they consider that their best friends live near them' (Gorer, op. cit., p. 51). See also the discussion in P. Willmott (1963), *The Evolution of a Community*, Routledge and Kegan Paul, London (chap. VI, especially pages 64-6).

house either. It doesn't seem right somehow. Your home's your own.'

This man typifies one kind of idea of sociability: it never occurs to him that friends might be shared with his wife. Nor is it likely to occur to him that he might share his wife's friends. The strict segregation of the men's world and the women's world—though beginning to die out in the South—is connected with this general feeling that 'your home's your own'. We are still in a social region where men and women are not really easy in each other's company. Although there is a growing conjugal companionship, men have traditionally had their own male groups outside the home, leaving the main responsibility for kin and neighbourly relations to their womenfolk. In this spirit, Mr. Newbolt is quoted as saying: 'Men have friends, women have relatives.' Where husband and wife share few interests, the men feel awkward and ill at ease, deprived of the opportunity to relax after the day's work, if they come home to find visitors, especially female visitors.

Visiting is the basic criterion which distinguishes intimates from other acquaintances. The front door is the symbol of the barrier.

> The first social fact [Mogey] noticed with the men is how strictly outside the home and inside it are kept as separate domains. Coming in from the outer world, the symbols operative there are removed: off comes the jacket, off come the collar and tie, off come the boots or shoes.

Hoggart sees the home as a refuge from the miseries of industrial life in the thirties.

> Where almost everything else is ruled from outside, is chancy and likely to knock you down when you least expect it, the home is yours and real: the warmest welcome is still 'Mek y'self at 'ome' . . . The insistence on the privacy of the home arises from this feeling, reinforced by the knowledge that, though the neighbours are 'your sort' and will rally round in trouble, they are always ready for a gossip and perhaps a mean-minded gossip . . . You can shut the front door, 'live yer own life', 'keep y'self to y'self'—that is, to the immediate members of the household, which includes the married sons and daughters with their families from

the streets nearby, and extends to the few friends on 'popping-in' terms. You want good neighbours, but a good neighbour is not always 'coming in and out': if she does that, she may have to be 'frozen off' . . . The hearth is reserved for the family, whether living at home or nearby, and for those who are 'something to us', and look in for a talk or just to sit. Much of the free time of a man and his wife will usually be passed at the hearth; 'just staying in' is still one of the most common leisure-time occupations.[1]

The feeling that 'your home is your own' is one means of preserving locally correct social distances and enabling people to cope with the strains of overcrowding. So are a number of other attitudes and practices we have noted in this sub-section. Zweig's 'model worker', for instance, is described as having certain virtues which lend themselves to the collective maintenance of the locally preferred levels of interaction. The great emphasis on 'being tolerant' is often expressed in very relevant interpersonal terms.

'Mind your own business', 'Don't interfere with others', 'Don't be superior', 'Don't snub people', 'Don't be a fanatic'. In sum, respect other people's feelings and points of view, don't persuade them of your own. The first principle is: Don't show up your fellow worker if he is weaker, older or less capable or efficient than you are.[2]

The distinction between good and bad gossip may also operate to preserve some areas of life as private and not to be intruded upon.

Retailing information about the way Mrs. —— spends her money at the pub and neglects her children may be permitted [write Smith and Hodges], but only because it is shameful to neglect children; if there were no children the speaker should mind her own business. But if Mrs. —— had just died, or her son had had an accident, it would be expected that her neighbour should stop people and tell them about it.

The practice of interacting in crises only also preserves more

---

[1] Gorer, op. cit., Tables 33–4F confirm this point. 'With my own family' was by far the most frequent response to the questions: 'If you wanted to spend a pleasant evening, in what sort of company would you like to spend it?' and 'In what company did you spend last Saturday evening?'

[2] See also pages 363 and 516.

distant relations at more normal times. Thus Firth and Djamour, writing of a South London borough, note that as far as close relationships were concerned the individual flat remains the dweller's castle. Outer doors are usually shut and there is little free-and-easy visiting. 'On the stairs, if the door is ajar and you happen to look in, they ask you what the b—— h—— you are looking at.' . . . In contrast to the fierce assertive separateness in ordinary mundane affairs, there is a sense of communal unity in *crises*. Some neighbourly help is often given, and communal help may be encountered in instances where only conventional sympathy might have been expected. For instance, at bereavements money is collected for a wreath and all the neighbours contribute.[1]

Hodges and Smith call this 'latent neighbourliness'. Neighbours willingly give help in exceptional circumstances. They pay the rent for others who happen to be out, they lend bread if someone runs short, they help in bereavements and confinements. This would be so even if they had not been on speaking terms for years. (But those who are unable to cope invent a conventional terminology of crises in order to procure neighbourly help. They, the cadgers, the roughs, just happen to be short of money this week, or just happen to have run out of bread. This may be much resented by those normally at the receiving end of such requests.)

It is no wonder that the solution to the many problems of social living involves the restriction of informal sociability to places outside the home. The street is an important meeting-place, especially for housewives. There are others: the market, the place of work, the fish parlour, the cafés, the youth clubs, the public houses. Most important, there is the small local shop where the shop-keeper and his family pass on information as well as the groceries. This is the clearing-house for local gossip. Here neighbours who happen to meet have an opportunity to exchange the news. Now if street or shop are the news-exchange, the socially important functions of gossip are fulfilled and yet very intimate relations cannot spring from such a source. The information is spread wide, with other shoppers

[1] R. Firth, ed. (1956), *Two Studies of Kinship in London*. University of London Press. See also next chapter, pages 274–5.

who happen to be there listening in, but close personal ties are avoided.

Meeting in the shop or the street also allows people to terminate the contact at will, and so its depth can be controlled. When one begins to feel uncomfortable one can say one must go. To turn a visitor politely out of a house is very much more difficult. The casual street contact allows both to feel that they are not imposing on the other, since both are free to walk away.

The attitudes and social conditions which keep informal relations outside the family as non-committal as possible also affect the more formal associational life of the community. On the whole, the people now under discussion do not join formal groups, though they may display a regularity in their social habits which resembles that required by formal organizations. The pub and its equivalent in many areas, the working-men's club, enable people to meet on the premises without enforcing regularity or punctuality. Zweig gives impressive examples of the strength of the habits governing visits to pub or sports-meeting. Whether men go once a week, twice or ten times, whichever they do, they do regularly, week by week, on the same days of the week, at the same times. If this is so for the majority of the pub-goers, they will see the same faces whenever they are there, and so an informal group is created. Mogey described one such group at the *Jolly Waterman*. 'The loyalty of this informal group to the house is remarkable. Most of the regulars know only the outside of the other public houses in the area.' The same kind of regularity is displayed, with the same consequences, by the women who meet in shop or market. The group exists, but it is not 'joined'. No demands are made on those who find themselves belonging to it. It is a non-committal, effortless sociability.[1]

ADOLESCENCE: A BRIEF FLOWERING PERIOD

We must now begin to consider some of the principal types of role-behaviour encountered in the traditional working-class family. In previous chapters this could be done by combining age and position in the family into a sequence of roles: infant,

[1] For further discussion, see pages 277–83 and 349–50.

child, adolescent, parent, breadwinner. In the three chapters of which this is the first, this is more difficult, partly because we have to be content with what our source-material provides, but partly also because the areas now under discussion are less isolated, so that the culture in each case is less unique: there would be less point in dealing with each locality separately (even if data were available to allow it). The adults are different enough; this makes it possible to write three chapters. On the other hand, the ways the children are brought up are so various, currently so subject to social changes, and so intricately related to the parents' personality and social position, that the whole topic has had to be dealt with in a separate volume. Adolescence occupies a position midway between these two phases of the life-cycle.

There is room for doubt whether the discussion of adolescence which follows is of more than historical interest. No conclusive statistics are available but it is perfectly possible that in the nineteen-sixties the number of typically traditional working-class adolescents is small. The new adolescents Colin MacInnes describes with such perceptiveness are so different from their predecessors that a social psychologist's courage may falter.[1] No attempt is made to incorporate into this book the scant data available on them; discussion of the traditional working-class adolescent has been confined to those aspects which fit into or throw light on other aspects of the traditional culture. These aspects are concerned with the adult's memory of his own grim childhood and the expectation that it will continue to be grim in the next generation, with the rather sudden and very marked restriction of all imaginative interests towards the end of adolescence, and with adolescent sex and courtship.

In a traditional community, roles are strictly defined and adhered to. The parallel with the Ashton miner is in some ways striking. It is not paradoxical to say that, in the traditional English working-class community, the role of the adolescent is strictly defined as involving great personal freedom. Hoggart described the phase as a 'brief flowering period' and shows

---

[1] Colin MacInnes (1957), *City of Spades*; (1959), *Absolute Beginners*, both published by MacGibbon and Kee, London. There is a brief but good description of some of the issues in Ronald Fletcher's *The Family and Marriage*, Penguin Special, 1962.

himself a good observer (and his people good sociologists) when he attributes the adults' permissiveness to a feeling that 'you're only young once'.

It is a working-class tradition of long standing to indulge not only children, but young people all the way up to marriage. Babies are smothered with love and attention, not allowed to cry, stuffed until their little bellies ache and then given dubious remedies in sixpenny packets; even today many of them are rarely left without a dummy and that probably dipped in syrup, jogged continually in their magnificent prams, hardly ever left alone by mother, by father when he gets home from work, by grand-parents, and kept up far too late. Later, though sometimes the girls may be expected to help a little in the house and the boys may take on a 'newspaper round', the remarkable feature, in view of how much the mother has to do and how short she is of spare money, is that they are asked to do so little and that spare-time money-making is so often regarded as for their own pockets. How often do children wash up? How often are they bought dispro-portionately expensive presents—bikes of the most splendid kind and prams almost full-size? Parents expect and encourage the children, even in adolescence, to do little to support the house in labour or money. A girl may be 'earning good money' and costing a lot to keep, but she is probably paying less than she costs to her mother. If this is a blind selfishness, it is a selfishness which the parents condone and support: there is all the rest of life to come and you cannot do much about that; you must let them "ave a good time while they can'; after all, 'yer only young once'. . .

The girls seem to be enveloped in the chrysalis of an adolescent day-dream. Everything they choose to do seems urban and trivial; it would be difficult to hold their attention for long to anything that was not part of the dream . . . They seem to fill the space between leaving school and marriage with thrice-weekly visits to 'musicals' and 'romantic dramas' at the pictures, with fantasy love-stories, and with successive hops at the Palais, the Mecca, the Locarno or the Public Baths. Their jobs rarely engage more than a small portion of their personalities, they seem to have little interest as committed individuals in anything, they take no inter-est in Trade Union activities and little in the home. Surely they are most of them flighty, careless and inane?

Matters are not always as bad as they first appear. Girls like these have only a brief flowering period, only a few years during which they have no responsibilities and some spare money . . .

Traditional Working-Class Life

This gay life of the 'teens is not regarded as finally 'real', as the real business of life. It is enjoyed and not regretted; it rarely affects the sense that, after all, the real business of life is getting married and having a family . . . Real life, questions of fun apart, is marriage . . . Marriage is the end of this temporary freedom for a woman and the beginning of a life in which 'scraping' will be normal. With most, this pattern is taken for granted; the free period is a kind of butterfly flight, giddy while it lasts, but short. There is a wealth of meaning in the phrase used as soon as a girl has found a man she is going to marry: 'I'm going steady now.' . . .

Those young wives who stay at work until the children come, or after, if grandma or a nursery will look after them, are not usually revolting against the demands of marriage, but rather prolonging, for what they know must be a limited period, the time when they can have spare money for little luxuries. When that goes, it goes: most working-class girls do not much pine for their lost freedom; they never regarded it as other than temporary.

Pearl Jephcott, considering a somewhat different population, holds the view that the knowledge of the future grimness of life may have a discouraging effect on the adolescent girl. Because that grimness is associated with adult status, the unfortunate consequence is that cognitive poverty appears to the girls as a positively attractive psychological state! Jephcott and her fellow-workers were much struck by the apathy among the young people they spoke to in the course of their enquiries.

This was very noticeable among the girls, and especially in those who held low-level routine jobs. According to what teachers remembered of them, most of these same girls had been reasonably alert as children. Whatever their I.Q., they had displayed a normal range of out-of-school interests, and had had their own modest skills. When they started work, however, they abandoned almost all their former hobbies, and their leisure became very desultory. This is not to say that they were openly unhappy. It was just that their mental life appeared to freeze up. The change may have been no more than a phase of adolescence . . . but if so, why was it less apparent in the Grammar School children and in those who held the better type of job? Or did the trouble perhaps correspond with a suggestion brought forward by other observers that, whereas boys tend to kick against an unsatisfactory post-school life by hostility and rowdiness, girls make their protest by

145

withdrawing from life?[1] There is a third possibility. Were the girls quicker than the boys to observe and reflect the view of so many of the adults of their own world that education should be directed at earning a living and that non-vocational skills are childish and unprofitable affairs, too frivolous for the serious interest of anyone who is practically grown up?[2]

The same depressing freeze-up is noted among boys by Mogey.

The adolescents are often prepared to use the skills they have acquired at school in the surroundings of a youth club, but, as they grow older, this willingness becomes less and less. The opportunities to break away from the traditional lack of scope are there but, at least at that time in St. Ebbe's, the boys did not grasp them firmly enough for a permanent change to take place. After some experimentation they remained loyal to their tradition.

SEX, COURTSHIP AND THE HOME[3]

Even today few working-class parents seem to tell their children anything about sex. They know they will quickly pick it all up from the street corner. But they are not deliberately leaving it aside because they know the street-gang will do the work for them; indeed, they are likely to be greatly upset if they find their children talking or acting 'dirty'. They leave it [Hoggart thinks], partly because they are not good teachers, are neither competent in nor fond of exposition, prefer knowledge to come incidentally, by means of apophthegm and proverb, and partly because of shyness about bringing sex to the conscious and 'sensible' level.

There are changes of attitude in the matter, however. An outstanding feature of the Grade III families in Radby seemed to be that they were less 'flummoxed by sex' than the adults in Grade I or II households. Mrs. Waters believed in sex-talks at school. She said she had such difficulties herself ('my mother never told me anything') and such worrying experiences as a girl ('lots learn the wrong road especially in the factory') that

---

[1] See also the contrast between youths and girls in Branch Street and Ashton, and pages 162 and 216.

[2] Pearl Jephcott (1954), *Some Young People*, Allen and Unwin, London. See also pages 152 and 589.

[3] See also M. W. Susser and W. Watson (1962), *Sociology in Medicine*, chaps. 6, 7, 8.

she was all for frankness. But old Mrs. Waters, her mother-in-law, did not hold with this. Two other Grade III mothers both gave their girls 'a good talking to' about sex when, at fourteen, the girls started to go out with a boy.

Gorer's information also suggests that feelings in this matter are changing. In that part of the questionnaire which concerns sex, he asks a number of questions about shyness. Slightly more than half his informants considered themselves exceptionally shy, two-thirds thought it natural for young people to be shy, but barely a quarter considered shyness a good thing. It could be argued from this that to be shy (i.e. modest and quiet) used to be a valued form of behaviour and was inculcated by respectable traditional parents, whose offspring duly consider themselves exceptionally shy. But values have changed, and the new generation no longer considers shyness a good thing.

Gorer asked a question about the age at which his informants first felt an interest in the opposite sex. The older the informant, the later the age at which this interest is reported to have begun.

Does this represent a real historical change or is it merely a difference in recollection? Did people now over 45 develop their emotions later than those now under that age? Or is there a tendency among English people, as they go toward their physiological decline, to increase in fantasy the number of years when they were still 'innocent' and 'uninterested in sex'? It seems at least possible that both elements are involved. Respondents now over 45 mostly grew up without the constant stimulation to 'love' and 'romance' which is so incessantly supplied to their juniors by the films, the radio and television and the lyrics of popular songs. Consequently, when the impulse was not particularly strong, there was much less propaganda to induce the young to attempt to manifest interest which they did not strongly feel; and the confused notions of 'psychological health' and the relative undesirability of one-sex groups had no currency. On the other hand, it does seem likely that the middle-aged and elderly tend to deny their own sexuality and to establish, even in an anonymous questionnaire, the picture of the absence of sexual feelings, as well as experience, before marriage, which was and still to a great extent remains the English ideal.

Slater and Woodside found that in discussions on happiness

and harmony in marriage 'the sexual aspects of love were mentioned but little, and this not so much out of prudery as out of a genuine disregard. Sex is not rapture but routine.'[1] Zweig is astounded at the same phenomenon:

> Why is it that among single working men I have met such a high percentage, I believe at least one in four, who either 'never bothered about women' or who after the age of thirty led a completely chaste life? Many men confessed, 'Sex never bothered me', 'I never had any interest in sex or women'. A few of them were effeminate, some were emaciated or undernourished, but the majority were apparently healthy men who could still argue that 'sex is a very overrated business' or that 'sex is largely a matter of the imagination'.[2]

And ten years later the great issue confronting Zweig's younger informants was whether to get married or stay single.

> What is better, a car or a wife? 'I was courting,' confided one, 'and should have been married by now, but instead I bought a car.' At first I treated this as a joke, but I heard it so many times in so many versions ('I can't afford both a car and a wife, so I drifted away from my girl') that I had to regard it as a major issue for youth at present.[3]

It is tempting to argue that sexual activity is highly rated only in the freedom of adolescence, during the brief flowering period before aspiration and feeling and enjoyment are muffled under a pall of resignation, stoicism and scepticism. For the older generation, Bott reports that Mrs. Newbolt seemed to feel that physical sexuality was an intrusion on a peaceful domestic relationship rather than an expression of such a relationship. It was as if sexuality were felt to be basically violent and disruptive. The even tenor of life, the absence of scenes, was more highly valued.

---

[1] E. Slater and M. Woodside (1951), *Patterns of Marriage*, Cassell, London. The two hundred couples interviewed came mainly from London, the men were mainly in semi-skilled or unskilled occupations. The interviews were made in war-time, the men were in hospital.

[2] *The British Worker* (1948).

[3] *The Worker in an Affluent Society* (1961). One must not be hasty to ascribe the attitudes here discussed solely to the working classes. Of Gorer's informants, regardless of social class, only just over half considered sexual love of major importance to the success of a marriage. The matter comes up for further discussion with specific reference to the middle classes on pages 336 and 620.

Traditional Working-Class Life

In adolescence, the boys hang about street corners and other conventional meeting places. 'No matter what you start talking about,' said one of them to Mogey's interviewers, 'it always comes back to girls.'

> Children after the age of ten, and especially boys [writes Hoggart], learn from the older ones in their group and later at work. With boys the emphasis is inevitably on both the enjoyment of sexual experience and on its dreadful and exciting dangers. From thirteen onwards, working-class boys' talk is very often of sex-adventures . . . By eighteen those who wish it can have had a great deal of sexual experience.

> My impression [Hoggart continues] is that more girls than boys escape this bitty promiscuous sexual experience. The names of the same girls who are willing crop up again and again; the easy ones are soon well-known. To me the surprising thing is that so many girls are able to remain unaffected, to retain both an ignorance about the facts of sex and an air of inviolability towards its whole atmosphere that would not have been unbecoming in a mid-nineteenth century young lady of the middle classes. It is wonderful how, without evident prudishness or apparent struggle, many of them can walk through the howling valley of sex-approaches from the local lads, and probably of sex-talk at work, and come through to the boy they are going to marry quite untouched both mentally and physically. Their best light has been the implicit assurance that they would marry, that they were 'keeping themselves for one man'.

In keeping with the principle of effortless sociability, the street is also the place where the first contacts of courtship are made.[1] The contacts are unplanned.

> Boys up to the age of twenty prefer their own company [writes Zweig]; from twenty to, say, twenty-five they are courting and going out with girls: after that age, if they haven't married, they come back to the company of their pals and stay there for life.[2]

First acquaintance is often by 'picking up', a form of behaviour generally recognized for what it is and in its way

---

[1] Slater and Woodside's figures show that the street provides the main opportunity for meeting, though closely followed by introduction through relatives, and to a lesser extent by work, dances and parties. The figures are 46, 36, 30, 23 and 17 respectively for their sample.

[2] Some men, writes Hoggart elsewhere, are felt to be born bachelors, it is characteristic of cognitive poverty that no one considers why this might be so.

respectable. The young man's problem then is, as one of Zweig's informants put it, 'to keep the conversation on neutral ground so as not to get entangled'. The boys generally prefer to meet girls in small groups, where the conversation can be less intimate and the atmosphere gayer and centred around games.

The whole process of mate-selection, on which Slater and Woodside spent a good of time in interview, seems a complete mystery to the actors themselves.

> It is something which 'happens'. From the non-specific sexual urge which forced them into one another's acquaintance at the beginning, together with the usually more or less indescribable nature of the primary specific and individual attraction, up to the logical culmination in a permanent bond, their feelings are vague in the extreme, though accompanied by a sense of moral certainty. 'It was instinct. Fate brought us together—you seem to feel it,' said the husband. And his wife: 'I just seemed to belong to him.'

Slater and Woodside also comment on the fact that it is very rare for any effort to be made at self-analysis. They relate this to the social tradition which favours the romantic attachment and would make it almost improper to apply common-sense and everyday standards to the loved one and the love-relationship. Mogey, who also noticed that in all conversations about courtship there appeared to be a lack of any definite criteria for liking or disliking, relates it to the idea that such vagueness of aspiration and tolerance of other people's attitudes are strong factors in adjustment after marriage. More profoundly than either of these connected attitudes, however, lies that complex which in an earlier passage was called 'cognitive poverty'.

This is found very characteristically in the difficulty Slater and Woodside's informants experienced in describing what it was in their partners that attracted them at the time of first meeting. Looks come first in the list of physical attractions, then facial expression. 'She was not bad-looking', 'She looked a nice type', 'young, fresh, good-looking', 'her general appearance and dress', 'she was clean-looking, she could look smart', 'I liked the way she smiled'. Mental attractions receive more mention, but are equally vaguely described: 'cheery', 'sporty', 'never miserable'.

Traditional Working-Class Life

There is [according to Slater and Woodside] a general and unquestioned acceptance of love as the basis for marriage, but it is more a popular ideal than a common experience. Love is taken for granted, rarely stated as a reason for marriage . . . Love at first sight is rare. The first meeting is usually on quite a low emotional tone . . . The average courtship begins with no very strong feelings on either side, and after petering along for one or two years, it has become a settled thing that they are to get married. Repeatedly one hears such phrases as 'we just drifted together', 'we fell in to going out together'.

One informant, who married at twenty-five, says he and his wife were playmates. He could not remember any attraction: 'We seemed to come together automatically.' She was his only girl. Slater and Woodside conclude that the married partners are less important for themselves than for the contribution that each can make to that complex of material and psychological factors that make up the home. Compared with middle-class or upper-class life the mutual relations of personalities, interests and the like play a much less prominent role.[1]

A slight insight into the English conception of love was afforded by the answers to [Gorer's] question: Do you think English people fall in love in the way you see Americans doing it on the films? Although this question was fairly vague, the pattern referred to is not unclear. In many American films the principal boy and principal girl are portrayed as being strangers to one another before the start of the story; attraction is immediate ('at first sight') followed by a speedy wooing of persiflage and endearments which leads to marriage as soon as the obstacles are removed. The English are vehemently of the opinion that this does not represent typical English behaviour . . .
The English pattern of love which leads to marriage is this. A young man meets a girl, courts her for a year or two, and is engaged for another year. More particularly in the North of England and more particularly among the working classes [i.e. the strongholds of tradition] she is likely to be the first girl he is seriously attracted to.

The expectation that everyone gets married is illustrated both by Hoggart and by Jephcott.

[1] Cf. pages 335-7.

Working-class men and women accept marriage as normal and 'right', and that in their early twenties. What a husband earns at twenty-one, he is likely to be earning at fifty-one; he probably married a girl from exactly his own class, and they set about 'getting a home of their own together' and living their lives inside it.

These adolescent girls of working-class homes were in general required to perform two duties. In the first place their parents expected them to hold the fort in any domestic crisis that might threaten the earning power of the other members of the family. Secondly she was expected to make a satisfactory marriage and to be reasonably quick about it. In Robin Wood (Nottingham) for example, from 'having a boy' to 'going steady' and from 'going steady' to 'getting married' were the proper steps of any dutiful daughter to take in her teens and to have completed by the early twenties. A girl who was sufficiently attractive and proper-spirited to proceed by this pattern brought credit to all. Aunties and uncles and grandparents were involved, since relatives were often as ambitious as parents that the girl should make a good match.

The Radby Report gives information on the proper rules to be observed vis-à-vis the interested families. Girls and boys in the respectable households, when they came to the age of fourteen or so, could go out together, provided that both families approved, and provided that the girl is invited to the boy's home before he goes to hers. In this way, the very beginnings of mate-selection are controlled, and the girl's family knows that the parents of the boy do not disapprove of the potential relationship.

Girls begin courting early and go on steadily until an early marriage. It is important, in this context, not to adjudge the frequency of pre-marital pregnancy sufficient evidence of sexual promiscuity.

> Most girls do not move from man to man, picking up fragmentary experience on the way [writes Hoggart] . . . Many have had some sexual experience before marriage, but usually with the boy they eventually marry; they have not been promiscuous. They are not sheltered: from sixteen they are regarded as in most respects adult; they meet the boy they 'fall for' and start courting. They are probably almost completely ignorant of the practice of sex. They feel romantically towards the boy, he presses, it does

not seem all that important to wait until marriage, and they yield. He will perhaps have taken precautions, but a proportion of men will not, being unprepared or inexpert. If a baby is conceived, the marriage takes place sooner than was expected, but the girl is unlikely to feel that she has been caught. It is my impression that most girls who lose their virginity before marriage lose it in this way—rather than from any deliberate passing from boy to boy 'for the fun of it'.[1]

The prevalence of first births which take place within the first nine months of marriage suggest that we have here a set of considerations which apply very widely indeed. The national statistics show that about one in every eight babies born in England and Wales in the last decade was conceived outside wedlock. About 60 per cent of these are made legitimate by the subsequent marriage of the parents.[2]

The kind of morality behind this seems to draw a clear distinction between pre-marital and extra-marital sexual intercourse. In the traditional working-class community, the former appears to lead, in fact and in principle, to marriage; the latter breaks up marriages and is condemned. Hoggart makes the point in connection with the stories in women's romantic fiction.

It uses words like 'sin', 'shame', guilt', 'evil', with every appearance of meaningfulness. It accepts completely, has as its main point of reference, the notion that marriage and a home, founded on love, fidelity, and cheerfulness, are the right purpose of a woman's life. If a girl 'sins', the suggestion is not that the girl has 'sinned against herself', or that she has fallen short in some relationship other than the human and social, but that she has

[1] Mogey suggests, in a private communication, that most girls have a not very satisfying initiation which arouses their interest, and next time, if satisfied with the boy, they 'stay with it' until they marry.

Before leaving this topic another more far-fetched but not entirely implausible suggestion by Pincus may be mentioned. He suggests that a young man who is very closely tied to his mother (of which there is always a likelihood when the mother is the dominant member of the household) may find it convenient to get his girl pregnant so as to be able to leave his mother without too much recrimination and guilt (L. Pincus, *Marriage: Studies in Emotional Conflict and Growth*, Tavistock Publications, London, 1961).

[2] See also V. Wimperis (1960), *The Unmarried Mother and her Child*, ed. by Clifford Whiting, George Allen and Unwin, London; in particular her chapter on the pregnant bride and the relevant tables in the appendix. Also Susser and Watson, op. cit.

spoiled her chances of a decent home and family. One of the commoner endings to this kind of serial is for the girl either to find again the man responsible, and marry him, or to find another man who, though he knows all, is prepared to marry her and be a father to the child, loving them both. One can appreciate the force of the mistrust of 'the other woman', the Jezebel, the home-breaker, the woman who sets out to wreck an existing marriage or one about to start. Even the man with a roving eye gets short shrift if he goes in for marriage-breaking.

The home, the marriage, the family, are the basic realities—of much greater importance to men and women alike than are the pleasures of sex or of romantic love.

Love is the sweetest thing in life, agreed Zweig's informants in 1958, but most of them added that they meant by this a home and children. 'It's the finest thing; something to work for, to look to and to look after', 'That's my life, wife and children', 'My love, that's my wife and children', 'My children and my home, that is my love'.

The perception of this has led Slater and Woodside to say that marriage and home are synonymous in many people's minds. The equation of the two is a characteristic feature of their sample. At this social level, practical advantages are given a higher rating than temperamental compatibilities. Marriage is less *to* someone than *for* something. Wanting a home is the most common reason given for marriage: 'It's somewhere to come home to', 'I thought I'd like a home of me own'. Both men and women feel like this. Marriage defines their position, their purpose in life.

In reviewing the differences in the position of married and single men [writes Zweig], I would emphasize as the strongest factor in happiness: *Purposefulness in life*. Married men have the feeling that they are cared for and at the same time needed by their womenfolk. They command a greater respect in the community. If a man has a purpose in life, he feels steadier, while without it he drifts and grows restless. A single man has more freedom, but less purpose, and we often overrate the blessings of freedom and underrate those of purpose.

For the women's point of view we may quote Pearl Jephcott who, after the account of the family pressures and expectations which guide a girl towards marriage quoted on page 152, continues:

> The girl herself was probably less bothered about these aspirations than with more personal concerns, the calls of romance and pride, the delectable possibilities of a home of her own and of the day that would transform her from just 'Johnson's girl' into 'the lady on the top floor'.

We must now begin to consider seriously the young couple and their relation to the social network in which they make their life. Our empirical starting point will be the conjugal relationship; other members of the family will be added to the account as the argument proceeds.

HUSBANDS AND WIVES

Early days

Our theoretical starting point is derived from the study of small groups, of which the family is, after all, a special case. In the pages which follow, some commonly observed regularities in the relationships between members of small groups will serve to coordinate the empirical data.

The first regularity to be used in this way is the simple notion that *interaction varies with liking.* In other words, if people like each other better, they will tend to interact more with each other and, conversely, if people interact more with each other, they will tend to like one another better. There is at least one exception to this general rule. Interaction normally varies with liking only if the interaction is freely chosen and can be broken off when desired. If a member is forced to interact with someone he does not like, the chances are at least as great that he will dislike the other more, as that he will come to like him after all.[1]

Where conjugal relations are concerned, it may be said that in most cases, initially at least, the interaction was freely chosen, in the sense that no external agency forced these two to get

---

[1] G. Homans (1950), *The Human Group*, Harcourt, Brace and Co., New York. J. Klein (1956), *The Study of Groups*, Routledge and Kegan Paul, London, chap. 7. See also pages 253 ff. in the next chapter.

married. According to Gorer, most couples claim to have been 'really in love' when they got married.

The reason why interaction and liking normally re-inforce each other is thought to be that with an increase in either comes also an increased understanding of the peculiar good qualities of the interacting members. (Of course, if with an increased understanding one comes to understand the peculiar bad qualities of the other, and neither is forced to interact, the relationship is likely to come to an end.) In the present context, given a period during which a mutual selection takes place, *interaction makes for understanding and greater liking, and liking makes for a stronger wish to understand and to interact.*

It seems fair to take length of courtship as a measure of the variables with which we are here concerned and to predict a correlation between interaction, affection and understanding. Slater and Woodside found a majority of the marriages contracted by couples who had known each other for no more than twelve months to be unhappy. The proportions were reversed for couples who had known each other for between one and four years before they married.[1] The difference was statistically significant. They comment:

> Courtship is a period when the two young people are getting to know one another, and this knowledge is of gradual growth. It generally lasts for two or three years before ending in marriage. If marriage occurs too soon, it is more than ordinarily likely to be unhappy...
>
> There is no difficulty in suggesting a reason why the abbreviated courtships are not of good omen. During courtship two processes are occurring. On the one hand the two people concerned are learning about one another and seeing how well they fit together and 'get on'. If they do not get on well, there is likely to be an end to the relationship before it is sealed by marriage. On the other hand, they are learning to make adjustments to one another. It is the first of these two processes which is the critical one, for mutual adjustment can, and necessarily must, go on after marriage. But if there is an undiscovered incompatibility, its discovery after marriage comes too late.

[1] It is of interest that couples who had known each other for over four years were also somewhat more likely to be unhappy. Obviously length of courtship is not the only significant variable.

We might also predict that the very early advent of a child would militate against a happy marriage, especially where associated with a forced marriage. For in this case certain of our conditions do not obtain—one: it may not have been for marriage that the two chose each other freely, and two: the early arrival of the child interrupts the normal process of mutual adjustment. The couple may come to terms with their situation and look forward to the child, but clearly they carry an additional handicap and the prognosis is to that extent less promising.

In Slater and Woodside's population, pregnancy featured as a reason for marriage in nine cases (out of two hundred). In general, their evidence suggested that pregnancy is not a good reason for getting married. In the nine cases cited, three of the marriages were unhappy, in two others prospects were poor, and in another the husband had not expected success and was surprised it turned out as well as it did. In the three cases where a happy marriage was made, the parties had either known each other very well, or had been really fond of one another, or had already planned marriage before the 'accident'.

Traditionally most young married couples have a period after the official honeymoon, in which friends and relatives allow them a greater degree of privacy and freedom from interruption. This gives the young husband and wife additional opportunity to get to know each other, and to understand and adjust to one another. At this time more than at any other they are exclusively devoted to one another. There are, of course, cultural differences in the length of time that this period is allowed to last. If, as in Ashton, there is much pressure on the young man to return to his group of friends, the chances of his arriving at any deep understanding of his young bride are thereby much reduced. In a close-knit network the period is likely to be short, in a loose-knit network longer.

There is a connection between the extent to which husband and wife share their lives with each other and the degree of network-connectedness. This is the crux of Bott's great contribution to the sociology of the family. When comparing the patterns of life of the different families she was interviewing, she was struck by the fact that there was considerable variation in the way husbands and wives performed their conjugal roles. At one extreme was a family in which the husband and wife carried out most domestic tasks separately and independently of each other. There was a strict division of labour: she had her tasks and he had his. This pattern, characterized in Bethnal Green by the Newbolts, Bott called a 'segregated conjugal role-relationship', which later is to be contrasted with a 'joint conjugal role-relationship' or partnership in marriage.

Bott realized that she had, in the concept of conjugal role-relationships, an important variable of social life, somehow connected with other aspects of a consistent pattern. She therefore wished to define more clearly the circumstances which accompanied variations in role-segregation. Thus she related it to social class as indicated by occupation, and found that the husbands whose lives were most sharply divided from the woman's world, i.e. who had the most segregated role-relationships, were manual workers, whereas the husbands who had the most joint role-relationships were professional or semi-professional people. But there were several working-class people with relatively little segregation, and there were professional families in which the segregation was considerable.[1]

She also related the degree of role-segregation to the type of local area in which the family lived, since the data suggested that the families with most segregation lived in socially homogeneous areas where population-turnover was low, whereas families with predominantly joint role-relationships lived in socially more heterogeneous areas with a high population turnover. Once again, however, there were several exceptions.

She therefore turned to the notion of the 'social network' and found a regular association between the degree of conjugal role-segregation and the degree of connectedness in the total network of relations maintained by the family. The families with a high degree of conjugal role-segregation had a close-knit network: many of the friends, neighbours and relatives of such a family knew one another. Families with a more joint role-relationship had a more loose-knit network: fewer of the friends, relatives and neighbours of such a family knew one another.

[1] See pages 168, 291–9 and 335–41 for further discussion of the families which were exceptional by these criteria.

Traditional Working-Class Life

It is not difficult to understand why this should be so. In general, and in accordance with our theory concerning the direct relationship of liking, interaction and understanding, the greater the extent to which the social network of kin or community imposes obligations on either partner of the marriage to interact elsewhere than in the conjugal bond, the smaller also the chances that the conjugal pair will arrive at any profound understanding of one another.

Bott adds a warning that these concepts must be used with due regard to the effects of the life-cycle. Her research couples made it clear that there had been important changes in the degree of their conjugal segregation during their married life. In the first phase, all couples had engaged in far more joint activities, especially in the form of shared recreation outside the home.

In these early years, and especially before the children come or if the wife is working, the couple are likely to maintain the frequent picture-going which played such a large part in their courtship. This common interest, uncreative though it may be, is, still, a common interest, a shared experience, something to talk about, and hence something to strengthen the bond.

Then arises the problem of finding someone to mind the baby if they are to go out together. Moreover, the way financial responsibility is distributed between man and wife may prove a disincentive for going out together. The expense has to come either out of the wife's budget, or out of the man's pocket-money. In each case there is likely to be a certain grudging feeling, because the idea of husband and wife going out to a place of entertainment together is relatively new and there is no tradition as to who should be financially responsible.

Also, [continuing the argument with Zweig] the hobbies and entertainments of husband and wife often do not coincide. She is more interested in knitting or listening to the wireless, or in going to the pictures, or, when young, in going dancing, and he primarily in sports of all sorts, in frequenting the public houses or going out to racing. In young days they had more common interests, in dancing and picture-going, in walks in the country and cycling, but later their interests often draw them apart. When the couple get used to spending their leisure time apart . . . the habit weighs heavily in later years.

Aspects of Adult Life in England

Data from group discussions which Bott conducted with her couples suggest that in a third phase, when children are adolescent or leaving home, opportunities for a closer conjugal bond exist, but the couples do not normally avail themselves of them. Other factors have intervened.

In a study of old people in Bethnal Green, Townsend found that men did come closer to their wives after retirement, because they now saw more of them than before. 'When people get older, they cling together more,' said one informant. 'You get to know one another better. You never see enough of each other at work,' said a sociologically more astute one.[1] But it was clear that the women did not by any means always share their husbands' new liking for domesticity. In the traditional setting, the barriers to a better understanding are maintained from both sides. Retirement is often a shocking experience in a man's life. But the life of a woman is less likely to change so drastically, especially if her daughters do not move far from her after marriage. There is no such emotional or social void for her as there is for the retired man, who has spent ten hours or so a day away from home for most of his life. The wife has filled her world with family, friends and children. Sociability, keeping the family together, had always been her function. This responsibility continues into old age without a break.

Thus during their married life the couple grow steadily further apart in interests and activities. Bott argues that they will normally find their emotional satisfaction and social interaction elsewhere, not in each other.

> When they marry, though husband and wife draw closer together, they do not break away from existing relatives. Rather the wife has to reconcile her new obligations to her husband with her old obligations to her parents, and the husband likewise . . .
>
> If both husband and wife come to the marriage with such close-knit networks, the marriage will be superimposed on these pre-existing relationships and both spouses will continue to be drawn into activities with people outside their own elementary family. Each will get some emotional satisfaction from these external relationships and will be likely to demand correspondingly less of the spouse.

[1] P. Townsend (1957), *The Family Life of Old People*, Routledge and Kegan Paul, London.

Traditional Working-Class Life

There are advantages to such traditions, since these marriages do not carry the immense emotional, social and economic burdens which the socially isolated couple may have to bear. In the women's magazines designed for social levels which take a loose-knit network for granted, there is always good advice to be found about the importance of 'outside interests' and the dangers of inward-turning marriages. In contrast, Smith points out that 'one contributory factor to the stabilization of populations is the process of intermarriage in a community. When a local boy marries a local girl, there are two families to help them in their troubles.'[1]

Nevertheless, there are also difficulties of adjustment in such a structure. To these we shall return later in the chapter. First, the mutual role-expectations of husbands and wives must be examined.

Role-expectations

It is easy to see how, in these as in other matters, a tradition is maintained. Bott asked husbands and wives: 'What are the rights and duties of husbands and wives?', 'When you got married did you have a clear idea of what family-life would be like?' People from close-knit networks found this easier to answer than did people from a loose-knit group. They were also more definite in their answers, speaking with more conviction.

Taking the population as a whole, we obtain from Gorer the following percentages:

What do you [husbands] think the three most important qualities a wife should have?		What do you [wives] think the three most important qualities a husband should have?	
good housekeeper	29	understanding	33
certain personal qualities[2]	26	thoughtfulness	28
understanding	23	sense of humour	24
love	22	certain moral qualities[2]	24
faithfulness	21	faithfulness	21

[1] C. Smith (1957), *People in Need*, Allen and Unwin, London.

[2] The phrase 'moral qualities' covers traits which Gorer considered would in a religious context have covered virtues: good principles, sincerity, integrity, honesty, etc. The phrase 'personal qualities' refers to traits with social or physical rather than moral significance: to keep oneself attractive and smart, cleanliness, good manners and good company, etc.

What do you [husbands] think the three most important qualities a wife should have?		*What do you [wives] think the three most important qualities a husband should have?*	
good cook	21	generosity	19
intelligence	18	love	17
good mother	18	tolerance	14
sense of humour	16	love of home	14
economical	16	fairness	13
certain moral qualities[1]	13	good father	13
patience	11	certain personal qualities[1]	12
tolerance	9	good worker	12
share husband's interests	8	treat wife as person	11
love of home	7	equanimity	10
equanimity	7	intelligence	8
		virility, strength, courage	8

Such statistics give an idea of the kind of wish that looms large in the minds of Gorer's informants, but it is not easy to know if the qualities listed are conspicuous by their presence or by their absence. We may, however, note in confirmation of the earlier discussion on mate-selection that neither sex pays any appreciable heed to the aesthetic qualities of their spouse. Beauty or strength, good looks or good figure are very seldom mentioned, and mainly by the single. It is also a very small group (less than one in twenty) who mention specifically sexual characteristics like being a good lover or 'staying sweethearts'.

We may also note in passing that the women's preferences are cast in more psychological terms; the men's in more functional terms. This lends support to a contention made in the previous chapter that in England men are culturally encouraged towards extraversion and women towards introversion; the men show a greater cognitive poverty and unimaginativeness than the women.[2]

Gorer concludes from his statistics that 'what Englishmen most wish for in a wife is the possession of appropriate feminine skills, whereas what Englishwomen most wish for in their husbands is an agreeable character'.

[1] See page 161, fn. 2.   [2] See also pages 108, 145–6 and 174.

Traditional Working-Class Life

The definition of appropriate feminine skills, that is, the normal role of the woman, embodies that of a good housewife, the care of whose home is the core of her self-respect. In Mogey's words:

> The wife must, in effect, see that the house as a centre of consumption is up to the expected standards. Comments on the role of the wife tended to centre on her triumphs and failures in this sphere . . . Success brings personal satisfaction and praise from others. Failure leads to apologies. Several wives said softly to us: 'I'm no manager.' 'He has to look after all the shopping for I've no head on me for that sort of thing.'

A very firm structure of norms supports the activities of housework. Not only is failure to come up to the standard associated with disapproval and grief, but failure by overshooting the mark is similarly subject to sanctions.[1] The question of standards will be discussed at the end of this chapter but it is worth noting here in this context that, as one would expect in this population, the expected standard is a mean and not a maximum. 'Good wives are those which can perform adequately but not superlatively,' says Mogey, and he quotes an informant: 'I call her a bad-good wife. She does far too much housework.'

In Oxford, at least, housewives are considered lucky, both by themselves and by their husbands, in that they can stay at home and do not have to go out to work. One aspect of this sentiment may be the general dislike of outside interference and supervision. Unlike their husbands, the women of St. Ebbe's could arrange their work as they pleased and they felt their husband's work was heavier for that reason.[2]

These St. Ebbe's wives were markedly relaxed. Mogey's interviewers were 'struck by the lack of any schedule or pressure to get things done, for over and over again when we called in casually, these women were pleased to see us, prepared to sit down and spend some time talking to us'. (It is only fair to add the pleasing comment that these interviewers must have been good at their jobs.)[3]

---

[1] See Homans, op. cit., especially chap. 11: 'Social Control.'

[2] But see, for a contrasting attitude, the middle-class wives described on pages 338-41.

[3] See also the discussion in the next chapter, pages 242 and 286-7.

Aspects of Adult Life in England

Just as the woman's role is domestic, and her self-respect and status depend on her performance in keeping house, so the man's role is financial and his status in the household depends rather stringently on his ability as a breadwinner: his self-respect is closely tied to his financial independence.[1] Hoggart recalls from the depressed years of the thirties that even when he is out of work, both husband and wife assume that he must still have his pocket-money.

> A man can't be without money in 'is pocket; he would then feel less than a man; for beer, cigarettes, or pools he must not be 'tied to' his wife and thus inferior to her; such a situation would be against nature.

For the man to remain in regular employment was not only of basic importance for his family, it was also likely to be a difficult problem for him . . . Because of its central importance and because of the rather high risk of failure, maintaining a steady income for the family seems to have become almost a test of manhood . . . A man who, for whatever reason, is unable to carry out his breadwinning role, unless the failure is only of short duration, falls a great distance in the estimation of himself, his wife and children, and his fellows. If his place as the breadwinner is taken by his son, then the younger man is likely to be treated with far more respect by the family, and given far more comfort and consideration than his father. There are cases to be found where a chronic invalid or cripple is treated by his wife and family as if he were some inferior kind of servant.[2]

In the prosperous nineteen-fifties, this association of the ideas of manhood, financial potency and general feelings of worth manifested itself mainly after the man retires from his work. Townsend notes the general agreement among his elderly informants in Bethnal Green that men deteriorated rapidly after retirement. They seemed to pine away.

> The man's position in the home and family became less secure . . . for his position has relied mainly on his traditional authority

---

[1] Self-respect is a word in common usage. There is a trend in social psychology to investigate certain phenomena under the heading 'sense of identity'. In the discussion here and on pages 202–5 it is interesting to note that self-respect *means* sense of identity.

[2] J. H. Robb (1954), *Working-Class Anti-Semite: a psychological study in a London borough*. Tavistock Publications, London.

in the home, derived from his role as bread-winner, and he was now bringing less money into the home.

However, Townsend was mainly concerned with elderly people, and Hoggart with an older tradition. The younger couples may have different feelings about this; their conjugal relations are based on a different conception of their roles, and the association of financial independence with self-respect may be declining. It is perhaps worth mentioning here that in Woodford, with which part of the chapter on the middle classes is concerned, and which is inhabited by a 'more modern' and 'smarter' set, the man suffered much less on retirement: the reason was found partly in the man's greater sharing of his wife's life.[1]

The division of labour[2]

Four topics are to be discussed under this heading: (1) the division of domestic duties, (2) financial arrangements, (3) social and emotional relations, (4) who is the boss?

(1) According to Hoggart, that is, according to the older and more Northern tradition, the husband is not expected to participate in *domestic* duties.

> If he does, a wife is pleased, but she is unlikely to harbour a grudge if he does not. 'When all's said and done' most things about a house are woman's work: 'Oh, that's not a man's job', a woman will say, and would not want him to do too much of that kind of thing for fear he is thought womanish. Or the highest praise will take the form, "E's ever so good about the 'ouse; just like a woman': if he does help much he is doing it in place of the woman whose job it should be; the household chores are not joint responsibilities. So it is a positive act of helpfulness if he decides to help with the washing up or the baby. In many cases a wife would not only 'never dream' of having his help with the washing, but does not feel she can "ave the washing around' when he is at home. There are often difficulties of drying-space, especially on rainy days, that are aggravated by the need for a complicated system of putting the damp stuff round the fire on a clothes horse and taking it off again into a basket or zinc bath when the husband wants to 'see t'fire' . . .

Yet there are a great many husbands who are thoughtful and helpful, who spend much of their free time at home, making and

---

[1] See pages 342-3.   [2] See also Susser and Watson, op. cit.

mending. Even so, there is the sense that the father occupies a special position. There are some things, difficult and men's things —such as chopping wood—which only he can do; there are other things which he may do without undermining the order, such as getting himself off to work or bringing his wife a cup of tea in bed occasionally.

Among some younger husbands there are signs of a striking change in the basic attitudes. Some wives press for it and find their husbands ready to modify the outlook they inherited from their fathers. Some working-class husbands will share the washing up if their wives go out to work, or will take turns with the baby if their job releases them early and not too tired. But many wives come home from work just as tired as their husbands and 'set to' to do all the housework without help from them . . .

If a wife has a conscious wish, it is probably not for a husband who does such things but rather for one who remains a husband in much the old sense, yet 'a good one' in the old sense, for one who is steady and a good worker, one who is likely to be kept on if the sackings begin, who brings home his money regularly, who is generous with his bonuses.

The Radby Report describes the conjugal relationship of the Grade III (normally respectable) households as 'solid'. The man takes his pleasure, the woman hers. The duties and obligations of husbands and wives are clearly defined and rigidly adhered to.

Farther south there is less rigour. About two-thirds of the households interviewed in St. Ebbe's had a marked division of labour. But Mogey observes that though there is a traditional separation of function between husband and wife in St. Ebbe's, households vary in the rigidity with which these separations are observed. He makes the interesting observation that a very rigid segregation of jobs into those done by the wife and those done by the husband, with a conscious awareness of this difference and a constant watchfulness for transgressions by either husband or wife, are indications that there is not a good marriage-relationship. Such husbands and wives, more than others, tended to bicker in front of the interviewer.

In St. Ebbe's, as elsewhere, the housework is the wife's domain. All the same, husbands seem often surprisingly helpful. One in ten is reported to help regularly with washing-up after breakfast or dinner. One in three does so at tea-time. At week-ends yet more help is given.

Mogey collected characteristic tributes which the wives paid to the 'good husband'. These may, of course, reflect the ideal more than the actuality. A good husband is steady at work, and comes home at regular times. He is quiet and undemonstrative, showing affection through actions rather than words. He is good at household repairs and decorations, and will do housework in an emergency. Husbands are praised for doing housework, which is acknowledged to be a favour on the man's part: the wife has no right to expect it. 'He polished the grate last Sunday because I wasn't feeling so good' and 'He cleans the silver and will do anything in the house if I ask him, but I hardly ever ask, it's not a man's place'. He 'does his best for all of us'. He grows vegetables on the allotment. He is not one for the pubs, though of course he likes his beer now and again. He is there as a court of appeal on the children, but 'not used to lift a hand to them'. He is faithful and not demanding sexually.

Still farther south, in London, Young and Willmott find their sample still farther along the trend. They quote Bosanquet on the Shoreditch husband of sixty years ago. He was not only mean with his money, he was callous in sex, harsh to his children and violent when drunk, which was often. The point, they add, is not that the old behaviour has not survived, but that it is no longer dominant. Whatever happened in the past, the younger husband of today does not consider that children belong exclusively to his wife's world, or that he can abandon them to her and her mother while he takes his comfort in the male atmosphere of the pub.

Even today cruelty is the commonest ground on which divorce is sought by working-class wives.[1] Gorer found that among the poorest and socially lowest class (but only there) drink and violence were mentioned as causes likely to break up a marriage. Zweig (1961) noted that 'the single and most potent reason for more satisfactory relationships in marriage is the decline in heavy drinking, and many women referred to

[1] O. R. McGregor (1957), *Divorce in England*, cited by Susser and Watson.

this as the most important factor', though in this connection it has to be kept in mind that an abnormally high proportion of Zweig's informants were steel workers, traditionally heavy drinkers.[1]

The impression that we are here dealing with a changing trend which has proceeded farther in the south than in the north, rather than with a specific cultural difference between north and south, is strengthened by another finding of Gorer's, that complaints about husbands' laziness are uniformly less often found among the younger informants. This suggests to him that there has been a marked change in the expectations of the help a husband should properly give in a household, with the dividing line among those born in the first decade of this century or earlier.

Bethnal Green is reported to be well aware of the change which has come about in the course of a few decades.

> Indeed, it is because the comparisons they make between the old and the new are so much part of their mentality, the source of much present exhilaration and perplexity, that the contrast belongs properly to an account of present-day life . . . In the home there are still 'men's jobs' like cleaning windows, mending fuses, and decorating, and 'women's jobs' like cleaning, cooking, baby-care, washing dishes and clothes, and ironing. But for most people the division of labour is no longer rigid. Of forty-five husbands interviewed, two-thirds gave some regular help to their wives with the housework.

Bott's Bethnal Green family, the Newbolts, were on the old-fashioned side: they considered that marriage involved a clear division of labour, albeit a harmonious one. All the same, 'a lot of men would not mind helping their wives if the curtains were drawn so that people couldn't see', said Mr. Newbolt. The Newbolts' definition of a good wife was clearly in terms of 'appropriate feminine skills': a good manager, an affectionate mother, one who kept out of serious rows with the neighbours and got on well with her relatives and those of her husband. A good husband was one who helped his wife when she was ill, took an interest in the children and did not waste money selfishly on himself but was generous.

[1] *The Worker in an Affluent Society*, Heinemann, London.

(2) In *financial matters* Mr. Newbolt was considered by his wife to be generous. He had control over the money and, in 1953, gave her £5 a week. (There were two children.) She had no clear idea how much he earned or how he spent the money he kept for himself. It was his habit not to comment when she indicated to him that she was running out of money, but to leave a pound note under the clock before he went out next morning. In view of the analysis made in the previous chapter about the difficulties of conjugal discussion it is worth noting that the gift was made as impersonally as possible, and that no conversation or 'argument' is recorded on the matter.[1]

The general traditional pattern seems to be as described by Hoggart.

> There are many husbands who regard all the family's money-affairs as a shared concern, who hand over their wage-packet on Friday night and leave its disposition to their wives. But an assumption just as characteristic in my experience is that the wage-packet is the husband's, and that he gives his wife a fixed amount for housekeeping each week. There are many households where the wife does not know how much her husband earns. This does not necessarily mean that she is poorly treated. 'Oh, 'e sees me alright', or, ''e treats me alright', she will say, meaning that she is not left short, but implying, in the phrasing itself, that the distribution of the wage lies with him. The wife is often responsible, out of this fixed amount, for any replacements—of crockery, furnishings, and so on; the more thoughtful of these husbands will be open to suggestion, will promise something out of the next payment of overtime. Quite often the wife's share of any overtime money arrives only quixotically.

A quotation from Zweig's *Women's Life and Labour* throws additional light on the financial role of the woman in the old-style family:

> Yes, the 'economic man' exists but 'he' is a female. So the economists should speak about the economic woman, not the economic man. To the question: 'Do you believe in saving?' you will get from women practically a 100 per cent answer: 'Of

---

[1] On financial arrangements in general, Michael Young's 'Distribution of income within the family', *Brit. J. Sociol.*, III (1952), is essential supplementary reading.

course', but not from the men. Every penny is used with a plan and a forethought. While working automatically with their hands, women think about the food they are going to prepare, and about their shopping, what is the best way of spending and saving, and how to economize on this and that . . . There is probably a certain amount of waste in women's spending in the working classes; but this is incomparably smaller than that in the men's sphere. Even women who go out to work have to scrape and count their pennies very carefully, to a considerable degree more than men.

A man of goodwill who knows this, and knows himself, may say: 'How much I spend depends on the company', and if his company is not to be trusted it is better to make a habit of giving the whole wage-packet to the wife.[1]

This sort of thing bears a marked resemblance to the Ashton pattern described in the previous chapter. No wonder, for these attitudes go with hardship and the fear of unemployment. No wonder either that Hoggart finds the woman often unable to discuss the budget with the man. This is also part of the traditional way of life, and goes with 'cognitive poverty'.

But changes are coming about. From Radby it is reported that in Dyke Street (a bad street) it is rare for husband and wife to have a common policy about spending, whereas this is often done in Gladstone Road (a good road). In Dyke Street one woman talked with envy of another whose husband gave her, in addition to her regular money, so much each week *for herself*. It was unheard-of generosity.

Farther south there is evidence of a new trend in finance as well as in other aspects of conjugal role-relations. Bott, with specific reference to London families in close-knit networks— i.e. more traditional families—reports that norms are changing, though apparently faster than practice. The wives living within close-knit networks said that husbands ought to give their wives a liberal house-keeping allowance, but they did not really expect such generosity. One wife complained about her husband's stinginess and another constantly stressed how fortunate she was to have a generous husband. The former thought that most women suffered as she did; in both cases it was clear that

---

[1] This last quotation is from Zweig's *Labour, Life and Poverty*.

the normal expectation was that husbands would not give enough.

Bethnal Green, in this as in other aspects, shows a transitional state. The man's earnings may still be his affair (as they were in the past) but when it comes to the spending of the money, his part of the wages as well as hers, husband and wife share the responsibility. 'To be truthful,' said Mrs. Sanderson, 'I don't know how much he earns, I only know what he gives me.' But later she went on to describe a discussion she and her husband had had about whether to buy a television set, which he would pay for. (This same Mrs. Sanderson also mentioned that her husband 'does a lot of the cooking, he's a good cook'.)

(3) With segregation of function in the domestic and financial spheres goes a separate *social life* for husband and wife. The Newbolts jointly entertained relatives, and went together to weddings, christenings, funerals and other family occasions. With the exception of such festivities, however, they spent little of their leisure time together. They did not consider themselves unusual in this respect. On the contrary, they felt that their behaviour was typical of their social circle.

The normal expectation is still that there are men's interests in which the women cannot share, and vice versa. There are little pockets of life defined as the prerogative of one sex or the other. In St. Ebbe's, one such men's grouping was located on the allotment. The allotment was, for the men, something more than just a place to grow vegetables. It was in a sense a married men's club. Many men went off to the allotment as soon as could be managed. 'It's what a lot of people quarrel over, isn't it?' said one woman. Another who had kept an allotment going when her husband was ill, had roused the 'astonishment' of the men working there, though in the gentler south she was not subjected to the treatment meted out to the Ashton wife who went to the bookie to place a bet for her sick husband.[1]

The Newbolts took it for granted that the husband should have some recreation away from the home, such as cycle-racing or cricket. He had his own friends, with whom he shared these interests. Mrs. Newbolt knew a little about these friends, although she did not share interests with them or entertain

[1] See page 213, op. cit.

them in her home. She nodded to their wives when she met them but did not make friends with them. 'Men have friends, women have relatives.' So when he went off to a cricket-match, she would be visiting relatives or, perhaps, go to a cinema.

During the day, the wife normally interacts with her kin or with friendly neighbours, or perhaps with acquaintances at her place of paid employment. Much of her interest will lie there. 'The wife's social life outside her family is found over the washing-line, at the corner-shop, visiting relatives, and perhaps now and again going with her husband to his pub or club' (Hoggart).

Even in the first years of marriage, when one might assume incentives to conjugal partnership to be strong, large stretches of time or interest are inaccessible to one or other spouse. The women know little about the men's day-time activities, and apparently take little interest even when they themselves also go out to work. The women of St. Ebbe's talked readily enough about what they enjoyed in their own outside jobs, but there was a lack of interest in the details of what their husbands did in the hours between the time he left in the morning and returned at night, a gap in understanding which surprised Mogey and his interviewers, since the topic appeared to them vital to the survival of the family. 'He makes all kinds of steel . . . (long pause for the right word) . . . things.' We may note here once again, besides the ignorance, the narrowness of interest and the accompanying poverty of thought and language. Not surprisingly, the world of politics, or even of 'news', tends to be left to the men. In a magnificent phrase, Hoggart refers to the 'close, myopic nature of most working-class women's lives'.

The theoretical commentary on family relationships began with the generalization that interaction, liking and understanding vary together. In so far as husband and wife share few interests and make their friends separately, there will therefore be a lack of understanding between them. This is in turn related to the difficulty they have in discussing matters of general interest, or even matters of family policy, at length and without anxiety.

> 'As a matter of fact, I don't discuss politics or religion with him. We don't agree and I think it's best not to talk about those things you disagree on, don't you? And men know best about these things I expect, don't you?'

In commenting on this remark, Mogey has recourse to a theory of masculine supremacy in the home, for it was a woman speaking. It may be argued, however, that, if we must relate the attitude which underlies it to the family structure, we should relate it to the difficulties of communication between husband and wife and to the traditional single-authority conjugal relationship. It does not matter whether husband or wife is the authority. What matters is that there shall be one authority, so that decisions may be made with the minimum of 'argument'. Even in the relaxed and equable Newbolt family, the husband simply left money under the clock to avoid discussion of the delicate topic. In conditions of cognitive poverty, discussion of domestic problems is fraught with danger. As Mogey writes: 'Taking into account the habit of talking almost exclusively in clichés and the poor use of words, these problems will be phrased in an uncomplete way and the real nature of the decision may never be revealed.'[1]

The discussion of domestic matters is, in fact, more or less taboo. It is interesting to note that this brings about situations which bear the classic hallmarks of psychological repression. Bott and her associates wanted to know the opinion of their informants on such matters as the normal husbands' and wives' duties and rights, the difference between their own family and others, or how ideal husbands, wives and children might be described.

> The usual reaction was either a prolonged uncomfortable silence or an immediate reply to the effect that there was so much variation that one could not generalize . . . We never became very successful at allaying this sort of anxiety or in asking direct questions skilfully. The question about ideal husbands, wives and children was particularly upsetting. Because we interviewed husband and wife together, it was interpreted as an invitation to comment on the other partner's conjugal deficiencies . . . This question upset the atmosphere of the interview so much that people did not give their full attention to the questions that followed it.

The fear of 'argument' is one reason why family relations strike the outside observer as often simple, stark, unsubtle. The

[1] See also pages 210–14.

alternatives open in this dilemma are few, simple and stark. If the husband wants his own way, he has to attain it by force or other authoritarian methods of an aggressive kind. Similarly the wife has to gain her ends by guile and authoritarian methods of a submissive kind. A certain kind of sentimental literature has glorified such feminine wiles and masculine woodenness. Whatever may be said in their favour, they cannot lead to conjugal understanding.

All the indications suggest that the Newbolts were very happily married. Generally speaking, however, the prognosis would seem less good. The more deeply each spouse is involved in a social sphere the other does not share, the more likely each is to see the division of function within the household as strict and exclusive: as instanced by the man who threw the dinner cooked by his sister-in-law into the fire. Mogey confirms that in those families where husband and wife did not get on so well, the emphasis on role-segregation was stronger.

(4) *Who is boss?* The husbands and wives discussed in previous chapters found themselves in situations where exploitation and hostility came easily to them. The families with which we are here concerned are more harmoniously constructed. They display a greater mutual tolerance and respect. In Bethnal Green, at least, there is evidence that this is a comparatively recent development, connected with shorter working hours and better living conditions. The men's world and the women's world are still very distinct, but conjugal role-segregation is here accompanied by peaceful co-existence.

For the more traditional northern areas, Hoggart's point of departure for an understanding of the position of the working-class father in his home is that

> he is the boss there, the 'master in his own house'. This he is by tradition, and neither he nor his wife would want the tradition changed. She will often refer to him before others as 'Mr. W.' or 'the mester'. This does not mean that he is by any means an absolute ruler, or that he gets or expects his own way in everything. It often accompanies a carefulness, a willingness to help and be 'considerate', to be 'a good husband' . . .
>
> But there is often a kind of roughness in his manner which a middle-class wife would find insupportable. A wife will say how

worried she is because something is amiss and 'the mester will be mad' when he gets home; he may 'tell yer off' harshly or in a few cases may even 'bash' you, especially if he has had a couple of pints on the way home from work. Or middle-aged wives will say to a younger one, "e's good to yer, i'n't he?', meaning he is not likely to become violent in word or act, or that he does not leave his wife alone every night, or that he will 'see 'er out' if she gets into difficulties with the housekeeping allowance.

In Radby (Nottingham) also, the 'meister' is definitely the master in three of the four Grade III households studied in detail. The eighteen-year-old Bonnington daughter cleans her father's boots on a Saturday morning; Mrs. Bonnington is careful to have his tea ready the minute he comes in.

Farther south, or perhaps more recently, or perhaps regarded from another point of view, the question 'Who is boss?' loses its meaning.

> The father's position in the family is difficult to describe [writes Robb]. The absolutely crucial nature of his role as breadwinner has already been indicated, but in some respects his position is very different. School-teachers, social workers and others who have contact with Bethnal Green families, nearly always agree that the real head of the family is the mother, but a few stress the importance of the man as the final authority. The disagreement seems to be based on a sharp division of labour between men and women, and a difference of opinion as to which is to be regarded as the more important.

The same difficulty is apparent in St. Ebbe's. Mogey begins his discussion of the role of the husband in the following words, surprising enough when contrasted with the Ashton man: 'The husband in many households is a shadowy figure . . . The ordinary husband was taken for granted as something in the background of the life of the woman and her children.' In some interviews with wives, a certain amount of prompting had to be used before information was given about the husband. Mogey attributes this more to a low level of interest in the husband than to an avoidance of talk about him, though in view of our previous discussion on the avoidance of delicate topics, it may also be an indication that his role is no longer clearly defined. Mogey does not doubt, however, that the husband has an established place in the home. He is expected to participate in the life of the family. He belongs inside the family circle, not outside it, even if he is rather peripheral. In his own sphere, he has his own important rights.

There are some houses in which, on coming in, the husband sits down without any expression of apology or explanation in the chair vacated as soon as his step is heard by the wife. There are even instances of chairs reserved for the exclusive use of the man of the house. These and many other small indicative words and actions all lead towards a picture of the man occupying an established position within the family circle. At certain times he appears for food, and food is placed before him; a chair is reserved for his leisure; and he is kept in a place, which he himself accepts, just outside the more intense mother-children relationship.

The children are the mother's sphere. 'My husband' (says a St. Ebbe's informant) 'says when the children ask him for anything: "Well, ask your Mum. If she says yes, well, I suppose it's all right", so I suppose I'm the boss.' And in this sort of way she is the boss. Moreover, the woman tends to be the more expressive and articulate of the two. Mogey notes that the wife is ready enough to give an opinion of the husband, but the husband rarely gives a direct opinion of the wife.

How can this discussion be summed up? We do not really know enough about the power structure in any of these families to come to firm conclusions. First, there is the fact of transition to take into account. The people of Bethnal Green commented frequently to the interviewers that times had changed and husbands were better than they used to be. Then regional differences have to be taken into account, and not only the coarser differences between north and south on which we have remarked. Where in the north the Irish have spread from Liverpool, the mother seems to hold sway, though the rest of the area is markedly male-dominant in power and privilege. Again, though husbands and wives in the south as a whole seem less competitive for power and privilege, Bethnal Green seems to show an unusually strong matriarchal pattern.

Another source of difficulty in interpreting the few data available is that observers themselves are fallible. Sociologists who concentrate on kin, as Young and Willmott do, are more likely to concentrate on the power of the mother. Sociologists who concentrate on the men's lives, as Dennis, Henriques and Slaughter do, are likely to take less notice of the mothers.

Therefore, although it seems safe to say that husbands exercise considerable power in their own sphere and wives in theirs, and that there is relatively little overlap between these spheres, it is not safe to point to either as the 'ultimate' source of power. Bott and Hoggart both make this point.

> The role of the husband–father in such families is often described as 'authoritarian', implying that he has clear authority over his wife and children in most or all of their activities. I think this characterization of his role is altogether too sweeping [writes Bott]. Male authoritarianism is often confused with segregation of conjugal roles. This comes about because authors assign to the financial and sexual arrangements of these families the same psychological meaning that they would have in families where husband and wife expect to have a joint relationship. This view is supported by the fact that authors also describe these families as 'mother-centred', although this description is not usually put side by side with male authoritarianism, because the two characterizations sound contradictory. But both are valid, for each partner has authority and responsibility in his own sphere.

> For most women there is, in varying degrees, a steady and self-forgetful routine, one devoted to the family and beyond proud self-regard [writes Hoggart]. Behind it, making any vague pity irrelevant, is pride in the knowledge that so much revolves around them. This can make the most unpromising and unprepossessing young woman arrive at a middle age in which she is, when in the midst of her home and family, splendidly 'there', and, under all her troubles, content. Her husband may be the 'mester' in the household, but she is not a door-mat. She and he know her value and virtue if she is, in her own way, a 'good mother'.

We conclude, therefore, that male dominance and female dominance are not necessarily mutually exclusive and to be contrasted with one another. Where there is role-segregation and a strict division between the spheres of the two spouses, each may be sovereign in his own sphere. This was not the case in 'Ship Street' or in 'Ashton': in these cases one sphere was defined as subordinate to the others.

177

Aspects of Adult Life in England

The lines in the diagrams below are best regarded in this way, that only a limited amount of ink is available for drawing them. If the line enclosing husband and wife is thick (i.e. there is much interaction between them) less ink is available for drawing the other lines (i.e. less interaction will take place in those other regions). The thicker one line, the thinner others must of necessity be.

Husbands' and wives' spheres of action

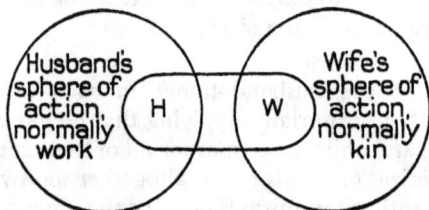

Husband's sphere of action, normally work

H

W

Wife's sphere of action, normally kin

The women's circle of interaction is shown in more detailed structure on page 191.

A special case: When the work is peculiarly hazardous or unpleasant, as in mining, the ties which bind a man to his workmates may be so strong as to draw him away from his family into constant interaction with them in leisure as at work.

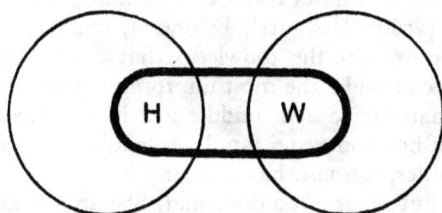

H   W

Normal case

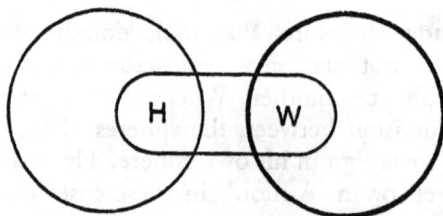

H   W

Special case

Traditional Working-Class Life

The generalization that interaction, liking and understanding mutually support each other applies as directly to the parent-child relationship as to the conjugal.

'Who is the proper person to punish a child who has done something really bad?' asked Gorer of the parents among his informants:[1]

> The father, according to 61%
> The mother, according to 35%
> The teacher, according to 6%

These figures were minutely analysed in a number of ways, with a rather interesting result: men's opinions of the role of the parents vary quite considerably in different regions, and to a certain extent by town size and economic level, but with a couple of exceptions, (mothers from the South West and in the £12-15 income range claim much less authority for themselves than do the women in other regions or income groups), the women's views of the different parental roles are remarkably stable . . . The fathers in the North East and North [in other ways shown to be highly traditional regions; Ashton is in the North East] are the most insistent on paternal authority; those from the North West [Liverpool is in the North West] and the South West least so . . . As family income goes up, the father claims more and more authority, from the poorest group where half do, to the most prosperous where it is claimed by four fifths . . .

In the more traditional areas, children are more or less exclusively the wife's domain. In the volume on child-rearing we shall note that this extends even to the regulation of their conception. In so far as changes are going on, they seem all to tend in the direction of a more equal and common responsibility for domestic affairs. Where there is relatively little change as yet, husband and wife do not much take over those parental functions associated traditionally with the other sex.

In the north at least, not many husbands will be seen pushing the baby round the streets in its pram. That is still thought

[1] Gorer had asked about punishment when the child had done something 'really bad'. In more normal circumstances, the mother is generally thought of as the natural agent of discipline. Both Goldberg's mothers and Shaw's agreed that if the child had to be punished they would do so themselves, and not wait for the father to come home.

'soft', and most wives would sympathize with the view. It happens in Bethnal Green, though, and Young and Willmott 'can watch from the windows of the Institute of Community Studies the sight of young fathers playing with their sons on the putting-green, or wheeling the prams up Bethnal Green Road, or taking their little daughters for a row on the lake'.

The Newbolts felt themselves to be jointly responsible for the children, though in practice Mrs. Newbolt was mainly concerned except in the evenings and at week-ends. Mr. Newbolt helped to keep the children entertained, occasionally put them to bed and sometimes got up when they cried in the night. He also bought them many presents. The transition between old norm and new norm shows up in that Mrs. Newbolt considered him an exceptionally good father.

Goldberg interviewed a number of East End wives and found a divided mind on the amount and kind of help a husband should give with the children.[1]

	Yes	No
Should I expect my husband to help with the baby?	14	7
Should I expect him to bath the baby sometimes?	10	11
Should I expect him to help in giving baby his meals?	8	13

The point at which tradition is changing most rapidly is suggested by a table in the recently published *Infant Care in an Urban Community*.[2]

Percentages of fathers undertaking various activities in the care of one-year-olds

	Play with him	Get him to sleep	Feed him	Take him out alone	Change him	Attend him in the night	Bath him
Often	83	31	34	29	20	18	15
Sometimes	16	49	44	39	37	32	24
Never	1	20	22	32	43	50	61

Traditionally children interact very much more with their mothers than with their fathers. The effects of such differences in the amount of interaction, on relationships within the family,

[1] E. M. Goldberg (1958), *Family Influences and Psycho-somatic Illness*, Tavistock Publications, London.
[2] J. and E. Newson, Allen and Unwin, 1963. The table cited includes parents from all social classes; half are manual workers in Class III.

must now be considered. It will be remembered that these effects are assumed to spring from a basic cause: that interaction, liking, and understanding vary together. Since voluntary interaction is assumed, it must be added that though children do not choose to interact with their parents—since children do not ask to be born—they do not normally feel interaction with their parents to be involuntary, i.e. forced upon them. (In those special cases where they do feel this, the effects also differ from the norm, but this is not our present concern.)

The greater frequency of interaction would in any case tend to increase the liking between mother and children at the expense of the paternal relationship. In addition, the mother, who performs her role inside the home, is seen by the children as doing much more for as well as with them than the father who, as breadwinner, performs a more remote service and one more difficult for the child to understand. And in the areas now under discussion, the mother was often seen by the children as doing more for them than could reasonably have been expected, especially in the past, in times of financial stringency. Most books comment on the mother's self-sacrifice in times of financial hardship, and on the grateful admiration with which her children regard her in later life. It is the maternal and not the conjugal aspect of the woman's role that tends to be extolled. The title of honour is not 'wife' but 'Mum'. As one Bethnal Green informant puts it: ' "Mum" puts a woman on a pedestal —where she should be.' Dennis, Henriques and Slaughter have argued convincingly why this should be so.

All those wives who brought their families through the depression period give an impression of strength, patience and consistency of character which asserts itself despite weariness and strain. Where the husband has not pulled his weight, the wife seems to retain this strength of personality but along with it goes a bitterness, or at best, a lack of sweetness in her relationship with her husband. This is associated also with an intensified relationship of affection between mother and children.

I was struck by a certain frequently recurring pattern in the father and mother relations. The relationship between the mother and son was warm and affectionate, often glowing with a deep sense of attachment and admiration, but the feeling of a son for his father was cold, and often hostile. I often met men who never married because they did not want to leave their mother alone and were afraid that a wife might not get on with her. Some even contended that they could not find a girl as perfect as their mother. One man said to me: 'Why should I marry?—to come home every night to see my mother, the way my brothers do?' Another: 'I haven't married because I have a strong sense of duty. I have seen my mother struggling all her life to keep us going, often washing up and ironing to the small hours, and I thought it unfair to subject any woman to such a life.'[1]

There was no sign of the same warmth in the relationship with the father. Is it just chance that I met so many men, most of them young, who, when they speak of their childhood, show contempt or even hatred for their father. 'I hated my father,' they have said, 'my father was a mug and a boozer.' Some told me that they have left home after a violent row with their father. 'One day I came home late at night and my father hit me. So I gave him a good hiding and left.'[2]

Zweig ended by asking himself: 'Can it be that poverty is conducive to a warmer relationship between the son and the mother than between the son and the father?' In the preceding pages, some reasons have been suggested why this may be so. The argument will be further pursued on pages 292–302.

There are good social reasons as well as emotional reasons for the woman's position at the centre of the family. After the children have arrived, the post-honeymoon period of intensive conjugal interaction is over. She learned to some extent to

[1] Zweig (1948). Note here also the expectation that things will not change for the better, an attitude further discussed on pages 238 ff. and 474.

[2] Zweig also relates behaviour in the home to experience in the world of work. 'A working man, especially if he is in one of the lower grades, is often kept down and ordered about; and it is perfectly natural for him to treat others as he is treated. "Remember the N.C.O.'s attitude to privates" (a labourer said to me, with some insight). For a long time he has been the underdog and then he finds himself on top having people to order about and shout at. He thinks that what he had to put up with is good enough for the other chap. "If I stood it, why can't he?" he says. A labourer often can't help behaving like that to his children. And, mind you, that treatment from his father is good training for a boy, because the world will treat him the same.' (Note here again the expectation that nothing will ever change; note also the type of socialization: very harsh, very pessimistic; note also the informant's appreciation of the socialization process.) A matching quotation for the newer, more relaxed situation will be found on page 298.

understand her husband when she had him to herself. Now, having the children to herself for most of the daytime, she stands in the middle position between husband and children. She knows the idiosyncrasies of each: it is she therefore who is best able to interpret either party to the other—the children to the father, the father to the children. She can say to her husband: 'John always does what you tell him if you ask him a second time', thereby shielding her son from his father's anger. Again, she can explain to the child that there are days when the conditions of his work are likely to make father irritable, and that he must then take care not to get underfoot. This aspect of the mother's role is generally well understood in England: those of Gorer's informants (a minority) who felt that the mother was in the main the better person to punish the children, gave as a reason—quite correctly—that 'she understands them better'. The diagram pictures this mediating role-position.

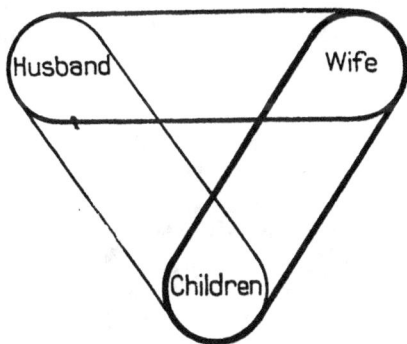

Husband, wife and children

The father has less common ground with the children. He interacts less with them. He does not know them as well as his wife does. How can he deal with them? In the nineteenth century, when the position of any father was highly authoritarian, he could behave to the children in an authoritarian way. There are survivals of this attitude in the more traditional groups (as well as among those with personality-needs that make this attitude congenial, but this is not here our concern).

How many fathers [asks Zweig] come home from their work tired, dissatisfied, frustrated, and thinking only of escaping from the family-life they dread to a pub or to the dogs? How many wives use their husband's name as a bogy to frighten small boys? 'Just you wait till your father comes home. He'll give it to you', they say. How many mothers warn their children to keep as quiet as a mouse when the father comes home, and not bother him with anything because he is tired from work? How many mothers give all the bacon to their husbands, and eat bread and potatoes themselves? Children are observant and notice that their father gets all the comforts and the best food. Their mother tells them that this is as it should be, because the father is the breadwinner.

Now that this pattern is changing, the father is in something of a difficulty. He may find himself, as in St. Ebbe's, 'taken for granted as something in the background of the woman and her children'. The man leaves his wife to cope, abdicating his own responsibility: 'Well, ask your Mum: if she says yes, well, I suppose it's all right.' He may, finding his position weakened, confine his interaction to what will please the child, as a sort of bribery, leaving his wife to deal with discipline.[1]

The men take a great deal of interest in the smaller children, especially at the toddler stage, and they may spend a great deal of money on gifts and treats for them [writes Robb]. Fathers frequently boast of the things they have bought their children: in fact the buying of rather expensive and elaborate though often unsuitable and unappreciated presents for his children, seems to be a man's regular method of demonstrating his goodness as a father. In spite of this, a father is unlikely to have much close contact, especially with the older children. Often he seems a rather remote figure, by contrast with the mother, and, even more than she, is he likely to be seen by the child as inconsistent and unpredictable.

A third alternative is that the husband may now take a fuller domestic responsibility, in a partnership with his wife. He will then interact more with his children than was the case in the past, and will find himself on a new footing with them, more intimate than before. This alternative is discussed in later chapters.

[1] See also pages 72, 337 and 565–6.

Traditional Working-Class Life

HUSBANDS, THEIR WIVES, AND THEIR MOTHERS-IN-LAW:
THE DEMETER-SYSTEM

Conjugal role-segregation was found to be a characteristic of the traditional working-class areas where people interacted within close-knit family networks. Clearly, if husbands and wives interact relatively little and have relatively little understanding of each other's lives, the women must either find themselves quite isolated, or else they must look elsewhere for help and support in the performance of their tasks and for the satisfaction of their social needs. For either purpose the larger family group is admirably suited. Sisters may see a lot of each other, and the women of two generations may be very close. Young and Willmott, who are mainly responsible for the greater emphasis on the mother–daughter tie in the sociology of the family, call this the Demeter-system.

Three characteristics are therefore likely to be encountered together: conjugal role-segregation, a strong bond between mothers and daughters, and a close-knit family circle.[1] The interrelationship between them must now be considered in detail.

In any area where there is little social mobility, grown-up children who have married tend to live near their parents. There may be two, three, sometimes even four generations living in the same street. In the Bethnal Green sample, half the married people who had parents still alive, had a parent living in Bethnal Green, another sixth or so had a parent living in an adjacent borough. Of those with parents living in Bethnal Green, the percentages show:

Parents' residence	Married men	Married women
In the same house or flat	14	28
In the same street or flat-block	14	23
Elsewhere in the borough	72	49

[1] And tradition. Townsend found in Bethnal Green that the more the women shared their daily lives with their daughters, the less they shared with their husbands, and the greater the strict traditional role-segregation. Young and Willmott found, however, little evidence of the same kind of segregation between younger couples. Patterns are changing and the old marital relationship is giving way to one based more on partnership. This trend is more marked still in the Woodford group, which is both younger and more up in the world, factors which between them seem to be the determining forces of joint role-relationships (see pages 342–3).

It is an interesting peculiarity, relevant to our general argument, that families tend to be matrilocal: a newly married couple is more likely to be living close to the wife's family than near the husband's. One reason is that the mother 'speaks for' her daughter to the rent-collector in the hope of obtaining a house for her. If such a practice is widespread in a district, it must clearly lead to a gradually increasing respectability in the area (as well as an increase in network-connectedness) since the mother has to persuade the rent-collector, and a regular payer is more likely to have her daughter favoured than one who is more slipshod.

Proximity makes possible the exchange of services between different members of the family. Mogey is impressed by the extent to which

> relations with kindred in St. Ebbe's are on the utilitarian basis of exchanged services. The facts conform closely to the picture many people hold in their minds when they think of personal exchanges in a friendly district. Thus the baby may be left with the grandmother while the mother shops; the rent-collector, the insurance-man and the laundry delivery-service may call and be paid for both families at the grandmother's. In the case of ordinary everyday kitchen needs, the first attempt at borrowing will be made within the kinship-group, surplus allotment-produce will, as a matter of course, be shared between its members without any ritual of offering and accepting or any compulsion to pay back soon.

A similar pattern was found in Bethnal Green. Mrs. Newbolt was helped by her mother, who, like the Ship Street Mum, might, when she felt lonely, borrow the oldest child for a fortnight or so at a time. An informant of Young and Willmott's went into hospital and came home to find that her husband and her father had decorated the kitchen in her absence. The womenfolk had looked after everything beautifully, not only in the way of direct care for the family, but also buying a new pram and other appropriate gifts.

Living so near, the older people, if they are ill or infirm, can be easily helped and looked after by their children. But very often, in middle age, the grandmother will just be getting her second wind. Life bears hardest on the woman after marriage and before her children are grown up and earning. During this period she may never be more than 'nobbut middlin'. But if she survives, Hoggart notes often a remarkable recovery of health and energy. (This recovery may also be partly connected with the menopause, since the fear of unwanted conception overshadows much sexual intercourse, and miscarriages may at this time impair the woman's well-being.) She is then at the centre of the family-network, which is kept in being by her.

One can have little but admiration for the position such a mother then naturally assumes in her household. She has an honoured place in most accounts of working-class childhoods. Her menfolk may appear careless of her for much of the time, but they like to buy ornaments inscribed 'What is home without a mother', and for years after she has 'gone' will speak lovingly of 'me mam'.

In early middle age, when she has fully established herself as the mother of the family [Hoggart continues], she comes into her own. She is then the pivot of the home, as it is practically the whole of her world. She, more than the father, holds it together, writing with difficulty to a son in the services or a daughter away at work. She keeps the close contact with those other members of the family who live near: grandparents, brothers, sisters, cousins.

The grandmother, or 'Mum' as she was universally called, was also the pivotal figure in Bethnal Green. The chief organizer of family-parties or of aid, she was something of a matriarchal figure. The local family group, linked together through her bond with her married daughters, was united on her hearth. 'Mum's is the central depot in this family,' said a respectful dustman of his mother-in-law. The network is knotted round Mum. 'Mum's is the family's rendezvous', and 'All my family,' said Mrs. Shipway, 'gather at Mum's every Saturday afternoon. We sit jawing and get amused with the children when all of them get together, play cards and listen to the wireless. No one leaves until tennish at night. It always happens on a Saturday.'

Because the men are absent at work during the day, whereas the women's work is at home, because of matrilocality, and because the women's occupation—housework—is a skill learned from and shared with the mother, conditions are ideal for a strong mother–daughter tie, especially upon the daughter's marriage. Thus an informant in Bethnal Green said to an interviewer: 'Since we've had the children I've got no more friends —outside the family, I mean', and another: 'I don't see my best friend much. She's married too and she's always round her Mum's like I'm always round mine.'

Matrilocality, a community of interests and the exchange of services maintain and strengthen a system based on a close emotional bond. Bethnal Greeners say:

> My son's my son till he gets him a wife,
> My daughter's my daughter all of her life.

> After breakfast I bath the baby and sweep the kitchen and wash up. Then I go up the road shopping with Mum, Greta (one of this wife's married sisters) and the three children. After dinner I clean up and then round about two o'clock I go out for a walk if it's fine with Mum, Greta and the children. I come back at about a quarter to four to be in time for Janice when she gets back from school. She calls in at Mum's on her way home just to see if I'm there. This is an ordinary day. If anything goes wrong and I'm in any trouble, I always go round to Mum's.[1]

The comforts and advantages of such a relationship are so great that if there is no Mum, some find it necessary to invent her. When Mrs. Brown was ten, her mother died, so she was grateful to have a mother-in-law.

---

[1] This is nicely matched by an account from Ashton: 'S. T. and his wife Jean live only four doors from the household of Jean's mother and retired father. With this father and mother live another daughter (Mary, aged twenty-one), her twenty-seven-year-old husband and two very small children. They are living there until they can find a house of their own in which to live. The sister, Mary, makes at least three visits a day with one or both children. Her father visits S. T.'s household at least once daily, to borrow something or perhaps simply to keep the child occupied. Jean makes the beds each night for her mother who is a cripple. Her two children, Stephen and John, obviously regard Mary and their grandmother as very close to them. Anything cooked for a meal and not eaten is taken to the mother's house to be finished. Jean says: We never have any letters or have to write to anybody, all our people are here . . . Jean and Mary will either go to the shops together and leave their mother in charge of the children or take turns to look after them while the other goes out. Both Jean and Mary joke about having four children instead of two. Their brother Ralph has gone to live with his wife some five miles distant in Burley, but each week-end the two of them come home and sleep alternately in the two households. On Saturday night two or three of these couples will go out together.'

Being so long without a mother, I suppose I took to her from the beginning. When I was younger I used to envy the other girls who had mothers. Mum—she's always been 'Mum' to me—Mum's always been helpful, she's always looked upon me as a daughter. Had I had a mother of my own, I expect I'd have stuck to her like anyone would, but as it was I was more than willing to accept someone who was willing to accept me.'

Mrs. Brown showed a sound intuition. But the need to love an older woman was not the only need she satisfied: there is also the need, for practical and emotional reasons, to belong to a family-network, and attachment to a Mum seems to be a necessary condition for this.

How do the men feel about this? According to Young and Willmott, the great triangle of adult life is Mum–wife–husband.

'My sisters are married, but they're not really married, if you see what I mean. When they finish work they go straight round to Mum's and don't get home till nine-thirty or ten at night.'

'Some people (said Mr. Warner pointedly) are too close to their mothers, if you ask me. They ought to stand on their own feet a bit more.' And the Manns decided to move to a new estate because, among other reasons, Mrs. Mann was pulled by conflicting loyalties. She said: 'I like to see Mum, of course', but she was also attached to her husband and understood his resentment when he complained: 'She doesn't mother you, she smothers you.' Mrs. Mann went on: 'If I don't see her every day, she says: "Oh, I thought you was ill, or something." She doesn't actually interfere, but she's always there making remarks. She says, "Baby seems to be crying a lot, doesn't he?" or "Haven't you put him on the bottle yet?" My husband doesn't like it, I can tell you!' This couple, having talked it over, moved. 'My husband says it will cost more and he'll have the extra journey, but we can make our own life out there.'[1]

In considering this triangle, Young and Willmott make an interesting prediction. The husband has as one alternative, to go his own way, spending a large part of his time away from his wife, not only during working hours but at weekends and in the evenings as well. Another alternative is for him to be drawn into the maternal fold, along with his wife. In the past, they

[1] Talking it over, moving and wishing to 'make our own life' are all more characteristic of status dissent, discussed more fully in the next chapter.

suspect that the second course was seldom followed, the pressures on the husband to exclude himself or be excluded from the family being too strong for him to withstand. Today, they think, if marriage is more often a partnership, then the couple is more likely to be partners in the extended family as well.

And in fact they found that the majority of husbands were good sons-in-law, visiting regularly with their wives. A minority were out-law sons, who did not visit. One man insisted that he never saw his wife's mother: 'Do you hear that, Alice?' he shouted to his wife in the next room. 'How often do I see your mother? Ho ho, that's good, ain't it? I never see her—never. I keep away from her.'

When the men are all day away at work, out of the ambience of the rest of the family, the women are left in charge of the family's social life. In these conditions, regardless of the local pattern of conjugal authority, it will be a woman—the Mum, the eldest woman and matriarch of the group—who keeps the family intact. Wives get practice in this role in earlier years. For instance, since a man's wife has the daytime in which to go visiting, while her husband is out at work, it is easier for her to

Interaction in the extended kin network

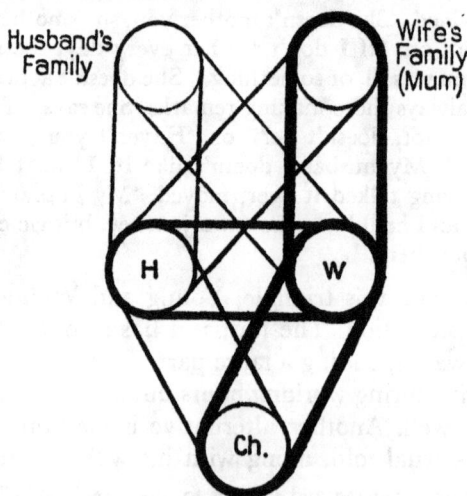

Husband's Family   Wife's Family (Mum)

H   W

Ch.

Three generations

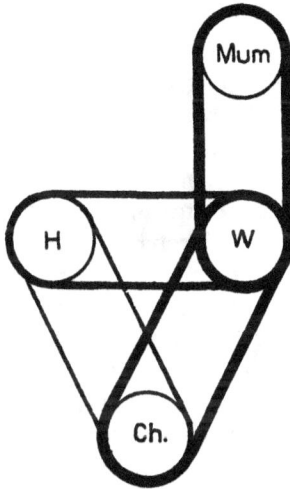

Family life from the wife's point of view

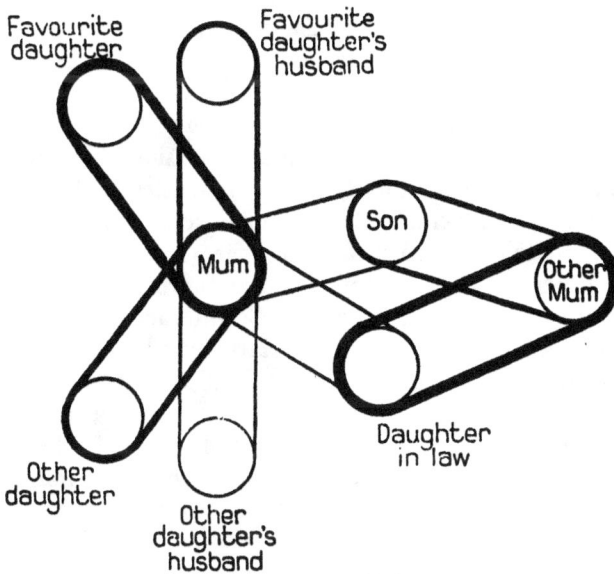

Family life from a Mum's point of view: 'the central depot in our family'.
The conjugal bond has not been represented, for clarity's sake

see more of the older generation. She can take the children to see them during the day, and this strengthens the ties across the generations further. The diagrams show the relative frequencies with the focus on various personalities in the network.

Little though we know about them, regional variations must be mentioned before we can allow ourselves to continue the main argument. The diagrams in these pages show what may well be an extreme of matriarchal dominance, extended-family sociability and so on. Certainly the Mum in St. Ebbe's is nothing like so important a figure, either administratively or emotionally, as she is in Bethnal Green. At the same time, the mother–daughter tie is weaker in St. Ebbe's. Mogey also found much less interest in family than was reported from Bethnal Green; nor was the network so extensive or contact between kin as frequent. In Bethnal Green, elderly women could recite lists of forty or fifty relatives; in St. Ebbe's, people who had the same name said neutrally 'I suppose they are relatives' but made no further effort to trace their relationship. Mogey gives an anecdote of two families of the same name living in the same street. The children of one family went to considerable trouble to verify that the man in the other family was a first cousin of their father's, but the adults never bothered to meet.[1]

In St. Ebbe's there is considerable confusion about what can be demanded of the kindred, just as there is less certainty about the exact way in which the roles of husband and wife are to be demarcated. Occasionally kin offer support when it is not wanted; permissive behaviour is much more difficult to sustain than conventional obligations are. So interaction is reduced in amount and content. As long as relatively minor functions and casual everyday visiting are involved, all is well. But the major emergency which calls for specialized skills, such as coping with serious sickness or with disagreements between husbands and wives or laying out the dead (which in very traditional communities is done by kin or neighbour), is beyond the kindred in St. Ebbe's, though this sort of aid is reported to be still forthcoming in old Bethnal Green.

Two possible explanations present themselves, at least. One

[1] Further comparative material is available in Mrs. Stacey's study of Banbury, op. cit., chap. 7, 'The Family'.

is, that we have here a long-standing cultural difference between two regions. Secondly, it is also possible that the explanation lies in the fact that fewer people have moved away from Bethnal Green than from St. Ebbe's. In the consequently more loose-knit network there is, as Mogey points out, good reason why the casual exchange of services should not be maintained at the Bethnal Green level. The restriction of acknowledged kinship-ties to a small group of individuals means that for many families such ties are possible with only one person, and then differences in personality or temperament may easily break them altogether. We have argued on page 136 that there is a critical level of network-connectedness: below that level there are too few people to be able to carry the burden for one another and there must then be an abrupt drop in the total exchange of services. But exchange of services is itself a form of interaction, and with the reduction of interaction we get a reduction in social conformity pressures, less certainty about the way to behave, less rigid role-definition and so on down. This process is to be discussed in very great detail in the next chapter, which concerns the families who have moved out of their neighbourhood. There the strength of conjugal role-segregation, network-connectedness and other related variables has declined still further. Indeed, those differences are so remarkable that differences between the areas now under discussion recede into the background.

THE SPLASH

As some of the quotations have already suggested, there are occasions when the whole extended family makes an effort to meet. In Mrs. Shipway's family, this was as often as every week. Normally, it would be at least on each birthday, with something special on Mum's birthday, at Christmas, at weddings and funerals.

Good cheer and an air of festivity accompany these family occasions. Here is part of an account of a Bethnal Green wedding.

The thirty-two guests squeezed down at the cramped tables for the wedding-breakfast of ham and tongue, salad and pickles, trifle and jelly, washed down with ale and Guinness. The heat became greater, the faces more flushed and talk louder. After an hour, the meal and toasts were over, the telegrams read, the trestle tables were cleared and stacked away. Sylvia and Harry concentrated on trying to bring the two families together. They were not to go off to their honeymoon until the next morning. In Bethnal Green, where they were born and bred, couples do not fly off to a honeymoon when the first reception is over. 'I'm going to stay till the very end, that's if we ever get away. We haven't actually booked,' said Sylvia. 'I wouldn't miss a minute of it.'

The deep feeling for home, the emotional significance of which seems to surpass all others, makes it congenial that there should every now and then be a joyous affirmation of the unity of the family in the home. The 'splash' is a rite in the religion of the family. But the need for an occasional outburst of this kind is also deeply rooted in the life-situation and personality-structure of this population. The splash is a short-term equivalent of the indulgence which marks certain age-groups, such as infancy and adolescence: the immediate gratification of impulses is a necessary counterpoise to the more rigorous conditions which obtain at other times and is justified by reference to the general harshness of the life. 'Gather ye rosebuds while ye may' can be taken to refer not only to age-groups but more generally to the rhythm of a life which is usually harsh and demanding but which allows well-defined occasions when the demands may legitimately be ignored and the rosebuds gathered.[1]

> In everyday life, the little bits extra add variety or colour or some gaiety [writes Hoggart]. They are among the freely springing things in a life which is largely an imposed routine, of clocking-in-and-out, of the family's washing, meals and repairs ... The good life is not simply a matter of 'putting up with things', 'making the best of it', but one with scope for having the 'bit extra' that really makes 'Life'.

A few pages later he identifies what lies behind these 'excursions into the Baroque'.

> In all these acts one is 'having a go', a fling, making a splash. It is a shortlived splash but a good one, because most of the rest

[1] See also the discussion on indulgence-periods in child rearing, pages 464–5.

of life is humdrum and regulated. One needs sometimes to make a gesture, even though finances do not reasonably permit it. A gesture like this, in sum, should have a suggestion of splendour and wealth about it—the charabancs are 'de-luxe coaches', the pantomimes are fond of 'extravaganzas', phrases like 'very fancy' and 'doing it in style'—that is, in the style in which posh folk are hazily assumed to pass their every day—strike the same note . . .

Hence the emphasis on a 'proper funeral', a 'decent burial', 'putting him away splendid '. . . The custom of laying on a good meal at a funeral, of 'burying 'im with 'am' is not simply an excuse for a good feed on the strength of the insurance policies. It is considered a suitable way of doing things, without for once pinching and scraping, on one of the rare occasions when the family gathers. We may be tempted, noticing how much the atmosphere lightens at tea and listening to the gossip which goes on for hours, to think that these are no more than gatherings for family gossip over a large meal . . . But behind it, too, is the assumption that neither the body nor those following it must go to the burial in the state of shabbiness which has been usual throughout life.

It has often been noted that festivities absorb a larger part of the working-class budget than the middle classes would expect. Cyril Smith found that a funeral in South London may cost £50, with the stone £20 extra (at 1955 prices). At Christmas a working-class family with children will spend at least £20 more than at other times of the year. Most relief agencies expect an increase in the volume of applications in the months before Christmas (though of course we must allow for the fact that this is also the season of cold and illness).

'Respectable' working people tend to be utilitarian. They are conscious of the limitations of their incomes and they spend their money wisely by taking care over what they buy . . . The old-style working man was much less rational and his satisfactions were more immediate and communal. Income was spent on social pleasures, not on improving the amenities and standards of the individual household. This decline in ritual has consequences that are not always realized. Ritual has the function of holding people together, of giving them something common from which to derive their loyalties. If it disappears and is not replaced, social solidarity weakens.

Especially when the lives are lives of hardship, when to help one another entails self-sacrifice, these occasional communal enjoyments are a necessary counterpoise for the perpetuation of the pattern.[1]

The same set of attitudes which makes the splash a congenial psychological adjustment is manifested also in the attitude to money in general, and to saving and budgeting in particular. Zweig (1952) asks himself 'Does poverty contribute to economical spending?' and answers firmly in the negative. Enumerating reasons for his opinion, he finally concludes with 'one more element which makes for uneconomical spending among the poor —the need for compensation for their drudgery and drabness of life, the search for substitutes or sheer escape in buying pleasures'.

Hoggart is clearly familiar with the same tradition.

There are many thrifty working-class people today, as there have always been. But in general the immediate and present nature of working-class life puts a premium on the taking of pleasures now and discourages planning for some future goal, or in the light of some ideal . . . Even of those who spend a more than usual amount of time worrying about how things are going to 'pan out', it is true to say that their life is one of the immediate present to a degree not often found among other classes. Wives will still 'slip out' with their purses at 4.30 on many a day to get something for tea. There is little on the shelf and that little is for special occasions. But this is not necessarily the living from hand to mouth which indicates poverty; it is not altogether indolence and forgetfulness; it is part of the climate of life; one moves generally from item to item. Wage-packets come in weekly and go out weekly, savings are traditionally for specific purposes, and a mistrust of saving is still quite common; you might get knocked down tomorrow.

[1] As the Ashton study showed, sometimes these conditions do not lead to the communal, cheerful, cosy family-splash, but to their harsher psychological equivalent: unbridled violence of groups of individuals outside the family circle. 'Come and have a riot of fun' advertises an Ashton dance hall. The riot of fun is also a counterpoise to the conditions of normal life, but because the family as an institution is weaker there, the counterpoise is less controlled by tender components. It is to be noted that the age-group is adolescence, when family-ties are at their weakest. See also page 292f n.

And, returning again to Zweig, we note a set of attitudes and circumstances already encountered in Ashton.

The fluctuation of a worker's income from week to week is great. The normal range of variations due to overtime, night-shifts and bonus can be as much as 20 to 35 per cent of his income. The worker has his ups and downs all the time. He cannot arrange his budget as smoothly as a middle-class man. He is used to living dangerously, one day having a fair amount of money and the next having little or none at all. But he does not worry about that and he rarely makes provision for the future. The mentality of the majority of workers is strongly 'in the present' . . . Most of those who do save, do so for clothes, holidays and Christmas. Some also save for a rainy day, normally up to a target, and saving is stopped when the target is reached. Most workers are against saving for old age, because you cannot save enough to make it worthwhile . . . There are born savers who enjoy saving, but they are rare. The majority of workers feel that when they have put some extra effort into work, they merit 'a treat' in extra pleasure or amusement[1] . . .

'If you have no spending-money you may as well be dead' is the common opinion of workers. Spending-money means pocket-money, or free money, to be spent on what a man *wants*, not on what he *needs*. Spending-money is the key to freedom, the freedom desired by the worker, not the freedom talked about by the politician.[2]

These, however, are becoming old-fashioned attitudes. Things are changing. By 1952 the Radby Report quotes an insurance agent who believes that very many miners, even from the 'bad' streets, save something each week through the colliery savings-scheme. A certain amount of savings for holidays is reported to be common. And in Gladstone Road, a 'good' road, not much haphazard buying is done. Spending is planned ahead and includes attempts to save. One woman is reported to put her money for rent, clothes, electricity, etc. in separate boxes 'so as to have it ready in time'.

[1] From *Labour, Life and Poverty* (1952); cf. pages 78-9.
[2] From *Women's Life and Labour* (1948). Mogey, in a private communication, points out that the need for spending-money ties up with maintaining one's position in the group of male friends; see also pages 111, 172 and 222-3.

Aspects of Adult Life in England

The traditional working classes have a tradition of poverty: saving is difficult or inexpedient for the same reasons as in Ashton. But the poverty is not feckless: the effort after respectability is there. Especially among the women (Zweig's 'economic men') there is a marked preference for a respectable, predictable, well-regulated existence. The very institution of the 'splash' bears witness to this: the splash limits and localizes episodes in which the harsh facts of existence may be temporarily disregarded and normal standards ignored.

There will be differences in the extent to which standards are attained, or indeed striven for, according to temperament, local culture and economic circumstance. It is clear that the range of effort will be very wide, and also the range of the attractiveness of the outcome. To sneer at some of the manifestations would be easy, and wrong: it is surely an admirable thing to set strict standards when in constant danger of submergence by fecklessness, hopelessness and the submissive, exploitative cunning of the poor.

> There is [writes Hoggart] a tendency among some writers on the working classes to think of all those who aim at thrift and cleanliness as imitators of the lower middle classes, as in some way traitors to their own class, anxious to get out of it. Conversely, those who do not make this effort tend to be regarded as more honest and less servile than those who do. But cleanliness, thrift and self-respect arise more from a concern not to drop down, not to succumb to the environment, than from an anxiety to go up; and among those who altogether ignore these criteria, the uninhibited, generous and carefree spirits are outnumbered by the slovenly and shiftless, whose homes and habits reflect their lack of inner grip . . .
>
> There is a clear dignity in that reaction to the pressures of the outside world which takes the form of insisting on 'keeping y' self-respect'. And the moment this idea of 'self-respect' and 'self-reliance' comes to mind, it begins to flower into related ideas: into that of 'respectability' first, which itself spreads outwards and upwards from some thin-lipped forms, through the pride of a skilled workman, to the integrity of those who have practically nothing except a determination not to allow themselves to be

dragged down by circumstances. At the centre is a resolution to hold on to that of which one can be rightly proud, in a world which puts so many stumbling-blocks in the way, to hold on at least to 'self-respect' . . . It is at work constantly in the hatred of 'going on the parish', in the worry to keep up sick payments, in the big insurances to avoid a parish burial, in thrift and the cult of cleanliness.

In sum, what distinguishes the respectable traditional working-class group from the rough is the effort they make to maintain standards, and not to let things slide. In the past the standards may have been impossible to attain because of the vicissitudes of life, and this would be a grief to the respectable, a glib excuse to the rough. But now the standards can be maintained and the effect of the difference in attitude is clear to perceive. In Radby, for example, the housekeeping in the rough (i.e. Grade II) households is described as showing 'intermittent effort, but no real interest in keeping the home clean and tidy'. In contrast, the respectable (i.e. Grade III) household evidently showed the 'effort made to ensure that the appearance of the house does not fall below certain standards'.

It is important to note, while these very delicate differences are under discussion, that the Radby Report continues its evaluation of Grade III housekeeping standards thus: 'No particular concern with maintaining high standards of tidiness, etc.' The standards which exist are apparently set with reference downwards. The aim is not 'to emulate those with higher standards'; it is 'not to resemble those with lower standards'. Regulation of behaviour is in terms of a 'negative comparison-group'.[1]

Another source shows that the men, separately considered, adhere to the standards appropriate to their own sphere. 'Is there', asks Zweig, 'a significant difference in attitude between skilled, semi-skilled and labourers? Definitely yes. Skilled men with few exceptions have a very negative attitude to shifts. This is because of the complexity of the work ("We are not so alert

---

[1] Negative comparison-groups are discussed in more detail in the next chapter, pages 249 ff.
The attitude to children shows the same rather unambitious, downwardly-oriented, but nevertheless clearly operative standards. See pages 556–7 and 592–3.

at night") and the difficulty of maintaining proper standards of performance ("It isn't fair to the job").'[1]

The number of normative words—italicized in the passage below—in the sentences with which the writers of the Radby Report describes the respectable households, is very striking.

In the good streets and grades, people are *proud of* the appearance of their house. They like to *take good care of* it whether they own it or not. They enjoy the garden which *must be cared for* as the house. If the walls get *shabby* they *must* be repapered. A broken chair leg *must* be mended *at once*. Things are housed in *appointed* places (e.g. the children have a cupboard for their toys). People take *particular care* of their own tools, books, bicycles, etc. Since they look after their own possessions they are *likely to accord similar respect* to other people's belongings in general . . . Each aspires to a *reasonably 'nice'* home. The elder Bonnington girl, for instance, was genuinely *shocked* at something she noticed about Buckingham Palace when she went to London on a Works' trip. The front curtains at the Palace did not match, and it was a sign of *pretty sluttish* housekeeping in her opinion.

It should be stressed that these families have coped relatively well with an environment that is no different from that of the squalidly kept homes. Mrs. Waters, for instance, had no larder and had to manage with her sink in the front room. What she minded most was that to get to the lavatory they had to go down nine steps from the living-room, through a cellar and up into the yard. She mentioned incidentally that this lavatory had been out of order for nine weeks.

The Radby (Grade III) respectables sound rather pleasantly less thin-lipped and censorious than some others. It is reported that living alongside the lower-grade families did not seriously perturb them, though they were observed to maintain a different set of standards with regard to behaviour and physical appearances, and to make a stand on certain matters: 'My Dolly and my Brian are *not* going to steal. I won't have it!' The authors comment that the policies of these families—unlike that of their rougher neighbours—is a long-distance one, and not just an occasional flash-in-the-pan effort.

It is also pleasant to note that we have here an instance of a

---

[1] From *The Worker in an Affluent Society*.

neighbourhood kept from deterioration because the acceptable leadership of the respectables keeps the community a going concern.

The four Grade III families were 'in good standing' in their street. This is not the standoffish superiority of the woman who will not let her child play out; it is reflected in such facts as that Mrs. Marks is one of the two women who always go to every house in the street if there is a collection for a wreath. For all the physical shortcomings of their houses, or even the low repute of the street itself, it is not really surprising that such families do not want to leave the district.

These people are the pillars of the local community: when they go, it totters. It is the disappearance of their sort which is saddening Bethnal Green. 'Shopkeepers and publicans say they are losing business, teachers that they will soon have no pupils. At annual meetings of the Labour Party, there is the familiar lament: "Once again many of our active members have moved out during the year".' This brings us to the next section.

IN-GROUP/OUT-GROUP RELATIONS

The psychological trait we have called 'striving after standards' is easily connected with a more general preference for well-defined situations. This preference manifests itself in social life as a preference for clearly-defined, generally-understood and rather rigidly-maintained personal relations. In sociological language, the role-structure is a simple one, allowing little choice or variation in behaviour. We have seen how this works out in married life. It is evident also in other social relations. Thus Barbu (a foreign observer, like Zweig), writing of English society in general, considers that

> there is no other community in which the individual resents vertical relationships with others with a greater intensity, and sub- and super-ordination in particular. A clerk, a servant, even a charlady, when taking up a new job, feel that their first concern is to find out what they are 'supposed to do'. Once this is achieved they have won their independence, for, later on, whenever someone asks for their services their first reaction is to make sure whether

they are supposed to do this or not, and to act accordingly. Thus any individual avoids being dependent on others in the exercise of his job; he makes himself responsible to a kind of abstract authority which consists of certain rules and requirements established by agreement or by tradition, and which define 'what he is supposed to do'.[1]

In this most interesting passage, Barbu not only stresses the importance of standards, but also indicates how a traditional society, while maintaining its traditional role-relationships, may yet allow new forms of relationship to be built into the traditional structure. This has great survival-value: the whole structure of roles can change, though slowly, in response to the new demands made by changing political and economic conditions. But this is not here our concern.

Our concern is with two interrelated psychological aspects of Barbu's analysis. We may note, first, the task-relatedness and the ability to react impersonally in a large variety of situations, a trait which becomes more important as we go higher up the social scale. Here this impersonality is applied specifically to in-group/out-group relations; in later chapters we shall see it manifested in a number of other forms.[2] Second, we must take note that changes in the environment which demand changes in the relations between people also create anxiety. Anxious people tend to be rigid as far as they can, in order to reduce the number of situations which they cannot predict or control.[3] Therefore it may be argued that it is easier for people to allow themselves some freedom from the prescribed forms of interaction when they live in a highly traditional society and that this would be more difficult for them in a society which is changing. When role-relationships become more uncertainly defined because of changes in social structure, the dangers of misunderstanding and misinterpretation are too great to permit such occasional laxities. Then firmly-defined role-structures and an insistence on everything being 'just so', that each shall act according to conventionally agreed expectations, becomes basic to self-

[1] Z. Barbu (1956), *Democracy and Dictatorship*, Routledge and Kegan Paul, London.
[2] See pages 380 and 391-2.
[3] See pages 89, 234, 523-4 and 558.

respect.[1] Doing 'what you are supposed to do', no more, no less, is one way of preserving the sense of privacy which has been noted as so important a part of the psychological make-up of this (and other) groups. It strengthens the tendency to restrict interaction whenever difficulties arise: 'When in doubt, do nowt.'

In a changing world, therefore, it is not surprising that the arguments and evidence set out in the previous pages to demonstrate that the avoidance of neighbourly intrusion and the preservation of some privacy is a major problem in these areas, apply equally forcibly to the avoidance of unregulated interaction with people who are not properly part of the local network of family or community: 'them'.

> The world of 'Them' is the world of the bosses. 'They' may be, as occasion requires, anyone from the classes outside (other than the few individuals from those classes whom working people know as individuals). 'They' are the people at the top, the higher-ups, the people who give you your dole, call you up, tell you to go to war, fine you, 'get yer in the end', 'are all twisters really', 'never tell yer owt', 'will do y' down if they can', 'treat y' like muck'.

The problem of the respectable traditional working man is to preserve his self-respect vis-à-vis 'them', and, in particular, to make 'them' appreciate his respectability. The relationship between 'us' and 'them' is part of the total set of external relations of this social group and cannot be fully appreciated without reference to those others which this group considers beneath them: the 'roughs'. 'They' take no account of the difference between respectable and rough working people, between those with standards and those without. If we are to understand anything of the in-group/out-group relations here, we have to keep in mind at least three levels: 'us', 'them' and 'the roughs'. Interaction with both these out-groups has to be regulated if self-respect is to be preserved.

'Respectability' and 'self-respect' are very clearly notions concerned with other people and other people's opinion of one

---

[1] See pages 80-3 and 112-13. What distinguishes this attitude from the Ashton contract-type is the frequency with which new bargains may be struck. Here again the close similarity of self-respect to the sense of identity may be noted—see also pages 163, 164-5, 250-2 and 407.

another. At another social level the word would be 'dignity', at another 'integrity'. Each of these words connotes an un-damaged self-image, undamaged at least in the sense that other people do not question its validity. It is this self-image that is very easily bruised in interaction with those outside the community.

We have argued that the respectables are at pains to attain or maintain standards of domestic behaviour and social inter-action which distinguish them from the roughs in their neigh-bourhood. They are different from them, but not in economic situation. A period of illness or unemployment, or some other misfortune, could until recently push a whole family below the poverty line. Then help from others would be needed. When this happens, it is very bitter to be mis-classified by an outer world which does not appreciate that one is managing as best one can, handicapped only by misfortune, not by a failure in character. The outer world, 'they', may think someone a cadger who asks for help, because 'they' cannot distinguish between those who are cadgers-by-misfortune and those who are cadgers-in-character.

The patronizing, contemptuous or bullying attitudes of 'them' are felt by the respectable and self-respecting working man to be more appropriately directed to a lower stratum than his own. At the other end, the traditional rough is more likely to react to 'their' exercise of authority with violence, subter-fuge, exploitation or indifference, and in any case without much psychic pain. In a respectable man, the resentment created when he finds himself mis-classified evokes rather a reaction of stoic independence, a determination to steer clear of 'them' as long as possible. With this are associated the mistrust of 'their' motives, the anxious definition of what one is 'supposed to do' and a marked pride in his independence, which is the other aspect of the coin marked 'Private—I keep myself to myself'.

> We may understand [writes Hoggart] why working-class people often seem not 'oncoming' to social workers, seem evasive and prepared to give answers designed to put off rather than to clarify. At the back of the announcement that 'Ah keep meself to meself', there can be a hurt pride. It is difficult to believe that a visitor from another class could ever realize all the ins-and-outs of one's

difficulties—there is an anxiety not to 'show y'self up', to defend oneself against patronage.

For obvious historical reasons, financial independence is an important component of self-respect. These more financial aspects are well illustrated by Townsend's investigations into the lives of old people in Bethnal Green. He found that more than a third of the retired had a personal income which entitled them to supplementary relief from the National Assistance Board. But the majority had not applied for help. Instead, they were helped by their families: people who knew how misfortune can come to the self-respecting, who would not humiliate them. They were unwilling to apply for state aid: 'I was never one to go running for help. I'm not a cadger. That's not the way I was brought up.' 'I don't want to tell people all my affairs. I'm too proud I suppose. They ask too many questions.' 'I'd rather starve than ask for a penny.' These informants seemed to feel that a pension was their right and did not damage their self-respect. But the supplementary assistance, from the National Assistance Board, was thought of as charity. The memory of the pre-war Poor Relief was strong.

This independence from external agencies is made possible to the extent that kin or neighbours are able and willing to help. Because this requires both good communications and the proximity of those willing to help, such independence is more likely to be found in the close-knit traditional community. The next chapter will show that in more loose-knit areas there is not this feeling against the welfare agencies. Concurrently—it is hard to guess the extent to which these two factors are connected psychologically—it may be noted that the younger people do not feel so strongly about the use of welfare agencies, perhaps because their need is less, perhaps because 'their' behaviour has improved, perhaps because their own self-respect takes different forms.

Zweig has imaginatively reconstructed this attitude of self-respect and independence from 'their' favours as it is experienced by the men. The attitude is experienced in association with the feeling of solidarity in a community of equals, and, like all in-group/out-group systems, it is accompanied by a denial of community with 'them'. Being men, the feeling appears more militant and less resigned: we see here why it is the responsibility of the Mum to deal with 'them' face-to-face in clinic or gas-board office. If you are too militant you cannot negotiate on personal terms.

The unions mean a great deal to the men, even to those who do not bother about attending the meetings or who criticize their policy or leadership. The workmen feel strongly their individual helplessness in more than one way; they could not formulate their demands, they would not dare to present them even if they could formulate them and nobody would listen to them if they made demands on their own. But if they appear in the mass . . . their helplessness disappears . . . The union is the worker's protector against injustice; it is his brain to think for him and formulate his demands and his voice to express them. 'It's so good to feel that you have someone to back you up, that your mates are behind you' . . .

The mass-organization gives the worker his individuality, his freedom, his self-esteem, his self-confidence. A middle-class man has no such experience and cannot understand it; it seems to him rather like a contradiction in terms. A worker does not lose his individuality in his trade-union; it is quite the other way around. By identifying himself with the union he gains status and strength in his own eyes and in everyone else's.

The first or perhaps even the only quality which rules in the union is solidarity of its members. If union solidarity is lost, everything is lost, because left to shift for themselves the old methods would return . . . The idea of the brotherhood of men is the governing idea of the unions . . . But the paternalism of the employers is opposed; what is given as charity and not as the worker's right is not appreciated. Favours are not sought and often not accepted; rights are bargained for and embodied in rules and agreement, but what is given beyond that is often regarded as suspect, and the men look for a hidden catch in it. 'Stand together and win' or 'Stand by your mates whatever happens' is another motto which expresses the enormous value of class unity.

FORMAL ASSOCIATIONS

Not only relationships which are explicitly *de haut en bas*, but also membership of formal organizations is affected by these considerations. The history of working-class associational life is bedevilled by the fact that leadership in many associations comes from the same classes who are thought of as 'they'. Before we consider this in detail, however, some factual problems require attention.

It is often said that 'joining' is a middle-class peculiarity. This is not contradicted by the evidence, but there are certain difficulties of interpretation. In Woodford, according to Willmott and Young (1960),[1]

> clubs and other organizations plainly attract middle-class people more than working class. Nearly twice as many in the middle class had attended in the previous month, and over half belong to an organization, compared with a third of working-class people. This is not peculiar to Woodford. Cauter and Downham found in Derby that middle-class people were 'easily the most interested in joining clubs; not only do more of them belong to a club, but when they do join they are more likely to join more than one club'. Bottomore, studying voluntary organizations in the country town of 'Squirebridge', found much the same there.

On the other hand, Gorer, asking 'Are there places outside your own homes and the street where you meet neighbours to have a chat?' found that social class was not correlated with frequency of more formal association in the expected way. Instead, those who qualified their class identification with 'upper', whether upper middle or upper working class, were above the average. These higher frequencies were due in both cases to attendance at mixed clubs, youth clubs, political clubs, and dance halls. The working-class informants also went frequently to sports grounds and scored high in the category 'other'.

These are important data because these are the kind of leisure activities often ignored when comparisons between classes are made. Since many social scientists were brought up in a middle-class culture there is always a danger that they may impose their own idea of associational life on the data, thinking in terms of the tennis club, the Park Residents' Society, the Floral Arrangement Group, the Monkhams Singers, the Knighton Players, the Snaresbrook Ladies Hockey Club and so on.[2]

[1] P. Willmott and M. Young (1960), *Family and Class in a London Suburb*, Routledge and Kegan Paul, London: fully discussed on pages 326–52.

[2] These charming names are taken from Willmott and Young's report on Woodford. I do not imply that these authors have fallen into the error here under discussion.

Working-class activities may be concentrated in the category 'other', and 'other' sometimes appears somehow less properly associational. We catch this tone even in the Radby Report:

> Any societies that the men mentioned, a Produce Association, for instance, or a Darts Team, were connected with a pub or Working Men's Club.

How oddly deprecatory the tone, as though these men had not really joined anything, as though it only looked like their having done so!

In fact the Radby Report gives details of what seems a quite extraordinarily full associational life in the four Grade III 'respectable' families which were studied at length. All four families had some effective link with a church, though only one set of adults were regular Chapel-goers and communicants. These, the Waters', were also members of the Labour Party. Mrs. Marks always went to church for the Anniversary and on special occasions. She saw to it that Mary went to Sunday School regularly, and was glad that Mary was now a Sunday School teacher. The Freeman adolescents and children frequented the Salvation Army organizations both weekdays and Sundays. The Bonningtons too were staunch Sunday School and Youth Club supporters. Margaret, aged 15, was said by her mother to 'live for' Peak Street Chapel Youth Club. Mrs. Bonnington used to go herself but some there 'wouldn't acknowledge me when in me muck', so she gave it up. But she saw to it that the two younger boys went faithfully to Sunday School and was careful to go herself to their prize-giving.

The Report calls this exceptional. But is it? What does seem to be true is that in some circumstances there is less *need* for voluntary associations, though they exist for those who like them.[1] Young and Willmott put the matter in a more plausible perspective:

> The informal ties that abound in the East End—ties with relatives who are also neighbours, with neighbours who are former school-mates or present work-mates, with a whole host of people familiar in one way or another—all these make for easy, unforced sociability. Of course, there are clubs in Bethnal Green—the

[1] These circumstances are specified by Bott and discussed on pages 349 ff.

place is well supplied with University Settlements and Youth Clubs, and there are the usual British Legion branches, political organizations and the rest—but for most people these are not essential for meeting others and mixing with them. The Bethnal Greener can do enough of that without joining anything. Sociability in such a setting needs no organization.

And according to Hoggart, the working man is far more of a clubman than is usually realized. In support of his claim he points out that there are today well over three thousand separate working men's clubs, with a total membership of more than two million. Membership costs ten shillings a year and control is vested in an elected committee. These clubs, independently controlled, but each affiliated to the Working Men's Club and Institute Union, are today the pub-cum-club for a very large number of working people.[1]

How, then, is this material to be interpreted? Firstly, the evidence cited so far suggests that a good deal of the energy that might go into formal associational life is absorbed by interaction within the kin-group in a traditional community. Secondly, there are people who have energy to spare over and above that required for the maintenance of kin-relationships. These will tend to join a formal voluntary association (at least once). Thirdly, the type of association they will join will tend to be one where there is no admixture of middle-class people, because middle-class people arouse all kinds of 'us'/'them' hostilities. They will tend to congregate in Darts Clubs and Produce Associations, pubs and clubs. These require relatively little organization or planning, both of which are activities which raise difficulties for the traditional working man.

There are traditional attitudes which prevent a man from being a 'leader' for any length of time. First and foremost there is the social and psychological pressure not to 'to stand out' or 'to put yourself forward' and to suspect the motives of those who do.[2] Secondly, leaders of groups are more likely to associate, by virtue of their role, with leaders of other groups, and are

---

[1] In connection with this, Mogey reminds me, in a private communication, that shop stewards are possibly the largest group of unpaid voluntary workers in this country today, and refers to an article by A.-Marsh in *Socialist Commentary*.

[2] See also pages 53 and 282.

therefore more likely to be in contact with middle-class groups or people.[1] In this way they are more open to the accusation of 'giving themselves airs' and thereby calling down upon themselves the sanctions of ridicule even if their own consciences are at peace in this respect. Since, in the traditional working-class community, solidarity is the great value, greater than leadership, association with others elsewhere is correctly perceived as weakening that solidarity, and disliked.

Some of those who might be 'joiners' are therefore deterred because they fear, with reason, that they will grow away from their primary groups if they interact too freely with those who do not belong to the community by birth and are often of a higher social class. Formally organized groups create especial difficulties because if a man is given an organizing role, 'leadership', 'responsibility', the stress is by so much increased; whereas, if he is not, this can be an alternative source of resentment. These considerations may explain Mogey's 'widespread lack of desire to be identified with a particular group, sometimes amounting almost to an inability to enter into any obligation which looks like a contract'.

Mogey believes this fear of commitment to be a sign of social insecurity, and so it is, though not of the kind he thinks. He associates it with the frequency with which he found people in ordinary conversation to manifest a belief in a hostile and dangerous world. This catches well the emotional tone of threat and unpredictability which interaction with 'them' in particular, and uncertainty in general, do create. Basic to the attitude is not superstition, however, but the fact that formal associations, and the demands they make, are the very opposite of the ideal of 'effortless sociability'. The fearfulness is therefore partly social: a dislike of being 'pushed around', and partly it is more intellectual: a doubt as to what one may be 'letting oneself in for', what one is 'supposed to do'.

The difficulties of communication between members of different social classes are worth investigating in a systematic way. This kind of social study is still in its infancy, but in connection with the problem of association in formal organization, at least

[1] See G. C. Homans, op. cit., chap. 8, especially the section on 'mutual dependence of sentiment and interaction'.

two points may be made. First, and perhaps most obviously, there is often a clash of norms when two cultures interact, and this clash is likely to be accompanied by ill-feeling, particularly when one culture imposes norms of behaviour on the other in the self-confident assurance that where the two differ, the other is wrong. This difficulty crops up in the most unexpected places. An American study discovered that not only did the (lower) working-class neurotics not get on with their psychiatrists, but the psychiatrists admitted to a dislike of these patients! The norms of the two sub-cultures were too different.[1]

Americans are more aware in these matters, partly because a continually renewed immigrant element does tend to make people more sophisticated about the barriers created by language. Another American study confirms and refines the point here under discussion. Bell, Vogel and Trieschman made a 'socio-cultural analysis of resistance of working-class fathers of children treated in a child-psychiatric clinic'.[2] These fathers, asked to attend for one afternoon, appeared genuinely puzzled at being thought concerned with their child's difficulties. They would point out that they worked hard and saw little of the child, that the mother could be more useful to the psychologists. They minimized the seriousness of the child's emotional disturbance and expressed the belief that it would soon be outgrown. Often they saw the symptoms as wilful misbehaviour. (It is easy to recognize a number of relevant traits here: the strict role-segregation of the sexes, the lack of interest in psychological matters, the tendency to concentrate on what is obvious, and so on.)

In considering the reasons for these attitudes, the authors arrive at some important general conclusions. They are struck, *inter alia*, by the difficulty working-class people have in believing that 'just talking will change anything'. Bernstein, whose observations on language difficulties were also considered in the previous chapter, analyses this problem in more detail.

The patient is placed in a situation where treatment depends

---

[1] A. B. Hollingshead and F. C. Redlich (1958), *Social Class and Mental Illness*, Wiley, New York; Chapman and Hall, London.

[2] N. Bell, A. Trieschman and E. Vogel (1961), 'A socio-cultural analysis of the resistances of working-class fathers', *Amer. J. Orthopsychiatry*, XXX.

essentially on the extent to which he can verbalize or be brought
to verbalize his particular relationships with the environment,
and eventually to understand and accept emotionally the implications of the pattern they form . . . This involves for the patient a
mode of communication and orientation which not only he has
never learned, but which has been positively discouraged by his
previous learning.

Bernstein makes it clear that he is referring here not to the
difficulty a patient may have in talking about such personal
matters as his sex-life, but in talking explicitly about anything
at all that he feels or wants. This experience is alien to him. 'To
the patient the situation is one of perplexity and bewilderment
—he is under pressure to give a response he has never learned
to make.'[1]

The higher social class is verbally the more agile and articulate, more capable of putting ideas easily into words and of
arguing convincingly. Since both cultures share an allegiance to
the value of rationality, there is a danger that the working man
feels he has been 'talked into something' and hence he is likely
to feel resentful at having been verbally bullied or beguiled.
This is one reason why he will tend to satisfy his need for an
associational life as far as possible in associations whose membership is drawn from his own class. It is as indicative of the com-
munication-difficulties between the two classes as any argument
can be, that the middle-class investigator tends not to consider
these 'teams' and 'clubs' convincing evidence of the existence of
associational life in the working classes.

What distinguishes these types of formal association from the
more middle-class type is that they are more compatible with
what we have called 'effortless sociability'. A member is likely
to hear of the next meeting in the course of everyday contacts
within his close-knit network, at home or at work. The notification is casual, the planning short-term, he may turn up or not
as he pleases, there are always others available if he is absent.

The more middle-class type of formal association presupposes
a more loose-knit network and requires more formal commitment. Then problems arise because future activities need to be

---

[1] Bernstein's theory is discussed in detail in the section on child rearing, for these
difficulties stem from experiences early in life. See pages 513-14.

planned farther ahead and notification has to be organized. At this point the other conclusions which Bell, Vogel and Trieschman arrived at may relevantly be mentioned. They point out that working people are less apt to organize their lives in terms of an orderly progression towards future goals. It does certainly seem as though a traditional group need not have such a long or such a highly-structured time-perspective as less traditional people. In very practical ways this makes formal associational life more difficult. To book a date in a diary for an appointment six weeks ahead is a middle-class act. To call a meeting for some future date then becomes an unreliable method of keeping an association in being, except if people know each other well enough, and see each other often enough, to pass reminders nearer the date in casual street encounters.[1]

The same authors also point out that working-class people are more inclined to take life as it comes, whereas middle-class culture tends to see problems as challenges. This problem-solving aspect of middle-class culture will be discussed at length in the appropriate chapter, but it is relevant here because middle-class people are much more apt to use formal organizations for the performance of particular tasks, for the solution of particular problems, for definite purposes. Because of this they cannot avoid planning a programme well in advance, to consider what the association should be doing this time next year and so on. Seeing life as an orderly progression towards goals, they are bound to want to plan towards them.

Planning common activities for the future involves making decisions now, arguing about alternatives, taking possibilities into account which are not now present. Here the theory of cognitive poverty in traditional communities encounters the theory of progressive individuation to which further reference will be made in the next chapter. In a traditional community there is little opportunity to exercise choice.

As the standard of living goes up, however, there is money to spare and time to spare and an increase in the awareness of opportunities. As people become accustomed to making use of the increased opportunities to choose for themselves, they begin to chafe at inconveniences which were in the past stoically

[1] See pages 141–2.

considered part of life itself. But the experience of choosing between alternatives is a relatively recent one and communal techniques for exercising such choices are not yet fully established. Formal associational life requires such techniques if highly individual members are to get on with one another. This contrast is neatly presented by Mrs. Stacey:

> Banbury today is a mixture of old and new and all its inhabitants are influenced by the old and the new. Its established practices and customs, its institutions and the values associated with them are being modified by men who practise new techniques and new forms of organization. This division between old and new is not one between Banburians and immigrants so much as between traditionalists and non-traditionalists. The former cling, so far as they can, to the old values based on personal face-to-face relationships, preferring the small organization to the large. For the latter the old ways are irrelevant. Non-traditionalists judge people as individuals, are not afraid of large-scale organizations and abstract ideas, and belong to groups which extend beyond Banbury.

The traditional working man lacks training in the sort of attitude which would enable him to confront large-scale organizations, abstract ideas or unfamiliar situations with self-confidence. The unfamiliar turns fearsome. The middle-class man seems to him more at home with these matters, and this does not ease the tension between the two groups.

> To come to terms with the world of 'Them' involves, in the end, [writes Hoggart] all kinds of political and social questions and leads, eventually, beyond politics and social philosophy to metaphysics. The question of how we face 'Them', whoever 'They' are, is, at last, a question of how we stand in relation to anything not visibly and intimately part of our local universe. Working-class people, with their roots so strongly in the homely and personal and local, and with little training in more general thinking, are even less likely [i.e. less likely than middle-class people, who, however, we shall see in a later chapter, are liable to other but equivalent ills] to bring the two worlds into focus. They are, if they think of it, ill at ease: this second and complex world cannot be easily dramatized, it is too vast, too much 'beyond them'.

Traditional Working-Class Life

The pivotal position of the Mum of an extended family militates against changes in tradition. Her function is in most respects conservative. Like any other leader, she is in charge of the external relations of the group. She mediates between 'them' and 'us'. By virtue of this position she can exert some control over the way in which the external world impinges on her family. She protects; what she disapproves she tries to keep out. There is a credit and a debit side to this.

On the credit side are the services rendered as mediator. It is she who has the long waits in public places, at the doctor's for 'a bottle', at the clinic with a child who has eye-trouble, at the municipal offices to see about an instalment on the electricity bill. She will speak for her daughter to the rent-collector.[1]

> 'When my mother was alive, she carried on my insurance policy for me. Now that she's dead, the collector still calls at her place every month. My sister Sarah took the place over when Mum died and she's gone on paying the collector for me. That's why I see her every fortnight—I call round to give her my insurance.'[2]

In a traditional society, in so far as women are responsible for such matters, the power of the oldest and most experienced woman of the family will be markedly enhanced. She may have to pay a price, however.

> Consciously or unconsciously, 'they' tend to treat the public from the working classes with a curt impersonality which verges on disrespect, and, at worst, with all the insolence of minor office, the brusqueness of the pettily uniformed . . . By all this, working-class women are easily made unhappy and [Hoggart continues in the same breath] so are more deferential than their menfolk towards small officials. A man is more likely to kick against it, and his kicking often takes the form of becoming really 'vulgar'. He is liable, if driven, to offer to 'knock 'is bloody block off if 'e doesn't cut out 'is bloody chelp'.

[1] In a similar way the men may 'speak to the guvnor' for jobs for their sons or other relations. Ten of a Bethnal Green sample of forty-five had the same occupations as their fathers—dockers, printers, or costermongers with a pitch.

[2] Sarah is obviously beginning to assume the role of Mum for this family.

This reaction is hardly likely to achieve the purpose for which the visit to the office was made, so the woman who swallows her hurt is clearly performing an important mediating function between the official and her family.[1]

The oldest woman is not only likely to be the most experienced in getting her own way in these circumstances; in mid-twentieth century she is also most likely to behave in a nineteenth-century traditional deferential manner which a younger generation would find exaggerated or humiliating and which the men, strengthened by their experience in their Trade Union, are no longer prepared to simulate. It may be noted in passing that, while the woman copes because someone has to, the whole system operates neatly to perpetuate a tradition of dependence on kin and independence of outsiders.

It seems a true social system: every component aspect maintains the total situation. The traditional respect with which Mum is regarded by her family, and the reliance placed upon her, may be ample compensation for her submission to the pin-pricks of minor officialdom. Tradition, respect, reliance, are terms which show on the debit side of the balance, however.

There is a debit side because Mum is not only the channel of much interaction between family and outside world, but also the gate-keeper, regulating the flow of influence and allowing to percolate through only what is in accordance with her own ideas.[2]

Hoggart is not unaware that the concentration of the mother's emotions and energies upon the family, and her position in it, may lead (as was in fact often reported by Dennis and his associates, and by Kerr) 'for those who are poorly gifted imaginatively or who have special trouble, to a turned-in-upon-itself world in which nothing that does not concern the family penetrates'.

She is apt to regard outside agencies with gingerly mistrust, not only because of the disagreeable experiences she has had of

[1] It is interesting that Hoggart takes it for granted, as it was also taken for granted in Ashton, that a woman turns her aggression inwards and a man outwards. It is a pity that there is no evidence at all on the way this sex-difference is acquired.

[2] See K. Lewin (1952), *Field Theory in Social Science*, chap. 8, for use of the concept 'gate-keeper' (Tavistock Publications, London).

'them' in her life, but because their advice may easily go against the traditions of which she, and the older woman generally, is the bearer. And so it happens that the younger generation experiences a conflict between home advice and institutional advice. Normally, as Mogey notes of the people of St. Ebbe's, 'children are brought up in the traditional way. The advice of the clinic is accepted only after a thorough testing to see if it agrees with local folklore.' Young and Willmott say the same thing rather more sympathetically, as is their wont.

It is natural that, with a new baby, a daughter should draw on the knowledge of her mother, who has been through it all before. When is she to stop work? What clothes is she to make? What should she eat and not eat?

'I take more notice of my Mum than I do of the Welfare. She's had eight, and we're alright. Experience speaks for itself, more or less, doesn't it? If you're living near your mother you don't really need that advice. You've got more confidence in your mother than you would have in the advice they give you. When I was in hospital, they taught me how to bath him. You're supposed to lay him out on your knees on a towel. But as soon as I got home Mum said: "Don't bother with doing it like that. Just put him in the water and wash him." Then they said that I ought to always bath him in the mornings, but Mum said: "You bath him in the evening. He'll sleep better that way." '[1]

Not unexpectedly, some grandmothers are reluctant to give up their traditional function as mentor and adviser, and this is probably responsible for the scarcely veiled hostility with which the advice of the midwife or health visitor is sometimes received. One maternal grandmother in our sample was determined to show her daughter that she knew better than the midwife. Mrs. Donovan [note the choice of an Irish pseudonym] was a woman of generous and imposing proportions, who from first to last dominated the interview; her daughter and son-in-law, a lorry-driver, lodged

---

[1] See also pages 549, 552 ff. and 569 where this attitude is contrasted with a more middle-class preoccupation with what the experts say. Not belonging to a close-knit network because more socially mobile, the middle-class mother is, for good or ill, less within reach of her mother's advice. Indeed, the pros and cons of a mother close-by are very evenly balanced. Mrs. Mann, whom we quoted on page 189, the same one who finally decided to move out of her mother's orbit and 'have a life of her own', said: 'Mum helped me when I was having the baby and I must say, she was very good. The trouble is, she still wants to help.'

with her, and were plainly well under her thumb. After the birth of the baby, we were told, the midwife said, before leaving them for the night, 'Now you are NOT to give that baby ANYTHING.' The baby cried; 'all that stuff she'd swallowed', Mrs. Donovan explained. She told her daughter that the other lodgers had to be considered, the baby couldn't cry all night, and she was going to give it some cinder-water.[1] Her daughter faint-heartedly protested, 'Oh, Mum, the midwife said . . .', but Mrs. Donovan was adamant. She got a cup of water, plunged into it a red-hot poker, strained the liquid and gave the baby two-and-a-half teaspoonsful of it. The baby vomited black mucus and slept all night. 'Haven't you ever heard of cinder-water?' Mrs. Donovan asked us with some scorn. 'Well, I'm surprised they don't teach you *that* at the University.' The interviewer asked, 'And what did the midwife say?' 'Huh,' said Mrs. Donovan, 'she never knew.'[2]

And this is how the school services for a physically delicate and nervously unstable child appear to his grandmother in St. Ebbe's, who had taken control, since her daughter (who lived in the same house) was 'not a motherly type'.

'I reared him and the doctor says I saved his life; when he had pneumonia I saw how ill he was but his mother didn't even notice.' Following more detail on the child's health, she said the school doctor wanted the mother to take him to a psychiatrist, but 'I think it's a cheek . . . When I went up to the school, I told the lady doctor so and the psychiatric worker who came here to see me, I said to her: "All this nonsense about giving a child paper to play with and matches so that he burns himself . . . and then comes home and sets fire to the house . . . just to see what he'll do; and asking questions about his home, what time he goes to bed, what he has to eat and why—you should ask me that and I'll tell you, and I'll tell you what he has to eat and why; . . . if you want to know why he's such a good boy it's because he's not allowed to do just what he likes at home and has to mind what I and his mother says. He's not allowed to do just as he likes, like the children in your clinic. It's as simple as that . . . There's nothing wrong with him. He's maybe a bit nervy but he'll grow out of it. I don't want you putting ideas in his head and making him ashamed of his home."'

[1] See also page 465.
[2] J. and E. Newson (1963), *Infant Care in an Urban Community*, Allen and Unwin, London.

Chapter Five

ASPECTS OF CHANGE IN
WORKING-CLASS LIFE[1]

IN this chapter some of the current changes in working-class life are analysed with particular reference to life on municipal housing estates. Although there are a number of studies of estates built before the war, attention will with one exception be confined to post-war ones, because in this period the move to better housing was accompanied by an improvement in the national standard of living. The one exception—a recent study of a Dagenham estate built in the twenties—will test the relationship between these two groups of determinants.[2]

Some of the people to whom reference is now to be made have come from areas discussed in the previous chapter. Young and Willmott interviewed a sample of people from Bethnal Green who had moved to Greenleigh. Barton has been the destination of a number of people from St. Ebbe's. Other information comes from a study made by Leo Kuper and his associates, of a new estate on the outskirts of Coventry, 'Braydon Road', and from a study of a Liverpool estate, by Mitchell and Lupton.[3] The latter two differ from the former in that the population is drawn from a greater variety of geographical regions.

The most recent information about newer ways of life comes

[1] For comparative material, see J. H. Nicholson (1961), *New Communities in Britain*, published by the National Council of Social Service.

[2] P. Willmott (1963), *The Evolution of a Community*, Routledge and Kegan Paul, London.

[3] L. Kuper *et al.* (1953), *Living in Towns*, Cresset Press, London. G. D. Mitchell and T. Lupton (1954), *Neighbourhood and Community*, University of Liverpool Social Research Series.

Aspects of Adult Life in England

from Zweig's *Worker in an Affluent Society*, published in 1961 and depending on interviews he conducted in 1958, much on the lines of his previous work. As before, his findings are not local but summarize what seem national trends. He warns us that the extent to which his data are representative of workers in general is difficult to assess. Firstly, he was concerned mainly with factory workers. Secondly, he was interviewing in large-scale, well-organized and well-conducted industries. Thirdly, the industries from which his sample of firms was drawn were on the whole prosperous and expanding industries, workers' rates of pay and earnings tending to be above average. (The industries concerned employ something like a million men—about one in fourteen of all adult male employees in the U.K.)

The Radby Report is again a source, this time in connection with households graded IV and V. These grades are simply farther along towards the other extreme of the same dimension which has the problem families at one end, followed by the traditional roughs, and with the standard-setting Grade IIIs in the middle. Grade V may be distinguished from Grade IV in that these households are even more ambitious for themselves and for their children, achieving higher standards of living from the point of view of home comforts and leisure-time activities, and striving more consciously to maintain the standards which they set themselves. The Grade Vs are more consciously 'on the rise'.

Some of these Radby people lived on new estates, but some did not: some of the roughest households lived in the new areas and some of the more ambitious in the old. Indeed, although our main concern will be with the period of adjustment immediately after migration to a new housing estate, the fact that changes take place at that time should not blind us to differences attributable in the main to other social and psychological sources. Housing estates are not to be thought of as the only places where changes take place. Rather, the argument will be that the break with tradition which a geographical move entails allows other social forces to make a relatively more forcible impact. The estates are convenient areas for the study of social change because the migrant's reaction to the impact of new situations is more emphatic.

Changes in Working-Class Life

The chapter is therefore not arranged in terms of 'before' and 'after' the move. Instead, alternative reactions to a number of changes in situation are discussed *seriatim*. These changes all seem to tend in the same general direction, though different aspects may come first in different cases, to be followed after a shorter or longer interval by other changes which are related to the earlier either psychologically or culturally. Since they are related, and since they will inevitably lose their sharp conceptual outlines in the discussion which follows, they are listed schematically here:

from a close-knit family network to a more loose-knit one;
from a community-centred existence to greater individuation;
from a community-centred existence to a more home-centred one;
from a community-centred existence to greater participation in associational life;
from a segregated conjugal role-relationship to greater partnership in marriage;
from traditional occupational choice to social mobility;
from status-assent to status-dissent;
from ascriptive values to achievement values;
from financial stringency to greater affluence;
from an emphasis on the breadwinner to emphasis on the child.[1]

The present chapter will be mainly concerned with people who experienced these changes in their own lives. The generation that has known no other way of life is only just reaching maturity. Little is as yet known of the newly-evolving stable patterns of living, either on the estates or elsewhere. At the end of the next chapter, however, a discussion of the 'middle-class manual worker' examines some aspects of the lives of those most deeply affected by the new trends, whose initial stages are the subject-matter of the present chapter.

The Dagenham study requires a few more introductory remarks. It was published too late to affect the structure of this chapter. Our main contention will be that it illustrates the thesis that rehousing creates a period of uncertainty and dis-

[1] Mogey adds a comment of his own: the problem moves from 'poverty' to 'privacy' and 'loneliness'; see also *Recherches sur la Famille*, III, 1958, Cologne, German Nat. UNESCO Commission.

ruption, which does not lead to a very great change in patterns of living, however, unless other social changes are taking place at the same time. These other changes—conscription and war, affluence and mass-media—came after the period of adjustment had come to an end in Dagenham. Dagenham therefore tends to resemble the old areas more than the new in some respects.[1]

ECONOMIC CHANGES

The move from an old area to a new one makes its impact on many aspects of family life. Economically, there is often a sudden, if temporary, decrease in real wages. The man has to travel farther to his work and spends more on fares. He is less likely to come home for his midday meal, and, unless he takes a packed lunch or eats at a relative's home in his area of origin, he has to pay for it in a café or canteen. The rent of the house takes a larger proportion of his income than was previously the case—it may be as much as double the amount he had to pay before. Moreover, it is generally felt that one has to 'live up to' such a nice new house, so that on top of the expense of the move there may be the expense of new furniture, often furniture of a kind not previously considered necessary. And if there is a financial crisis, those who would normally help out are more inaccessible.

To meet the higher costs at Greenleigh, people economized on other things on which they used to spend money. Many of the husbands gave up drinking, a change made all the easier by the absence or inaccessibility of pubs. 'I was a very heavy drinker before,' said Mr. Minton. 'I'm a teetotaller now.' The move away from the influence of the traditional routines of life in the old area helps to make this change. In 1952, Zweig, chatting to working-class men about their saving-habits, heard one say, 'If I come out at 5 p.m. I can't stay at home the whole evening and when I go out it costs money.' Another: 'I only started to save when I was on the shift from 3 to 11 p.m. or on

---

[1] Brief footnotes refer to pages in the Dagenham study where material similar to that discussed in the main text is to be found. These footnotes read 'Dagenham, page 123' where the evidence is in support of the main text and 'But Dagenham, page 123' where the evidence is in contrast.

a night shift.'[1] On the estates there is often nowhere to go out to again, the other men on the estates are not lifelong friends and the home is more attractive. The home and family become more important emotionally and in some ways cost less money for their maintenance than the traditional male group does. According to Zweig, the ethos of saving is undergoing a very deep transformation. In the late fifties,

> the phrase 'I don't believe in saving' or 'You may be dead to-morrow' is rarely heard; instead one can hear 'I look after the money all right', or 'I got so used to saving that it became second nature', or 'We both save and each of our children has a savings book'. An elderly man, asked whether he had a nest egg, referred to social change in such terms: 'Unfortunately not. The big money came only after the war. There was nothing worthwhile saving previously; you might as well enjoy life.' Those who do not save, use more frequently the phrase: 'Unfortunately I can't save anything.' Savings conceived as deferred payment were previously the rule; now savings conceived as investment, or for old age, or for a rainy day are more frequently admitted. Life insurances are also more frequent and 'good nest eggs' are not such a great rarity as they used to be.

When farsightedness is likely to be rewarded, a number of people respond appropriately. In Radby, in the Grade IV and V households, expenditure and saving are carefully planned in accordance with chosen standards and criteria. People ask themselves: 'Can I afford to go out for the evening, or will it mean a delay in purchasing a new coat for the children, or a washing machine for the wife?' One Grade IV mother does not draw her family-allowance weekly but lets it accumulate until there is sufficient money to purchase new clothes for the children. The Radby Report considers this sort of thing typical of this group, adding that the delayed earning caused by letting a child go to a Grammar School is not here a source of discontent. These attitudes must not be too glibly related to affluence. Having regard to the fact that few of the wives are employed (at any rate full-time) and also that fewer members of the household other than the chief men are employed full time, the authors count it fair to say that the income of these IV and

[1] Dagenham, page 87.

V households is less—often considerably less—than that of households in the lower grades.

As is suggested by all this, many of the changes in consumption-pattern—either forced on the migrant or due to a change in preference—are in the direction of greater respectability. Cyril Smith has an impressive passage on the change in expenditure currently taking place. He does not like the change, but that is a matter of opinion. (It is also worth noting that he is contrasting two ways of life in one geographical area. This serves as a reminder that changes of behaviour may occur independently of geographical mobility, though the latter may accelerate the process and intensify its effects.)

> The cultural gap between succeeding generations is often very great. When the old people die, and their possessions are to be shared among the children, these often do not want them: they are out of date. As opportunities change, so do ideas. Now more than ever before we have the ideal of the individual household—the family—supplanting the notion of wider responsibilities. The family must remain self-supporting and independent of all other households. It must maintain its reputation of being able to look after its own affairs. Trouble is not a thing to be shared with other people, it must be sorted out with the resources of the family. Other families are expected to do the same—'We look after our own'. This trend in family life is obviously connected to the improved standards of living of working people and the urge toward respectability that has gone with them . . . Respectable working people tend to be utilitarian. They are conscious of the limitations of their incomes and they spend their money wisely by taking care over what they buy.[1]

Smith remarks that respectable families do not splash at weddings or funerals. They don't buy the appropriate white or black: it is not sensible for later. Yet, he continues, these are the rituals which keep people together, something in common from which to derive their loyalties. The neighbourly tie is weakening as the family tie becomes stronger. The common attitude is: 'We're all right, Jacksons.'

Similarly, in the Radby Grade IV and V households 'it is recognized that, in the matter of expenditure, choices have to

---

[1] See also page 195.

be made—and the choice is made in favour of the home first and foremost'.

These views are confirmed and expanded by Young and Willmott:

> The first essential is money for material possessions. When people move to Greenleigh, the standard of life, measured by the quality of housing, is at once raised. They attempt to bring the level in other respects up to the same standards. Furniture and carpets have to be bought.

With the higher standard goes a change in taste and style of furnishing. Moreover, the house is only a beginning (Young and Willmott continue). A nice house and shabby clothes, a neat garden and an old box of a pram, do not go together. 'My sister gave me a beautiful pram,' said Mrs. Berry. 'Because I was going to such a beautiful house.' Other things go with the changed way of life. In the early fifties the figures for residential subscribers for telephones were 13 per thousand in Bethnal Green, 88 per thousand in Greenleigh. Television-sets were 32 per thousand in Bethnal Green, 65 per thousand in Greenleigh.[1]

The children are also affected by the new pattern of expenditure. Toys are more lavish on the estate and require more care, imagination or activity: Barton children had dolls' houses, radiograms with records, tools for making elaborate models, rocking horses, dogs, cats, goldfish. In St. Ebbe's the children had generally fewer and less elaborate toys.

CHANGES IN THE LEVEL OF INTERACTION AND IN NETWORK-CONNECTEDNESS

The families described in previous chapters were generally of the kind that belonged to a close-knit network. When such families move, the network-connections become fewer and more tenuous. To some this is a desirable state; others fear it.

In a Birmingham study of the housing-satisfaction of municipally re-housed tenants, Mrs. Norris asked how the new situation compared with the old. This was an open question and was

---

[1] Over one-tenth of the Dagenham sample of households had a telephone, over four-fifths a television-set. This was in 1958-9.

answered by over half the informants not in terms of their new dwelling but in terms of their new social situation. Obviously, then, social factors loom large in the minds of the new residents. Of those who answered her question in social terms, over half spoke approvingly, indeed with longing, of the old central district: its friendliness, the help given by neighbours, the community-feeling and so on. But the rest, a large minority, thought back with disapproval and remembered quarrels, too much mixing, too much popping in and out.

This might be a reaction governed by individual differences, but the importance of past social experience is illustrated by a related finding. A much smaller proportion of those who had lived most of their lives in the central area (with presumably more traditional and close-knit relationships) were glad to think they would be leaving it, as compared with those who had not lived mainly in the central area.[1]

Coming from a close-knit network of the Bethnal Green type, the young housewife may at first feel overwhelmingly lonely. She has been accustomed to a constant cheerful bustle. Now friends, relatives, old neighbours, all live far away. It is too quiet. The streets seem deserted. There is nothing to do, nothing to see, nothing going on. She has to spend her day alone, 'looking at herself', as they say.

> The husband was congratulating himself on having a house, a garden, a bathroom, a T.V. ('the tellie is a bit of a friend down here') when his wife broke in to say—'It's all right for you. What about the time I have to spend here on my own?' This difference in the lives of husband and wife [write Young and Willmott] may cause sharp contention, especially in the early years. 'When we first came,' said Mrs. Haddon, 'I'd just had the baby and it was all a misery, not knowing anyone. I sat on the stairs and cried my eyes out. For the first two years we were swaying whether to go back. I wanted to and my husband didn't. We used to have

---

[1] J. Norris (1960), *Human Aspects of Redevelopment*, published by the Midlands New Towns Society. Age and willingness to change are also related factors. Mrs. Norris found that the proportion of those who had been glad to leave decreased as the informants' ages increased. Over three-quarters of the under-fifties had been either 'quite glad' or 'very glad' to leave. Similarly, Mogey found three times as many older married couples among those who had returned to Central Oxford after a spell at Barton.

terrible arguments about it. I used to say: It's all right for you. I have to sit here all day. You do get a break.'

Most deeply-felt of all is the reduction of interaction with other members of the extended family. Instead of dropping in on a mother or a sister, visiting becomes an activity that has to be planned. But where the distances are not too large, a new pattern of family relations may spring up. Mrs. Soper, one of Young and Willmott's Bethnal Green informants, took her two children every fortnight 'on the underground to my sister at Hainault. We have a nice afternoon there. It's quite a little outing.' In this way, the migrants become the destination for little trips from the old area. In the summer, the new house may receive city-relatives as a sort of holiday-resort. A new cheerfulness and festivity may thus come to be associated with a visit to the migrants, though often a greater formality as well, because it needs more 'arranging'.[1]

There may also be more permanent migration. Relatives may come to live on an estate after the first wave of re-housing has subsided. Of the Greenleigh sample, one-third had relatives on the estate by 1955. Mitchell and Lupton note a similar second wave in Liverpool.

In the second generation the situation changes again, of course. After the move, children are born, grow up and marry on the estate. Willmott compared the proximity of the nearest married child in Bethnal Green and in Dagenham. (General sample—people with at least one married child.)

Residence of married child	Dagenham	Bethnal Green
Same dwelling	16	23
Within five minutes' walk	15	27
Elsewhere in same district	14	9
Not in same district	55	41

The availability of housing for the second generation is obviously an important factor here, and there is pressure now on the housing authorities to keep sites available to allow the children of those living on the estate to find a house nearby after

[1] Cf. pages 213 and 333.

marriage. The good effects of such a policy are obvious, but the total balance of advantages and disadvantages has not been cast. It would slow up changes normally accelerated by mobility.

Whereas some migrants suffer badly from loneliness, there is evidence that others, or perhaps the same people in a different mood, are grateful for at least some reduction in the level of interaction. Mogey, for instance, finds that more people in St. Ebbe's—which everybody spoke of as a very 'friendly place'— spoke rejectingly of their neighbours, whereas in Barton the majority spoke of their neighbours with approval. Among the many reasons for this difference in attitude, we may surely include the fact that people on a new estate live less on top of one another.

> Mrs. Painswick of Greenleigh was favourably impressed by the seclusion her new surroundings afforded. She had been more averse to the quarrels among the rowdy, shouty Bethnal Greeners than appreciative of the mateyness to which the quarrels were the counter-part. She found the less intense life of Greenleigh a pleasant contrast. 'In London people had more squabbles. We haven't seen neighbours out here having words.'

From Kuper's account one finds that people may actually be discomfited, not by the secluded life, but by the lack of seclusion.

> In Braydon Road, they complain: 'When one goes out the back way, one is immediately right on top of one's neighbours'; 'As soon as she comes out of her door, we are face-to-face'; 'Being so near, people can see the sort of thing you have and want to borrow them'; 'We are putting up a partition. Every time you open the back door, you see your neighbour. Children quarrel, and with the unbroken view, it makes it difficult to keep the peace.'

Because of the large front windows, there is a general feeling of being constantly observed, both within the house and on the street:

> 'There is no privacy . . . You look across at the houses there —they must feel as though you are looking at them. You look out of the bedroom windows into their bedrooms . . . You turn

228

the corner coming home and everyone's eyes are on you in the cul-de-sac. For the amount you pay, it's degrading.'[1]

Such reactions are partly the result of the way the houses were built and disposed along the road, partly due to the high social standing of Braydon Road tenants, and partly accounted for by the fact that this was geographically a very mixed group, which would make mutual adjustment more difficult. (Only a third were native Coventrians.)

When relatives are no longer next-door, or in the next street, it becomes more difficult to rely on them for the kind of services described in the previous chapter. In Bethnal Green, people with relatives close-by seldom go short of money in a crisis.

'You notice the difference out here,' said Mr. Tonks of Green-leigh, 'when you fall on hard times. Up there you were where you were born. You could always get helped by your family. You didn't even have to ask them—they'd help you out of trouble straightaway. Down here you've had it.'

Then there is the care of the sick, normally undertaken by some relative who does not go out to work, often by Mum. After a move, especially in cases of illness or a confinement, many problems are created for the young family, and at such times the loneliness is deeply felt.

More generally also, loneliness in the early stages is created by a cumulative impact, as the families become increasingly aware of the many quite simple services which are no longer forthcoming and which had been normal in a community in which everybody knows everyone else's needs: baby-minding, fetching children from school, shopping for someone else, advising whether a skirt hangs straight when dress-making. In the old area kin helped, or, in their absence, neighbours. On the estate there are no relatives, at least to begin with, and neighbours do not know each other or each other's needs: 'When the baby was ill, not a soul knocked at my door to get me an errand.' The Dagenham study suggests that this period does not last, both because more kin come to live near and because neighbours eventually do re-establish this kind of relationship.

[1] But later the cul-de-sacs, 'banjos' they were called in Dagenham, were very friendly easy places to live in.

With a much more loose-knit network, information spreads with much greater difficulty. Not only do people not meet on the streets in casual informal fashion, but other facilities for the unobtrusive spread of necessary information are also absent.

It was all very much easier in the older, traditional communities, with their regular meeting-places—shops, clubs, pubs —where neighbours could meet and exchange information. None of these places where all kinds of people may gather and get to know one another, or where people come on legitimate errands and cannot avoid meeting their fellow-men, was present on the Barton estate.

> In Bethnal Green, your pub and your shop is a 'local'. There people meet their neighbours. At Greenleigh they are put off by the distances. They don't go to the pub because it may take twenty minutes to walk instead of one minute. They don't go more often than they must to the shops and these are now grouped together into specialized centres and often of the large clean, chromium, self-service type, instead of being scattered in converted houses through the ordinary streets. And when they do get there, the people are gathered from the corners of the estate instead of being neighbours with whom they already have a point of contact.[1]

Indeed, help may be more easily forthcoming from the older area with its established information-exchange. A couple living at Barton used to go back to a pub in St. Ebbe's on Saturday nights. When they stayed away, the pub sent a delegation to see what was wrong. They found that the man had been put on short time and was in financial straits. They passed the hat round at the pub and sent him money to help out.

In this connection a point may be made, not mentioned by the research workers in this field, but surely valid. In a close-knit network people are not only accustomed to get help, but also to give it. There must be some damage to self-esteem when the opportunity to perform simple services for others is no longer available. Such occasions then have to be re-invented, this time in connection with a non-kin network, and this may prove too difficult a step to make without help and encouragement.

[1] Dagenham, pages 88–9.

Changes in Working-Class Life

Again, this matter may adjust itself in the second generation. The longer people lived in Dagenham, the more they knew of those they met outside the house.

'When I come along from the shops,' said Mrs. Mitchell, 'everybody sort of stops and has a chat because they've known me since I was a little girl.' 'We know all the people in this turning,' said Mr. Gale. 'They're mostly old neighbours.' Mrs. Rank explained, 'You've got a lot of the same neighbours you've had all along. People's children have grown up and got married. The parents have lived down here for a long time and you've seen them right through it all.'

Meanwhile, on the newer estate, mothers do travel out to help their daughters in emergencies whenever they can. In addition, the husbands help more than was customary in the old area, and to a certain extent neighbours help. As may be expected from the argument in the previous chapter, the attitude of neighbours seems to be that they will help in a real emergency, when relatives are unable to do so and no formal agency exists to cope. They regard themselves as last-resort helpers. An account from Braydon Road shows how a neighbour's helpfulness is in the first place directed to advice on how to avoid troubling your neighbours unnecessarily.

The Hanleys, a migrant family, were worried about arrangements before the birth of their fourth child. A Coventry woman had advised Mr. Hanley to save up hard and take a fortnight off... Yet when the time came, the neighbours did in fact help: one with the family washing, another with the shopping, and the Coventry woman did the cooking.

The general effect of all these changes tends to make the families more dependent on the formal associations which exist to enable people to cope in the absence of traditional kin-and community-ties: the savings bank, the hospital, the home-help, the hire-purchase system, the Wives' Club, the Elks. Illustrations of this point will be made later in the chapter; a more theoretical issue must be introduced here.

In the traditional close-knit network of the old communities, everybody knew about everyone else, and by virtue of this knowledge could react swiftly to bring back to the traditional way any member who had deliberately experimented or unconsciously strayed. In this way, traditional ways of behaviour are maintained. On the new estates, the social pressure exerted by the close-knit network is removed. (This partly accounts for the feeling of loneliness and isolation many migrants experienced.) When there is less interaction, there is more opportunity for experiment, and we shall see that in fact there is a good deal of experimentation on the estates, both with new forms of behaviour and with new norms.

Before considering the new norms emerging from such ventures, we may consider those changes which are forced upon the migrant more or less directly by the change in his circumstances.

CHANGES IN NORMS

All geographical changes are accompanied by social and psychological changes. A new inhabitant finds that he lives nearer a church—or near a more active church—or nearer an ante-natal clinic than before. If the related activities were previously marginal to him, he may now use them more readily. He is in this way subject to new influences. Other facilities will be somewhat farther away and he may now give them up, their attraction not being sufficiently strong to compensate for the extra trouble that would be required to continue them. So, at St. Ebbe's, adolescents who joined a formal organization would go to a youth club; in Barton, they would join a Sunday school. The difference is a reflection of the different opportunities in the two districts.

The new house itself may require a re-adjustment of normal habits. A woman on a new estate told Zweig's wife how the old kitchen was gradually losing its appeal as the centre of the family. 'In the other house the front room was never used except for Christmas. If I lit a fire in the front room we always seemed to get back into the kitchen. I suppose we were used to it. Now it's different.' Zweig adds that 'of course the T.V. has also contributed to this, and moves to new housing-estates break some of the old habits', and concludes: 'One can say that the kitchen mentality is gradually being replaced by the living-room mentality.'

In St. Ebbe's, similarly, Mogey never observed any uncertainty about the purpose of a particular room. In Barton, some of the non-traditional houses set just this problem.

The Barton houses were carefully matched to the 'need' of the family. There were temporary bungalows with a square kitchen large enough to take a dining table, and a living room as well. These bungalows, apart from occasional families who took all their meals in the kitchen, were used as the architect intended. Then there were two types of semi-detached dwelling, each with three bedrooms. The principal difference lay in the design of the living room. In one this room was large and L-shaped; in the other there is a small dining-room separate from the living room. Both had the modern narrow corridor-kitchen. The architect's intention was clear; the kitchen was meant for preparing and cooking meals, the dining space—whether separate or part of another room—was to be used for eating, and the living room for leisure-time activities. This functional separation accorded ill with the habits of the people, and many households were found preparing, cooking and eating their meals in the narrow corridor-kitchen and making other changes accordingly. Some of the more enterprising husbands in Barton erected partitions to create a parlour type space in houses where these were not provided. But they felt dubious about it. The partitions were contrary to the agreement of tenancy, and a few timorous families took them down every week before the rent-collector called.

This again may be a transition phenomenon. In Dagenham redecorating and rebuilding seems almost the major leisure-time activity of the residents.

In adjusting to the novelties of his situation, the migrant discovers something of the extent to which he has in the past relied on the tradition of his group, especially if he was a member of a close-knit network. When many of the people one knows interact also with each other, the members of the network tend not only to reach consensus on norms, and to exercise consistent social pressure on each other, but also to protect each other from a full impact of new ideas and practices. With a decrease in the level of interaction—which may itself be experienced as painful—a man is correspondingly more exposed to other pressures. In this transitional state of uncertainty, with new goals perceptible and old goals inaccessible or accessible only by new paths, a man may find his sense of direction impaired. He will find it difficult to envisage the consequences of his actions at all clearly. Psychologically he resembles a man who has lost his way. He will view each step he takes with ambivalence, since he cannot tell for certain whether it is bringing him nearer to his goal or whether he is unintentionally moving away from it.

He must learn to become sensitive to the reactions of his new neighbours. This may induce him to become more 'other-directed' than he was. In due course he learns that, in his new neighbourhood, evening classes are generally held to be enjoyable and confer prestige, or that they are not and do not. He learns that here it matters—or does not matter—if his wife does the washing on Sundays. He may have to learn the locally proper overtures to friendship, to borrowing, to refusing to lend. He has to learn the finer shades of difference in behaviour which afford others the cues according to which they regulate their own conduct. He has to learn what are the socially important role-discriminations here and what are the appropriate actions that go with them. He has to review behaviour he had taken for granted since childhood. It is not surprising that Mr. Adams of Greenleigh complained: 'You're English, but you feel like a foreigner here. I don't know why. Up there you've lived for years and you knew how to deal with people there. People here are different.'

To the outside observer, a man in this kind of situation may seem to go to extremes, either acting and interacting with a total lack of discrimination and crashing through the conventions he does not perceive, or cutting himself off from normal and legitimate interaction for fear of making a mistake.[1] He may become either a 'rough'—unable to discriminate finely in his new social situation (and this is presumably related to the training in discrimination, reasoning and reflection he has experienced previous to his move)—in which case no 'respectable' will have anything to do with him; or he may become a rigid, isolated respectable, like the man who said to Mogey:

---

[1] This point is developed on pages 253-6 of the present chapter. For the general characteristics of people in this kind of uncertainty see K. Lewin (1952), *Field Theory in Social Science*, Tavistock Publications, London.

Changes in Working-Class Life

'You get to know your neighbour on either side, but you don't get much further. I did pass the neighbour of next-door but one and *gave him the opportunity to greet me,* but nothing happened.'[1]

The problem of moving into and adjusting to a strange neighbourhood is aggravated in the case of moving to a new estate, because all the migrants are in the same case. As Young and Willmott say, it would not matter quite so much if they had moved into an established community. The place would then have already been criss-crossed with ties of kinship and friendship, and one new friend would have been an introduction to several. But Greenleigh was built in the late forties on ground that had been open fields before, and Barton estate was begun when fifty-four houses were added to a small hamlet of six or eight cottages clustering round two public houses.

On a new estate, most people are new arrivals. There is no established set of norms or relationships for any of them to perceive: 'Barton estate is in a state of flux—lacking norms of its own it can have no cohesion.' In this situation, the new inhabitant has not just to learn what is proper behaviour, he has to *create* proper behaviour, new standards, a new way of life. There may be the additional difficulty that he has not yet realized that a new way of life is to be created.[2]

Migrants, to the United States or to housing estates, always take part of their home-land with them, our informants like everyone else. They take with them the standards of Bethnal Green . . . Unfortunately, not everyone else comes from Bethnal Green. No doubt if they did, they might get on much better than they do;

---

[1] Gorer quotes a woman from Grantham: 'They are waiting for me to speak and be friendly, but I am waiting for them to speak and break the ice.'

[2] 'The newcomer in an established neighbourhood always runs the risk of attracting other people's friends or of finding a social life which has no spare places. The first few months are critical because this is the period of exploration during which there is a chance of selecting friends and deciding at which level to engage them. It is also a testing time when the established residents are likely to make their overtures and to decide whether to become involved. It seems likely that the northerners in Sonniton Street (Banbury), because of their different concept of neighbouring, failed during this critical period. At whatever point the failure comes, it may be said with a fair degree of certainty that working-class families from the north of England or from Scotland are very unlikely to settle on intimate terms as neighbours to Banburians.' M. Stacey (1960), *Tradition and Change,* Oxford University Press. For further discussion, see pages 252–4 and 351.

many of them would have known each other before, and they would have had at least a background in common. But as Mr. Abbot says: 'You've not grown up with them. They come from different neighbourhoods. They're different sorts of people and they don't mix.'

It is with these 'different' people that he has to co-operate to create a new community.

In the old areas there must have been strains due to undesired interaction, but because people had lived there a long time, conventions (differing, of course, from place to place) had developed to reduce the strains.[1] On a new estate there are fewer commonly accepted conventions and the differences in expectation are only corrected through bitter experience. In Braydon Road, the complaints about unfriendliness can almost be reduced to aggrieved statements about other people's normal practices.

> 'Most people keep you on the doorstep. In Lancashire, the clubmen just lift the latch and walk in, and stop and talk; here they're kept on the doorstep.'
> 'In Wales every front door was open; you'd just walk up to the door and go in. In Coventry they have their front doors shut.'
> 'In Scotland people were in and out all the time. People are neighbourly enough here, but they don't come into each other's houses.'
> When people have been used to a high standard of friendliness [write Young and Willmott], they will be all the more censorious about other tenants of the County Council. They are harsh in their comment, when someone arriving from a less settled district, or from another and even newer housing estate, might be accustomed to the stand-offishness and, by his canons, even impressed by the good behaviour of the same neighbours.

Because no conventions are generally established, everyone worries about the proper type and proper amount of inter-action: of friendliness between neighbours, of visiting, of

[1] As in Dagenham, see chap. VII.

borrowing and lending.[1] It is for these that new norms have to be created. The Braydon Road study is particularly useful in this connection because it directs attention to the problems of transition: a stage at which the old norms are no longer practised but still verbally acknowledged.

Braydon Road inhabitants 'don't believe in' visiting, popping in and out, borrowing or lending, as the case may be. These norms are stated in firm and absolute terms: 'My mother laid down the rule—never borrow, then you'll never be under obligation to anybody.' Borrowing is generally felt to be a departure from the ideal of the independent and self-reliant household. The general standard of the group is disapproval. But even when they expressed such disapproval, they often said in other sections of the interview that they themselves borrowed and lent. Practice and precept are no longer in concord.

This conflict between the proper and actual behaviour is resolved in various way, as one would expect when there is no single standard to which all must conform and conformity to which is generally rewarded.[2]

One compromise was reached by Mrs. Hatfield. Talking of her friendship with Mrs. Jones, in one section of the interview, she said: 'I go to Mrs. Jones a lot. As a matter of fact, I've borrowed her iron.' However, when interviewed on her feelings about borrowing and lending, she said, 'I don't mind lending, but I hate to borrow myself. I'd much rather do without.' Then she remembers: 'Of course, with the iron, it was absolutely hopeless with me.' Mrs. Hatfield tried to reconcile her replies; occasionally informants left conflicting responses, without any effort at explanation, as if they were quite unaware of the contradiction. Only one informant faced her deviation from the ideal: 'I don't believe in it, but, of course, I do it.'

[1] Sociologists have occasionally expressed doubts about the value of studying these phenomena but it is not difficult to put up a defence if one is interested in community-life at all. One assumes that the typical forms of interaction in a community are, like other social relationships, legitimated by norms concerning the right and proper relations which ought to obtain. One discovers who interacts with whom in order to infer from this the norms of conduct so valued in this social region that people choose their social contacts accordingly. The discussion on status-assent and dissent, roughs and respectables, illustrates this procedure.

[2] Festinger would call this a cognitive dissonance (*A Theory of Cognitive Dissonance*, Tavistock Publications, London, 1957).

Aspects of Adult Life in England

At this point an additional pair of concepts may be introduced: status-assent and status-dissent. At their most general, these concepts belong primarily to psychology, rather than to sociology; they describe attitudes of mind. Being states of mind they may of course be found, *mutatis mutandis*, in any social stratum, but Mogey, who evolved the concepts, uses them for his purpose with reference to the working class only, where the status-assenters are clearly thought of as belonging to traditional communities.[1] Mogey himself uses some sociological as well as psychological criteria in defining the two concepts more closely; this somewhat confuses the conceptual level at which they are to be used; he also ties them too closely to a particular social stratum. However, their basic meaning is quite clear.

Characteristic of [working-class] status-assenters are such remarks as 'I'm working class myself. You can only have a few bosses and then there's the rest.' 'I like this area. It's central and I know a lot of people. I never like to go away for a holiday. It's alright to go away for a day. Then you know you can come back again at night. I hope there will never be a change to a housing estate. I dread the thought of that.'

If we call people who feel and speak in this way about their position, or status, in society, the status-assenting people, we shall be able to recognize an important division within those who are usually referred to collectively as the working classes.[2]

Zweig must have had a similar distinction in mind when he wrote, in *The Worker in an Affluent Society*:

The working classes may be divided into three groups, numerically not very far apart. One group tries to acquire property; the second does not think about house property at all as it is beyond its possibilities and its ken; the third group rejects the acquisition

---

[1] Mrs. Stacey (1960) does not confuse the issue in this way. On 'traditionalists' and 'non-traditionalists' see e.g. pages 18–19, 158 ff., 180–1 in *Tradition and Change*, and pages 306, 307 and 309 in the present book.

[2] Dagenham has its quota of status-assenters. 'To tell you the truth, I hope my husband doesn't win the football pools, because if he did I suppose we'd have to buy a house and move away. I wouldn't like that. I said to him the other day, I said, "I'm settled here, I'm contented, I've got good neighbours. I don't ever want to go away from here."'

of house property as downright undesirable and even pernicious for the working man. People in this last group would often say: 'A house of your own is like a millstone round your neck', or 'I wouldn't touch it, it's only worry', or 'They want to catch you in that way'.

The latter two groups might be called status-assenting, the first group status-dissenting. Zweig notes that the general trend is toward a desire for property; in other words, working-class status-dissent is on the increase.

House-ownership and the attitude towards ownership of property is one important and easily observed index of working-class assent or dissent.[1] The Radby sample shows that there is a relationship between house-ownership and the general pattern of living.

	Grade I	Grade II	Grade III	Grade IV	Grade V
rented	24 in 24	38 in 40	60 in 80	21 in 35	3 in 16
per cent	100	95	75	60	18

(The total in each case is the total number for whom information was available. The remainder in each grade either lived in their own house or were buying.)

Once again Zweig brings further support.

> In the affluent society of 1958, possessions often went in clusters: some families had most of the items, others had very few. The highest standard of home equipment was to be found among the house owners, the lowest among the privately rented houses. The differences were most marked where property was concerned which does make life easier: washing-machines, refrigerators, cars, rather than T.V., radiograms, pianos.

The improvement of housing conditions in the last decade is considered by Zweig to have been one of the most potent factors in the transformation of the working man's way of life. 'A house', argue Young and Willmott to the same effect, 'is the bearer of status in any society—it most certainly is in a country

---

[1] In Dagenham many of the second generation had to move because of the local housing shortage. Willmott followed up sixteen of these—a very small number whose statistical significance is further reduced by the distinction between voluntary and reluctant leavers. The former are more likely to be status-dissenters, and more of these owned the houses they had moved into, more of the reluctant leavers rented theirs.

where a semi-detached suburban house with a garden has become the signal mark of the middle classes.' And this is where the ways of assenters and dissenters diverge.[1]

Mogey's summary description of working-class status-assenters has a familiar ring; they are traditional.

> They are less vocal; they accept the habits, standards, word usages and values typical of their area and their street; they talk little about problems of class conflict, about trade unions, work or any other general topic. They are interested in specific people, in the details of daily living, and they make no general observations other than clichés or headlines from recent papers. They are not worried about the future, they make a few plans for their children.

Their strength lies in kin-solidarity. Status-assenters tend to live in a close-knit, somewhat isolated community, beyond which they have no real understanding or interest, and within which they are reasonably well content. They put up with things. For instance, though most of the stock of condemned houses in the city was located in St. Ebbe's, three-quarters of the sample found something to praise about their house there, while only a quarter were consistently critical.

Status-assenters will find it difficult to adjust to the new requirements and opportunities of a housing-estate. They are not only found in Barton. Mr. Wild of Greenleigh complained: 'They're all Londoners here, but they get highbrow when they get here. They're not so friendly. Coming from a turning like the one where we lived, we knew everyone. We were bred and born among them, like one big family, we were. We knew all their troubles and everything. Here they are all total strangers to each other and so they are wary of each other. It's a question of time, I suppose.' After four years at Greenleigh, he still expected the old pattern eventually to reproduce itself in these new surroundings.

Others, however, adjust more happily and take part in creating a new pattern. For these, the general flux of ideas and the temporary lack of informal social controls offers an opportunity. These are the ones Mogey calls status-dissenting. They show

---

[1] But only where other factors reinforce the divergence. In Dagenham the status-assenters were equally busily engaged in improving their homes.

signs of an aspiration to move higher in the world, occasionally recognizing that though this is not possible for them, their children can do so. They are very conscious of the difference between themselves—the nice people—and others, whom they described in various derogatory ways. Mrs. Painswick (page 228) was one of these. She was emphatically glad to be out of the rowdy streets of Bethnal Green. She was not lonely or discouraged in Greenleigh.

Status-dissenters are found in Radby also. The Grade IV families are described as making more obvious efforts to achieve higher standards than those of the Grade III families—standards, the authors continue, which are often *above* those which the present parents knew in their own childhood homes. And the Grade V families are described as 'houseproud'. Even more than the Grade IVs, they put their money into the house, which is the centre of their family-life. If this distinction relates to status-assenters and dissenters, it is worth noting that the high-grade families live in the same local area as lower-grade households. The 'good' inhabitants of Gladstone Road have lived there for as long as the 'bad' Dyke Streeters. From Mogey's discriptions of his St. Ebbe's people, and from Cyril Smith, it is clear that dissenters may be found in the old areas.

Although there are dissenters in the old areas, the chances are that there will be more in the new. Many on the margin between the two approaches to life will only be pushed into a dissenting pattern after they move.

> The house is a starting point for many new acquisitions [writes Zweig], it whets the appetite for more. Once the barrier of non-possessing has been crossed, a new wave sets in . . . He (the man on the crest of the new wave) knows that money can bring something more lasting than a few hours' enjoyment.

Having to some extent, for one reason or another, broken free from custom, the way is open for other changes to follow. The status-dissenter is not a negative character. He assents: and what he assents to is a materially richer, socially more ambitious, more open, freer way of life.

Mogey quotes, as a typical assenter's remark: 'I'm working class myself. You can have only a few bosses, and then there's the rest.' From Zweig comes a contrasting illustration. 'I am working class only in the works, but outside I am like anyone else', 'The class distinctions are at work, but not otherwise', 'Here I am a worker but outside I am a human being'. Zweig concludes that 'class distinctions seem to be much stronger in the works than outside. The specific status of hourly-paid men, with the canteen divisions, forcibly remind the workers of their definite place in the social ladder. Outside, class distinctions are now less pronounced.'

The cake of custom once broken, status-dissenters are open to many sophisticating influences. They become less accepting, more demanding, more questioning, more aware of the forces which shape and modify the society in which they live. To take a simple example, Barton residents took Mogey's right to interview them less for granted than did the inhabitants of St. Ebbe's; they asked the interviewers for their credentials, tested their sincerity, wondered visibly how they could make use of them. The Radby research encountered a similar attitude.

> A research problem of specific significance was that of gaining entrance into 'equivalent situations' in the sets of streets being compared. It was comparatively easy to gain access to situations involving people coming from Dyke Street, but it was more difficult to gain entry into situations involving people coming from Gladstone Road. This difficulty arises from one of the differences which distinguishes the two streets, namely that the people who live in Gladstone Road live more private lives.

In spite of this, the social intercourse between interviewer and informant is eventually less gingerly at Barton than at St. Ebbe's. Once the interviewers had established themselves, they were treated more nearly as equals, less as 'them'.

In general, dissenters should be more capable of interaction with those not born and bred in exactly their tradition. At Barton they feel more free to go and meet others—40 per cent there, as contrasted with 10 per cent in St. Ebbe's, joined a voluntary association of some kind.[1] And Zweig reports that the men who made the distinction between their status at work

---

[1] In Dagenham, 20 per cent; see pages 84 ff. Mogey writes in a private communication that his differences are partly attributable to the greater number of children at Barton.

and their status outside (thereby defining themselves to be status-dissenters) often belonged to clubs of a socially mixed character, such as the British Legion, ex-Serviceman's clubs, Conservative clubs, Catholic clubs, or Buffaloes.

Status-dissenters seemed to Mogey more in charge of their lives. They placed less reliance on luck or destiny. They felt more responsible for their own shortcomings and hence a little more on the defensive also. They expected more from life in general and from the institutions of society. They could complain to the local authority about their condition. They made demands; they were less likely to react with stoic acceptance to discomfort. They had what Mogey calls 'a heightened ability to communicate their desires', they had also heightened aspirations. Whereas only a quarter of the St. Ebbe's sample were consistently critical of their housing, only a quarter of the Barton families did not criticize theirs. And this not because they wanted to go back to their former abodes: they wanted to move to a yet better house. Norris comments on the same phenomenon.

> As the great majority of the sample were experiencing the advantages of modern housing—bathroom, indoor lavatory, kitchen—as a result of their move, many of them for the first time, it is interesting that less than a third thought to mention amenities which it is certain all appreciated. Already in many cases they were being taken for granted.

Status-dissenters are more likely to adjust well to the change from old area to new housing-estate. Norris found that of those who had been glad to hear that they were to be re-housed, a larger proportion settled down well than of those who said they had been sorry to leave.

Hence another reason for finding more status-dissenters on the new estates than in the old areas is that those who cannot adjust to the new conditions—in other words, the assenters—will want to flee back to their old area when the opportunity offers.[1] This may be seen in terms of difficulties about rent-

---

[1] Dagenham, page 21. But in the second Dagenham generation, it is the status-dissenters who leave, see chaps. IV and V: 'Pressures on the second generation' and 'Voluntary emigrants'.

payment. Norris found that those showing severe anxiety about the rent were much more likely to want to move back. The higher rent may act as a selective factor, as Kuper suggested. But according to Norris there is perhaps more here than the obvious connection.

The rebate-system means that those who cannot afford the rent do not have to pay it all. The people who feel anxious about the rent and who want to move back, do so not because they cannot reasonably pay but because they do not feel that what the rent buys is worth the price. Their scale of values is involved and modern suburban housing does not rank particularly high on it. They were satisfied with their old house and their old way of life, of which the budget is an index. They never wished to change.

The proportion of status-dissenters is likely to be higher on a new estate for another reason. Local housing policies tend to select 'better people' to go to the 'better estates' while others, among whom are the less effortful and ambitious, are re-housed in dwellings scattered throughout the city, a little less rickety than their previous houses, but not so impressive as the nice neat semi-detached little houses on the new estates.

Because the mixture on the new estate is not as before, but has a rather larger proportion of dissenters, and because the creation of new opportunities may itself create dissenters, those who have not changed their aspirations notice the difference with discomfort. They do not find it difficult to identify the cause of their discomfort:

'They all come from the East End, but they seem to change when they come down here.' 'I deliver milk all over the estate, so I think I know practically everybody. And I can tell you that when they move down here—I suppose it's just that they've got a new house—they think themselves a cut above everybody else.' 'I don't like it, the atmosphere. People are not the same. I don't know if they get bigheaded because they've got a house.'

And that is it. More people on the new estates are 'big-headed'. Big-headedness is status-dissent. What other people notice is not the changed social situation but the psychological changes which accompany dissent. This is well illustrated by the Newbolts—status-assenters discussing those who had moved away from them in one sense or another. Whether they felt that relatives considered themselves 'posh' was not for them a matter of whether the relatives had better jobs. The two families they most strongly condemned had not been occupationally mobile, and four families who had moved up the occupational ladder were not felt by the Newbolts to consider themselves posh. Bott found that their class-sentiment emerged most strongly about relatives who had moved away from the old neighbourhood to a new estate and who had, presumably, become 'different'. When the Newbolts felt a family had moved primarily because of the housing shortage, they remained in contact, regardless of whether the family had been occupationally mobile. But when they felt that a family had moved so as to 'better themselves' they were condemned for being posh and contact was reduced.

What the Newbolts felt subjectively, Mitchell and Lupton were able to confirm objectively. They found two mutually hostile groups on their estate outside Liverpool. The superior group felt superior, but was not so by sociological criteria like occupation or income. They spent their money differently and their attitudes were different. Young and Willmott similarly note that relations mostly remain good with those who had moved up in the world, but not if they had allowed their move to make a difference to their behaviour with their kindred. They were especially blamed if they avoided their obligations to their parents and to their family in the place they had left. (Little awareness was shown by those who were left behind that, with reduced contact, there is less knowledge of their needs and less opportunity to do something about it from the greater distance.)

Moreover, with reduced contact, people grow apart. There is evidence that visiting is often successful and cheerful. But Mogey draws a convincing picture of the widening split which may separate initially similar kin. The reason is obvious. Interaction, liking and understanding normally vary together. So do interaction and similarity of behaviour and of norms, for the greater the social interaction, the greater the social pressure not to change from what is accepted in the group as proper.

Now [according to Mogey] for many of the families, visiting relatives in the former neighbourhood becomes an affair for the weekend or for special occasions. Dressing up is required, everyone is on their best behaviour, stiffness and formality creep in, enjoyment escapes away, and the social contacts are subsequently broken. An important consideration in this break is the fact that estate families rapidly acquire a set of aspirations different from those of the older neighbourhood: *wanting different things they soon become estranged*.[1]

Gorer has some data on the other end of this process; its effect on those who have gone up in the world. He found that many people are disturbed by the belief that their neighbours are jealous of their success. He found it impossible to judge from his data whether this jealousy actually exists or is a mildly paranoid projection. He is inclined towards the latter belief, but the evidence from our other sources seems rather to suggest the former. The belief in question is especially prevalent among those who call themselves 'upper working class'; these refer to the others' 'obvious dislike of our hard work which has resulted in our owning our own house and car' and to 'the way they begrudge what we have (when these others spend their money on drink and gambling)'. Gorer concludes that 'improving one's position is not without danger in England'.

THE CREATION OF NEW NORMS

(a) The social comparison process
Upon moving to a new estate, people are presented with a serious emotional and intellectual problem. The neighbours don't know them and they don't know the neighbours. They are obviously different. They may feel the attraction of alternative ways of living, and may for a while be conscious of inconsistencies in their own behaviour or values. There is the increased opportunity to become status-dissenting, to cut oneself off from the old network. The question of where one stands in relation to other people is likely to present itself with greater force than ever before.

This leads to a 'social comparison process'. Patterns of neighbourly interaction and consumption-patterns are not arbitrarily

---

[1] The Dagenham study shows that if they do not want different things, they do not become estranged.

chosen as processes of interest to the social psychologist in his analysis of areas such as those now under discussion. The new migrants themselves are more preoccupied with them than appears to be the case elsewhere. The increased interest may be attributed to the variations in practice which the migrant notices on the estate. Festinger would say: *The availability of comparison with others whose (patterns of behaviour) are somewhat different from one's own will produce tendencies to change one's evaluation of the (behaviour pattern) in question.* He and his associates have evolved a number of generalizations which are surprisingly useful for our purpose, although they were first constructed to bring order into a different field of study: the behaviour of members of small experimental groups.[1] Social comparison processes in small groups are generally concerned with abilities and opinions. We are concerned with patterns of neighbourly relations like visiting, borrowing and lending, and patterns of consumption. Yet *mutatis mutandis* the generalizations apply very well. They are printed italicized and in modified form below wherever they fit into the discussion. It will be as well to remember that they form a set of interdependent hypotheses: some of the later and more refined statements qualify the more general ones stated first; used singly they are not good predictors.[2]

When a discrepancy exists with respect to a pattern of behaviour, there will be tendencies to change others in the group so as to bring them closer to oneself, and to change one's own position so as to move closer to others in the group.

Things become popular among the people you know. You see a T.V. someone's got and you think it would be nice to have one like it. Or someone will get a new washing machine and they'll

[1] L. Festinger *et al.* (1954), 'The social comparison process', *Hum. Rel.*, VII.

[2] The behaviour-patterns which are subject to conformity-pressures are here only generally stated. The source-literature itself is not very specific. This is the more to be regretted because there exists a body of theory concerning groups in culture-contact which could have been checked against actual practice. This body of theory makes predictions concerning the traits which one group will take over from another, the traits which will be modified in the process of perception or adoption, and the traits which will not be taken over; see Max Gluckman (1958), *Analysis of a Social Situation in Modern Zululand*, Manchester University Press, and S. N. Eisenstadt (1955), *The Absorption of Immigrants*, Routledge and Kegan Paul, London.

show it to you and say how good it is and how much of a help to them. It's not envy or anything, it's just recommendation. And if you don't get the same thing, they often share it with you. The woman next door has got a spin drier, for instance. She comes in and takes my washing for me two or three times a week and dries it. She does several people's drying round here.

I was telling the young woman over the road about the Marley tiles my husband had just put down in the scullery. She seemed interested, so I said, 'Why don't you come over and look at it?' Now she's seen it she'll tell her husband about it. I gave her a sample, as a matter of fact. I expect her husband will put some down for her in their scullery. We don't mind about that. Why should we?

Peter Willmott, from whose Dagenham informants these quotations are taken, considers that in the main people on the estate seem to see their fellows not as adversaries but as allies in a general advance. Social comparison need not lead to competition.

One cannot, of course, rely entirely on what people say about this kind of thing. One does not know how far they are misleading themselves about what is really happening. But, to the outsider, competition between neighbours certainly seems less keen, anxiety over possessions less sharp, at Dagenham than elsewhere, in the private suburb of Woodford, for example, or in the new estate of Greenleigh. There is little sign of 'status-striving'.

In what circumstances will there be status-striving and competition? It is sometimes argued that affluence encourages them. But as the quotations showed, affluence and stress do not necessarily go together. Uncertainty is a factor which accounts for much of the kind of stress often connected with competitiveness. *Any factors which increase the strength of the drive to evaluate some particular pattern of behaviour will increase pressure towards uniformity concerning that pattern.*

In Bethnal Green [write Young and Willmott] the people are less concerned with getting on. Naturally, they want to have more money and a better education for their children. But the urge is less compulsive than in Greenleigh. They stand well with plenty of other people whether or not they have net curtains and a fine pram. Their credit with others does not depend so much on their

'success' as on the subtleties of behaviour in their many face-
to-face groups. They have the security of belonging to a series
of small and overlapping groups, and get from their fellows the
respect they need . . .

In Greenleigh the new arrivals watch the first comers and the
first comers watch the new arrivals . . . All are under the same
pressure for material advance; they naturally mark each other's
progress. Those who make the most progress are those who
have proved their claim to respectability, Greenleigh fashion. The
fact that people are watching their neighbours and their neighbours are watching them provides the further stimulus, reinforcing
the process set in motion by the new house, to conform to the
norms of the estate. There is anxiety lest they do not fit.

Because people on the Dagenham estate have lived there for
a considerable time, their reference-groups are different from
those of the people on the new estates. *Any factors which increase
the importance of some particular group as a comparison group for some
pattern of behaviour will increase the pressure towards uniformity
concerning that pattern.* This gives us, in the present case, both a
negative reference-group—the status-assenters of the old area
—and a positive reference-group—the status-dissenters on the
estate. Young and Willmott describe how the new resident finds
his own position with reference to both. On the one hand:

> The house is one bearer of status in any society—it most
> certainly is in a country where a semi-detached suburban house
> with a garden has become the signal mark of the middle classes.
> When the migrants compare the old with the new, is it any wonder
> that for a time they feel 'big-headed'? In their mind's eye the
> people with whom they compare themselves may be less their
> fellow residents at Greenleigh with their identical houses than
> their old neighbours at Bethnal Green. And compared with them,
> they are in this one way undeniably superior.

On the other hand:

> People struggle to raise their all-round standards to those of
> the home, and in the course of doing so, they must look to their
> present neighbours for guidance. To begin with, the first-comers
> had to make their own way, but the later arrivals have their
> model at hand. The neighbours have put up nice curtains. Have
> we? They have their garden planted with privet and grass-seed.

Have we? The new arrivals watch the first-comers and the first-comers watch the new arrivals.

Under the same pressures, Kuper's informants from the high-status streets of Braydon Road would discuss furniture in terms of what should or should not go into each room. A new set of norms was beginning to establish itself.

The visibility of material possessions is a third factor. There are two aspects to this, one closely related to the point just made about reference-groups. Dagenham is a one-class estate, unlike Woodford. The people in Dagenham are less frequently confronted with major, class-linked differences in behaviour and consumption patterns.[1] The other aspect is the simpler one; material possessions are more easily perceived than psychological qualities. The less is known about the latter, the more visibly the former stand out.

> In Bethnal Green, people belong to a close network of personal relations. They know intimately dozens of other local people living near . . . In this situation, Bethnal Green is not, as we see it, concerned to any marked extent with what is usually thought of as status. It is true, of course, that people have different incomes, different kinds of jobs, different kinds of houses—in this respect there is much less uniformity than there is at Greenleigh —even different standards of education. But these attributes are not so important in evaluating others. It is the personal characteristics which matter. The first thing they think of about Bert is not that he has a 'frig' and a car. They see him as bad-tempered, or a real good sport, or the man with a way with women . . . He is judged, if he is judged at all, more in the round, as a person with the usual mixture of all kinds of qualities, some good, some bad, many indefinable. He is more of a life-portrait than a figure on a scale.
>
> How different is Greenleigh . . . Where nearly everyone is a stranger, there is no means of uncovering personality. People cannot be judged by their personal characteristics: a person can certainly see that his neighbour works in his shirt sleeves and his wife goes down to the shops in a blue coat, but that is not much of a guide to character. Judgment must therefore rest on the trappings of the man rather than on the man himself. If people have nothing else to go by, they judge from his appearance, his house,

---

[1] Dagenham, pages 101–2, 112.

even his Minimotor. Once the accepted standards are few, and mostly to do with wealth, they become the standards by which high status is judged . . .

In the absence of small groups which join one family to another, in the absence of strong personal associations which extend from one household to another, people think that they are judged, and judge others, by the material standards which are the outward and visible marks of respectability.

And so relationships instead of being face-to-face become window-to-window. The reliance on ascription becomes a desire for achievement. Young and Willmott are apt to see the behaviour of the people at Greenleigh as an inexplicable immoral phenomenon: normally pleasant people have suddenly become madly competitive and achievement-oriented. This colours their comment, but from their descriptions, it is clear that they have, perhaps unconsciously, correctly perceived that the new resident at Greenleigh is seeking new standards to share with others, and with which he wishes to conform from the moment that the differences are noticed. And they have clearly understood why the more obvious 'materialist' standards are of primary interest to the migrant: 'it starts with the new house, the bearer of a new status and in itself an encouragement towards a new pattern of consumption'.

The Barton housewife, proud of her new home, would often insist that the interviewer go round the house to see every room. And no wonder. As Young and Willmott put it, the man's status is the status of his job, which has not necessarily changed with the move. The woman's status is the status of her home. She has moved up in the world, she is only realistic to recognize it and be proud of it. And so the item for comparison is likely to be the consumption-pattern in general, and the more visible items of expenditure in particular. This is what Zweig called the 'surburban drive of status-seeking through the home'.

Differences in the extent to which items of expenditure are 'visible' aggravate the concern with privacy to which reference has been made on earlier pages. The insistence on the privacy of the home is bound up with a preoccupation about social status which seems to run right through most levels of

English society. Because the home contains many symbols of social status—carpets, lino, firedogs—keeping all but intimates out of the house is a simple technique for controlling other people's opportunities to assess one's status more closely than one could wish. It will be remembered that Gorer found complaints about neighbours' gossip to decline as income rose. As income rises, people live farther apart from their neighbours and, in any case, neighbours are less likely to know one another, having lived less long in the area.

The normal English preference for privacy is given additional strength by the social comparison process. For one thing, the need for privacy, or more precisely, the need to control the level of interaction and the people with whom one interacts, is particularly important for those who are experimenting with patterns of expenditure which are new to them. It is important to those who are moving up because they need to be able to experiment out of sight of prying eyes with the acquisitions acquired for the sake of conformity to a way of life which is not clear to them in its finer details and with the uses of which they did not become acquainted in the every-day life of the parental home. It is also important to those who fear they are sinking, for it may enable them to maintain in others the belief that there has been no change in expenditure-pattern, even when only the more obvious objects remain while the rest of a way of life has perforce altered in response to the reduced income. The more the neighbourhood is one in which the inhabitants are experiencing mobility at different rates, the greater the emphasis on privacy is likely to be. When one of Kuper's interviewers first called on Mrs. Dudley she opened the door only a few inches:

> 'I was praying you wouldn't ask to come in.' She does not like people to see her stairs and hall, which lack the prestige-giving carpets and rug. Similarly, the sofa of her three-piece suite in the living room is placed against the large windows and the curtains are kept partly drawn, so as to shut off from observant eyes the slightly shabby furniture and the lino squares which serve for rugs.

Poverty may exert pressure to maintain a higher standard of privacy. Conversely, those who feel they have 'arrived', like

Kuper's informants the 'Gardeners', do not object to neighbours looking in at their windows. They say they have nothing to be ashamed of. In point of fact they are exceedingly proud of their home. But to a neighbour, the Gardeners' behaviour is simply exhibitionism: they don't even draw the curtains at night!

We now turn to other factors which affect the level of interaction in a neighbourhood.

(b) Roughs and respectables

A person will be less attracted to situations where others are very divergent from him than to situations where others are very close to him. When a discrepancy exists, there will be a tendency to cease comparing oneself with those in the group who are very different from oneself.

In the previous chapter it was held that interaction and liking vary together, except in special circumstances. Interaction must not, for instance, be felt to have been enforced by some outside agency. People must feel that their interaction is by choice. In present housing conditions, few people choose their house or their neighbours. There is therefore no *a priori* reason for believing that people have chosen to interact with their neighbours, and no *a priori* reason for believing they will like them when they do interact.

As we have seen in the previous chapter, neighbourly interaction is in any case a sensitive matter for the English psyche. But in the more traditional areas, a set of conventions governing interaction has evolved. These social conventions relate partly to the *amount* of interaction. When the amount of interaction is higher than the local norm allows, privacy is felt to have been violated. But there is also a conventional side to the *kind* of interaction. Interaction will evoke no sense of outraged privacy when common custom determines what the proper response shall be.

Where norms are shared in a neighbourhood, there need therefore be less concern about privacy. Conversely, where norms differ among neighbours, privacy will be a constant preoccupation. The complaint that neighbours 'take advantage' or are intrusive then means that they start 'dropping in' on you when you greet them, and you come from a group where formal invitations have to be issued first. To complain that the neighbours are 'stuck up' may be translated as meaning that when you say good-day to them, as is customary in the society from which you came, they do not return the greeting for fear that you will drop in on them, because they will interpret it as an overture to further interaction. In a traditional society, minute cues may serve to indicate the behaviour people expect of one another. When norms differ, cues are not recognized. In Braydon Road, a woman who had failed to perceive the differences in situation which had governed a neighbour's reactions on two occasions, complained: 'One day she'd speak to you, and another day she wouldn't. You never knew where you were with her.' But, as Kuper points out, the other woman may only have been trying to secure her own standards of privacy.

Our hypothesis is, therefore: the greater the difference in norms, the greater the concern over norms (shown in the example below as concern about the effect on the children of living in a particular neighbourhood), the less good relations between neighbours are likely to be, the greater the concern about privacy, and the less liked the area. Supporting evidence is provided from Mitchell and Lupton's Liverpool estate. They studied in detail three blocks, each of six houses in a row facing six others. Occupationally, these blocks were pretty similar, except that Block III had three householders of different blocks from the staff/technical category, whereas the others had none or one. But the inhabitants had come from different types of housing-area.

	Block I	Block II	Block III
	(initial differences in norms)		
From a congested working-class area	2	2	4
From a normal working-class area	5	8	7
From a suburban area	5	2	1

An obvious point is that more people from a suburban area live in Block I than in any other block, and these people are more likely to be respectable. Less obvious, perhaps, but equally important, is that Block I is more 'mixed' in character, Blocks II and III having a normal preponderance of people from normal

working-class areas. To illustrate our hypothesis, all that needs
to be done is to show certain tables:

	Block I	Block II	Block III
	(concern other norms)		
Serious disagreements over children	**8**	2	4
Some mention of disagreements	1	2	–
No mention of problem	3	**8**	**8**
	(relations with neighbours)		
Undesired contacts, difficult personal relations, strong personal criticisms	**6**	0	1
Little contact, no adverse comment	3	4	**7**
Mutual assistance and expressions of good neighbourly relations	0	**8**	3
	(concern over privacy		
Keen discussion about lack of privacy	**6**	--	2
Mention of problems in general terms	2	3	2
	(liking for area)		
Strong objection and wish to move	**7**	–	3
Minor criticisms of estate	4	2	4
Satisfaction, no wish to move	1	**10**	5

Significantly, these authors describe privacy as the 'freedom
to choose one's social contacts and exclude those which are not
desired'. 'Privacy', they add, 'is essentially a co-operative enterprise.'

In the previous chapter it was argued that one reason why
interaction and liking vary together is that interaction leads
to greater understanding (whereupon those who on further
acquaintance proved uncongenial could be dropped). What follows, then, when interaction leads to misunderstanding? Where
norms are not shared, actions are likely to be misunderstood
and interaction will prove confusing. The level of interaction
may then be reduced in order to reduce the uncertainty.[1]

There had been trouble between the neighbours in one block
(on the Liverpool estate). But now everyone had settled down.

[1] See also pages 201-6.

The inhabitants had learned what was expected of them, and what was not. *Social interaction was minimal, but then so also was friction.*

So it is not surprising that Young and Willmott find that even when neighbours were willing to help, people were apparently reluctant to depend on them too much, or to confide in them too freely. One reason is that when people become aware of variations in practice, any thought of initiating interaction may arouse anxiety. If you are wanting to borrow something for the house, what will the reaction be? A willingness to lend? Or will you be unlucky enough to pick the type of person who 'will laugh in your face'? People do not care to initiate interaction, for fear of an unrewarding response by the other person, or for fear of a response which they will be unable to control, so that the situation may get out of hand. There may be a thin-end-of-the-wedge aspect to this fear. People are afraid to interact now, in case it commits them to more interaction later. 'It's a bad policy,' they said to Mitchell and Lupton, 'to make friends on the estate, because sooner or later you fall out with them and that creates unpleasantness.' Similarly at Braydon Road it was explained to the interviewers that 'one little thing leads to bigger things, and then it's money' and 'people can keep borrowing and not paying back, till in the end you have to refuse them, and that is unpleasant'.[1]

This suggests that a lack of appropriate social techniques enhances the uncertainty, and hence the isolation of the newcomers. They are afraid to get friendly in case they get too friendly and see too much of each other, because they have no generally understood and agreed conventional way of maintaining interaction at the level they prefer. 'I was always afraid I might pick on the wrong type and then you would not be able to get rid of them.' They are able to help one another in emergencies and crises, not only because of their common humanity, but because illnesses and bereavements are clearly defined situations with a beginning and an end, so that they know there will be no difficulty in reducing the level of interaction when the episode is terminated.

Still in the late fifties, a population with largely status-dissenting attitudes, Zweig reports

[1] But Dagenham, chap. VI, 'Friends and neighbours'.

a pattern of neighbourly relations, well-established and nearly uniform, which can be summed up in two phrases I often heard: 'friendly but not too friendly', and 'keep apart from neighbours but be friendly'. The majority of the men I talked to were on 'good morning' terms with their neighbours, willing to help and oblige if the need for help arose. A cat or a dog may be taken care of, garden plants may be exchanged, a hand may be given in repairing a fence, a school child may be taken in while the mother is at work. But visiting is in the main discouraged.

Gorer's summary was, 'The typical relationship of the English to their neighbours can probably best be described as "distant cordiality".' This has not changed with growing prosperity. But other shifts have taken place.

In the previous chapter it was argued that as kin moved away from the local community, some of those who are left become more dependent on their neighbours for help.[1] (Meanwhile others, left freer from social pressures, begin the development that characterizes status-dissent.) The neighbours may react by becoming less helpful than they had been when they were called upon only in exceptional circumstances. We could call this the 'undue strain' theory of privacy. The same process may be at work on the new estate. Certainly the move, and the demands it makes on the character, appear to have the interesting consequence that a deeper rift separates those who can cope from those who cannot, than was ever the case in the old environment.

Such a rift is partly based on realistic considerations like the undue strain placed on those who do not need help and are therefore called upon to help others. This may explain the phenomenon Ruth Glass has called 'Watlingitis'—'a common disease after eight or ten months living on the estate in great friendliness and helpfulness. The patient is attacked by a sudden desire to do nothing, see nothing, help no one and go nowhere.' The 'patient' is likely to be the energetic, status-dissenting, let's-all-pull-together type who has had more calls on his good nature than he had resources for.

---

[1] The Dagenham study also suggests that status-dissenters are more likely to leave the area voluntarily. Status-assenters are more likely to be reluctant to leave and may make arrangements to stay behind—see chaps. IV and V.

Though the rift has some realistic aspects, others are less rational in origin and practice. Once people begin to distinguish two social categories, the temptation to exaggerate the characteristics of each seems overwhelming. Now, these people are likely to be familiar with two social-group designations because of their life in the old area. There were the respectable working-class people and a rougher element. This terminology is carried over into the new life, sometimes appropriately (some traditional roughs are in fact moved to some new estates), but often less correctly. Then the words 'rough' and 'respectable' come to denote the traditional status-assenting respectable working-class and the status-dissenting people respectively. Schematically, and pretending that the categories have definite boundaries instead of flowing into one another, the language shifts thus:

	Traditional status-assenting rough	Traditional status-assenting respectable	Status-dissenting respectable
In the old areas	'rough'	'respectable'	'stuck-up'
On the estates	'rough'	'rough'	'respectable'

Mrs. Stacey in her Banbury study makes the same point.

The working-class concept of neighbouring in fact changes with status and changes also with the traditional or non-traditional attitude to life. Within the working class in Banbury there are three status groups: the 'rough', the 'ordinary', and the 'respectable'. The self-styled 'ordinary working-class' people follow closest the traditional concept of neighbouring. The 'roughs' and the 'respectables' deviate most from it. The 'roughs', often the poorest families, would like to lean heavily upon their neighbours, but they are discouraged. Their personal appearance and the state of their houses add to their unattractiveness as companions. The 'respectables', on the other hand, are not expelled; they withdraw: they are 'stand-offish'. They are bent on improving their own social positions and intimate neighbouring is a part of the life of the social class they wish to leave behind.

Having carried over the labels from an older tradition, by the usual processes of selective perception people will be seen to have the characteristics attributed to them by the labels.

Changes in Working-Class Life

Mutual prejudice then magnifies the actual differences, and interaction between the members of the two groups is reduced.

'We don't mix very well in this part of the estate. At first I used to lend every Tom, Dick and Harry my tools, or lawn mower or anything. Then I had twenty pounds pinched from my wallet. Now we don't want to know anyone. We keep ourselves to ourselves. There's a good old English saying—an Englishman's home is his castle. It's very true.' . . . Mrs. Chortle of Greenleigh had broken off trading as well as diplomatic relations with one of her neighbours. 'These people are very dirty,' she said. 'And I've told them I don't want to lend or to borrow.'

Almost all the studies of a move from an old to a new area reveal a progressive polarization of this kind, though Dagenham presents an interesting special case. This was a pre-war estate and, for reasons discussed on pages 271, 277 and 288, lacked opportunity for status-dissent to develop among the new residents. Dagenham shows two groups which differ in social interaction but which lack the mutual animosity which seems to characterize the rift on the newer estates. The greater similarity of norms is one important factor here. Dagenham resembles Bethnal Green more than Greenleigh. Though the respectables keep themselves more to themselves, they show little of the enterprise in choice of friends which characterizes the status-dissenter and they are not hostile to those who live in rougher ways. Dagenham is in many ways half-way between the old traditional way of life and that of the newer estates. Mr. Wild of Greenleigh will hope in vain that eventually the place will be like Bethnal Green; such a dream has come true for Mr. Adams.

The majority were divided fairly evenly, as far as I could judge from what they said in the interviews, into two views. One described social relationships at Dagenham as 'friendly' but somewhat distant . . . Such people distinguished sharply between their 'friends'—that is those out of the people nearby with whom they might exchange visits or go shopping—and the rest of the neighbours. Mrs. Snell said, 'I don't mix with many of the neighbours. The women on both sides and the woman opposite—they're my friends. I say good morning to the others, but that's all.' Mrs. Pink was another: 'My only friend round here is Mrs. Noble. The rest are just neighbours—we hardly speak.'

Not, they insisted, that neighbours at Dagenham are unhelpful to each other. 'Underneath that aloofness,' said one man, 'they're every bit as helpful when you need it.' But there are limits to sociability, boundaries to neighbourliness . . .

The pattern of relationships these people describe—more 'reserved', more 'aloof', 'not so familiar'—is close to the stereotype of 'suburban' social life. And indeed, apart from the fact that people in the middle-class suburb of Woodford had friends in their homes more often, and tended to draw at least some of them from farther afield, the relationships of many of these Dagenham residents seem similar. 'Dagenham is like the other suburban areas in this way,' said one man, who put it, I should explain, more strongly than most. 'They suffer from the same common factor—suburbanitis, a withdrawing, a shutting of the door.'

What was described by the other main group of informants at Dagenham was not at all like suburbia; it was like Bethnal Green. They saw the estate differently—or at least the part where they lived—and apparently had very different relationships with those living near them. They might have special 'friends', but they did not distinguish so sharply between them and the others. 'We're all good pals round here,' said Mrs. Croom. 'Everybody's very friendly with everybody else in this little community.' Some explicitly drew the parallel between their present social relations and those of the East End . . .

Mr. Adams, who had arrived from Shoreditch in 1927, thought that time had re-created the spirit of the old district: 'At the beginning the atmosphere was more of the off-handed, but now it's more of the amicable. At first people weren't bold enough—they didn't like to speak to each other—but after a while they began to speak and get more friendly. Now Dagenham has moulded itself into a place where most people know each other. The atmosphere has originated itself to more or less what it was back in Shoreditch.'

But Dagenham is not typical of the way the new estates develop. More characteristically, Mitchell and Lupton could divide their Liverpool population into two status-groups, into those who did and those who did not manifest their belief in their own superior social status by such remarks as 'This estate is very mixed and there aren't many of our kind here', 'Where we live is the better end of the estate', 'The people who live here are very scruffy'. Those who did not were presumably the ones to speak of big-headedness. The superior group did not differ from the other in income or occupation. Status-assent and dissent, roughness and respectability, are psychological variables.

Kuper and his associates, in their Braydon Road study, found similarly that a stereotyped classification of styles of life emerged from the responses of their informants. One stereotype was of the 'very rough', the 'scruffy', the 'low-class', the 'slum-family'. Scruffiness implied lower standards of cleanliness, neatness and housewifeliness. ('They don't look after their houses so well, and the houses are dirtier, as also the children.') In Braydon Road, scruffiness was associated with large families, plain speech, free use of taboo words, perhaps an over-readiness to cuff the children, a forthright approach in personal relations and a lack of neighbourly reticence. Working out a classification on the basis of such considerations, Kuper found that there was little difficulty in placing the majority of his informants on the estate. There were forty-two respectables, of whom eleven were ultra-respectable; there were forty-five ordinary families, of whom eight were really scruffy.

Mogey found the same distinction in Oxford. He wisely qualifies it, however, with the reflection that, to some extent, a mechanism of projection is here at stake. 'The estate family, lacking the support of a traditional set of behaviour-patterns and of a way of finding out what is expected, projects its uncertainty on to a largely unknown world which it labels "the children at the bottom of the avenue".' At Barton, those who are considered rough are described by their neighbours as approving of the (rough) children at the bottom of the avenue. They drop in on their neighbours uninvited, often, say the exasperated neighbours, at tea-time. They talk about their own affairs. They complain to outsiders about their house or about the estate. They borrow from their neighbours and, the neighbours say, they don't always return what they borrow. They are felt to be intrusive, to pry on their neighbours. They don't cultivate their gardens. In these respects, it is obvious that they behave in their customary pre-migration way. Some other characteristics seem to be simply chance deviations from the norm of the local respectable families: they are atheist or too religious, they discuss politics, they attend services in the wooden hut on the estate instead of going to the church, they use the community-centre.

The characteristics of the Barton respectables, on the other hand, show them to be managing their environment better and planning farther ahead in order to be able to manage better. Everything is obviously neat, tidy, orderly. They find more satisfaction in doing things instead of just talking: that is, they are less person-centred:

> They collect things, such as dolls; or they make things, like model aeroplanes or radios; they garden. They have pets. They read 'good books'. They see 'good films'. They exchange magazines with their neighbours. Their house is tidy, their wives are good cooks. They use the separate dining and living spaces as intended by the architects. Their furniture matches. They have framed photographs of weddings and proficiency certificates hanging on the walls. They are clean and dress neatly. They are polite. They are more willing to lend than to borrow. They have no debts. They join clubs and Trade Unions, though (in Barton) they no longer attend the community centre. The respectable thing is to have helped build it. They keep themselves to ᵗhemselves and don't talk of their own affairs, they value privacy. They keep their children in the house or in their own garden. In general, they *choose* their own activities, their own companions, and their children's companions.

Like to like, and 'ordinary people' will tend to feel that they have more in common with other 'ordinary people': they get on better with them and interact more with them than with the 'stuck-up' people farther along the road. These latter, 'respectable people', will feel the same about others of their kind, and will avoid the 'roughs' down the road.

This is how the polarization into roughs and respectables maintains itself. A man cannot easily move away from the neighbours with whom he does not wish to interact. Willy-nilly he is subjected therefore to some of the pressure towards conformity which the sight of other people's behaviour must exert upon him. Nor can he entirely avoid subjecting others to similar pressure. But over and above this minimum, in so far as he can, he restricts his interaction on a voluntary and pleasurable basis to those whose way of life he finds or has learned to find attractive, and he will avoid those whose way of life he (now) feels to be alien. This, after all, is why liking and interaction and homogeneity of norms all vary together.[1]

Clearly, such effects will be cumulative. The more he interacts with those to whom he is attracted, the more opportunity he will have to see how they behave, and if this confirms the attraction he will seek to conform more, to interact more, and so on.

This process of choice, and the way it may lead to a widening of the rift, is well illustrated from Braydon Road. Kuper had classified his sample into ultra-respectables, respectables, ordinary families and roughs. All were asked which of their neighbours they really liked best. The respectables most frequently chose ultra-respectables, after that other respectables, after that ordinary families. Those classified ordinary chose first the roughs, then other ordinaries, then respectables. Across the rough/respectable barrier there were relatively fewer choices. The same relationship can be stated the other way round. Of thirteen informants who said they disliked their next-door neighbours, ten were on the other side of the barrier.

From the descriptions of the interaction-patterns of roughs and respectables it appears at first sight that the roughs interact more with their rough neighbours than respectables do with their like. A general rule can be laid down, writes Zweig, 'the higher the level of prosperity, the higher the fences'. In Braydon Road, this was borne out in the descriptions of what a good neighbour is like: *either* not very particular about maintaining privacy and willing to borrow, lend and visit, *or* very particular and unwilling to interact.

A Radby woman in a Grade V household spoke of 'two classes of people' in the district. She deplored the habits of those who drink a lot, neglect their children and so on. This 'lower' class does much neighbouring, she says, and works up strong alliances which often end in argument and a breaking of the relationship. But

[1] This is a straightforward application of Homans' theory of the interrelation of the internal and the external system, see *The Human Group*, especially the beginning of chap. VI. If they are given the opportunity to move around, as the Dagenham housing authorities allowed for a period, similar people may congregate in certain streets.

after a short time visiting will probably be resumed. She says there is much borrowing and lending among these people. She and others in Grade IV and V state that they 'have some good friends in the district but they do not mix a lot', they keep themselves to themselves and do not neighbour. They do not pop in and out.

It will be noted that generally the behaviour with which the respectables reproach the roughs is the more sociable behaviour. Reserve seems a more respectable attitude to neighbouring. This may in some cases make those who value respectability appear isolated in their neighbourhood. But it does not necessarily mean that the respectables have fewer friends in their lives. Zweig rightly points out that with growing prosperity, when the need for mutual neighbourly help is not so pronounced and everyone can manage by and for himself, the need for freedom may come to the fore. In this case, it is a freedom to choose those with whom one shall interact.[1] Zweig found that skilled men interacted more outside the factory than the non-skilled did. He attributes the fact that they sought each other out to shared hobbies and interests. We may also note that in Kuper's study the choice of the respectables for their own groupings (respectable and superior) was statistically significant and the choice of the ordinaries for their own groupings (ordinary and rough) just missed significance. Kuper concludes that the former are more fastidious. That is probable, but we must also consider that the respectables we now have in view are status-dissenting, and therefore less likely to put up with a situation they dislike. Hence Kuper also concludes that 'respectable residents show a greater tendency to go further afield in their choices, while ordinary residents are apparently more ready to come to terms with their immediate neighbours'. If some people in a local area do go farther afield to find the contacts congenial to them, then they may appear in a sociologist's local sample as isolated simply because their friends are not on the estate.

The Radby Report confirms the greater selectivity of the more respectable households, and their consequent tendency to go farther afield for the satisfaction of their sociability. The people

---

[1] But Dagenham, page 63.

of (the high-grade) Gladstone Road led more private lives and had a greater variety of interests, but more especially an interest in their homes. The result was that they tended not to go out to the pubs and the clubs as often as did the people of (the lower grade) Dyke Street, and when they did go out, their range of interests acted against the tendency apparent in Dyke Street, to cluster together in particular pubs and clubs.

> Cars [writes Zweig] have a deep social effect on the degree of interaction of local communities and social life at large. Those who have a car move out of the reach of the 'local'. (Many of these new men say that they can only afford one major hobby: gambling, beer, or a car.) Previously they visited their own public house or club or other local centre of amusement where they could see their friends and neighbours. With a car they can visit more distant places of entertainment. There they are no more known as 'working class', there they come into contact with wider circles and layers of society.

In the chapter on the traditional community it was argued that habit brought the inhabitants regularly together and that the interchange of information which resulted from this 'effortless sociability' kept the local community intact. The opposite tendency here observed is more conducive to a more varied and more associational social life.

In short, status-dissenting respectables may maintain non-local social networks. This could explain why Kuper found that the measurement of responses dealing with sociability and mutual aid showed a bi-modal distribution: people tended to engage in either few or else all the relevant practices. When Kuper took samples of smaller areas, the distribution was uni-modal. Maybe those who were not sociable or helpful neighbours were suffering from *anomie*, maybe they were influenced by the idea that respectable people do not interact a lot, but maybe they had a car and friends elsewhere in the town. (Status-dissenting ex-roughs who aspire to respectability may of course not be so aware of this, and be under the impression that the maintenance of reserve is synonymous with 'better class'. These would then be isolates.)

Provided, therefore, that a largish area is taken for analysis, one may find within the area several rough communities whose members do not look outside their streets for company, the interstices being filled by respectables.

Roughs and respectables tend to be mutually contemptuous and mistrustful. In Festinger's view *the cessation of comparison with others is accompanied by hostility or derogation to the extent that continued comparison with those others implies unpleasant consequences.* Young and Willmott consider the unemphatic but continuous grumbling mutual hostility and derogation to be part of a projective mechanism.

> Do they label themselves as unfriendly? No one admits to it, some indignantly deny it. If they themselves are hostile, they do not acknowledge it but attribute the feeling to others. Yet mostly they reveal that the behaviour they resent in others is the same as their own, that—since *others* are unfriendly—to withdraw will avoid trouble and keep the peace. Co-existence is safer, because more realistic, than co-operation . . . Mr. Young told his wife: 'When I walk into these four walls, I always tell her, Don't make too many friends. They turn out to be enemies.'

But it is arguable that in our highly stratified, highly status-conscious society the fear of being mis-classified, to which reference has already been made in the previous chapter, is here again at work. And this time it is not in circumstances where the individual is securely embedded in a social group whose members at least know him for what he is, whatever they may think of him, but in circumstances in which the other inhabitants of the neighbourhood are the very people who would mis-classify him. Is it surprising that Kuper's interviewers found that there were deliberate omissions when they asked informants for the names of others living in the streets around? People leave out the names of certain others for fear they should be thought to know the rougher types.

Informal interaction between the two groupings is kept to a minimum because, it being difficult to draw clear distinctions, the respectables fear that they will be classified as roughs if they are seen to interact with them on a friendly footing, just as some white men fear to interact with coloured men because from there to having aspersions cast on their white ancestry is only a step. The more easily a mis-classification is made—in this case the more two groups approximate in appearance and other obvious aspects—the greater the circumspection with which they will interact.[1] Williams' list of the mutual appellations of neighbours of different status confirms that hostility is directed particularly at those whose social level is only just different from one's own.

What the 'upper upper' group called the

Upper upper: Our social level. Better class.

Lower upper: Social climbers. Not quite our class. He *tries* to behave like a gentleman, but . . .

Intermediate: Neither here nor there, more intelligent than the normal run of people around here. Quite well educated and very handy when you have about a dozen village organizations to see to.

Upper medial: Social climbers in the village.

Medial and Villagers and farmers. Decent lower class people. The *lower medial:* country people.

Lower class: The immoral element in the village. The worst kind of country man. The worst of the lower orders.

What the 'lower upper' group called the

Upper upper: The Upper Ten. The people who have more breeding than sense. They have no money, but because they talk like a B.B.C. announcer and their great grand-father was a tuppenny-halfpenny baronet they think they own the place.

Lower upper: Ambitious people. Go-ahead people.

Intermediate: In between.

Upper medial: The village aristocracy. They try their best to get ahead but everything is against them.

Medial: Farmers and small professionals. Farmers and village tradesmen.

Lower medial: The village.

Lower class: Dirty people. I can't understand them. Some of them are quite well off, but you'd never think it to look at them.

What the 'intermediate' group called the

Upper upper: The Nibs. The usual well-off people you find in the countryside these days. Mostly retired people. Very few of them are old established.

[1] Evidence on page 282 suggests that this means, among other things, that community centres (and perhaps by analogy other community-facilities) are used either by one section of the community, or by the other, but not normally by both.

Aspects of Adult Life in England

Lower upper: The money-maker class. They have ambitions of climbing but they don't seem to have much luck.

Intermediate: We are a class of our own. Our position is not a very easy one to understand.

Upper medial: The kind of people who don't mix with their neighbours. Usually they are social climbers.

Medial: The majority of ordinary people with good jobs—including farmers of course.

Lower medial: The average villager.

Lower class: An unfortunate minority. You can tell them by the way they live. Most of them are dirty.

What the 'upper medial' group called the

Upper upper: The sort of people you really can look up to. The proper gentry. The better class people.

Lower upper: They are not the Upper Ten but they like to think they are. They are not all that different from us, except for their money.

Intermediate: School teachers and that sort. I think folks make far too much fuss about them.

Upper medial: People who keep themselves to themselves. Decent people who try to get on. The sort of people who try to improve themselves a bit.

Medial: Farmers and such.

Lower medial: Village people. The ordinary working-class people.

Lower class: People who don't try to lift themselves.

What the 'medial and lower medial' group called the

Upper upper: The people who are higher class than we are.

Lower upper: Folk like X who have plenty of money and plenty of cheek. They want to get on in t'world.

Intermediate: In between because of education.

Upper medial: Snobs. Stuck-up folk.

Medial and lower medial: Ordinary Gosfer folk.

Lower class: Folk who don't care what they look like.

What the 'lower class' group called the

Upper upper: Them posh folk living in the big houses. They won't acknowledge you and the way some of them behaves you'd think you was some mak o' animal.

Lower upper: The folk with brass who acts like they was big nobs.

Intermediate: Don't know much about them. A lot o' bloody barrack room lawyers if tha ask me.

Changes in Working-Class Life

Upper medial:	A lot of —— —— —— snobs.
Medial and	Village folk like us, but some on 'em is very high and
lower medial:	mighty.
Lower class:	Decent folk. Folk that like to do what they wants to.[1]

(c) The individual individual

It has been argued by some sociologists that the state of 'anomie', or normlessness consequent upon a loosening of the social network, weakens the individual and his society by increasing his uncertainties and his opportunities for aberration. Others have argued that the changes to which man in modern society is subjected will tend to obliterate individual differences and bring about a uniformity of personality and behaviour. These two arguments do not seem to have cancelled each other.

We shall argue that there are circumstances which counteract the feared ill effects, and that there are effects arising out of anomie which are not ill at all. In particular, the opportunities for experimentation, and a greater awareness of individual dignity and potentiality, may be connected with a break in tradition. For, as was argued in previous chapters, certain aspects of traditional life encourage cognitive poverty. Economic poverty is not the least important of these aspects. As the standard of living goes up, what had been considered superfluous luxuries increase in availability and variety. Then people, having more money at their disposal or watching their better-off neighbours, become accustomed to using the increased opportunities to choose for themselves, and they learn to chafe at inconveniences which in the past were stoically considered to be part of life itself. Prosperity is more-ish, and so is the taste for making individual decisions.

In favourable conditions, migration furthers this trend. There was a feeling among Mogey's status-dissenters that they must accept responsibility for many things which never even became conscious problems for the assenting. The adverse conditions on many new housing estates—which can be very primitive: unmade roads, no shops, too few buses—force upon some who would otherwise have 'put up with things' more decisions, more

---

[1] W. M. Williams (1956), *Gosforth, The Sociology of an English Village*, Routledge and Kegan Paul, London.

269

forethought, more activity than had previously been required for survival. (The roughs will be the people who get more depressed than ever without taking action.) Things have to be done and the more energetic get together to do them. Community Associations form to push the authorities into building roads and altering bus-routes. Some people are for the first time in the position of dealing with the powers that be: 'them'. And if they are successful, this whets the appetite for more. Hence Mogey found the status-dissenters to be more demanding. They see no point in 'putting up with things'.

Moreover, when the individual moves to a new estate he is very forcibly presented with the sight of other ways of doing things. On a minor scale, we have something like a culture-contact. In a traditional society, a man's behaviour is governed by traditional, unquestioned rules and role-expectations. If there are contradictions in the culture, they are not likely to be perceived by the individual. He takes the customary reactions to customary situations for granted as obvious, natural, correct. In such societies it is relatively easy to describe how people behave, because most people behave in the same way.

But when the neighbours come newly from areas which, though their ways of life resemble his in some respects, are yet in other ways very different, a man is confronted more forcibly than before with the idea that there are alternative ways of action open to people like himself. Conscription in war-time has much the same effect and, as with conscription, the impact comes just at a time when the social control of the customary network is at a minimum—the old is disrupted, the new not yet formed.[1] At the same time, certain hopes and ambitions incapable of fulfilment in the old environment may now look more capable of attainment. When a man perceives alternatives of action, he perceives that he must make a choice.

Choice is what makes a man aware of himself as an individual. This happens when, upon encountering a problem in his life, he has to ask himself: 'What must I do next?' 'Why am I doing this?' instead of following without reflecting upon the solutions traditional in his society and therefore so obvious to

---

[1] It has been suggested that mining communities are so very traditional partly because miners were not subject to conscription.

him that he can hardly be said to have made a choice. These questions are likely to arise with more ineluctable force when, upon migration, a man is faced with more and new alternative possibilities of action.

In these ways, the move away from a close-knit community increases the number of occasions on which individual choices are called for, and may thereby set in motion a progress of individuation. So will that other classic condition for anomie: a marked increase in income.[1]

Before the evidence is seriously examined in detail, the case of Dagenham merits some discussion. By the time Willmott studied the estate, all the factors which, when they coincide, make for change, had appeared: a new house, a loosening of the network, affluence, and so on. But they had not coincided, and so the general pattern of life in Dagenham is status-assenting.

What happened in Dagenham suggests that the period of disruption is one of rather short duration. After ten years or so, most people had new routines of help and sociability. After twenty years nearly half had relatives on the estate. The next generation lives in an environment only a little less traditional and close-knit than those who moved there can remember from their own younger days in the place where they were born. Many of the old traditions of role-segregation and status-assent reappear in Dagenham.

This has interesting implications. There is a relatively brief period in which the opportunities for change are at their optimum—when conditions are such that the individual is at his most receptive. The changes that are made then 'take', becoming established and perpetuated. The circumstances which keep people flexible for long periods are difficult to identify and may be rather rare.

The exercise of the new freedom would show itself in a number of ways, but a general index would be in terms of the frequency with which the individual treads a path of his own choosing instead of following the traditional mode in which he

---

[1] It is of course perfectly possible that others, frightened by such freedom, escape into a cramped and compulsive conformity, though there is no evidence of this (E. Fromm (1946), *The Fear of Freedom*, Routledge and Kegan Paul, London).

was reared. For example, Zweig remarks that many working men are venturing into new fields of hobbies which were previously closed to them on account of their empty pockets.

> The inclination, widely spread among members of the British community, to have a hobby, and particularly the institutionalization of this inclination, constitutes another proof of the possibility for individual differentiation offered by the British culture pattern. For a hobby is obviously rooted in the individual's desire to develop his personality along a particular line which makes it possible for him to break away from his role as a member of society and thus to be himself. Hobbies are, on the whole, expressions of the feeling of privacy and the desire to differentiate which are experienced with a unique intensity in this country.[1]

Of more immediate social importance is evidence from Radby:

> The smaller size of the Grade IV and V households is usually a matter of choice—the parents decide they can afford so many children and no more, and that it is convenient from the point of view of housing-space and facilities to have a certain number.

In all the sources used in this chapter, the recurrent use of words like 'choice', 'decision', 'selection', is to be remarked.

> In Grades IV and V it is recognized that in the matter of expenditure, choices have to be made.
> Their dealings with other people are a matter of choice and selection: constant coming and going between relatives and friends is not desired, whereas privacy is.

Social interaction is by its nature very vulnerable to the effects of progressive individuation. At one extreme, there is Mrs. Newbolt: traditional and very assenting. She took it for granted that a friendly relation with a neighbour would come to an end if the other moved away. It required too great an effort to decide, and to implement the decision, to keep in contact with those outside the neighbourhood-network.[2] On the other hand we have Mogey's dissenters described in terms which show them to be more demanding, more striving, less easily

---

[1] Barbu, op. cit. For support see also Dagenham, pages 63 and 92 ff.

[2] Cf. the story of Mary and Jean in the chapter on Ashton, page 109.

resigned. 'In general, they *choose* their activities, their own companions, and their children's companions.' A more modern Mrs. Newbolt would not lose touch so soon with a neighbour she had liked. She would take a bus and go to see her.

The absence of deliberately chosen 'friends' is correctly associated by Mogey with the absence of deliberate choice in social relations. In St. Ebbe's, and in Dagenham also, 'friends' were mainly neighbours (not necessarily next-door ones) and school-mates, with a few work-mates.[1] These were the people with whom interaction was in any case enforced by circumstances. At Barton, half the friends reported came from the neighbourhood in which the informants had previously lived, about a third lived on the estate, the rest came from work. There was a greater variety, therefore, and their upkeep required more effort.

The kind of interaction which marked non-kin friendship in the older areas persists. It is in the additional relationships that the change is noticeable. This seems confirmed by Zweig, who asked in 1958 a series of standard questions for comparison with 1948. One of these was: 'How do you get on with your mates?' and the current answer was, in the overwhelming majority of cases, 'Very well', or, 'The finest lot'. But actually, he continues, the comradeship as revealed in the answers seemed cordial but not intimate ('distant cordiality', Gorer called it). It entailed men helping one another during work and conversing during the break, mostly on such topics as sports or T.V. or girls, but talking only rarely of their own home-life. Zweig would describe the trend as a widening of contacts with, at the same time, a definite decline in intensity.

Only those who are able, for one reason or another, to detach themselves from the old neighbourly and family network feel the need for new social relations and are thus tempted to make the effort to create them for themselves. Being cut off from the older providers of advice and service and companionship may itself be one such reason. Thereafter, the migrant is more likely to rely on *congenial* people, wherever he can find them. These do not necessarily live next door (though more people at Barton than at St. Ebbe's are thought by the interviewers to have

[1] Dagenham, pages 61-2.

'accepting' attitudes to the people immediately next door). To find a friend, the migrant has to make a bit of an effort, and he has to make a choice. This may provide an opportunity for greater personal individuation than was previously possible. At least at Barton, it seems that people availed themselves of this opportunity, as the following little table indicates:

	At St. Ebbe's %	At Barton %
Families reporting no friends	60	30
Families who have one friend	30	30
Families reporting more than one friend	10	40

This may be no more than a straw in the wind.

> The change is probably not one of importance in real activities ... but the choice of words indicates a shift from passive acceptance of a neighbourhood to the selection of friends, a matter involving choice and therefore a more active behaviour, a sign of the use of social skills.

Mogey's reserve concerning the extent of the change may be justified where Barton is concerned. From a different source the same argument is put forward with evidence that the trend there has affected activities as well as verbal expressions of feelings. In Firth's comparative study of kinship-networks, a contrast was drawn with primitive tribal communities where, when a gap occurs in the network it tends to be filled by other kin, and a South London borough where

> should an elementary family be denuded or dispersed, or should dislikes weaken contacts, the kinship structure is immediately broken. This breaking-up is due to the high degree of *personal selectivity* possible in the borough. In primitive societies, kin may be bound by elaborate and firm obligations which are apt to bring them into frequent contact with one another. Even if their sentiments are lukewarm, the chain of relation is usually sufficiently strong, especially through their children, to keep the system in force. But in the South Borough the lack of formalized kin obligations leaves the tie without that necessary support of periodic repetition which gives it content. On the other hand, the kin-relations in force have a high emotional content, and pattern

the kinship system according to the individual personalities of the members.[1]

The authors then show how this personal selectivity is manifested in visiting, some of which is with kin and some with others, and in the exchange of simple services, which is also undertaken with those outside as well as with those within the family. The following may be a particularly telling observation.

> In the same fortnight of July 1948, there were in that seaside resort ten persons of the same kinship set, all staying in the same boarding house . . . The group also included people not related to the informant, as a personal friend and his wife, who had come to share their holidays with him.

In the previous chapter it was argued that the idea of 'friends' did not fit well into traditional working-class life. One reason was, that it implied a difference between types of social interaction which did not there exist. Zweig provides some evidence for our expectation—arising directly out of the present argument—that with changing circumstances such differentiation becomes possible.

> The majority of workers would subscribe to the saying often heard, that 'mates are not pals'. As one man put it: 'In the environment of work we are friends, but outside we are more choosey.' 'It but rarely happens that you work with a mate who is your personal friend.'

In these quotations we see a new terminology evolving to keep pace with the new psychological refinement. As distinctions between relationships emerge, words are allotted to stiffen the distinctions.

The prerogative of choice shows not only in the personal selection of friends, but in a new approach to other social groupings. Those who are feeling more emancipated from the traditional community are more likely to feel free to join other associations. This very plausible hypothesis is confirmed by a curious negative instance. Even in the traditional area there are people who join associations, just as there are people who

[1] R. Firth, ed. (1956), *Two Studies of Kinship in London*, University of London Press.

do choose friends. Now it turns out that in St. Ebbe's not a few friendships are a *consequence of selection among the members of such associational groups*. This may be considered together with a similar finding by Willmott and Young that in Bethnal Green those who were most sociable at home were also most sociable outside it. These people are a minority; they are status-dissenters who still live in the old area.

Mogey has argued that the selection of friends is a sign of greater social confidence than is the uncritical acceptance of neighbours. More generally, the individual individual does not confine himself uncritically to the more obvious and traditional opportunities which his environment affords him. Selectivity in other areas of life may therefore be expected. It will be argued here that the mass media of communication further this trend towards selectivity, though many have maintained the opposite view—that mass media induce conformity.

It can be agreed that when social norms have to be created because the old ones are no longer congenial to status-dissenters, the mass-media will have considerable impact. The argument is stated by Mogey in the following terms.

The fact that people on the estate have changed may be attributed in part to the change in physical environment, to the break in the pattern of daily exchanges within an extended family of several households, and also to an interruption in the older gossip exchanges which maintained, as good and acceptable, former standards of outlook and behaviour. In the old areas, there is only a slow penetration past the barriers of inertia and local groups, of middle-class ideas current in magazines, in cinema and wireless programmes. So long as the audiences of these mass media report back to a local gathering, whether in a public house or a mothers' meeting, before they accept the outlooks and standard of values shown in these media, so long will the change be slow. But as the reference-group on which they base their ideals ceases to be a local neighbourhood one, it becomes more and more a national one as depicted in the mass media of communication. The break-up of local face-to-face groups will not inevitably lead to the rapid adoption of new standards, but if such disruption of social life takes place as a result of transportation to a new environment, and of isolation there, the tendency to believe what is heard on the wireless, what is read in the picture magazines, and what is viewed on television and cinema-screens is re-inforced.

In these circumstances a man is not necessarily driven towards conformity and mass-society. He may move towards greater individuation instead. Initially this may show itself, as in the status-dissenter's behaviour, in efforts to move away from the traditional pattern. Having learned how to emancipate himself, he may apply his knowledge so as to differentiate himself from his neighbours. There are signs that on a relatively trivial level, such as house-decoration, this is indeed happening. Psychological differentiation may be slower to come about; as yet there is no evidence one way or the other about it, except in the matter of hobbies. The trends being described in this chapter suggest, however, that conditions favourable to greater individuation do now exist.

As was argued at the end of the previous chapter, the closer the members of the extended family, the closer the community and hence the slower the response to the new opportunities which affluence and the Welfare State afford. Because the latter were lacking at the time when people moved into Dagenham, the response there is in fact slower. In the two sub-sections which follow, formal associational life and the trend toward greater partnership in marriage are to be considered. In both aspects the Dagenham population resembles the old areas more than the new.

(d) Formal associations

Logically considered, there is nothing to prevent the trend towards individuation from occurring simultaneously with a trend towards mass-society: different people or different areas of life may be subject to either. So it is that Mogey has felt justified in ending his book on a truly optimistic note:

> The absence of any commonly accepted standards of belief and action distinguishes Barton from the community of St. Ebbe's. Barton is in fact not a localized society nor do its inhabitants feel loyal to an isolating set of social customs. They have lost their ties to a neighbourhood and gained in return citizenship in the wider and freer atmosphere of the varied associational life of a city.

In the previous chapter it was noted that Gorer had found that those who troubled to specify that they belonged to the upper strata, either of middle or of working class, took a much greater part in formal associational life than the rest of his informants. Status-dissenters welcome new opportunities. Certainly only 10 per cent of Mogey's St. Ebbe's sample belonged to any organization, 40 per cent on the new estate. Dagenham falls between these two, at 20 per cent.

As a man becomes more demanding of life and impatient of the restraint he now feels traditional social expectations to be exerting upon him, he is more likely to turn to impersonal agencies for the satisfaction of his needs. For in this way he can avoid feeling under obligation. But with this goes a deeper change in attitude, already touched upon when the distinction between status-assent and status-dissent was first mentioned. The greater tendency for dissenters to join formal associations was there associated with their greater freedom from that form of self-consciousness which is basically a consciousness of inferior class-membership. Dissenters are less resigned to, or perhaps more free from, the tendency to perceive the social world as divisible into an inferior 'us' and a superior 'them'.

Consequently they feel freer to associate in grouping where they will meet 'them'. Thus, for instance, in the Radby Grade IV and V households the parents co-operated with the school authorities through such means as the Parent-Teacher Association. The men in these grades applauded the principle of a training-scheme for lads interested in the (mining) industry. Like Gorer's informants, some feel that they cannot accurately be called 'working class', they qualify the term in some way. Zweig also finds that when he asks manual workers about their social class, some make a distinction between their status in the works and their status outside. If they make this distinction they more often belong to clubs with a socially mixed membership: in the employer–employee context they are aware of status-differences; outside the factory these are of less significance.

Mitchell and Lupton noted the same trend some years previously: 'When the individual, and this applies particularly to the manual worker, leaves his work and returns to the housing-estate where he lives, a change in attitudes and relationships takes place. He ceases to be a fitter by the name of John Smith and becomes instead, John Smith, a person who happens to be a fitter but who, as a person, likes to feel that he excercises a wide choice in ordering his relationships with others, and who will attempt to satisfy his social needs and live up to his scheme of values by using such social skills as he may possess. When a large number of "John Smiths", each attempting to exercise the prerogative of choice in relationships, are placed together, a complex pattern or even number of patterns of interpersonal and inter-group relationships will emerge. In such a situation, although manual workers as such have no status which they can carry over from the factory to the estate some of them will tend to assume superior status.' They feel less inhibited by their group if they want to mix with others or even if they want to exercise their talent for leadership.

The question of class-consciousness in this situation will be dealt with more fully in the next chapter. Here only a few quotations from Zweig are presented to support the argument Mitchell and Lupton put forward. 'I'm working class only in the works, but outside I'm a human being'; 'I'm working class but I'm not conscious of it'; 'There are no (class) differences. I live in the same neighbourhood as my manager, have the same kind of house and have a car.' In this psychological climate many of the difficulties that beset traditional working-class associational life do disappear.

This more general change in attitude has worried Raymond Williams, who views with alarm the trend towards individuality because he sees it not in contrast with the uniformity and mass-society of the traditional working-class community, but in contrast with the practice of solidarity which he feels to be a characteristic virtue of that group at its best.

> Another alternative to solidarity which has had some effect is the idea of individual opportunity—of the ladder. Many working-class leaders, men in fact who have used the ladder, have been dazzled by this alternative to solidarity. Yet the ladder is a perfect symbol of the bourgeois idea of society, because, while undoubtedly it offers the opportunity to climb, it is a device which can only be used individually: you go up the ladder alone. This kind of individual climbing is of course the bourgeois model: a man

should be allowed to better himself . . . The process of reform, insofar as it has not been governed by working-class pressure, has been, in large part, the giving of increasing opportunity to climb. Many indeed have scrambled up and gone off to play on the other side; many have tried to climb and failed.

Judged in each particular case, it seems obviously right that a working man, or a child of a working-class family, should be enabled to fit himself for a different kind of work, corresponding to his ability. Because of this, the ladder idea has produced a real conflict of values within the working class itself. My own view is that the ladder version of society is objectionable in two related respects: first, it weakens the principle of common betterment which ought to be an absolute value; second, it sweetens the poison of hierarchy, in particular by offering the hierarchy of merit as a thing different in kind from the hierarchy of money or birth.[1]

The idea that the more fortunate worker complacently accepts his absorption into a middle-class style of life is supported by Zweig, quoted below. The difference in the emotional tone of these two writers arises from Zweig's assumption that nobody will be left behind, that the betterment is in fact common and that it is effortless.[2] Williams assumes that children will have to abandon their parents and their community, as Bott has described.[3]

In the five works I visited I found little signs of what is often called the 'alienation' of the workman from his work, or 'estrangement from society'. I had no feeling that the worker was estranged from society, or from the firm employing him. The tendency, I think, was for the worker to be brought nearer to the firm which gives him good treatment, a relatively good livelihood and a measure of security, and—this is perhaps the most significant development—for him to lose the sense of identity with his own class, to which he is bound no longer by the links of common hardship, handicaps and injustices, and the constant call to arms in class-warfare.

[1] R. Williams (1958), *Culture and Society*, Chatto and Windus, London. This quotation is reconsidered on page 429.
[2] As in Dagenham, a single-class estate, where the absence of status-anxiety is to be noted.
[3] See the discussion on pages 244–5 of this chapter, and page 331.

Changes in Working-Class Life

The important point for consideration here is clearly brought out by both writers. The intense us/them mistrust is on its way out. One of the hindrances to a richer associational life is thereby removed.

The move to a new estate may in many ways reinforce a tendency towards associational life. Because in the very early days there is a feeling of crisis and emergency (traditional occasions for neighbourliness), many sources report at first a good deal of spontaneous helpfulness. Among the families in Barton were some who had been living on the estate since 1946. Their description of the first days of the estate was confirmed by other families not in the Barton sample, and by accounts of other estates. There is at first a period of great mutual friendliness, when groups of people help one another in all sorts of ways: shopping, baby-minding, helping with the garden, lending, welcoming newly-arrived families, and so on. Sometimes this informal interaction is accompanied by the creation of more formal bodies. Residents' Associations agitate for remedies against the worst features of the estates: better roads, more buses, something for the children to do. In Barton—very typical of other estates in this respect—

> out of this intense social activity, leaders began to emerge and to organize the children into cricket and football teams. From these men a Residents' Association was formed through the intiative of the Youth Officer of the City Council, and a movement began which led to the erection of a community-centre building.

But though some of the preconditions for a more varied associational life exist, it is not likely to flourish among first-generation status-dissenters. The attitudes of the past, described in the previous chapter, may be too firmly established to allow it to persist. Hence neither in Barton nor in the other areas on which evidence is published do the new associations act for any period of time as a cohesive agent for the whole community. The cards are stacked against successful long-term ventures. The tradition is against it. Watlingitis sets in ('The patient is attacked by a sudden desire to do nothing, see nothing, help no-one and go nowhere'). This is partly attributable to the extreme strain of inventing, as one goes along, in a variety of unexpected and novel situations, the most sensible and most proper way to behave, putting up the while with the mistakes that others make and with one's own inadequacy in coping. After a while the will is sapped.

Moreover, the lack of commonly-accepted norms means that the Association is normally captured after a while by one or other subgroup with a greater internal uniformity of norms; in practice this will be a group either of roughs or of respectables on the estate. This process, once begun, is difficult to reverse. We may apply here a conclusion reached before: the more easily a misclassification is made, in this case the more people look similar but feel different, the greater the circumspection with which they will interact.[1] In Coventry this mutual avoidance was manifested very delicately because there were two foci for association. There was the Social Club preferred by the roughs and nicely demonstrating the characteristic of 'effortless sociability'. Its membership decreased regularly the farther away the people lived, fading out beyond a radius of a mile. And there was the Community Centre, favoured by the respectables and attracting its members by more discriminating criteria than proximity. On the Liverpool estate the better class kept aloof from formal sociable activity: supervisory and clerical grades entirely, the skilled manual workers more than the other manual workers. On this estate the less respectable were the joiners. They were the ones who went to the Community Centre, belonged to the Residents' Association, and had a generally favourable attitude to community life.

A third reason for failure in associational life is that leadership is a skill that most people are not born to. Normally it has to be learnt by experience. Here we have a population whose values in the past have been very strongly against 'putting yourself forward', 'getting big-headed', 'shoving people around', and sturdy enough often to find middle-class leadership unsatisfactory. The lack of past experience in organizing social activities, and particularly in co-operating with each other in a formal way to develop new activities, tells against new ventures in associational life, as does the fact that they have little experience of being led by one of themselves. An extreme form of the

[1] On people looking similar but feeling different see also page 245.

difficulties this engenders is illustrated in Frankenberg's *Village on the Border*, if for once a rural setting may be referred to. No member of this community could stay leader for long, because ere long the other people would be asking themselves why they should do as he suggested—in spite of the fact that he had been elected by them. Their solution was ever to revert to an earlier pattern and find some stranger to their community—the squire in olden days—to take over the responsibility.[1]

Frankenberg's study also suggests that one important factor for success, if people are to adjust to such major changes as arrival on a new estate, is the ability to let go of kin-supported attitudes and behaviour. In *Village on the Border* the change-over from community to associational life was never success-fully made, partly because each time the village had elected someone, who, obviously, belonged to some kin-group or other, the other kin-groups would not for long respond to his leader-ship-role. Nor was this sheer cussedness on their part, for the members of the leader's kin-group tended to expect, and often obtained, favours from the leaders in a way which is normal when, in a traditional community, one member of a family is more fortunate than another.

If, however, the kin-group is renounced, this leaves people freer to work through formal associations and agencies, and it also occurs to them more easily to 'see someone about it'.

Finally, in this brief discussion on some of the causes for the relative failure of associational life in the new areas, we must take into consideration the development of other new interests, particularly in the home and the family. Home and family compete with outside associations, and so far, the latter have lost to the former.

(e) *The home-centred family*

In a small-scale relatively closed society, the local group and the kin-group mediate between the family and the total society; in an urban industrialized society there is no single encapsulating group or institution that mediates between the family and the total society. One result of this difference in external relationships

[1] R. Frankenberg (1957), *Village on the Border*, Routledge and Kegan Paul, London.

is that urban families have more freedom to govern their own affairs. In a small-scale society the encapsulating groups have a great deal of control over the family. In an urban industrialized society the doctor looks after the health of individual members of the family, the clinic looks after the health of the mother and child, the school educates the children, the boss cares about the individual as an employee rather than as a husband, and even friends, neighbours and relatives may disagree among themselves as to how the affairs of the family should be conducted.

In brief [Bott continues] social control of the family is split up among so many agencies that none of them has continuous, complete, governing power. Within broad limits, a family can make its own decision and regulate its own affairs. The situation may be summed up by saying that [like individuals] these families are more highly *individuated* than families in relatively closed communities. I think this term describes the situation of urban families more accurately than does the more commonly used term 'isolated'. By individuation is meant that the elementary family is separated off, differentiated out as a distinct and to some extent autonomous social group.

The elementary family is forced by the move to become aware of itself as, at least potentially, a self-sufficient unit.

At Barton, husband and wife are reported to share more interests, to go on holiday together more often, to take more interest in the children and their future. They all go out together: to the cinema, for walks in the country, maybe to a country pub with a garden for the children. The associations they join they may join together. In general [Mogey comments] the status-dissenters demand more from their family-life.

The television keeps men at home with their families and procures a family-entertainment [writes Zweig], while a car provides for a family outing and once again keeps them with their families. A car outing is a family-affair. 'The car's for the kiddies.' Both innovations strengthen the family circle, while weakening the ties with work-mates. Only rarely do the men invite their friends in their car or arrange outings with their mates (though they may take them to work).

The growth of television also compensates for the absence of amenities outside the home, and serves to support the [Greenleigh] family in its isolation. Instead of going out to the cinema or the pub, the family sits night by night around the magic screen in its place of honour in the parlour. 'The tellie keeps the family together. None of us ever have to go out now.'

The people in Grades IV and V know how to enjoy themselves without spending a lot of money. Much of their leisure-time is spent with their children in the home, and they spend on the home itself to make this a pleasant place in which to pass their spare time. Leisure-time is spent decorating the house, cultivating the garden, watching T.V., listening to the wireless and so on. In these grades, leisure-time seems to be considered in terms of activity on the part of the children as well as the adults. The family spends much of its leisure together—children get taken into the country, or to see the Ideal Home Exhibition, or 'his father takes him to the cinema when there is a jungle-film on'. Three households were met where the family are keen readers. For people like these [the authors continue rather acidly], a visit to the countryside is not so expensive as it might be for a lower-grade family. Where the latter are concerned, the licensing laws are likely to curtail considerably the actual time spent 'in the country'.

Young and Willmott are more preoccupied with the unattractive aspects of migration.

Their lives outside the family are no longer centred on people, their lives are centred on the house. This change from a people-centred to a house-centred existence is one of the fundamental changes resulting from the migration. It goes some way to explain the competition for status which is in itself the result of isolation from kin and the cause of estrangement from neighbours, the reason why co-existence, instead of being just a state of live-and-let-live, is frequently infused with so much bitterness . . . 'I don't mind saying hello to any of them, or passing the time of day with them, but if they don't want to have anything to do with me, I don't want to have anything to do with them. I'm not bothered about them. My wife and my two children—they're the people that I care about. My life down here is my home.'

Mogey, on the other hand, likes the changes; he speaks of a family-centred group which he contrasts with the neighbourhood-centred group of St. Ebbe's. Although St. Ebbe's appears a somewhat different culture from Bethnal Green, the resemblance between Barton and Greenleigh is clear. One may conclude, therefore, that what Young and Willmott call the achievement-oriented, house-centred group, Mogey calls the family-centred group; which is certainly a more pleasant, less derogatory appellation. To avoid controversy we may call it, as Mark Abrams does, the home-centred society.[1]

The home-centred family does not necessarily isolate itself from other people. Zweig set himself to elicit reactions from his informants which would enable him to compare the affluent worker with his less fortunate counterpart ten years before. He did this by making 'provocative remarks'. One of these was 'when we are married, all the company we need is at home'. Twenty-four of the men agreed with this, either in terms of affection for home or in terms of 'keeping ourselves to ourselves'. The other thirty-five objected, often very emphatically. The women's proportion was much the same. Nor is the picture drawn in the Radby Report an unattractive one.

> The women in Grades IV and V are houseproud, but this is not just a mania about having a speck of dust in the house. It is an integral part of their lives. Deep satisfaction is gained from having a 'good' home and from conforming with the standards which they set themselves.

House-work in these 'good' grades is an important part of family life, and is considered both necessary and a valuable contribution to the construction and maintenance of a pleasant home. It is recognized as a skill, and there are standards of excellence in operation.[2] These women were pleased to have the opportunity to attend a cake-making demonstration at the Community Centre.

Some of the housewives have a strict time-table which governs the performance of their domestic duties, and they feel called upon to explain, in an apologetic way, if they are found not conforming to it. Keeping the home spick and span is a matter of principle in Grades IV and V. At one house the woman was busy cleaning when the interviewer called. He was invited back on another day: the house-cleaning could not be interrupted for him. A contrast is evident here with the lower

---

[1] M. Abrams, 'The home-centred society', *The Listener*, November 26, 1959.

[2] The psychological traits mentioned in the passage which follow are later discussed in greater detail with reference to the parental behaviour which encourages their growth in young children. The references which follow direct the reader's attention to those further discussions. Here *vide* page 609.

grades, where in many cases no set time was allotted for house-keeping, and a visitor provided a welcome excuse for breaking off from work—this was also the experience of the interviewers in St. Ebbe's.[1]

Most of the houses in these grades are reported to be neat and clean and in a good state of repair. Interviewers often comment 'spotlessly clean' or 'a very pretty spotless, expensive room, new tiled grate, pretty loose covers, flowers in bowl'. In several cases the husband does all the house decorations—working on it at week-ends and evenings for several months.[2] The home plays an important part in these people's scheme of values. They set up their homes with the intention of improving them as it becomes economically possible. Many are buying their home, or already own it, believing that it is a good plan to expend a little more at the moment in order to provide for the future.[3]

These trends are characteristic of affluence, and more will be said of them in the pages which follow. To round off the discussion on associational life it is now only necessary to state explicitly that here interest in home and family have taken priority over the joining of more formal organizations. Individuation has shown itself less in 'joining' than in a new ideal of home life.

Some of the loss of social life may be made good within the home, write Young and Willmott of the Greenleigh couple. Husband and wife are together and a closer partnership here can make isolation bearable. Both are cut off from their previous networks. The wife may now discuss with her husband some of the problems she would normally have talked over with the other womenfolk. He talks to her more because his work-mates may not live on the same estate, so that he is more likely to be at home in the evenings. This is the more important since the house, as far as amenities are concerned, is a more attractive place than the old housing, which was after all the primary cause of their move.

---

[1] See page 163.
[2] See pages 500-5 and 508-11 for further discussion on the value and consequences of longer time-perspectives.
[3] See pages 490, 497 and 524 on the ability to tolerate a delay in gratification.

The pressure towards a greater self-sufficiency in the family was also experienced by two of Bott's sample families, the Dodgsons and the Butlers. They were working class and had not been occupationally mobile. In this, and in their general cultural background, they were like the Newbolts. But their networks had become disrupted when they moved away from their old neighbourhood. Both couples recounted how, when they moved, they felt strangers in a land of people all strangers to one another. At first they did not know how to cope with the situation. In both cases husband and wife had turned to one another for help, especially at first.

This is a touch-and-go transitional phenomenon. If, as in Dagenham, the move is not accompanied by other social changes, the old patterns re-establish themselves. 'The great majority—four-fifths—of the married men and women in the general sample who grew up on the estate and whose parents are alive have them living there', and here the life of the extended family is as described in the previous chapter. Whatever may have been the conjugal relation in the early days of the move to Dagenham, now the majority of mothers and daughters are closely tied, and the men relatively separate. There is less individuation of the elementary family in Dagenham. In spite of affluence and the Welfare State, the greater interest in the home is not accompanied to the same extent by a strengthening of the conjugal bond. The persistence of the Demeter-system may be held accountable for this.

Normally in the post-war period, however, the change in social relationship may be schematically represented as tending from the first sketch (reproduced from page 190 of the previous chapter) to the second.

(f) The disappearance of the stress syndrome and the emergence of partnership
It is a common finding in small-group studies that when the group's task is considered supremely important by the members, or, which may be the same thing, when the environment of the group makes survival difficult, the relations of group-members towards one another tend to take on a characteristic form. Interaction between the members tends to be restricted, more

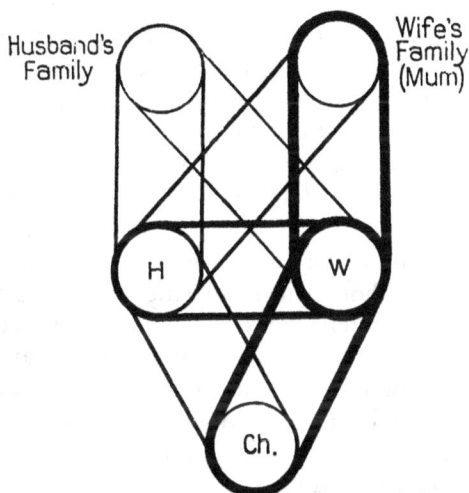

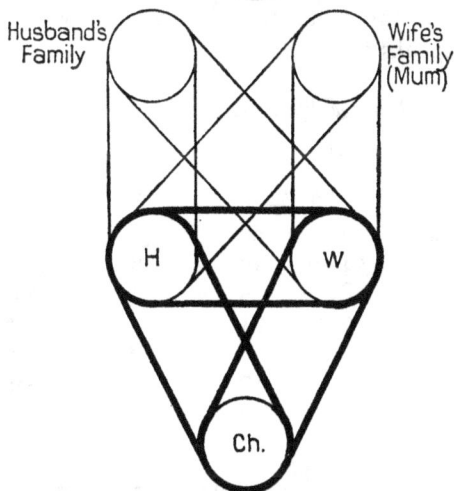

than is normally the case, to matters arising from the task itself, and less interaction is devoted to the maintenance of a happy social and emotional life between the members. After a critical point, which of course varies in different circumstances, members tend to like each other less than in the past or than is normal, and they also tend to begin to resent the task they are performing. Thirdly, a more authoritarian structure tends to evolve, with one strong leader whose followers are submissive to him. We may call these characteristics the 'stress syndrome'.[1] It is not difficult to see a resemblance between the effects produced by stress in the small experimental group, and the effects of stress in family life. Stress is of course always to some extent a subjective phenomenon, as students of the problem-family are well aware. Lack of skills, lack of health, and a relative inability to tolerate frustration combine to produce stress in one family while another is still managing well on the same income. The housewife's efficiency is often crucial, but it is rarely an independent variable: it relates to income, health (often affected by income), husband's support and so on. In traditional working-class families, as Hoggart pointed out, what with frequent childbirth and miscarriages, with neither time nor money nor courage to see the doctor, a woman may from her early thirties onward be 'nobbut middling'.

The following table, taken from a recent book on marriage counselling, speaks for itself.[2]

Marriage difficulties and family income

Weekly family income (1953)

	up to £5	£5–£10	£10–£20	over £20	No record
Personal defects	52	50	50	59	41
Health	24	23	22	15	21
Income	18	5	2	1	3
Living conditions	19	21	11	3	16
Separation	12	6	5	3	7
Infidelity	21	16	19	29	17
Incompatibility	12	15	17	20	15
Sex difficulties	15	25	33	29	27

Given that personal defects make the greatest single category, distressing conditions of a non-psychological kind cause more difficulties in marriage in the lower-income groups; more psychological conditions cause difficulties in the higher.

[1] J. Klein (1956), *The Study of Groups*, Routledge and Kegan Paul, London (chap. VII).
[2] J. H. Wallis and H. S. Booker (1958), *Marriage Counselling*, Routledge and Kegan Paul, London.

Changes in Working-Class Life

In the traditional communities whose family-structure was discussed in the previous chapter, when financial stress intensifies, the rift between husband and wife must deepen. The man will work more overtime, and so be in the house less than before. The woman will rely more on her kin, and hence be less involved with her spouse than before. The poorer the family is, the more restricted their lives will become, and the less man and wife will have to share emotionally and socially.

Conversely, in groups under less stress, or, since it may be necessary to think in relative terms, where the stress is lifting, one tends to find more affectionate relations between members, or at least more interaction which expresses and demonstrates such affection, more consultation between the members, and a less authoritarian structure. These conclusions seem to apply to families which have, in their own life-time, risen above subsistence level or markedly improved their standard of living. A new book, *Infant Care in an Urban Community*, devotes its final chapter to a comparison of 'Then and Now'.

I think we're more *interested* in the children. I remember them singing to us after our baths, but we never had interesting *conversations* with our parents, the way I do with my children.

Children these days, it is said, are able to 'talk to' their parents in a way which, for a considerable number, seems to have been quite impossible before. Partly this reflects a new feeling of equality between parent and child, which allows the parents to accept correction from the child and even to take pride in it; partly, it seems also a matter of frankness: a willingness on the parents' part to answer the child truthfully, without continually taking refuge on the parental pedestal.

I never had what you'd call—any love—from my mother. Now with ours I think that's the main thing, because even with our Patricia (five)—I'll put her on my knee and nurse her and love her, and she comes and asks me for it; well, I can never remember having any of that. I could never hold a conversation with my mother, well even now I can't—seems as though we're distant somehow, funny isn't it? Yet I think a lot *of* her, but I just couldn't talk to her like I'm doing you. We can't get near each other . . . I don't know if it's because of me being a bit timid of my mam, but my little girl has her say; I have to listen to her say, you see; and then I'm not right, you see, the little one knows it all, I don't know nothing![1]

It is along these lines that an explanation may also be attempted of the tendency towards a more joint conjugal role-relationship—partnership in marriage—which has been noted by so many writers.

Another problem deserving investigation is the relation between the sexes in the working class [wrote Zweig in 1952]. Any observer of working-class communities will be struck by a certain segregation of the sexes in their leisure-time activities. It is more pronounced among the older generation than among the younger, more in the slummy than in good working-class districts, more in the North than in the South, more among the heavy labourers than among the factory workers. The phenomenon itself is receding and the older generations are used to their separate outings much more than the younger ones . . .

I believe poverty, slummy conditions, unsatisfactory working-conditions and educational backwardness are somewhat conducive to a certain segregation of the sexes in their leisure time. Poverty means that both partners cannot afford to pay for their outings as they would wish to. Slummy conditions drive men from their homes more frequently than otherwise. Unsatisfactory working-conditions make men irritable and create a real need for more entertainment.[2]

Zweig believes that the home of the affluent worker is more insulated against the adverse effects of factory life.

Previously a man used to bring work home in the form of dirt in his clothes; now more often he has a bath provided by the firm. He used to bring work home in the form of anxiety, perhaps as to whether he would be able to hold his job; now security of employment is much more general. He used to be more tired, working longer hours under more strenuous conditions. Now when he gets home he not only wants to forget about his work, but is also more able to do so as the job rarely carries a great load of frustrations,

---

[1] On the importance of conversation, see pages 493, 505 and 512-13. On pride in the child's ability to correct the parent, see page 596 also.

[2] A popular novel by Alan Sillitoe, *Saturday Night and Sunday Morning*, recently described with imaginative insight the relation between the dully exasperating working conditions and the taste for violent, intense experiences in one's time off. See also the discussion on page 182 fn.

anxieties and conflicts. He is rarely pushed and driven, he is rarely offended in a way which could involve his self-respect. He does not need to keep his resentment or grievances to himself, he can voice them freely, and he can lodge his complaints. He still, so to speak, wears a mask while at work, but wearing it is not such a strain as it used to be. He feels better adjusted all round, so when he comes home he is not so 'bottled up' as he was.

The general trend towards the more home-centred family has already been noted; it remains to show one particular aspect of this: the greater equality of husbands and wives, and the stronger feeling for partnership in marriage when stress lifts. This is the family's equivalent of more equality of status and better group-morale in the small experimental group.

With a decline in financial difficulties, more relaxed attitudes towards financial matters become possible. Zweig asked a small sample of some sixty husbands and wives (in London) whether they knew what the other earned. Most of them did. In thirteen cases the wives did not know what the husband earned, but the husbands in these cases did not know what the wife earned either! Dennis, Henriques and Slaughter present more complicated supporting evidence:

The more irresponsible minority of [middle-aged Ashton] husbands and wives have now passed their most difficult days of managing with money. As it happens, those years were difficult not only because they had to build the household and bring up their families but because they were years of depression and grinding hardship. In the families of this less responsible element there is a continual haggling over money, the wife accusing the husband of deceiving her as to the money he has in his pocket, the husband trying to think of ways of 'scrounging' a few shillings without telling his wife. All the worst examples found of this tendency were among those workmen who had returned to day-wage work, had not adapted themselves to new spending-habits, and had not a sufficiently smooth relationship with their wives to effect a peaceful transition to the new level of life.

This quotation may be contrasted with a more forward-looking one from Zweig.

One can say that the majority [of the 1958 workers' sample] enjoyed a comfortable and well-equipped home although a fair proportion were still living in poor conditions. They were very conscious of their home comforts and their attachments to their homes. One might hear such remarks as: 'I have achieved many things which would be unthinkable to my father' or 'I have achieved something which I thought would have been impossible for me'. It is reasonable to conclude that more of the spare money of these people is spent on the home, which assumes a possibly romanticized image of refuge, giving delight as well as status.

And a Bethnal Green informant reminisces about the bad old days when 'my dad used to say: "I'm the man of the house. Here's my money, and if anyone wants me, you know where I am—in the pub." ' This man went on: 'If they want a drink of beer now, they go and fetch a bottle in, so they can watch the telly at the same time.' With more money, the house becomes a more attractive place. So better housing conditions have played their part in bringing about a better conjugal relationship.

With the house a more attractive place, the man is induced to stay home more often. This may in turn encourage the man to take a greater interest in what goes on in the house and how it looks. For instance, Chapman notes that with a rise in social status as judged by type of house occupied, husband and wife are more likely to consider together furnishings for their house.[1]

Housing groups	Main interest in furnishing taken by		
	Wife	Husband	Both
Small bye-law	46	6	48
Larger bye-law	56	5	39
Council house	33	2	65
Semi-detached	24	2	69
Detached	14	2	79

This Liverpool (1949) finding may well be typical of the new national trend. There are certainly many more opportunities for husband and wife to do things together than there were and, it will be remembered, the probability is that with an increase in interaction will go an increase in liking and understanding. For instance, now that real incomes have risen there is more

[1] D. Chapman (1955), *The Home and Social Status*, Routledge and Kegan Paul, London. The sample consisted of 275 Liverpool families more or less equally distributed over the social scale.

money about than there was and this, as well as lifting stress by affording more opportunities for the gratification of wants, allows more elbow-room for conjugally-shared decisions on how it is to be spent. (That this does not necessarily follow was noted in the account of the Ashton way of life, where more money meant only that the man had more 'free income' than hitherto.)

When man and wife discuss the way they shall spend money, the fact that they talk together is not the least of the benefits more spending-money confers. Parallel to this, the fact that television keeps the husband from the pub is not the only benefit T.V. confers. Like purchases for the home, television provides a talking-point for husbands and wives who have not learned the arts of conjugal conversation in their parental homes. Television-advertisements provide a common background of ideas on which husbands and wives may base the decisions, about home-furnishings and other purchases, which they make together.

There is undoubtedly an increase in the number of topics about which husbands and wives now find it possible to talk together. The home itself is one of these topics. The adults in the Radby Grade IV and V households, it will be recalled, were reported to have few hobbies or leisure activities unconnected with the home, 'which is for most of these people the one great interest in life'. The relative lack of interest in formal organizations had surprised the investigators, who, however, attributed this without difficulty to 'the concentration of their informants' interest upon the home and the children'.

The shared conjugal interest in the children will merit a section for itself below, but it is relevant here that the investigators found it

> obvious that the parents of these children (in Grades IV and V) not only discuss their children constantly, but also talk over other things of interest to them. Several women informed their husbands of the interviewer's calls, and subsequently discussed the topics with him. Other parents argued over the topics in a friendly way, while the interviewer was there. Unlike in the I and II homes, there seemed to be little hesitation on the part of the women about discussing matters in their husbands' presence.

Zweig relates understanding, liking and conversation very neatly.

> It is notable that whenever the wife is conversant with the kind of work her husband does—if for instance she was on similar work during the war, or has a similar job, or when the wife is especially affectionate or concerned about her husband—talking shop more frequently occurs.

In fact, there is evidence that with a lightening of the load, husbands and wives talk not only more with each other, they also talk with each other more pleasantly than before. They like each other better. Mogey has an interesting set of correlations.

	St. Ebbe's	Barton
	in percentages	
Bickering in front of interviewer	35	15
No bickering in front of interviewer	65	85
Strong division of labour in household	65	20
Weak division of labour in household	35	80

Although Mogey stresses that these figures are no more than indicative, it is worth while noting that on the new estate, where things are easier, relations between husbands and wives are better, or at least more considerate, and that here the division of labour is also very much weaker. Partnership and good relations go together. Zweig makes the same point.

> The husband–wife relationships of the workers in an affluent society were described by the overwhelming majority as happy. Very few men referred to tiffs of any consequence, perhaps one in twenty or less. Of course I realize that such accounts may not be accurate, but I have the impression that they were truthful. Of the London sample, three-quarters of the men claimed that wife and husband had absolutely equality or near equality; only one in four claimed absolute superiority for the male.

Similar results were obtained in interviews with the wives. The same point may be made from negative evidence.

> Still today in that part of Ashton known for its backwardness and its nearness to slum-conditions there are families with reputations among neighbours for their 'rows' which periodically break into open fighting. All the evidence suggests, however, that this

violence in marital relations has declined considerably since the years of depression.

As Mogey's little table suggests, rigid conjugal role-segregation becomes psychologically difficult to maintain in conditions of greater equality. Mogey also compared wives' description of 'good husbands' in St. Ebbe's and in Barton.

If this series of statements is closely examined, it will appear that there is a difference between the two. Barton, in fact, shows that a husband who is prepared to take his part in routine household-tasks, who will share experiences, and who will take the wife out occasionally is preferred. The co-operative family-unit, where necessary jobs are done by anybody, rather than the rigid unit where division of labour is insisted upon, has become a numerous type among the families on the new estate.

We [Young and Willmott] can see that husbands not only do more to aid their wives in emergencies. They also spend less on themselves and more on their families. When they watch the television instead of drinking beer in the pub, and weed the garden instead of going to a football-match, the husbands have taken further the partnership mentioned as one of the characteristics of modern Bethnal Green . . . Husbands do more. Children do more. The family is more self-contained in bad times and in good . . .

Moreover, the husband's role in the social world of the family has changed. He is now the one who leads the active life of society, not only on the job, but sometimes too in his round of the relatives after work is done. He is the messenger who brings back to Greenleigh the news from the larger world of work and the smaller world of kinship. She is more dependent on him, for news and for the financial sacrifice which will sustain their domestic economy. If, now that he does not have to share her with so many others, he plays well his role of messenger, earner and companion, the strains of the new life are not without compensations.

The greater partnership is something the men may benefit from, in that it enriches their psychological world, and reduces the cognitive poverty of which so much was made in previous chapters. The greater interest in the home may then be seen as an effect, as well as a cause, of the trend towards partnership.

It seems to me [Zweig ends his 1961 section on 'Masters or Partners'] that we are witnessing a considerable social change in husband–wife relationships in the working classes, and that this has a bearing on the world of the man's values. The more he accepts his wife as an equal partner, the more he acquires, mostly unconsciously, her values and standards. He is no longer contemptuous of women's ideas, as he used to be. They may differ from his, placing greater value on domesticity, for example, but are more frequently nearer to his own. Once his was the specifically masculine world, standing for self-assertion, sturdiness, force and pungency. Now he tends to find room for softer and more feminine values.

With more and better relationships in the home, goes a decline in the authoritarian type of husband. Before we consider how this manifests itself, we may, with Zweig, relate this trend to a general trend in society and in industrial life particularly.

Is the husband–wife relationship still under the dominance of the male, or is the relationship moving toward greater equality of the sexes? A manager with whom I discussed this subject put his view in a most pungent way, linking this with the social change in the factory: 'The age of authority and its abuse has passed. Men were bullied at work and they bullied back their wives and children. Now you cannot order your men about, you have rather to coax and humour them. The same change is reflected at home. There is not the same authority at home as there used to be.'[1]

There is, of course, nothing new in this idea of linking authority in the workshop with authority at home. Frederic Le Play, the French social thinker of the last century, linked the authority of the master in the *atelier* with that of the father in the household at home. The link between the two kinds of authority has a deep psychological foundation as the attitude in one sphere is often transferred to the other: instances of this could be seen most clearly in the attitudes of foremen. But in fact both attitudes have a deeper background in the general decline of authoritarian behaviour. Ours is not the age of authority.

The differences between past and present are beautifully brought out by some other evidence from Zweig. Nearly one in three of the families he interviewed in 1958 owned a washing-machine. The standard joke of the older men is unthinkable in the context of the new, more tender relationship between

[1] See also page 182 fn.

Changes in Working-Class Life

husband and wife: 'I don't need a washing-machine, my wife is my washing-machine.'

But it is also significant that he adds that the women who went out to work frequently invested their first earnings in a washing-machine. For if the man is not so keen to give up his supremacy, there are now more opportunities for a woman to maintain herself apart from her husband, and social condemnation of a wife who leaves an unsatisfactory husband is not what it was. A truly authoritarian structure is really only possible where there are no alternatives (subjectively or objectively) to submission. The husband can no longer afford to be unthinkingly authoritarian, and so partnership, in finance as elsewhere, becomes more feasible. On this, as on so many matters, Zweig is a perceptive commentator.

> Why is it? [he asked in 1952] that so many husbands, in spite of the fact that they derive great benefit from the work of their wives, dislike their wife's work outside and speak so contemptuously about it, although they do not openly discourage it? The fact is that the whole relationship of husband and wife changes basically, although none would admit it. She is no longer dependent on him economically; she has a practical alternative to his support. If he walks out, the whole world does not collapse over her head and she can still carry on. The less reliable the husband, the less satisfactory their relationship, the better she feels for having a job and showing him that she need not accept all his whims, that she is not at his mercy.

> In other respects also [Zweig writes in 1961] the husband is not the paymaster who can call the tune to the same extent as he used to be. His wife may be working. The Welfare State, with children's allowances, Welfare Services, and the Assistance Board, may also supplement a man's wages. The phrase describing house-keeping money as 'Wages for the Missus' is very rarely used nowadays.

(g) *'We're different with our boy: we make more of a mate of him'*

The social services have in many ways already made the family of three generations not less but more viable . . . The health services have made a great and obvious difference to the well-being of the family, especially to mothers and children. Old-age pensions, inadequate though they often are, have enabled children to care for their parents all the more effectively. Anthropologists have reported how much even the old non-contributory pensions sweetened relations between the generations in Ireland, and what is true there, is just as much true in East London.

With the general though gradual and incomplete easing of stress, there is a greater hope for the future. And the future, in family terms, means the children. It is not easy for a man to change his social class in his own life-time and, for a manual worker, not easy to increase his income after his twenties, when he is at his strongest and most energetic. But a more liberal educational system makes it possible to achieve such ambitions in the second generation. In a status-dissenting family the focus of attention shifts therefore from the father as breadwinner to the child as a potential credit to the family. It is not surprising that in Ashton, where the general expectation was that the boy should go down the mine, this shift in emphasis was not noted. In somewhat the same way, parental aspirations for the child in the traditional culture of St. Ebbe's were only vaguely expressed; parents wanted the child 'to do well', 'to get on well', but made no reference to a specific course of action. Willmott considers that the one-class uniformity of Dagenham is a cause of the lack of parental ambition in Dagenham: 'I don't care a lot myself. The main thing is for the children to be happy.'[1] But in Bethnal Green, there were parents who were much more ambitious for their children: 'I want the boy to be a doctor or a farmer, not to work in a factory or be a porter like me.'

Zweig (1961) bears witness to the same effect. The men he talked to rarely had ambitions for themselves, but they had a deal of ambition for their children. One of his standard questions to family-men concerned their interest in the upbringing and education of their children, and he gathered from the replies that the overwhelming majority took an intense interest. The standard phrases which came up again and again were: 'We want to give them a better chance than we had' or 'That's

[1] It is not perhaps surprising, he writes, that in 1951 Dagenham showed the third highest (among 157 towns listed) of children leaving school under the age of 15 (84 per cent) and the very lowest proportion of people between 15 and 24 in full-time education (4 per cent). The whole topic of parental ambition is discussed in detail in the volume on child-rearing, under the heading 'Parental care and aspirations for achievement'.

the finest thing—to give them every opportunity' or 'They come first'.

Because both parents are interested in this kind of improvement, this gives them another interest in common which, as partners, they can discuss and act upon together. In this way the segregation of men's interests from women's interests is further broken down. Indeed, the new focus of interest in the family circle affects the very nature of conjugal interaction, as a Radby Grade IV informant explained to the interviewer.

> The parents must set a good example to the children. Me and my husband never disagree before Peter.

And with more time available for interaction, there is more opportunity for the husband to interact with wife and children than was previously possible. An informant of Young and Willmott's lends this generalization a historical perspective.

> One good thing is that we have much shorter working hours now than before the war. I'm all for the five-day week—the forty-hour week. I remember my father used to work 72 hours one week and 60 the next. He was on shifts. The week he did the longer hours was on the day. We didn't see anything of him. I was in bed when he got back at night. People get more time with their families now.

Now, therefore, as another informant in Bethnal Green put it, 'it's all for the kiddies'.

> Dad used to be very strict with us. We're different with our boy, we make more of a mate of him. When I was a kid, Dad always had the best of everything. Now it's the children who get the best of it. If there's one pork chop left, the kiddy gets it.

And in St. Ebbe's:

> The father used to be the most important person in the house, but not now. Now he's more or less in the background.

Even the Newbolts, in some ways the most traditional family of all, 'make more of a pal' of their children. Shaw gives an indication of what this means in practice.[1] The younger families

---

[1] L. A. Shaw (1954), 'Impressions of family life in a London suburb', *Sociol. Rev.*, II. See also Volume Two, pages x, 441 and 552.

in the group she studied gave the children noticeably more freedom to play, making fewer demands on them to help in the house and imposing fewer restrictions on their play. When the children played indoors, the whole family had to put up with quite a bit of mess, for they then cluttered up the general living and kitchen space. The father's changed position is exemplified by one young man who could not stand the noise his children made in the house when he came back from work. He solved his problem not by going out again, as the old-fashioned father might have done, but by playing with the children to keep them quiet. Thus the father is drawn into the family circle.

> The spread of the five-day week has created the week-end, a new term and a new experience for the working man. With it has come the sight of young fathers wheeling prams up Bethnal Green Road on a Saturday morning, taking their little daughters for a row on the lake or playing with their sons on the putting green in front of the windows of the Institute of Community Studies.

And Zweig, in almost the same terms:

> Fathers of babies often push the pram, give them baths, see them to bed; fathers of toddlers often read them stories, play with them, take them for a walk at week-ends; fathers of school children often go to the school for progress reports and supervise their homework; fathers of adolescents try to apprentice them or find them suitable jobs . . .
>
> His hobbies and pastimes also centre round the house. So he is becoming more of a home-maker all round, much more than his father was.[1]

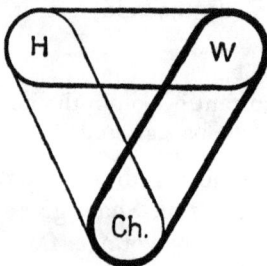

Then and *Now*

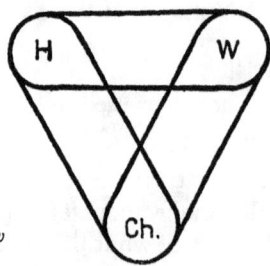

[1] For further discussion of the new significance of children, see pages 557–61.

Chapter Six

ASPECTS OF MIDDLE-CLASS LIFE

INTRODUCTORY[1]

THIS chapter could have been the most laborious and least rewarding to write. People who read books on *Samples from English Cultures* are likely to have come from somewhere in the middle-class range, so that there is one area which they know very well from the inside, and they are also likely to be readers of novels and biographies which describe life in these classes. To collect evidence from such sources, very few sociological descriptions being available, would have been pleasant. It would also have been very time-consuming and in the end one would still be left wondering how representative the fictional and semi-fictional accounts of presumably 'interesting' people are. One might also wonder how far current literary traditions have substituted for social realities a conventionally recognizable set of character-types. And it is uncertain whether the ultimate result would have convinced a sceptic. What has been done, therefore, is partly to concentrate on new and unfamiliar aspects of middle-class life, which seem not yet to have been absorbed into the imagination of those who read novels and biographies, and partly to review rapidly some aspects of middle-class

---

[1] This chapter is not intended as a contribution to the sociology of class but rather as an essay in social psychology. It has been written mainly because the argument of the book as a whole required it: it is needed so that current knowledge of child-rearing practices (discussed in the second volume of the book) may be related to whatever is known of adult personality and work-situation. Only selected aspects of middle-class life are presented, in particular those aspects of adult life whose childhood roots it is possible to discern. Although social stratification is of necessity discussed, it should not be thought that a representative sample of middle-class traits is to be set forth, if, indeed, such a phrase has a meaning.

working life, with particular reference to the attitudes which would make the work more, or less, congenial.

Until quite recently, psychologists interested in personality-formation—if they showed any awareness at all of the relevance of social class—tended to contrast a group they called 'middle class' with a group they called 'working class' or 'lower class'. Love of contrast tended to lead them, for one sample, to some 'Branch Street' with its shiftless work-shy population, and for the other sample to the professional and often traditional upper middle class. But, ranging from the clerk at one financial extreme to the judge and the industrial magnate at the other, the middle classes are not more homogeneous than the working classes, although the detailed differences which interest the social psychologist are still largely in *terra incognita*. Some attempt to map them out is to be made in this chapter and in the section on child rearing later in the book, but much systematic research is needed before we can attach to the social psychology of the middle classes even that small amount of credence which is now justifiable in the case of the working classes.

The social scientist may have inherited from the facts of the past, when the gap between the classes was much wider, his reliance on a two-class model of the social structure. Certainly popular mythology, normally a generation or so behind the times, used to incorporate the same dichotomy. When Zweig, writing in 1948, contrasted his working-class informants with the (relatively few) lower-middle-class people he talked to in the course of his enquiries, he felt justified in writing:

Their whole mentality, attitude and behaviour are so markedly different from those of the working class that it struck me as perhaps the most outstanding single fact brought to light in my inquiry. First of all there exists a great consciousness of the two strata—the middle and the working class, the people who work mostly with their brain and the people who work mostly with their hands—while there is absolutely no class-consciousness between the craftsman and the labourer. The craftsmen are better organized and have stronger unions—that is all: they do not treat the labourer as something lower or different, nor do they dislike him.[1] There is a fine gradation and interchange between them and

---

[1] There are regional differences in this respect.

Middle-Class Life

nearly complete intercourse with full *commercium et connubium*, while there are barriers between the middle class and the working class. The average working man dislikes the middle-class man, although in his heart he may regard him as somewhat superior. He does not dislike in the same sense and degree the upper class —on the contrary, he considers that the rich man is as genuine and true as the working-class man, while the middle-class people are snobbish, imitating the upper class and sneering at the working classes. 'The middle-class people think', contended the people with whom I talked, 'that working men are stupid because they can't work with anything but their hands'. 'Middle-class men are grabbing and money-minded; they only think of accumulating money and save every bit they can'. 'They like to run with the hare and hunt with the hounds', or, as another man expressed it: 'They like to keep a foot in both camps.' Those are the words which I heard often from my worker friends.[1]

One labour manageress put the differences in the following way: 'A middle-class lady expects service all the time, she thinks a lot of herself, she has more leisure anyway, she does not go out to work. She is made a fuss of, all eyes are on her, everything is for her. You can see that in her expression, in the way she walks and behaves, all head up. She has a strongly developed ego. A working-class woman gives service all the time. She is a meek domestic drudge, often expected to go out to work as well. She is overburdened like an ox, with no time for herself. And she accepts her lot with equanimity, thinking she does not deserve anything better. You can see her sense of inferiority in her eyes and bearing.'[2]

One of the men explained to me why in his view middle-class men are more disliked than the rich. The latter have already made their money and are often concerned in handing back part of the surplus they have made to the community in the form of charity. The people who are born to riches and brought up accordingly do not care for money, and are often modest and kind-hearted men, sincere and ready to help. It is otherwise with the middle class, who are on their way to making money and are often ruthless, snobbish and less human in their desire to accumulate.[3]

These passages, dating from 1948, are clearly written from the point of view of the traditional working man, with whom

[1] From *Labour, Life and Poverty.*
[2] From *Women's Life and Labour.*
[3] From *Labour, Life and Poverty.*

Zweig found himself most in sympathy. In passing, we may note also the rather touching references to a third class, a good class, an upper class, which serves the function in popular mythology of blackening the bad bourgeois by means of contrast with the good aristocrat. In these passages we can hear the affection of the old-fashioned traditional 'other ranker' for his officers.

The changing facts of social structure are changing the consciousness of class-differences, however, and the division of English society into two, or at most three, major classes is coming to have a curiously old-fashioned air about it. New conditions have created a situation which is much more difficult to analyse. For one thing, the range of incomes and occupations which are thought of as middle-class has widened, not in the sense that the extremes are farther apart, but in the sense that more points on the range can be distinguished. Secondly, just as a distinction had to be made between traditional and changing aspects of working-class life, so now we must distinguish between new and traditional middle-class occupations and occupants. This is the more confusing because it makes a hierarchical arrangement of social levels impossible.

By 1955, when Bott was interviewing, only two of her twenty informants thought strictly in a two-class way. All the others used more than three categories into which they sorted people. None used three. This is perhaps not surprising: people at the top and at the bottom of the social scale are easily enough distinguished and in a two-class model of society these are the ones which are contrasted. But when people are accustomed to a society with much mobility, attention is directed to the range between the extremes. Then an immense variety of possibilities becomes conceivable, and numerous sub-divisions are needed to do justice to the realities of people's experience.

What happens when one attempts to construct a realistic image of social structure from a more psychological point of view, i.e. in terms of the attitudes and conscious experience of actual people living actually in a town, has been frankly and sensibly stated in the course of Mrs. Stacey's discussions of the problems she encountered in her study of Banbury.[1]

[1] M. Stacey (1961), *Tradition and Change*, Oxford University Press.

Middle-Class Life

It was not possible to construct for Banbury and district a simple n-fold class system. That is to say, the total population could not be placed in a series of horizontal groupings, members of each group being assumed to have parity with each other and able to recognize each other as social equals should they meet. Nor was it possible to place people upon one social scale, ranked on a basis of commonly agreed social characteristics. There was a reasonably clear-cut status system within the traditional society, linked with the traditional class system. Among non-traditionalists there were numbers of status groups based most often on occupational status, but on a variety of occupational hierarchies rather than on one single system. Prediction about the class and status position of a traditionalist may be fairly accurate; only the roughest prediction is possible for the non-traditionalists.

The traditionalists are part of the traditional social structure, living by traditional values. They can judge each other according to 'who they are', by reference to a total social status to which family and social background contribute as much as occupation. They are actively aware of fine status divisions. They accept their own and other traditionals' position and behave with the manners appropriate to the status situation in which they find themselves. 'Although they do not all know each other, it is possible to think of traditionalists as belonging to one social system. For traditional society is made up of a network of face-to-face groups, based on family, neighbours, occupations, associations, status.'

This was not true of the non-traditionals who formed a considerable and increasing part of Banbury, where immigrants made up about half the adult population.[1] Many of these were professional people of a kind new to Banbury, coming from the great industrial cities, and from the North. Susser and Watson have called them 'spiralists'.[2]

The balance between the traditional professions of medicine, law and religion and these new professions has been altered considerably: today engineering, building and scientific professions outnumber the traditional professions by two to one, whereas thirty years ago they amounted to less than half. Whether the new

[1] According to Mrs. Stacey's analysis of a sample of over 1,000 households.
[2] M. W. Susser and W. Watson (1962), *Sociology in Medicine*, Oxford University Press.

professions are scientific or non-scientific, they all show certain common characteristics, and these characteristics foster mobility, both social and residential. They are all organized in the same way into professional associations or institutions, they qualify by university training, they attempt to achieve a monopoly of their function, and they all have similar careers, although their rewards might not be the same. They tend to work for salaries and not for fees . . .

The formal hierarchy of statuses of large-scale organizations provides the new professions with a ladder of promotion through which to advance their careers. The similarity of bureaucratic structures allows a professional man to start as a junior in one, climb through intermediate positions in several, to a senior position in yet another. But even if he remains in the same organization, they operate on such a large scale that he is obliged to move his place of residence as he leaves one branch for another. Thus mobility in status and responsibility is often accompanied by residential movement. This mobility in career and residence is characteristic of persons with scientific, technical and administrative professions, and for this reason they have been termed *spiralists*. This movement of professional persons through the status hierarchies of large-scale organizations and a series of communities is inherent in the structure and operation of these organizations, and influences both their functioning and policy. Within the organization itself, the age and career expectations of individuals helps to determine the composition of both formal and informal groups, and in turn, this affects the policy of the organization. Moreover, it also affects the social relations of the spiralists with other members of the communities through which they pass, for their social relations within each tend to reflect their particular age and prospects.

The people of Banbury find it difficult to place a man such as a department head who is employed (a sign of low status) and yet has more power (a sign of high status) than many in the town who are their own masters; or again, a metallurgist, a skill previously unknown in the town, who appears to have little or no authority (low status) and yet has a university education (very high status). The confusion is increased because people of this sort are usually immigrants whose family background is unknown and many of whose associations are outside the district . . . Highly mobile, geographically as well as socially, they typically belong to loose-knit social networks and have the characteristics which foster and are fostered by them. They are a puzzle to traditional Banbury. They do not choose to identify with it. Their occupations are non-traditional and so, often, are their attitudes, for instance towards work and towards religion.

Non-traditionalists, whether immigrant or local status-dissenters, by definition do not adhere to local values and customs. This negative may be the only quality they have in common. In Woodford, a modern middle-class suburb described by Willmott and Young and discussed at length in the next sub-section, it appears that attempts were made to create a new social life, though of a rather different kind from that of a traditional community. In Banbury, a traditional county town, they did not share any common social system among themselves, nor with the older inhabitants.

Spiralists are distinguished from those other persons of professional occupation with the same education and social class, like general practitioners, consultants, and solicitors, who have a practice and take fees, and thereby have an economic, professional and social interest in the area within which they practise. Although doctors and solicitors in practice may have a greater potential of mobility than men of non-professional occupations, their interest remains localized. Similarly, the owners and managers of small businesses or factories, or small shopkeepers, the *burgesses*, all have an economic and social interest within one area. The spiralist has no such economic interest in a limited area; his economic interest lies within the hierarchy of the organization, at least during the years while he can still reasonably hope to be promoted.

The consideration of non-traditional immigrants in a city brings the argument back to Bott, who was led to the conclusion that the difference between people who have moved many times in their lives and those who have moved little—the difference between those who live within a loose-knit network and those who are part of a close-knit one—was more indicative of differences in the families' style of life than income or occupation or position on any of the social-class scales constructed by sociologists.[1]

Bott ranged her informants according to the degree of

---

[1] These are briefly outlined in the appendix.

connectedness displayed by their social networks. At one extreme was the sort of family exemplified by the 'Newbolts': closely knit into the community, often characterized by the segregated conjugal role-relationship which seems associated with this type. The Newbolts had moved only twice in their lives. At the opposite extreme were a number of families with very loose-knit social connections, where husband and wife viewed their marriage as a partnership. In Bott's collection of these, the average number of moves per family was around twenty.

Some social characteristics of the five very loose-knit families

Name	Position on the Hall-Jones social-class scale	Occupational group	Occupation	Numbers of areas lived in
Bruce	5	Clerical	Temporary clerk in Gas Board	22
Denton	3	Professional	Accounts executive in advertising agency	26
Woodman	2	Professional	Pottery designer working as occupational therapist in hospital	19
Daniels	2	Professional	Deputy manager of fire department in insurance firm	19
Bullock	1	Professional	Statistician in welfare agency	9

Between these two extremes among Bott's informants were nine 'intermediate' families, averaging eight moves each. In four of these families the breadwinners were professional or semi-professional; in one he was a clerk; three were skilled manual workers and one was unskilled. The intermediate families are of particular interest because Bott's description of their manner of life shows that they resemble the people of Woodford in a number of other significant respects.

The reason why Stacey and Bott found it impossible to apply the current sociological ideas on social stratification directly to their own work was, of course, that they were interested in the more psychological aspects of society. The present chapter, which is concerned mainly with those elements in social differentiation which have a bearing on the formation of characteristic personality-patterns, suffers from the same difficulties, writ even more largely. The evidence on what would be useful *differentia* for this purpose is sparse; the evidence on what differences exist is scarcely less so.

The device of presentation which proved most expedient was to make the most of the very plentiful recent literature on the Civil Service. There seemed not nearly enough reliable material about teachers' work and personality requirements, or doctors', or business-men's, and so rather than use what existed, with elaborate discussions on reliability and generality, they have been neglected. People from all levels of the middle class seem to go in for Civil Service careers. If they are not very able, or not very pushful, they stay more or less at the level at which they enter. If they are either or both, they move up or possibly out, in which case we lose sight of them, or, if they stay in, dissatisfied, they tend to write critical appraisals of their situation, to which we have access.

Accordingly I have drawn on a number of accounts of the Civil Service: Frank Dunnill's *The Civil Service, Some Human Aspects* (1956), 'C. K. Munro's' *The Fountains in Trafalgar Square* (1952), E. N. Gladden's *Civil Service or Bureaucracy?* (1956), Nigel Walker's *Morale in the Civil Service* (1961). Lewis and Maude's *English Middle Classes* (1949) and *Professional People* (1952) have provided valuable evidence on the psychological situation of the traditional upper middle class. On the middle and lower middle range of occupations there is sadly little except for Lockwood's invaluable *Black-Coated Worker* (1958) to which a great debt is owing. Without it, there would have been no way of writing about this very large section of the English population.

One of the disadvantages of this approach is that one obvious fact had to be ignored: people get promoted. A man may start off in one grade and in the course of his life go right to the top of the ladder. But there are no longitudinal studies of the careers of successful and less successful English middle-class people. Little is known of the careers of spiralists. With one exception —Clements investigated the characteristics of over 600 managers in 28 firms in the Manchester area (*Managers: a Study of their Careers in Industry*, 1958, Allen and Unwin). The range of management-levels is very wide, and so is the range of the social origins from which the managers came. Yet useful additional evidence is provided by this study and the present chapter is indebted to it.

On the whole, however, the procedure of considering the typical work and life situations at each level, and the attitudes which make that situation congenial or inhibit promotion, has had to be used. It is therefore important to keep in mind the fact that at each occupational level described will be people whose attitudes and abilities will move them to a higher stratum before retirement.

Mrs. Stacey's sketch of Banbury's social structure provides a means of identifying the relative positions of some of the sets of people which are to be distinguished and discussed in the present chapter. Her framework allows us to keep in mind, at a middle-class level, the old distinction between status-assent and dissent, between traditional and established middle-class people on the the one hand, the socially mobile and newly arrived spiralists on the other.

With Mrs. Stacey's 'upper class' we shall scarcely be concerned. The first row on the chart to interest us is the 'upper frontier'. This group lies between the middle and the upper classes. The majority of its members had the same sort of education as the upper class; their manner of life and their attitudes are in many ways similar. But they 'work for a living', many of them in the older professions.

> This 'upper frontier' group is perhaps nationally most often called upper middle, but since in Banbury some of its members associate on terms of ease with some members of the gentry who are definitely upper class (as well as with middle-class people) this title has been avoided. Further, the rather loose common use of 'upper-middle' also covers groups of professional and business men who do not share the upper-class characteristics of the Banbury upper frontier.

At the top, then, as far as this chapter is concerned, we have a set of people who have been traditionally at the top of the middle-class range, both by virtue of their occupation and by birth. Mingling with these are others, whose family background

places them lower in the social scale and whose schooling may
have been on different lines. There is a general feeling, not
easily substantiated in every case, that their access to the upper
reaches depends markedly on the occupation they have chosen:
that, for instance, the higher Civil Servants, the Bishops, the
Headmasters of Public Schools, tend to be more exclusively
recruited from those whose family is traditionally upper class
or upper frontier, whereas this is less true for men in the higher
professions or for those in business and industry. We shall deal
with all these as a traditional set of people, including not only
those who come from established upper-middle-class families
but also those who have more recently arrived at this occupational and income level, *if* they have adopted the way of life
of the established families. The criterion is that they tend to
value traditional responsibility in social matters, tiaditional
leadership roles, traditional politics, a creative use of leisure,
gracious living. (Mrs. Stacey mentions also 'connoisseurship'
and much entertaining in the home.) Many but by no means
all show a high degree of self-confident ambition, an interest in
intellectual matters with a problem-solving, task-related approach, and an intense feeling for psychological independence.[1]

These are the people Spinley thought of as middle class—the
people social psychologists generally have tended to resort to
when they needed a middle-class sample for comparative study.

In terms of the social-class scales most often used by sociologists (reproduced in an appendix here) we must be including
mainly Class I (professionals) and Occupational Group 3 (higher
administrative, professional and managerial) as classified by the
Registrar-General; those in category 1 on the Hall-Jones scale
(all occupations calling for highly specialized experience and
frequently requiring a degree or comparable professional training); Lockwood's top category (professional occupations, owners
of large businesses, middle and higher management, officers in
the Armed Forces). From Cole's sub-groupings one might
recognize:

> (*b*) the main body of salaried administrators, managers,
> salaried officers of a wide range of institutions and societies [at
> least those who live and work in London],

---

[1] See pages 357–8, 360–3.

Some distinctive characteristics of Social Class and Status Groups
'Tradition and Change' by Margaret Stacey (1960), p. 150

Social Class	Social Status Groups		Education	Occupation	Hall/Jones Scale	Source of Income	Social Circle			Verbal Communication		
	Traditional	non-Traditional					Outside Banbury	Inside Banbury	Home and Neighbours	Speech Grammar Accent	Size of Vocab.	Command of Written Word
UPPER	County		Public School and Oxford, Cambridge or Sandhurst	Various, with directorial authority	1	Inherited means, profits and fees	Centre; county, nation	None	No	Accurate 'U'	Large	High
	Gentry		As above	Various	1	As above	Centre; county, nation	Slight connection	No	Accurate 'U'	Large	High
		Industrial Upper	Various	Owner, director, large-scale industry outside Banbury	1	Profits and fees	Centre; nation some international	None	No	Accurate, possibly some local accent	Large	High
Upper Frontier			Public School and Oxford or Cambridge	Professions, especially doctors	1	Profits, fees and some salary	National connections	Yes	No formal relationship	Accurate 'U'	Large	High
MIDDLE		Banbury Senior Directors and Managers	Various	Director or senior manager large-scale industry in Banbury	1	Profits, fees, salary	National and international connections	Yes	No formal relationship	Accurate, possibly some local accent	Large	High

		Education	Occupation	Groups	Income	National connections					
MIDDLE	Newer Professions	Grammar (probably State) and University (probably provincial)	Metallurgists, etc. Grammar School teachers, Senr. exec. Civil Servants	1, 2	Salary	Some national connections	Yes	Some	As above	Large	High
	Middle	State Secondary, some Elementary only	Proprietor or manager large shop or factory in Banbury	2 Some 1	Profits, fees, salary	None	Yes, centre	Some	Reasonable, some solecisms	Reasonable, some misuse	Reasonable, little reading
	Lower Frontier ==	Elementary, some State Secondary	Manager of branch shop, independent shopkeeper, some skilled manual workers	3, 4, 5	Various	None ==	Yes ==	Yes, centre	Less than reasonable, local accent	More limited	Some, little reading
	Industrial Technicians and staff	Elementary, State Secondary or Technical	Technical or clerical in industry, jnr. exec. or clerical Civil Servants	3, 4	Salary, wage	None	Yes	Yes, centre	As above	As above	As above
WORKING	Respectable	Elementary	Skilled manual, some clerical, some semi-skilled manual	5, 6	Wage	None	Yes, limited extent	Yes, centre	Inaccurate local accent	Limited	Little command
	Ordinary	Elementary	Semi-skilled manual, some skilled and some unskilled manual	5, 6, 7	Wage	None	Informal only	Yes, centre	As above	As above	As above
	Rough	Elementary	Unskilled manual, some semi-skilled	6, 7	Wage	None	Informal only	Yes, centre	As above	As above	As above

(*c*) the members of the principal recognized professions, whether salaried or working as consultants and remunerated by professional fees, including medical men, lawyers, ministers of religion, officers of the Armed Services, the upper ranges of the teaching profession and the upper range of the artistic profession [again, at least in so far as they live and work in London],

(*d*) the higher grades of the Civil Service and other public and semi-public administrative and voluntary services [again, at least in so far as they are London-centred].

One problem in this game of social snakes and ladders is clearly brought out by Cole's classification as it is being used here: there are differences between London and the provinces. In so far as they are London-based, those who fit into Cole's sub-groupings (*b*), (*c*) and (*d*) do seem to belong to the upper frontier. Those who live in the provinces may be distinguished into at least three different categories. There are those who will stay there and whose social background, education and way of life puts them firmly in the middle range of the middle class; there are spiralists who have not yet achieved London; and there are those whose social background, education and way of life places them in the local social élite. A footnote of Mrs. Stacey's makes explicit reference to such regional variations.

> It is an apposite comment on occupation as an index of status that the social class of doctors of the same medical rank varies from one part of the country to another, from middle class to upper class, including the 'frontier' cases. It may be relevant to their status in Banbury, where they mostly fall in the upper-frontier group, that there it is possible for general practitioners to live in, or almost in, the country, a characteristic piece of upper-class behaviour.[1]

The useful category of 'spiralist' pinpoints also a related problem. Both where present occupation is concerned and in the matter of the origin from which their upward spiral started, spiralists cover a range from teacher to top management.

[1] Cf. Jackson and Marsden: 'There are, plainly, many groups to be distinguished within the term "middle class", just as there are groups within the term "working class". We use the general phrase "Marburton middle class" both knowing what other truths it conceals, and hoping that it will not be confused with the Southern England image of a quite different "middle class"' (*Education and the Working Class*).

Middle-Class Life

Many spiralists are also occupationally mobile, in the sense that the demarcation of skills between many professions is not yet so rigid as among other occupations. A spiralist who acquires certain key qualifications can move from one profession to an allied one. Moreover, every professional qualification, whatever its basic skill, carries with it the potentiality of achieving high managerial or executive position: a schoolmaster can become an administrator in the educational system, an Air Marshal become a bank director, a chemist become the chairman of the nationalized railways, and a university professor become an ambassador. The abilities considered necessary for the top executive position in bureaucratic organization are not as yet ascertainable by examination, as are basic professional skills; promotion depends on such imponderables as 'administrative ability', 'qualities of leadership', 'drive', and 'personality'. This seems to apply to many large-scale organizations, whatever their basic function; the general manager in industry may have begun his career in any one of the specialized departments, as an engineer, accountant, administrator or chemist.

But this description is in terms of people who have arrived. Those who have not (or not yet) arrived must also be considered. Little is known of the psychological characteristics and social situation of all these different sets of people. While some are therefore discussed in the sub-section on top professionals, others may resemble more those discussed later in the chapter.

The second sub-section, for instance, glances cursorily at wealthy businessmen who are not traditional in the sense defined above. Little is known of them, the most useful material for our purposes being American.[1]

Thereupon we cross the borderline (because no one knows quite where it is, it might be more accurate to call it a no-man's-land) between what is normally thought of as upper-middle and what is thought of as the middle-middle class. The complexity of this middle-middle range faces us with a formidable problem of categorization and presentation.

Below the 'upper frontier' Mrs. Stacey places a status-group 'middle' which is in her eyes the centre of the middle class. It is the stratum of the traditional tradesmen and local businessmen,

---

[1] See, however, Anthony Sampson (1962), *Anatomy of Britain*, Hodder and Stoughton, London.

from which the traditional political and social leaders of Banbury are drawn. 'Mr. Shaw' may be cited as an example.

> A prosperous tradesman who owns a business which has been in the family for three generations and in which his son works also, he is an acknowledged leader in the town. He knows where he stands in the old-town society and accepts his position. He considers that 'service to the community' is a duty. He has been Mayor of the town and gives freely to local charity.

Those of Cole's groups already mentioned belong here in so far as they work and live in the provinces, and so do those of his subgrouping (*d*) who are in the middle grades in the Civil Service or in Local Government, and his subgrouping (*e*), 'the big and middle shopkeepers, garage keepers, hotel keepers and the analogous groups of employed managers, accountants and other officers employed by joint stock companies operating in this field'.

Here are included many spiralists who have not gone traditional on arrival, or are still on their way up, and Mrs. Stacey's newer professions, as well as the proprietors and managers of large shops and factories in Banbury. Many of the Registrar-General's Intermediate Class II and socio-economic group 4 (intermediate administrative, professional and managerial, including teachers and salaried staff) belong here, as well as some group 5 (shopkeepers and other small employers). On the Hall-Jones scale this is the level of category 2 (Managerial and Executive: those responsible for initiating and/or implementing policy, e.g. personnel managers, headmasters of elementary schools) as well as some of the provincial members of category 1. The provincial members of Lockwood's top category, as well as some in his second and third category, belong here (lower professionals, such as teachers, nurses, qualified technicians, as well as self-employed persons with small businesses, people in lesser management in shops and offices).

Our source material deals mainly with the Executive and Senior Executive Civil Servant, but in general we have in mind Weber's bureaucrat, who was to be found in the administration of 'political parties and armies, of large-scale private organizations, of churches, of profit-making businesses and charitable organizations, as well as of the State'.[1] To use a modern phrase, we shall be concerned with the 'organization man'—though not with the personality-type to which this term has come to belong.[2] Weber's bureaucrat is *par excellence* a rational-legal character, to be contrasted with those who derive their authority from tradition or from personal characteristics. He is, as far as our argument is concerned, a man who has got to the top but has not adopted the gracious-living style of traditional top people. We shall consider a 'rational-legal' kind of personality, which does not go in for the more imaginative qualities so much as for effort, hard work, hard-headedness and other such traits conducive to upward mobility. The end of the sub-section examines briefly the reactions of those who have not achieved the position to which they aspired.

From here on, the possibilities of mobility, up or down, have increasingly to be kept in mind. The middle classes do not form static categories. In each social category, in each occupation, will be some who have entered because it was their father's or their uncle's. Others are on their way up, others on their way down from fathers in the higher professional or business world. Geographical differences, with a related difference in the local definition of social strata, further complicate the picture. Any of these people may move to another town. Each generation increases the possibilities for change. The children make fuller use of their educational opportunities and may choose occupations very different from those of their parents or brothers. They are more likely to be non-traditional, rejecting the advice of their parents on the best way to live, or, since social and geographical mobility tend to go together, unable to copy the patterns of adult living exemplified by their parents because they have moved to another place and cannot take advice.

Living side by side in the same street, often intermarried or due to intermarry in the next generation, may be found people whose parents (living in another district) are commonly regarded as below them in social standing, others whose parents

---

[1] Max Weber (1922), *Theory of Economic and Social Organization*, translated by A. R. Henderson and T. Parsons in 1947 (William Hodge and Co., London).

[2] The reference is to W. H. Whyte (1956), *The Organization Man*. This is an American book about a phenomenon which still seems more American than English, but see pages 350–1.

are above them, with children whose occupations similarly classify them as higher or lower.

In this highly fluid, highly mobile situation, some are more mobile than others. Some occupational groups and some unlucky individuals are left behind. So we approach the ranks of the lower middle class. These, who had more than their fair share in the fiction of fifty years ago—Wells, Bennett, Gissing—have had little attention from more modern observers, except from detractors who make much of their alleged narrowness of outlook, their primness, their cramped self-satisfaction. These are the characteristics which people seem to have in mind when they speak contemptuously of the middle class. It is appropriate to remark here that practically no one described himself to Bott as 'lower middle class'.

This category contains, from among the less successful self-employed middle-class people, the independent poor shopkeeper, the struggling small businessman, the professional man in a small provincial town who would have preferred to be elsewhere, and others such. Also to be included here are the members of the less prestige-carrying professions, who work in an organization but have no share in running it: teaching in lower-prestige schools, some kinds of engineering, lower-level management, nursing, some kinds of accounting.

These can be considered the top people in this very wide range. The gradations within the range are hardly known systematically, but the sociological and psychological characteristics of the people here included are varied indeed. Sociologically, there is a sense of constant ebb and flow over the generations. People may 'marry well' into the secure executive range, or not so well, among themselves, or beneath themselves, into that group of routine clerical workers whose occupational status has been declining steadily. Their children may follow in their footsteps, do them credit, disappoint them. They may decline into manual work. Little being known of them, we shall deal with them under the general heading 'black-coated', and divide them according to social-psychological criteria into the relatively privileged and the relatively deprived. The relatively deprived are assumed to be the more traditional middle-class types, coming from families whose breadwinners worked in occupations of the same social standing a generation or so ago. Because these occupations are declining in prestige, or being flooded by people with other social backgrounds, or for other reasons examined in the relevant sub-section, these people are especially liable to experience the current social changes as disadvantageous to them. The relatively privileged will be those who are assumed to have come up from the manual working classes.

Within this range is the region Mrs. Stacey called the 'lower frontier'.

> Its members include both manual and non-manual workers; among non-manual workers it includes both those who work on their own account and employed office workers; among manual workers it includes skilled men working on their own account and employed skilled workers. This group might be called 'lower middle class', but equally some of its members might be called 'superior working class'; it is in fact a frontier group and has therefore been so named.

It is doubtful whether many of these people would in fact call themselves working class; most would place themselves without hesitation in the middle class.

One reason why classification is so confusing here, is that even the breadwinner's occupational history may be much more eventful than is often assumed in discussions of this kind. Lockwood, for instance, quotes a finding to the effect that nearly 40 per cent of a sample of men who started their career as clerks found their way into managerial and professional strata, while another 30 per cent moved into manual work.[1]

Clements found that managers coming from this stratum most often had dreams of setting up independently in business, though those who had tried had on the whole not succeeded. He also found, it may be noted here, that the lower the social origin of the managers, the more mobile they had been in the sense of changing from firm to firm in the course of their career upwards.

Douglas and Blomfield show one half of this process. They

---

[1] G. Thomas, *Labour Mobility in Great Britain 1945–9*, an enquiry carried out for the Ministry of Labour and National Service (mimeographed).

found that their sample of families had seen significant changes in occupation, and hence in social class, during the years of their study, 1946–1950, and in particular a drift upward.[1]

	Profes-sional	Em-ployer	Salaried	Black-coated	Skilled manual	Other categories	Total %
1946	3·1	0·6	4·1	10·9	48·6	32·7	100
1950	3·4	0·7	5·7	11·5	44·2	34·5	100
% increase or decrease	+ 9·2	+ 15·0	+ 40·3	+ 5·4	− 8·9		

They found, moreover, that those moving upward in the social scale were the better-educated in each group, and in this context the wife's education appeared to be almost as important as the husband's. In the case of those moving to self-employment it was even more important. Families moving upward had also fewer children than the group from which they came, whereas those moving downward had more. The importance of the education of the wife, the mother of the family, will become evident on many later pages.

Jackson and Marsden, on the other hand, investigating the social background of eighty-eight men and women from working-class homes who had completed a grammar school education, found that to do justice to their material they had to evolve a theory of a 'sunken middle class'.

> These were all manual workers' homes; yet manifestly this did not always fit either with the bountiful display of material posses-sions or, more importantly, with their whole style of living. Six of the fathers had once owned their own small business and had turned to their present manual work when that collapsed. A further twenty-five couples had a middle-class father on the husband's or the wife's side, or on both.[2]

The indications are that Jackson and Marsden are here look-ing at a border stratum, a 'lower frontier' somewhat similar to Mrs. Stacey's, where people move up and down, from manual to non-manual and back, over the generations or in their own life-time. Marsden and Jackson remark that in these

[1] J. W. B. Douglas and J. M. Blomfield (1958), *Children under Five*, Allen and Unwin, London.

[2] B. Jackson and D. Marsden (1962), *Education and the Working Class*, Routledge and Kegan Paul, London.

families attempts were made to preserve more middle-class ways —these families felt a little different from the others.

People move into a social stratum, from above or from below; they move out, up or down, by marriage also. Lockwood asks himself: 'How far do clerks marry clerks, and how far do they take spouses whose occupations and social origins are different from their own?' He finds that half the wives in one random sample of over 700 clerks were in what might be called middle-class occupations, predominantly office work and the lower professions. Only a quarter had distinctively working-class jobs.[1] Clerks of middle-class origin were more likely to marry women in middle-class occupations than working-class clerks were. Of the married women clerks, rather more than half were married to husbands whose work placed them in the middle class, and here also there was a marked difference in husband's original class according to whether the wife came from a middle-class or a working-class home. Regarded either way, however, the minorities are substantial, ranging from a fifth to a third. Hence Lockwood feels justified in concluding that:

> Clerks as a group are definitely not endogamous. Because of the numerous marriage-ties they establish with working-class individuals and families it becomes difficult to draw a clear social division between clerks and manual workers.

Social class identification is further complicated by the fact that there are occupations to which the dichotomy manual/ non-manual is not really appropriate. It is surely by conventional agreement only that the more routine forms of office work are defined as non-manual and some kinds of supervisory activity as manual. No such convention has even been agreed on for the occupations in the Registrar-General's occupational group 7: the shop assistants and salesmen, commercial travellers and insurance agents. And if we solve the difficulty by looking at the colour of their collars, how shall we justify our opposition to the stand taken by Willmott and Young when they had to identify the social class of people in their Woodford sample?

[1] His source reference is the sample enquiry into social mobility in Great Britain, which is reported in chapter four of David Glass, ed. (1954), *Social Mobility in Britain*, Routledge and Kegan Paul, London.

There are a number of occupations which we have classified as 'manual' which might well have been regarded as 'non-manual'. Foremen are an obvious example. The difficulty about them is that, while some are virtually administrators, others do manual work alongside those they are supervising. In preliminary analysis, we distinguished thirty-four 'foremen, inspectors and supervisors' in the general sample; when they turned out to be, in all sorts of ways, more like manual than non-manual workers, we decided to include them with the former.

Similarly, we examined people in a number of other occupations that could be regarded as 'non-manual'—policemen, telephonists, laboratory assistants . . . Since they also, in the ways we could measure, were not markedly different from manual workers generally, they too were included in this category.

Lockwood allows for this ambiguity when he considers the social class position of the clerical worker of whom it is 'equally likely that he is drawn from the higher ranks of the working class or the lower ranks of the middle class', keeping in mind, moreover, that 'if the definition of the working class is extended to include foremen, shop assistants and similar groups, the proportion is considerably higher'.

The subjects of enquiry being so varied in social form, it is not surprising that the collectors of statistics make decisions which are inconvenient for our purpose. The Registrar-General does not distinguish between manual and non-manual work in Class III. This may represent a social reality, but also makes it difficult to check whether it is or not. The related socio-economic groupings range from 4, which includes elementary schoolteachers, through 5, where are placed the small shop-keepers and small employers as well as those on the verge of bankruptcy after years of struggling with a shoe-repair shop in a slum district, and 6, where we find most clerical workers, to 7, whence we derive shop assistants, salesmen, commercial travellers, and insurance agents, while the highly skilled foremen come in group 9 and skilled men in group 10. Many of the sociological investigations used as sources for this book, however, do divide Class III into a manual and a non-manual category.

These occupations may in the past have been the prerogative of distinctive social groups with characteristic ways of life. Now they are exogamous, brothers, sisters, sons and fathers might be found in almost any of them. In one life-time, a number of groups may be joined and abandoned.

Taking all these considerations together, it is clear that there will be a considerable proportion of clerks who have fathers and brothers in manual work. A related set of questions then arises. To what class are their families of origin to be allotted? In *The Worker in an Affluent Society* Zweig compares the occupations of a sample of fathers and sons over eighteen. He finds that 63 non-skilled, 25 skilled and 6 fathers at a supervisory level had 52 non-skilled, 48 skilled and 35 sons either at supervisory level or above it. Another of his samples shows how the flow over two generations may be either up or down.

	Status and skill of fathers			
	Clerical or business	*Supervisory*	*Skilled*	*Semi- or unskilled*
Fathers of				
32 supervisors	4	9	9	10
107 skilled men	21	13	39	33
272 non-skilled	41	24	57	144

In view of this table it is not surprising that he found the supervisor's way of life to resemble that of the manual worker. Nor is it surprising then that many manual workers will feel that they belong really to the middle class. It may be argued that the lower end of the middle-class range is represented by a kind of manual worker whose allegiance is to a middle-class way of life, and not to the community of manual working people. They make the quotations at the beginning of this chapter appear entirely out of date. We shall discuss some aspects of their way of life at the end of the present chapter to illustrate their evolution. They are also to be found in Woodford, at all stages of their life-history from recent arrival to final assimilation.

In the sub-section which now follows, life in Woodford is discussed, interesting in itself as a local area with a mixed population and interesting as providing a point of comparison for a more general examination of the relations between parents and children, husbands and wives, friends and neighbours in more loose-knit social networks.

Thereafter other aspects of middle-class life will be considered under the headings

TOP PROFESSIONALS

FIRST GENERATION TOP BUSINESSMEN

EXECUTIVES: THE RATIONAL-LEGAL ATTITUDE

THE CONCEPT OF RELATIVE DEPRIVATION

THE BLACK-COATED WORKER

(1) the relatively deprived

(2) the relatively privileged

THE MIDDLE-CLASS MANUAL WORKER.

WOODFORD

Woodford is a 'middle-class' sort of place. It is

almost entirely without what many people would think of as an 'upper' or 'upper-middle' class. Not only are really wealthy people scarce, but there are very few surgeons or architects, stockbrokers or barristers. The professions are represented by people like bank managers, accountants and surveyors, and such company directors as live there work far more often in small (mainly family) concerns than in large public companies. They seemed, from the interviews, to have lives not sharply different from those of other white-collar workers—the bank clerks, insurance agents, shopkeepers, Civil Servants and teachers who appeared so often on the interview schedules. These people represented just over three-fifths of the sample. The rest were manual workers.

The locality has a middle-class air.

How few people there seemed to be in Woodford, and how many dogs [write Willmott and Young on the first page of their book]. This is perhaps what Orwell was talking about when he wrote of the 'huge peaceful wilderness of outer London . . . sleeping the deep, deep sleep of England'.[1]

They remark on the trees with which Woodford abounds.

The older trees are oaks, elms, hawthorns, chestnuts, limes and sycamores. Then, after 1918, a new phase of planting began.

---

[1] Peter Willmott and Michael Young (1960), *Family and Class in a London Suburb*, Routledge and Kegan Paul, London. The density of population in Woodford was 16 to the acre, as compared to 64 in Bethnal Green and 100 in Paddington.

There was a demand in the newly-built streets for trees which would give a country air to the place while preserving the tidy appearance proper to a respectable suburb. Flowering cherries (pink rather than white), crab apples, almonds, mountain ashes, purple plums and laburnum now line hundreds of local streets.

These streets are more likely to be exclusively middle-class. There is some mixing of social class along single streets, but in the main the working class in Woodford live in 'recognizably working-class enclaves'. 'Still two classes' announce Willmott and Young as the final subheading of their chapter on the tensions of social class. 'Inside people's minds, the boundaries of class are still closely drawn.' 'Yet', they are able to write on another page, 'the suburb as a whole certainly bears a middle-class stamp'. Woodford in fact reflects the current changes in social structure very faithfully.

We saw something of the variety [of social origin] in people's lives as we went about our interviewing. Our informants sometimes engulfed us in deep velvet-covered settees, and handed us glasses of sherry which we had to hold gingerly in the left hand while unchivalrously scribbling notes with the right. In another street we were seated on hard upright chairs next to drying nappies and given a large cup of sweet tea and sterilized milk . . . We encountered neat grey suits, gold watch chains, bow-ties, clipped moustaches and shiny brown shoes; also men collarless and in shirt-sleeves, with waistcoats and over-size carpet slippers. As well as the middle-aged mothers with faces made up and hair colour-rinsed, wearing two-pieces and nylon stockings, there were plump 'Mums' of the same age wearing lisle stockings and enormous flowered overalls.

Yet the suburb as a whole certainly bears a middle-class stamp. On their way to work, electricians and bank clerks wear the same sort of clothes, and what is more, so do their wives. They sometimes drive the same sort of cars, and sometimes the interiors of their houses are indistinguishable too . . . In the homes of the young couples there are plenty of signs of the post-war redistribution of incomes which can be viewed instead as the general adoption of middle-class standards.

These may be called the 'new' middle class, or the 'new' residents of Woodford. According to Willmott and Young the old

and more traditional Woodfordians are moving away.[1] Even
if they do not, their significance must be declining as the population expands. Although we do not know the number of moves
made by couples who ended up in Willmott and Young's
Woodford sample, there is abundant evidence of movement.
Only twelve per cent were born in Woodford. Fifteen per cent
were born in the East End of London; a quarter in the inner
Essex boroughs of Leyton, East and West Ham, and Waltham-
stow; a fifth from elsewhere in Greater London. 'People from
the inner London districts are still the core of suburban society,'
Willmott and Young conclude.

Woodford offers a vivid picture of the upward-moving working-class family. (We may note in passing that 'Woodford
itself is not a haven—more people flock from East London
because the suburb is desirable, and by doing so make it less
desirable for those who were there before them. The older
people were only too well aware that the newcomers detracted
constantly from the value of the district.')

> Often they arrive in stages, they and their parents having
> moved, while they were yet children, from Bethnal Green or
> Poplar to Walthamstow and Forest Gate, and from there on to
> Woodford. For the move outward from London is also a move up
> the social scale. When Mr. Lloyd said that he had come a long way,
> he was not thinking of miles. Woodford is a step up the ladder.
> 'I've come quite a long way from being a Shadwell boy earning
> 5/- a week to having my own house out here,' said Mr. Lloyd.
> At twenty-eight he had married a girl from Hackney and to begin
> with they had lived in two rooms at Bow. 'The house came up for
> sale after a couple of years,' he explained, 'and I tried to buy it.
> But I couldn't afford it. After that, I said to the wife, "I'm going
> to work hellish hard for the next five years. You help me and I
> promise you you'll have your own house." And I did it. Six years
> later I paid the deposit on a small house at Leytonstone. We
> couldn't afford to furnish the whole house at first so we let off
> half of it. But it was a footing, a foundation, something I could
> build on.' By 1936 he had enough money to pay the deposit on

[1] They are reported as moving deeper into the country as the suburb becomes
more 'suburban'. It seems, from Mrs. Stacey's description, that the traditionals in
Banbury are more firmly established, presumably because they are farther away
from London, that inexhaustible supply source of ambitious working-class people.

his present house. 'It's a good feeling that you've achieved something. Something you've done, something you're proud of. I could have stayed in the East End, but it didn't appeal to me. I wanted something better for my family. There's always something better than what you've got if only you're prepared to work for it.'

Mr. Lloyd manifests a number of traits, later to be discussed in more detail, which characterize certain sections of the middle class and which, if possessed by a manual working man in favourable economic circumstances, will soon land him in those sections. We may note in particular the liking for individual achievement, the ability to work for long-term goals, and the confidence that success rewards effort.[1] Such traits are characteristic of the socially mobile in a society with a rapidly rising standard of living. There are less attractive concomitants. With the tough-minded optimism so apparent in Mr. Lloyd's recital goes also a dislike of those with other aspirations, of those without aspirations, of those with other values, and indeed, as Robb noted, a dislike of all outgroups. Thus one other resident in Woodford complains about the Jews in Bethnal Green and a third confided that 'we don't tell people we come from Bethnal Green. You get the scum of the earth there.' Precisely parallel passages can be found in Willmott's chapter on those who had voluntarily migrated from Dagenham.[2]

The move upward requires hard work, and during this phase the man sees little of his family. It is clear from Mr. Lloyd's account that the ideal of partnership in marriage, which is more typical of families with loose-knit social connections, cannot be realized until the desired social level is attained. At least four related social processes have therefore to be kept in mind simultaneously: hard work and social mobility, hard work and little family life, geographical mobility and loss of everyday community-life, loss of community and greater conjugal partnership. These are not to be directly related to social class.

At one end of the Woodford social scale we have . . . Mr. Lane, for instance. He manages his own small factory nearby. He gets to work every morning at eight and often doesn't leave for home until ten or eleven at night . . . Mr. Milner, an accountant in a

---

[1] See *inter alia* pages 422 and 605.
[2] See, for example, the quotations cited on page 425.

large company, did not have such long hours in his office, but almost every night and every week-end he brought papers back to work on in his study. At the other end of the Woodford spectrum, there are manual workers who snatch at every chance of overtime and stay in their factories night after night to earn money for a washing machine, a refrigerator or a small car.

Some presumably continue this grind all their lives. But, as the quotation suggests, others change. Producer-mentality becomes consumer-mentality.[1] Mr. Lane was an example of 'the executive who spends nearly all his time out of the home, not so much spending money as making it'. But spending money together on objects of common interest like the children and the house is exactly what draws husband and wife together.[2] Having arrived at a certain income, having moved house, with his wife now rather more cut off from her original community, the husband feels freer to partner his wife. This phase seems to have been most characteristic of Woodford when Willmott and Young were there.

Most Woodford men are emphatically not absentee husbands. They hurry back from their offices and factories, arriving between six and seven, to spend the evenings at home, and they are there, at home, for two full days at week-ends. It is their work, especially if rather tedious, which takes second place in their thoughts. They are as devoted as their wives to the house they share.

The growth of what Young and Willmott called 'house-centredness' in their discussion of Greenleigh life has here gone a step further, or perhaps it is better to say that the pattern has here become established with a true conjugal partnership ideal. Two-thirds of the Woodford sample lived in privately owned houses. Putting in new gadgets, making improvements or simply making changes was a favourite occupation and interest, both with husband and wife.

The competitiveness which played its part in the world of industry and commerce may now find a new outlet in the community. We may note here, as in the chapter on working-class status-dissent, the tendency towards competitive consumption. Woodford informants disagreed on how general and how impor-

[1] See also the discussion on pages 247-52 and 422-7.
[2] See also the discussion on pages 295-303.

tant the competitiveness for material goods was. But the interviews gave several examples of this motive at work.

'As soon as next door knew we'd got a washing machine, they got one too. Then a few months later we got a fridge, so they got a fridge as well.' . . . 'It seems to worry her if we have anything new.' . . . 'During the course of conversation a neighbour told me they were getting a new car. Then she mentioned someone else in the road who'd just got a new car and she said, "That'll be a knock in the eye for *them*".' . . . 'My wife is always getting on to me. She says, "I see the so-and-so's have got a car. Why don't *you* get a car?"'

PARENTS AND ADULT CHILDREN IN MORE LOOSE-KNIT SOCIAL NETWORKS

Because they expected to follow whatever opportunity offered for getting ahead, most people in Woodford felt no deep concern to live near their kin. 'A man's got to go where his work is, and a wife's got to go where her husband's livelihood is. You just can't stay near your parents if your job pulls in another direction.'

Many of the parental generation supported this point of view: there seems to be little evidence of an inter-generational conflict of norms in this matter.

'They mustn't be tied to their parents,' said one parent. 'My family's got a motto,' said Mrs. Archer. 'When you're married you're on your own.' Another: 'I'd be broken-hearted if I thought I'd done anything to prevent them going off and becoming people in their own right. I think this possessiveness and tying them to you all the time is all wrong.' Such remarks are reminiscent of the emphasis on individual development and individual choice which Mogey associated with his status-dissenters, who had upwardly mobile aspirations.[1] In this connection we may also mention Gorer's finding that more of his informants who called themselves 'middle class' had moved to their present address in the past year, and fewer of them had lived at their present address for more than ten years. More of

---

[1] See pages 272-3 and 352.

them also had parents who live in another town.[1] Willmott and Young conclude that 'localized extended families—family groups spreading over two or more nearby houses, the distinctive feature of kinship in the East End—are rare in Woodford'. It is easy to misinterpret the evidence and to under-estimate the amount of family-contact among the mobile. The barriers raised by physical distance may be removed by techniques which middle-class incomes and education make possible. There is a greater facility with pen and paper. Woodford people write letters.

Cars make a difference. Mr. Devon, a school teacher, is one man who uses his car regularly for this purpose; he drives an elderly sister to church in Barking every Sunday and on the way back picks up his brother and brings him back to dinner. Mr. Prior, a bank manager, explained that he goes over to Harringay to pick up his mother for the week-end occasionally. He drops her back there on his way to work on Monday mornings.

The possession of a spare room is a great help in such contacts. It enables a family to spend part of their holidays with their kin. Then there is the telephone: 'We ring up my parents every month to see how they are.' 'I've got a sister in Ealing, I'm always talking to her on the phone.' 'I speak to all my sisters at least once a week on the telephone.'

With all these technical aids, the middle-class people of Woodford keep in touch with relatives almost as much as working-class people do, although they do not live as close.

Comparing three main categories, we find Woodford working-class people more likely than middle-class people to live near their parents, but that more working-class people lived near their parents in Bethnal Green than in Woodford.

Parents' residence	*Woodford middle class*	*Woodford working class*	*Bethnal Green*	*Dagenham*
	%	%	%	%
Same dwelling	8	11	12	17
Within 5 mins. walk	6	10	29	15
Elsewhere in district	12	21	13	12
Outside the district	74	58	46	56

[1] These middle classes are likely to be non-traditional, for the obvious reason of mobility. *Exploring English Character*, Cresset Press, London (1955). See Tables 10, 11, 15, 16.

Middle-Class Life

The Woodford working-class sample was more 'middle-class' in attitude than the Bethnal Green counterpart, having experienced more moves. More of them called themselves middle class. These differed, in ways one would expect, from those who did not. 22 per cent of Woodford manual workers who called themselves middle class had been visited by a relative in the previous twenty-four hours, as compared with 32 per cent of those who called themselves working class. More of the former also attended church more often, and more belonged to formal organizations.[1]

Social distance as well as geographical distance affects class differences in contact between parents and children. Together these two factors account for the somewhat more formalized interaction between the two generations which Willmott and Young noticed in Woodford. The beginnings of this trend were perceptible in Greenleigh.[2] Meetings are much less casual than in Bethnal Green, much more dependent on definite appointments. When an informant says 'We don't see much of our parents except by arrangement; it's better that way' one guesses at other embarrassments beside the fear of finding the others not at home after a journey. There is for instance the awkwardness of mixing parents of one social class with the new friends and acquaintances (who gain in importance as the network loosens) of another social class.[3]

[1] We may remind ourselves once again that 'middle class', in this context, cannot mean traditional middle class. These are socially mobile people who are better off than their parents and want a different way of life, status-dissenters with money and a better education than those discussed in the previous chapter.

[2] See page 333.

[3] M. B. Sussman found that parents and children in a U.S. sample were more likely to keep in touch if the children married people of the same cultural background ('The help pattern in the middle-class family', *Amer. Sociol. Rev.*, XVIII, 1953). This supports the argument frequently encountered in sociological literature that close family-relations clash with occupational mobility. But Litvak, reacting against this, concluded from a small study of American patterns of visiting that geographical rather than social mobility accounts for the decline in the number of family-visits in large cities. The upwardly mobile are admired by their kin, and are pleased to entertain them *in a city large enough to afford anonymity so that their friends don't know about them and don't meet them.* He calls this pattern 'the modified extended family'. Whether this precise psychological analysis is applicable to Britain we cannot know, but the reference to 'arrangements' in the quotation above and some quotations below about difficulties in getting on with parents who live with them provide some supporting evidence. (E. Litvak, 1960, 'Occupational mobility and extended family cohesion', *Amer. Sociol. Rev.*, XXV.)

The life-cycle also has obviously important effects on parent–child relations. Bott notes that, even in the very loose-knit families, there is likely to be a rapprochement between the two older generations when a grandchild is born. And when parents can no longer look after themselves as they used to, or when they are widowed, they often come to live with their children. Gorer's tables, for instance, show *both* that the higher up the social scale informants place themselves they less likely are to be living in the same town as their parents (in other words, they are more likely to be in a loose-knit network) *and* that the higher up they place themselves the more likely they are to have a widowed parent actually living with them.[1]

Strain may be felt because the new level of interaction is not freely chosen but imposed by circumstances, by illness or widowhood. Then people chafe at the unaccustomed noise, the presence of the other in kitchen or living room; they miss the spare room. And the parent may attempt to exercise the authority which was appropriate at an earlier stage in the life-cycle.

There may be strain because the life-cycles of the two generations do not mesh well together. A young married couple of the highly mobile kind would not be living near parents just at the time when they needed them most: during confinements, for baby-sitting, to help with shopping when the children are small, nursing babies through illness, and so on. Parents come to live near when they need to, and children may feel that there has been no proper reciprocity in the exchange of services.

Moreover, when they come together again, the problem of mutual adjustment is aggravated, either because one family has moved to a different social level, with all the changes in pattern of living that this entails, or (or additionally) because during the period of separation the two families have grown apart simply because they have not been exerting such strong social control on one another as is possible when people live in constant interaction.[2] It would in fact be a very lucky chance if parents and

---

[1] Gorer's tables 13 and 14. Willmott and Young indicate that parents tend to join daughters rather than sons, but Gorer shows no such tendency for widowed fathers and only a very slight tendency for widowed mothers to live with daughters.

[2] See pages 231–2 and 245.

children developed along the same lines. By definition, there is no traditional solution to this problem. So one daughter complains:

'You're pulled both ways—you've got obligations to your mother, of course, but you've got obligations to your husband and your own family too. Sometimes it does create tension.'

But a young man has the opposite complaint.

'She doesn't seem to feel she's sharing with us. She seems to want to keep her independence. She won't join in and accept our ways. I feel she should try to integrate herself more with the family.'

Reactions to such strains must also be affected by the knowledge that living together has become a practical solution to a practical problem; often it is not, at least for the younger generation, of emotional value in itself. The younger couple are emotionally dependent on each other, then on their friends, and only thereafter dependent on their parents.

CONJUGAL RELATIONS IN MORE LOOSE-KNIT SOCIAL NETWORKS

In Woodford as in Greenleigh, when interaction with kin is less frequent, husband and wife will tend to depend more on each other for the satisfaction of their social and emotional needs. To put the correlation the other way round, when the conjugal bond is satisfying and strong, it matters less that kin are living far away.

Hence it is not surprising to find the ideal of marriage as a partnership most pervasive among the middle classes, or more precisely, among those who are subject to social forces which induce a more middle-class way of life, that is to say, among those who are mobile either socially or geographically, or in both ways. Accordingly, Bott's account of the marriage-ideal of 'loose-knit' families is in contrast to that of the traditional close-knit families.

It was felt that in a good marriage, husband and wife should achieve a high degree of compatibility, based on their own particular combination of shared interests and complementary differences. Their relationship with each other should be more important than any separate relationship with outsiders. The conjugal relationship should be kept private and revelations to outsiders or letting down one's spouse in public were felt to be serious offences.

The feeling that the marriage bond is pre-eminent and other ties comparatively unimportant is well illustrated by three wedding-memories. At one extreme is Sylvia's wedding in the traditional close-knit Bethnal Green community, part of which was quoted on page 194. An 'intermediate' couple, the Hartleys (seven moves), were married in church, 'with me in a white dress and all the trimmings'. Six of the wedding guests were relatives, five were friends of the young Hartleys, two were friends of the parents.

> The Daniels (nineteen moves) got married in a Registry Office. The only relative who came was Mr. Daniel's sister. All the other guests were friends. Although the Daniels got along very well with their parents and had introduced each other to their respective parents before they got married, they did not feel that it was essential for their parents to come to the wedding. The parents were living in the country at the time.

For the Daniels, marriage is not an act which cements the community; rather it is the mark of independence from the older generation, the beginning of a new and separate life. As Bott put it, 'the contrast between the Hartleys' wedding and the Daniels' suggests that the latter conceived of the wedding purely as their personal union, not a bringing together of their relatives'.

The exclusiveness of the conjugal pair makes for a greater intensity within their relationship. Bott found that, in general, the greater the emphasis on shared conjugal interests and joint organization of domestic activities, the greater the importance attached to sexual relations. The achievement of a successful sex-life was felt by these couples to be a very important part of a happy marriage. Bott considered that they talked as though they felt 'almost a moral obligation to enjoy sexual relations'.[1] This is not surprising since sexual relations distinguish the conjugal from other family relationships.

The children who resulted were considered of equal interest to both parents. Co-parenthood was reported by Bott to be a

[1] Cf. page 148, also pages 618–19.

deeply felt value. Among these families there was no feeling that the father was the more authoritative of the two. Indeed, Bott noticed that fathers tended to specialize in entertaining the children.[1] Both parents were thought of as equally warmly disposed towards the children.[2] Nevertheless, in practice, they felt just as deeply that the mother had a special relation to the child which could never be achieved by the father, especially when the child was young.

The more loose-knit the network, the less sex-determined the performance of domestic duties. These couples conformed to social custom in recognizing the basic differentiation between the husband's role as primary breadwinner and the wife's role as mother of young children. But in other respects they felt such division of labour as did exist to be more a matter of convenience than of inherent differences between the sexes. The division of labour was an extremely flexible one, with a good deal of shared activity as well as interchange of tasks. Financial affairs among these families were managed jointly and it was taken for granted that there should be joint consultation on all major issues.

Leisure too was more often shared than was the case in the previous types of family studied. Joint entertainment at home, or going out together, was a major form of recreation. (In spite of the fact that after the advent of children this became more difficult because of the necessity of finding baby-sitters and other such disadvantages of the loose-knit social network.)

There was no strict division of labour in dealing with the outside institution. The husband usually dealt with financial and legal ones, and the wife with those that catered for children, but either partner could, and when convenient would, take over the other's activities in this sphere. (It may be added that this may not be such a strain on a recognizably middle-class family with its obvious respectability, which is less apt to be subjected to pin-pricks from jacks-in-office. Certainly neither partner felt these services to be alien to them and they were not

[1] See also pages 184 and 468.

[2] A family in Woodford illustrates what is perhaps the most extreme achievement of parental partnership ideals. 'We have the same routine every night. I put one child to bed and my husband puts the other. We take it in turns to tell them stories too.'

worried about using them. They were well informed about the possibilities that they offered. This is all in marked contrast to the account on pages 203–6.)

Other attitudes were congruent with these practices. It was a favourite topic among these families whether there were any real differences between men and women, apart from the obvious reproductive ones. In relation to their own families of origin there was much less concentration on one parent at the expense of the other. The Hartleys and the Daniels, both more loose-knit than the Newbolts, also placed less emphasis on the mother than the Newbolts did. When they talked about past events, they mentioned their fathers as often as their mothers. Bott concluded that they thought of their 'parents' more as a unit, rather than considering 'mother' and 'father' separately. The Daniels and the Hartleys also took it for granted that the younger couple would normally be on equally intimate terms with both sets of parents: maternal preference is not here the norm. Compared with more close-knit families, however, whereas the cleavage between the sexes is felt less deeply, the cleavage between generations is felt more—parents and children do not so easily make good company for each other. This has been discussed in terms of the contact between the two adult generations already, we shall note it in connection with young children below.

Daytime occupation is one area in which the ideal of equality and conjugal partnership is difficult to put into practice. The general feeling among Bott's informants was that the woman should, if she wanted it, have a career or some special skill or interest 'comparable in seriousness to her husband's occupation'. All the wives wanted to work. But they also felt that the young child needed his mother's care, and that ideally a mother should relinquish her career until the last child had reached school age. The women thought of themselves as having sacrificed a career in order to marry.

Hence among these couples the question of whether wives should go out to work or stay at home was a highly controversial one. Money was not the only consideration; these women wanted to work for the sake of the work itself. Without it, they felt that not all their potentialities were being used. They had

Middle-Class Life

in fact the normal professional middle-class attitude towards the exercise of skills.[1] They did not think housework gave them sufficient scope for their talents. They regarded it as drudgery and—in contrast with Mogey's housewives—they considered the man the more fortunate partner because he went out to work while his wife was confined to the house. The Newsons have described the wife's situation in vivid modern terms.

> With the growth of large-scale public and business organizations, many young men in this occupational class enjoy higher standards of material luxury and comfort in their working environment (in heating, lighting, air conditioning and quality furnishing, for instance) than they can expect to provide initially for their wives and families at home; furthermore, their wives are often quite well aware of this discrepancy. It may well be difficult for a woman to match her husband's status position at work by contriving a domestic environment which similarly enhances his reputation among friends and neighbours at home; and while she may privately blame this state of affairs on his financial inability to provide her with labour-saving gadgets or domestic help, she may still feel guilty if she fails, within her means, to achieve the kind of home which does him credit.[2]

Connected with this, both as a cause and as effect, is the wife's reluctance to apply her mind whole-heartedly to domestic work as though it were a job to be done well, for the good performance of which she reaps a reward in self-respect and praise from others. There may be a change in this direction when husbands

---

[1] See pages 355–8. Viola Klein analysed the replies given by a national sample of working women in answer to the question, why they went out to work (*Working Wives* (1957), published by the Institute of Personnel Management, London).

The classification she used is that of the Hulton Readership Survey. A and B represent the upper and upper middle class, C represents the lower middle, D and E manual workers of all grades of skill.

Main reason given for going out to work	Class		
	AB	C	DE
	%	%	%
Financial	43	67	79
Independence (money of one's own)		4	2
Works with husband to help him	25	10	2
Need of mental stimulus (not enough to do)	14	20	11
Need of social stimulus (likes meeting people)	4	12	4

[2] From *Infant Care in an Urban Community*, by John and Elizabeth Newson.

come to appreciate the high degree of skill needed to run a home well—a probability which must increase as conjugal role-segregation declines.

The arrival of young children inevitably restricts her horizons rather drastically to begin with; if she has aspirations to an active intellectual life, this may be a time of frustration and despondency, and at best felt as a temporary phase to be tolerated and lived through . . .[1]

The resulting state of conflict may be shown in a variety of ways. She may live nostalgically in the past, remembering her early adult life, when she was still at work, as a time of unfettered freedom and gay adventure. Alternatively, she may see the humorous side of her present predicament, and put it to social use by telling funny stories against herself: how the elderly visitor, arriving unexpectedly, was guided deftly past the unemptied potty behind the front door, only to come upon the toddler admiring her naked stomach in the hall mirror; or how the cake for a party, collapsed when its baking was interrupted by the baby, was filled up with chocolate icing and passed off as a special new recipe.

Each of these expedients makes it less probable that the housewife will take pride in the efficient performance of her tasks.

Bott evoked a rather different set of responses from her sample. One mother was looking forward to the day when her youngest would be going to school, and she herself able to take up her special interest again. Another had a hobby which her husband shared and which took up almost as much time as a job would. A third worked at some other occupation at home. The other two mothers in Bott's group of families in loose-knit networks had solved the problem by continuing to work outside, making expensive provision for the care of their children. The husbands helped them a good deal with domestic work. Nevertheless, there was a strain. As Margot Jefferys put it:

> Women who choose to do two jobs are subject to considerable strain . . . Few were able to reduce their routine domestic tasks to less than twenty hours a week . . . It seems clear that at present the husbands of working professional women leave the main burden of domestic arrangements to their wives.[2]

[1] The discussion of this reaction is continued at the beginning of the sub-section on the socialization of the privileged child.
[2] M. Jefferys (1952), 'Married women in the Civil Service', *Brit. J. Sociol.*, III.

Middle-Class Life

For all these reasons, wives tend to feel separated from their husbands and somewhat hard done by. Many of them complained to Bott at one time or another of their drudgery, their boredom and their isolation. Especially when the children were young, they felt 'tied to the house'. 'You must forgive me if I sound half-witted,' said one informant, a highly educated woman, to Bott. 'I've been talking to the children all day.' The Newbolts felt no such gap between the generations. But we may also note in passing what must be considered in detail in the volume on child-rearing, that she *had* been talking to them all day—an important experience in the life of the middle-class child.[1] It should be added, as Bott does, that all these mothers achieved a good deal of satisfaction from their maternal role.

Bott found that the 'intermediate' families were less self-conscious about themselves as parents than were those in very loose-knit networks, and also less conscious of the gulf between themselves and their children, though on the whole the division of labour was the same, both as regards child-care and in other matters. The differences are, as would be expected, that they felt somewhat more that they could rely on help from neighbours, or from kin if these lived near. And though these families also stressed the importance of conjugal privacy, the precedence of the conjugal relation over all others, and the sharing of interests and activities, they were more ready to acknowledge the possibility of social or temperamental differences between the sexes and to maintain a more marked division of labour in the domestic activities of husbands and wives.

In most respects Woodford is closest to the 'intermediate' pattern. In the constant improvement of the house, in painting or rebuilding, 'each step is discussed in detail with the wife'. She did not normally have to do anything, but, as one informant puts it:

> In the old days, the husband was the husband and the wife was the wife and they each had their own way of going on. Her job was to look after him. The wives wouldn't stand for it nowadays. Husbands help with the children now. They stay more in the home and have more interest in the home.

[1] See pages 512–15.

Some of the husbands now dry up for their wives, lay breakfast, hoover on Sundays, polish floors, as a matter of routine, without embarrassment, not behind closed curtains.

The garden provides further opportunity for joint activity, and here the opportunity is taken as it never seems to have been, for instance, on the allotments of St. Ebbe's. The co-operation in the garden is touchingly indicated by the informants' use of personal pronouns:

'Frank dug a small patch for me to plant a new Japonica bush. I joined him and we planted the bush, hoping it would survive...'

'Spent the afternoon with John. We put in the spring bulbs—daffodils, narcissi, tulips. Then I disbudded the chrysanthemums.'

Both these speakers were older people. The drift towards a less traditional way of life affects old as well as young in Woodford. Willmott and Young found that old people of all social classes held a more companionate conception of marriage than they had encountered in Bethnal Green. In four out of every five couples in the Woodford sample of old people, the husband helped his wife regularly with the housework, compared with less than half who did so in Bethnal Green. Mr. Harding, for instance, a retired bank clerk, helped his wife with the weekend shopping every Friday afternoon, did some of the washing, made beds because she was not strong enough to turn the mattress. Another informant said they went fifty-fifty in all the jobs in the house.

Willmott and Young suggest that one reason for this change is that the daughter is likely to have moved away from Woodford and 'with the children off the scene, middle-aged mothers and fathers are much more likely than in Bethnal Green, to lead shared lives, to develop common interests, and to deepen their attachment to each other'. There were admittedly some retired manual workers who felt they had no real place in the home, that they were useless and in the way. Mr. Garner complained: 'What's the good of mooching around here all the time? I see enough of the wife without sitting here all day.' And from a wife's point of view, when there is no family tradition of sharing the work of the house: 'He just sits around here all day since he gave up work. He gets in my way more than anything.'[1]

[1] See also pages 160 and 164–5.

These were exceptions. Though financially the working-class retired men in Woodford are worse off than the middle-class, in other important respects they are more like them than like the manual workers of Bethnal Green. On the whole, even working-class fathers in Woodford do not feel excluded from the home. On the contrary, their relationship with their wives is a close one . . . Woodford fathers and mothers more often own their homes and have gardens to tend, and the interest in the house and garden is something the couples hold in common.

FRIENDS AND NEIGHBOURS IN MORE LOOSE-KNIT SOCIAL NETWORKS

'The contrast between the Hartleys and the Daniels,' wrote Bott, 'suggests that the latter conceived of their wedding purely as their personal union.' She continued: 'Friends rather than relatives were needed as an audience for the establishment of the new relationship.'

We must now consider the social contacts of people who are not connected by family ties. There is a marked difference here between couples in a very loose-knit network and those in an intermediate situation. The five families in Bott's sample who had very loose-knit networks did not think of the neighbourhood as a source of friends. They regarded their neighbours with caution, and the neighbours reciprocated. The neighbourhoods were like that: everybody cool and distant. Bott surmised that one reason for this may have been that all neighbours felt they had little in common with the others. It is a bit of a puzzle why they should feel this, since to an outsider's eye they seem no more dissimilar than the inhabitants of other places. It may be that, like Mogey's status-dissenters, they were more demanding in all areas of life, including social relationships. They were looking exclusively for friends in the middle-class sense of the word.[1]

Gorer gives some relevant further information on this point. He asked his informants if they would say that their best friends lived near them (that is, within walking distance), a short distance away (say a mile or so), or far away. The replies show an

[1] See the discussion on pages 137–8 and 272–6.

age factor: particularly the younger and married informants, those between twenty-five and forty-four, were likely to have their friends live far away. Those older or younger than this group, and the single, were more likely to have friends at hand. There is also a class factor. The higher the social class which the informant attributed to himself, the more likely it was that he had friends 'far away'. Class and age amount to a career factor. These are socially mobile people moving about the country following their best opportunities.[1] Susser and Watson paint a rather rosy picture and have possibly been over-impressed by the social life of the university, itself idealized:

As they share a generic culture and a common set of liberal values, they can readily interact in these terms with colleagues, friends and other associates who are their economic and social equals. The nearest equivalent to a close-knit network the spiralist family possesses is possibly the professional association or institute to which the spiralist belongs, particularly if his skill is highly specialized. For although his colleagues are dispersed throughout the country, they meet regularly to discuss professional matters, read about each other in journals, and soon learn about changes in status and residence among their associates. Hence, the spiralist family also gains material and emotional satisfactions, but they seek their social support in a less direct way, have more varied demands, and are less dependent on kin relationships. Indeed, their view of such relationships may be cool and detached.

More plausibly, Bott found that the friends of people in very loose-knit networks had been made at diverse times in the lives of these couples. In the places where they had stayed at various stages in their careers they had met people they had liked enough to keep in touch. They were, in the full sense of the word, chosen friends. Being at some distance they maintained

---

[1] If we identify as more traditional the people who think of themselves as simply middle class or working class, i.e. in terms of a simple two-class model, we find that those who qualify their class in some way, especially the upper middle and the upper working class, are most likely to have friends far away. These people, who feel they must specify in which stratum of their class they belong, are just the sort of people who are likely to be mobile, if we argue that the qualification suggests that they are more aware of the class-structure. This suggestion is given some weight by a correlated finding of Gorer's, that they are also more politically conscious and belong to more formal organizations. This discussion is relevant to pages 207, 278 and 259–66.

contact in the usual middle-class way: telephone, letters arranged visits. This Susser and Watson put rather more acidly. 'They work with one set, play golf with another, entertain another, and live beside yet another. To operate their dispersed networks they need expensive material objects, large homes, motor-cars, and telephones, as well as appropriate social skills.'[1] In accordance with the ideal of conjugal partnership, these friends are friends of both husband and wife. Bott found some rare exceptions, but in her experience no-one was happy about them. Joint entertainment was the norm, and the major leisure-time activity. It had for these couples something of the social and emotional meaning which being with kin has in other social regions.

By hypothesis and in fact, people in very loose-knit networks rarely know more than a couple of others in the same network: friends don't know the friends of friends, they don't know the relatives, relatives don't keep in touch much, no one knows the neighbours. Families in these circumstances are subject to relatively little social pressure; they will find few others who exactly agree and support the combination of norms and practices they have created for themselves. At the more practical level, they have no easily available solid body of helpers such as people in other social circumstances might command. Loneliness is therefore a problem.

The men have their professional relationships during the day. Munro has a remarkable passage in which he likens the satisfactions of the team-spirit experienced by the Civil Servant at work with those of the community-spirit in the past. He contrasts the traditional close-knit community with the world of today, 'where most people, even our friends, are comparative strangers'.

> In shared work and enterprise the old state of affairs can in a sense be recreated, because this involves none of those personal and family matters out of which reserves and reticences arise. Thus Jones' wife and Smith's wife might not get on if they knew each other, but they don't and are never likely to, for Jones lives at Ealing and Smith at Blackheath. Jones may be a studious man, Smith a worldly man, whose tastes would not fit at all, did they

[1] There is a further discussion of social skills on pages 350-2.

345

ever meet in their home lives, but they don't. In the office, on the other hand, they may develop the strongest bond through years of common endeavour and common interest. When two of these men lunch together, as often they do, a superior person sitting at the next table will be heard remarking afterwards with a smile that the whole time they talked nothing but 'shop' . . . But what should two such men talk about except the one and only interest they share in common?

It is the women who feel the loneliness in the daytime. Bott asks herself whether this problem could perhaps be solved if families moved to areas which were felt to be homogeneous and composed of people similar to themselves, for then the wives might be able to find friends among the neighbours. But she finds it difficult to imagine that people such as these could feel that any local area, however homogeneous by objective criteria, could contain potential friends, since their experience of moving about and their very varied social contacts would have made them highly discriminating in their choice of friends.

On the other hand, in a more typically 'intermediate' setting like Woodford, many women did feel that they and their neighbours had something in common. Four of the couples Bott designated as 'intermediate' lived in 'suburban' areas, five in mixed working-class areas; five lived in or near the area where one or both had lived since childhood. Some of these people's friends did know each other. Many of the neighbours knew each other. There was not the very great familiarity built up through continuous residence, as was the case with the Newbolts, but there was not the stand-offishness typical of the families with very loose-knit networks. Several had had considerable continuity of relationships since childhood, and they had not developed the pattern of ignoring neighbours and relying chiefly on friends and colleagues for social contact, which characterized the others.

Bott makes the interesting point that these women complained less about being cooped up with their children not only because they had more help from neighbours and relatives, but also because their children spent more of their time playing outside with neighbouring children. They were less uneasy about such play than the mothers in very loose-knit networks, because they felt they lived in an area where the neighbours were socially similar to themselves, less likely to be offended or to offend.[1]

In Woodford, nearly two-thirds of the sample thought that the people around them were easy to get on with. Most of the rest 'did not notice them much'. Less than a tenth complained of standoffishness.

> 'The day I moved into this house, the lady opposite, whom I'd never seen before in my life, told the milkman to leave a pint of milk and call back again at dinner time to see what we wanted.' 'My wife is the sort of person who endeavours to entertain new people whenever they arrive. If anyone new comes to live on this estate, they are invited to one of her coffee evenings.' Another informant was taking her dog for a walk soon after she had arrived when another young woman living in the same road went up to her and asked if she'd been in the WRENS. 'She didn't know I had been,' said Mrs. King, 'she'd never met me before but she said she just guessed I'd been in the WRENS like her.' Now these two are close friends.

So in spite of the mobility which marked Woodford, most of the people there had friends locally, often living in the immediate neighbourhood, in the same road or the next one.[2]

> 'I've got a lot of friends,' said Mrs. Long, 'most of them in Corncroft Crescent. There's May at number 4, Eileen at 16, another friend at 24, another at 29 and another at 21.' . . . 'We all get on very well in this road,' said Mrs. Sturgis. 'Every morning someone takes it in turn to have the others in for coffee.'

Mrs. Matthew's time-budget bears comparison with its Bethnal Green counterpart, quoted on pages 131–2.

8.45. Got Susan ready for school and took her round there.

---

[1] Cf. pages 556–60 in the volume on child-rearing.

[2] Banbury, which has a greater proportion of traditional people, has also its share of 'intermediate families'. The Trubshaws, for instance, have as strong friendship with people outside as they had with their neighbours in the Drive. They had also maintained friendships with people in other towns. They, like everyone, can rely on their neighbours in emergencies. When her child had an accident, Mrs. Trubshaw called on her neighbour for immediate help. As for other middle-class people, middle-class substitutes for community-help are available and used. If the young mothers cannot leave the house they can telephone friends, doctors and (since in Banbury there is still a large traditional element) the shops.

Then went on to the shops. On the way back saw Mrs. Rayburn who has been ill with 'flu and stopped to ask her how she was feeling.

10.0. My friend Joyce called. She wanted to know if I would go over to her house for tea that afternoon instead of the next day as previously arranged. I agreed. We started discussion about washing machines.

10.45. Joyce having gone, I took Dennis (the dog) out for his morning walk in the forest. We have made a lot of friends on these walks—dog-owners seem to find it easier. Saw my friend Shirley . . .

Mothers also meet through their children. Then they entertain each other, help each other by taking turns in escorting children to and from school, or having them in to play. The tie between them can assume the social and emotional significance normally accorded to kin. 'We're more like sisters than friends,' said Mrs. Kendrick of the woman living opposite her in Woodford. The children grow up to call their mother's friends 'auntie'. They exchange services too, shopping for each other, watering each other's plants and looking after each other's pets on holiday. A neighbour may mend a fuse for a widow, another will dig her garden for her.

There is a good deal of visiting in Woodford. Forty per cent of the Woodford sample had had a friend or neighbour in the house during the previous twenty-four hours, another third during the previous week. These friends were mostly local, often living in the same road or the next. It was normal here to belong to a small intimate network of 'friends' coming mostly from the surrounding twenty or thirty houses, though some people, especially those nearer the upper range of the middle classes—i.e. those in professional and managerial jobs—also had friends living farther afield. The size of the network varied —sometimes just a pair, sometimes three or four, sometimes ten or twelve, sometimes an even larger group. This network, organized and run largely by the women, is the analogue in Woodford of the extended family of the East End. Willmott and Young were much struck by the similarity. The husband was drawn into this largely female system in much the same way as they were related to the family in Bethnal Green.

Middle-Class Life

In Woodford, as so often elsewhere, the women are the organizers of social life for their families. They are the links between two or more households. If they do not go out to work, they have more opportunity than their husbands to meet the neighbours. The husbands are still somewhat on the periphery of social life; they tend to follow their wives' lead in the matter of family friendships. The accounts of Bott's 'intermediate' families also sometimes give the impression that the man's working day absorbs most of his sociable energies and that it is the wife who makes, maintains, even insists on social contacts outside the family. From some of the descriptions it almost seems that the men feel that 'friends' are 'an interest' for 'the little woman' and that they play along for her sake:

> Wives in the intermediate range often wanted some special interest of their own other than housework and children, but they were able to find activities such as evening classes or local clubs *that could be carried on without interfering with housework or child care.* [Italics added] . . .
> Husband and wife were able to form independent, segregated relationships with the neighbours. Many of the wives spent a good deal of their leisure time during the day with neighbouring women. Husband and wife joined local clubs, most of them uni-sexual.

In Woodford, it is the women particularly who are the great joiners of formal organizations: of tennis clubs, Women's Institutes, Townswomen's Guilds, Parent-Teacher Associations, Conservative Associations, and so on. Often these associations are the source of friends for people newly come to the district.

> 'We didn't know many people,' said Mr. Milner, 'until my wife got going with the Health and Beauty lark. We've met quite a lot of people through that.'

Woodford has a very rich associational life, and this may be thought to confirm Bott's dictum that 'voluntary associations appear to thrive best in areas where people are similar in social status but do not know each other well; the common activity gives people an opportunity to get to know one another better'.[1]

Formal associations may fulfil, for people who move about,

[1] See also pages 208–9.

the sort of function which needs no special institution in the traditional close-knit community: they enlarge the population from which intimates may be selected. Accordingly we find that those who are active members of Woodford organizations also invite friends in more often. Of the (177) people in the general sample who had attended a club in the previous week, 83 per cent had been visited by a non-relative in the same period, as against 69 per cent of those (548) who never go to a club.

Clubs and other organizations do not of course account for all the friendly contacts in Woodford—after all, over two-thirds of those who never attend them had friends in. The social and psychological background to these friendships is worth some comment.

We do not say that friendliness has the same character in Bethnal Green as in Woodford. In Bethnal Green people took each other very much for granted. In Woodford relations are not so easy-going. Standards are harsher. A newcomer has to show that she is worthy of the neighbourhood group, she has to be the right sort of person, have a decently furnished home, speak with the right accent, be neatly dressed, enjoy living in Woodford but not so much that she would greatly mind moving, have a readiness to engage in conversation, and above all, be rather extroverted, able to march out and meet people without being too shy about it. Sociability becomes a sort of profession. To get on well, people have to some extent to put on a front of *bonhomie* and maybe leave out some part of their personality in the process.

The people in this sub-culture may bear some resemblance to those described in Whyte's *Organization Man*: the same qualities which help a wife to support her husband in his career enable her also to adapt to the frequent moves which promotion brings. She is able to make new social contacts easily, though at a rather shallow emotional level which suggests that this is not an ideal solution for those who value individuality and self-expression.[1]

To put this in a different way: those with the personality which suits a mobile middle class will be able to get on reasonably well with one another. They are adaptable to many circumstances. They expect to have to make an effort to find

[1] See also pages 335 and 336.

congenial social contacts. In their circumstances it is not possible to rely on the 'effortless sociability' which characterizes so many traditional working-class communities, and indeed, as Mrs. Stacey has shown, traditional middle-class communities as well.[1]

> 'We expected that Woodford would turn out to be another Greenleigh. This has turned out not to be so. People in the suburb are on the whole friendly, neighbourly, and helpful to each other. Long residence and kinship were the clues to this kind of behaviour in Bethnal Green. But obviously this explanation will not do for Woodford, since both of these conditions are for the most part absent. The explanation seems to be that many people, particularly middle-class people of the sort who live in Woodford, have a certain capacity or skill at "making friends". Bethnal Greeners do not need this capacity: they have plenty of friends around them whether they make any effort or not, and this is presumably why they were so lost when they were transported to the strange environment of the housing estate.'

Mrs. Stacey confirms this social difference in the ease with which friends may be made. She was able to say 'with a fair degree of certainty, that working-class families from the North of England or from Scotland were very unlikely to settle on intimate terms as neighbours to Banburians. No such prediction can be made for the middle class. In Larkin Drive immigrants came from many areas and all were equally acceptable. The middle-class concept of neighbouring is apparently sufficiently common to North, South and Midlands.'

Middle-class people of the mobile kind probably are more status-conscious and less locality-conscious where values and customs are concerned. But other factors have also to be taken into account. For instance, it may be difficult, from a purely intellectual point of view, to perceive the circumstances in which particular behaviour is called for. The norms in Banbury are stated.

> Neighbours are to be acknowledged, but they are less often close friends. At Christmas, when social impulses are nearer the surface, they may be invited in for a drink, but at all other times of the year the principle is 'hedge green, friendship green'.

[1] See pages 307 and 347 fn.

It would be quite difficult to learn this set of norms, Christmas coming but once a year. It takes rather a marked ability to discriminate, to perceive and use fine shades of meaning, to indicate and preserve delicate social distances if the chances of making friends are not to be impaired by a wrong move in the initial stages. The new residents of Braydon Road (Coventry) lacked this sort of skill which, we shall later argue, is more often associated with a middle-class type of child-rearing.[1]

Mobile middle-class people may also for other reasons not need to worry so much about neighbourly differences.

> Mr. Brown, a technologist on the staff of the aluminium factory, and a graduate from a provincial university, did not inherit this position but earned it on merit. He came to Banbury to work, and, if he does not get promotion in the factory, he will apply for a better post elsewhere: his social aspirations are more closely linked to his job than to the status 'sets' of Banbury.

The discussion on associational life among the working-class status-dissenter began with Mogey's words that

> Barton is in fact not a localized society nor do its inhabitants feel loyal to an isolating set of social customs. They have lost their ties to a neighbourhood and gained in return a citizenship in the wider and freer atmosphere of the varied associational life of a city.

We may end the present discussion and introduce the next subsections by an equivalent quotation from Willmott and Young:

> Today's children are growing up with their own ideas. Our time has its own values, perhaps prizing more the individual and less the group, whether of the family or any other kind. To grow up may mean increasingly to grow away. The virtues of movement, from area to area, from one job to another, from one set of beliefs to another, may be stressed more than the virtues of stability, tradition and community.

TOP PROFESSIONALS

When its admirers think of the middle-class way of life, they tend to think of it in terms of the professional and upper middle

[1] See pages 254 and 256 for discussion of Braydon Road; pages 513–14 and 521–4 for the discussion of socialization for discrimination.

classes. To this group belong many social commentators, social scientists and writers of fiction. In fact, most members of the middle classes (here defined simply as those not engaged in manual work) when they think of 'the middle-class way of life' or even, often, of 'the English' think of this top group, which therefore finds itself in the peculiar position of exemplifying a stereotype. In a different terminology, it is a reference-group.

'Reference-groups', according to Sherif and Sherif, can be defined as 'those groups to which the individual relates himself as a part, or to which he *aspires* to relate himself'.[1] This definition does not require that members of a reference-group should interact on terms of familiarity with one another. They need not belong to it in any other way than by allegiance to its attributes, actual, perceived or imputed.

It is the tenor of much writing, both in the sources used for this sub-section and more generally in fiction and biography, that what unites the (self-identified) middle classes as a whole, and distinguishes them from (self-identified) working-class people, is a common devotion to the way of life of a more or less dimly perceived reference-group: the way of life of the traditional upper middle class. Because this is not a membership-group for the vast majority, there is a good deal of room for misunderstanding, both on the part of aspirants and on the part of social scientists. The idea of that life of service and leisure and culture is as much perpetuated by myths, hearsay and novels, as by the biographies which some people who belonged to that group write in their later years, thinking back now to the Edwardian era or to the twenties. The discussions in the forties about the decline of the middle classes suggest that it is rapidly disappearing from the visible social scene, though not from the emotional; they suggest also the tendency of members of any middle class to assume that they belong to that particular section of it.[2]

Not by any means all men in this category are professional men, but for the sake of convenient presentation—more is

---

[1] M. Sherif and C. W. Sherif (1956), *An Outline of Social Psychology*, Harper Bros., New York. See also pages 249 ff. and 418 ff.

[2] See, for instance, a series of articles on 'The Decline of the Middle Classes' in *The Economist* (1943).

known of them—we shall start with them, or more precisely, with the professional attitude. We have in mind here the kind of people who have been trained to enjoy and make the fullest use of the opportunities provided by a middle-class career. That pattern at its best is a training for professional attitudes, in which the only status-distinctions are those of age and experience, which time and life will inevitably alter for the better. Each recognizes each as an expert *in esse* or *in posse*, and interpersonal relations are regulated in this light. How this affects husband–wife relations has been outlined in the previous subsection, the volume on child-rearing considers the same attitudes as manifested in the parents' handling of their children.

It is not our purpose here to arrive at the most telling definition of a profession, any more than we were previously concerned to go very deeply into the sociology of social class, status and stratification. One illustration, chosen for convenience, will do what is required, namely, to give an idea of the kind of psychological demand made upon the professional man, for which his social background and the way his parents treated him may have fitted him well or less well.

We may place first a *Body of Knowledge* (science) or of *Art* (skill) held as a common possession and to be extended by united effort.

Next is an *Educational Process* based on this knowledge and art, in ordering which the professional group has a recognized responsibility.

The third is a *Standard of Professional Qualifications* for admission to the professional group, based on character, training and proved competence.

Next follows a *Standard of Conduct* based on courtesy, honour and ethics, which guides the practitioner in his relations with clients, colleagues and the public.

Fifth we may place more or less formal *Recognition of Status* by one's colleagues or by the State as a basis of good standing.

Finally, there is usually the *Organization of the Professional Group*, devoted to its common advancement and its social duty rather than the maintenance of an economic monopoly.[1]

---

[1] W. E. Wickenden in the *Journal of the Engineers' Guild*, March, 1950, quoted in Lewis and Maude, *Professional People*. See also Susser and Watson's description of some spiralists on page 344.

Middle-Class Life

A body of knowledge, long training to acquire skill at the proper standard, high standards of performance and conduct, and the power to exclude those who do not conform, are means by which continuous good performance may be encouraged in those professions—the university, medicine, the church, the law —where work is frequently done without supervision and without the constant presence of others doing similar work. But the professional approach as here defined is not alien to the Civil Servant working in an office, nor to some kinds of business management. Co-operation does not necessarily preclude individual enterprise or independent judgement. Much depends on the extent to which the individual's contribution can eventually be recognized and valued by those whose approbation he esteems.

What is required for contentment with work at this level is a feeling that the job must be done, however harassing or personally disadvantageous it may be. Good performance should be felt to be a duty. More, a feeling of pride should follow good performance even when colleagues and supervisors feel that nothing exceptional has been done, or when no one is there to give credit. Self-employed people need, because of the nature of their work, an internal regulator which ensures pride in good work, anxiety over slackness. This is *task-relatedness*. By ensuring devotion to the task itself, the need for immediate extrinsic reward is done away with.

How this internalization is achieved is one of the major topics in the volume on child-rearing, but we may note here that the traits which make for such psychological independence are already sufficiently marked to show up in psychological tests by the late teens and early twenties. Spinley, for instance, contrasted her Branch Street population with a 'privileged' sample: University students who had been to a 'good public school' paid for by their parents.[1]

Looking at the results of psychological tests and at the life-histories of this group, Spinley would say that, typically, the young man follows his own conscience and does not feel that he is much under pressure from extraneous forces. He believes, for instance (if the belief is incorrect, the naïve self-confident

[1] For details of this sample, see Volume Two, page x.

assumption is itself evidence of a personality-trait to which we shall refer later in this discussion), that he was allowed to choose his own career. His parents may have put forward suggestions, but he believes he followed them only if they coincided with his own inclinations.

> The young adult follows his conscience, he does not feel that he is influenced by external standards and does not feel tempted to change his own convictions when these are challenged. There is also implied here the probability that the ex-Public School pupil will not conform to the standards and customs of any other social group no matter how powerful in the community this other group may be . . .
>
> If in later life he enters a situation in which he is subject to an authority which asserts rights and wrongs differing from his own, it seems likely that he will resist such authority.

Two things are worth noting about these findings: the marked psychological independence they refer to, and the high value attached to being independent in this sense. Not all English people would speak with approval of this reluctance to give in to personal pressures and persuasions.[1]

Another test, on boys still at school, has a bearing on their ability to take and carry responsibility.

> The general emotional development is amazingly mature for subjects of the ages involved; they are trying, however, to keep a control of themselves which is rather too rigid. The time when this control slips would seem to be when emotional stimuli reach the subjects abruptly from the environment; but even when these stimuli are experienced as disturbing, anxiety-provoking and unpleasant, the children do not escape by leaving the field [as the Branch Street children do]. They show considerable powers of recovery in the sense that they can make an adequate response if they give themselves time. New situations tend to be grasped in their entirety with an awareness and understanding of their important components.

In effect, these young people are less likely than others to experience lack of supervision or lack of social support as frightening or coldly impersonal. Near the top of the social ladder, among the self-confident, secure and successful, the im-

[1] See e.g. pages 140 and 516.

personality of a bureaucratic or independent professional environment may be felt to be stimulating. Private enterprise will have been found rewarding. At the top, too, there is greater freedom of spirit; here a man may be called upon to decide in accordance with what he thinks best. He is less often required to act as instructed. His decisions will of course be determined largely by the rules operating in the situation, but he will have at the back of him the skill to analyse the situation correctly. He is a kind of craftsman working with intellectual tools on refractory material. This is of course especially true of the more or less independent professionals, the top Civil Servants, and the top businessmen who gave the name 'enterprise' an economic connotation.

'Why do Civil Servants work hard?' asks Munro. One answer comes from pride in work well done.

> Consider the position of a manager of an Employment Exchange. He has no rivals or substitutes. The citizens of his town depend entirely on him for a certain range of services, which may be of vital importance to them. By doing his job really well, he can render immeasurably valuable service to the community of which he is a member . . . The consciousness of their responsibilities, and of the opportunities for doing good that these provide, does give many members of the Civil Service a pride in their position which is wholly admirable and a strong incentive to hard work . . .
> One of the most powerful factors I believe to be an innate objection to leaving things half-done. The Gestalt school of psychologists have published the results of some experiments with children which seem to illustrate this. A number of children were given a considerable number of small tasks to do. Some of these they were allowed to finish, and in the case of the rest they were stopped before they had finished. Some days afterwards they were asked to make a list of the tasks which they had been given. In the case of the tasks which they had been prevented from finishing the proportion which they could remember was always greater than in the case of tasks they had been allowed to finish. It is as though, when one sets oneself to do a task, then a pressure is generated driving one along to the end; if one is stopped in the middle, this pressure remains unrelieved, thus leaving a stronger mark on the memory.

The interest in the task itself, and the urge not to leave it half done, is not now considered by most psychologists to be innate, but rather to depend on early training. The discussion of task-relatedness and its connection with achievement-motivation will therefore be taken up again in the next volume. What is of interest here is Munro's contention that task-relatedness is at once the peculiarity and the intrinsic reward of many in this sub-culture.

> Taken as a whole the work can be regarded as a tremendous and continuing task which is never finished. At any given moment there are parts of it just finished, parts half done, parts just begun. But subconsciously one is always trying to get this great task done. So one drives oneself along, day after day, to reach a goal which is ever receding.

These are not work-conditions which would commend themselves to everyone as highly desirable or enjoyable. The task is abstract, the achievement never more than temporary, the end-result rarely obvious, yet Munro feels this to be rewarding and stimulating rather than discouraging.[1] The motive for work is here certainly very different from that wish to see the completed product which is often alleged to operate among manual workers.

The pride in work and the recognition of skill, which were last referred to in the discussion of Ashton, find their emotional counterparts here. Munro gives an attractive picture of the way the respect of fellow-workers is felt at this level:

> Here is a world in which a Civil Servant can expect, if he reaches a certain level, to have an acknowledged importance; and this is a kind of importance which many men would prefer to a blaze of notoriety in the greater world. For the respect and attention of a comparatively small number of persons, who are themselves of some distinction, is in some ways to be preferred to the stupid gaping of the mob.

After identifying the team spirit as one incentive to good work, Munro discusses good leadership in terms which make it very clear that he is thinking of a work-group in which the quality of the work is obvious and good performance gains

[1] See pages 507–9 for the discussion on 'achievement-motivation'.

prestige with fellow workers (though not necessarily with the superior, if he is not himself competent). Fellow-workers and status-superiors are therefore seen best as people who will appreciate one's capabilities, not as people who enforce control.[1]

The leader who is the superior of the members of his team in general capacity can be perfectly free and frank, and fearlessly expose any particular weakness he may have, without any question arising as to his right to leadership.

Whereas it is normally assumed that traditional people break down for lack of social pressure to conform when they are isolated from their group, we find in this sub-culture many who are expected to be capable of carrying on as usual. The classical stereotype of this kind of personality is that of the district officer in the colonies who, in the middle of his jungle, is said to eat his dinner in attire judged suitable for the purpose in good London society. Kipling's 'If' similarly celebrates the character which, undeterred by fatigue or inconvenience, is capable of resisting great pressure to alter behaviour for the sake of personal preferences. This is the sort of stress which ought to be sustained without too much psychological discomfort by professional men who are not in constant touch with others of their educational or social background, and also by some kinds of businessmen.[2]

'Task-relatedness' seems to be the factor which reconciles the high degree of psychological independence of other people's support or approval with 'devotion to duty' and 'social responsibility', traits which Lewis and Maude connect with the middle-class way of life at its best:

> The ability to back one's own judgment without fear or favour is all-important, whether the case is that of the professional man advising a client, or of a businessman deciding to go ahead with jet propulsion without State support, or of the farmer campaigning for the use of compost against the artificial fertilizers made by a great combine.

[1] For more detailed argument see Klein (1961), *Working with Groups*, chapter nine, 'Structure, function and morale'.

[2] So much so that Miller and Swanson call this personality type 'entrepreneurial'. The difficulties raised by these authors are, however, many. (See the discussion on pages 547-8.) Riesman calls these characters 'inner-directed', but the contrast he draws between tradition-directed and inner-directed cultures makes it difficult to apply his work to English society. See, however, page 562 fn.

The independence of the English middle classes does not derive from the fact that all their members can throw up their job if they dislike the terms. Most of them cannot do so. The point is that many of them can, while all of them are interested in the conditions under which responsible persons discharge their duties.[1]

Rightly, therefore, Lewis and Maude, who consider that 'until recently the essential characteristic of being middle-class in England has been independence', add at once that this independence is only partly a matter of economic life. One must look for the social and psychological pre-conditions which make this independence possible, as well as for the economic factors which can support this personality-type.

To regard the English middle classes as merely an organizing or managerial cadre would be to miss the fulness of their function. It is all too easily done. But a salariat is not a middle class as we know it, for it has neither social power nor independence. A distinction based on a standard of living can be quickly swept away. Only one based on a way of life endures.

This way of life, Lewis and Maude admit, requires some concentration of wealth and reserves. The kind of people they have in mind have either some capital of their own, or they tend to be self-employed and independent of others in that sense, or they are engaged in an occupation where tenure is secure, or in a profession which is always in demand. They are, in short, financially secure. But other qualities accompany this security, qualities of social responsibility, cultivated mind, gracious living.

'With independence has gone a sense of psychological security which has made it easier to shoulder greater responsibilities to the community.' And this in turn may be associated with the leisure which makes the assumption of this kind of social responsibility possible. 'There should be leisure because anyone with leisure will presumably devote part of it to the voluntary and creative activities of citizenship.'

'Leisure' has in this context the full connotation of gracious living which appertained to the traditional leisured class of the past. The point at issue is not that the top professional with

[1] R. Lewis and A. Maude (1949), *The English Middle Classes*.

whom we are here concerned has more leisure than other sections of the English population, but that his upbringing and schooling, the late age at which he starts to earn his living, the ability to arrange his work as he likes to a relatively large extent, the tradition of saving and the income which encourages it, are conditions which create a feeling of leisure and a capacity for the creative use of what leisure there is.

Barbu, in the course of a discussion on the democratic way of life which he considers the English people to exemplify (like many foreign Anglophils he rather tends to think of the class with which we are here concerned as 'the English'), suggests that 'it is leisure that enables a man to develop cognitive refinement' and thereby links a number of very relevant social and psychological variables. We may start by recalling Pear's dictum:

> Can a cultured person be psychologically described? It may be suggested that he shows unusual delicacy in discriminating between situations and people, and in graduating his responses to them.

Barbu relates leisure to a long period of security which facilitates the development of a flexible social organization and a flexible habit of mind. In such circumstances, he argues, the individual is allowed a high degree of freedom in his social adjustment. The opposite happens in a group under stress: both individual and social organization tend to become rigid.[1]

The long extract which follows provides an invaluable background for the discussion on cognitive aspects of socialization in the second volume of this book.

> To start with, leisure constitutes a necessary condition for the functioning of the critical mind. Why this is so can be easily understood when one takes into account that the main function of the critical mind is to facilitate the individual's adjustment to distant and comprehensive goals in life.[2] Any feeling of pressure minimizes the chances of such adjustment.

[1] Z. Barbu (1956), *Democracy and Dictatorship*, Routledge and Kegan Paul, London. For other aspects of this connection between stress and rigidity see pages 89, 202, 288–90 and 298.

[2] See pages 620–2 in the volume on child-rearing.

Leisure is also a necessary condition for the functioning of the ego. While the Id urges the mind to react according to the rigid pattern of instincts, and while the super-ego takes the 'clichés' of adjustment existing in the cultural milieu, the ego resorts to flexible schemes in order to enable the individual to work out for himself the forms of adjustment, and in this case the feeling of leisure is necessary . . .

The most important aspect of an act of intelligence lies in the individual's capacity to grasp the specific nature and therefore the novelty of a situation, and to work out the most suitable form of adjustment. Thus any act of intelligence involves a strong tendency towards exploration and adventure; the greater the independence from old forms of adjustment, the better . . .[1]

The main feature of an intelligent type of reaction consists in the distance the organism puts between the stimulus and the final form of satisfaction, or in the capacity of an individual's mind to bear the tension aroused by a stimulus as long as the search for an adequate reaction requires. At the instinctive level of behaviour, reaction is direct and urgent. An act of intelligence is, on the contrary, a 'detour' reaction in which a certain degree of leisure is necessary. The aim of such a type of reaction is not only the release of tension, but also mental efficiency. This means that the organism, while reacting, disposes of enough leisure and detachment from its own action to grasp and retain the best ways and conditions leading to the pursued goal, and thus, to improve the mechanism of reaction itself.[2]

Barbu then proceeds to associate these purely psychological factors with their effect on social relationships. In this discussion we see some of the characteristics that make committee-work and unofficial decision-making via an 'old-boy network' so congenial to people brought up in this group.

In the absence of strong authoritarian trends, an individual carrying out a specific task, or performing his social duty, defines his position in the function of two factors: the accepted norms of action, and the individuals with whom he is in contact. The particular way he himself, and the other individuals involved, feel about the situation, is always reflected in the performance of his actions. Thus the guiding principles of life are never rigidly

[1] See pages 521–6 in the volume on child-rearing.
[2] See pages 518–20 in the volume on child-rearing.

applied. This is due to a series of modes of social experience or inter-personal relations, which we call personal feelings.

Among these personal feelings is 'politeness' defined as

> a tactful intervention in a system of inter-relations, with the main intention of facilitating the free manifestation of the personalities of the individuals involved. This is done by arousing in them the feeling that their weaknesses are spared, their good qualities are noticed, and that their personalities occupy a necessary place in the situation. Decency is another form under which personal feelings can be shown . . . Decency can be defined as a tactful withdrawal from social situations with the view of producing in others the same feeling of ease which we have just defined. [We may note that the feeling of ease may here be equated with the feeling of leisure.] Thus what the polite man does through his intervention, the decent man does through his non-interference.

Such traits make these people delightful to be with. The discussion so far has in the main conformed to the favourable stereotype of the upper middle classes, displaying their exceptional talent for gracious and responsible living. This is the image exploited by advertisements which rely for their appeal on the attractiveness of being a 'top person'. The unfavourable stereotype would be of an 'establishment person'. We must therefore now have a look at the other side of our coin, at the way these traits appear to less tolerant eyes and at the defects which appear when the virtues turn sour.

To begin with, it may be asked if *at its most typical* the upper middle-class personality is as creative and cultivated as the previous choice of quotations has perhaps suggested. Impressive theoretical arguments have been put forward which sharply contrast, as mutually exclusive by definition, the traditional mode of life and the individually enterprising.[1] Lewis and Maude balance the matter rather carefully:

> By and large, middle-class homes are distinguished (as are their working lives) by regularity, order, and even ritual; sometimes within a framework so gracious as to represent an almost perfected art of living, sometimes oppressively or meaninglessly, most often between the two.

[1] See pages 544 ff.

As ill luck will have it, this sort of problem is especially difficult to solve if the Civil Service is the illustrative occupation.
At the top, the leisured tradition is likely to be mixed with a
goodly proportion of professional and managerial spice. That
the enterprising element in the traditional upper-middle-class
personality may be rather slight is suggested by Spinley's
account of the 'privileged' personality in late adolescence, as
indicated by the results of psychological tests and interviews.
Though pleasant to get on with and rather charming, there is
a certain imperviousness to unfamiliar ideas.

> As the child grows up he feels that he rules his behaviour
> according to his own individual standards and not to those of an
> external group. Tolerance he regards as the greatest virtue and he
> does not have any strong desire to influence the opinions of other
> people.
> As a late adolescent or young adult he is contented with his life
> and with his own personality; he realizes that he has certain faults
> but he does not worry very much about these, although he is at
> pains to inhibit his anger and aggressiveness. He believes that he
> is generally calm emotionally, and that this calm is not easily
> destroyed.[1]
> The confidence he expresses in his relations with the opposite
> sex is present in other areas of his life. From earliest childhood he
> plays with other people of his own age, he feels accepted by them
> and likes their companionship. He makes close friends as well as
> acquaintances, and feels able to mix with all kinds of people
> without awkwardness. Socially he feels that he is a success, that
> other people like him and recognize his good points.[2]
> When deciding upon his future career he is influenced by
> several wishes. He wants to be a definite success, he wants both
> security and social status, he wants to exercise authority or at least
> not to be under the authority of someone else. He has no marked
> ideals of service; his aim is 'success', but he does not want this
> success 'at any cost' to others. Once he has selected his future job
> he feels confident that he can achieve his aim and avoid frustra-
> tion.

There is little enterprise in this character, though with a good
educational start, a nicely-balanced and well-stocked mind, and

---

[1] 'He has, however, periodic depressions which are deep and which, while they
last, make him feel unhappy and worthless.'

[2] See pages 513–14 and 628–9 in the volume on child-rearing.

a situation which requires little improvisation, he is likely to be successful, and capable of working on his own in some independent profession, or of making a success of a bureaucratic career.

One may note also the characteristic calm confidence with which he is reported to face the various points at which life so easily turns into a crisis. Where the balance would rest if correct appraisal of good qualities were weighed against easy overconfidence is difficult to say. Walker, summarizing answers to questionnaires submitted to a sample of Administrative Civil Servants, to whose records he also had access, finds that the average of the efficiency-ratings for this group was higher than that of other groups. These people felt that they fitted into their jobs, were not inclined to think the work below their capacities, enjoyed their work. They tended to estimate their social status highly, higher than that of people occupying the upper levels of industrial companies.[1]

This chimes in well with the findings from Spinley's personality tests, which led her to conclude that 'he feels he is able to assess his own performance with considerable objectivity' and 'is content with his life and with his own personality'.

Such an easy and more or less unimaginative assumption of his competence, and the self-confidence that accompanies it, makes him an admirable parent for most children. Spinley is left with an impression of a relatively unharassed childhood without any great experience of guilt, worthlessness or deprivation—a childhood which permits an easy cheerful acceptance of the present state of affairs.

> The strict super-ego is the most obvious characteristic of the Public School child . . . The parents have affection for their child and the child realizes this, and at the same time the parents clearly define good and bad behaviour. Discipline is firm, it is consistent and it begins almost from birth. At school this discipline is even more rigorous and punishment for detected infringement is inevitable and often severe. The fact that during childhood an individual is seldom punished seems to point to early conformity and internalization of standards, in other words to an early development of an effective super-ego.
>
> Both at home and later at school, the child has to take his place

[1] N. Walker (1961), *Morale in the Civil Service*, Edinburgh University Press.

365

in an authoritarian hierarchy; he learns to obey other people. But the homogeneity of the group in which he grows up means that the notions of right and wrong which are held by those in authority are also his own, kept active by his super-ego, and that therefore little conflict is aroused.

This must make it easier for him in later years to work in organizations with a hierarchical structure, unhampered by irrational fears, jealousies or rebellions left over from his childhood days.

So it is that Walker finds that the Administrative Civil Servant has a high opinion of 'the men at the top', whom he has had a good chance of seeing at work. His views on the organization to which he belongs—his family as it were, or his school—also show this relaxed uninhibited regard. When asked to compare his own Ministry with others, he is less likely than his juniors to sit on the fence, and more likely to say either that it is better or that it is worse. Walker also finds him willing to trust his subordinates, and especially apt to regard his colleagues as likeable. (The equality-of-experts aspect of this has already been touched on; here the emphasis is on brothers-without-rivalry.) In general, his social world has no snakes in the grass.

It is obvious that a collection of people of this kind will get on very nicely with one another. 'The homogeneity of the group in which he grows up means that little conflict is experienced.' His upbringing, his public school and his work keep him in contact with people very much like himself, as one would expect in a traditional culture.

So Munro, continuing his ruminations on the reasons why Civil Servants work hard for relatively little reward, refers to 'another factor which, he believes, is important in providing a stimulus to work: not the spirit of competition, but that of co-operation or "the team spirit" '. After the remarkable passage which was quoted in the sub-section on Woodford, suggesting that the office where team-spirit prevails affords at this social level the type of satisfaction which is associated with the community-spirit farther down the social scale or farther back in time, Munro concludes that 'official comradeship is at the basis of a team spirit which may include a whole staff; and where it

Middle-Class Life

does, it is a great incentive to hard work and interest in the job, for no member of a team likes to let the team down'.

But Gladden, another commentator on Civil Service personalities, points out that the matter-of-fact assumption of competence, team-spirit and pride of work, are all too easily accompanied by that contempt for others which is found, *mutatis mutandis*, in practically every English sub-culture on which there is any evidence at all. Among top professionals it takes a 'public school' form.[1]

> There is a distinct sense everywhere of the *we* and the *they*. The specially brilliant top *we* are of a different clay from the lowlier *they*. The *we* are too sure of their superiority to be arrogant, but they can hardly help showing this superiority even when their condescension is masked with the charm that long established members of the Administrative Class almost invariably cultivate. Their very virtue creates more than a commensurate vice in other reaches of the Service. Members of senior grades outside the Administrative Class who have worked in headquarter offices will appreciate fully how this almost indefinable difference so clearly exists as to weigh upon their souls. They are made to feel in subtle ways that they do not belong to the inner circle . . .
>
> It works in wider fields, for there is a similar gap between headquarter offices and the regions, where the Administrative Class has no particular interest. Headquarter staffs tend to despise the regional workers as simple hewers of wood: regional workers, certain that the tempo and difficulties of their work in close contact with the public far transcends the stresses of the specialist work at headquarters, despise the headquarter staffs for their inflated assessment of their work while at the same time envying them their opportunities.[2]

It works in wider fields than this, affecting and impoverishing the social life of communities. Mrs. Stacey recounts an anecdote of a Colonel's wife speaking to a newcomer in the village, on whom she was calling.

'I think you'll like the X's,' she said, 'and there are the Y's and the Z's; otherwise I don't think there is anybody. But of course it's

[1] Nigel Walker, in a private communication, points out that Gladden is depicting the 'Method I' direct entrant and not those promoted from the lower grades. It may therefore be useful to remind ourselves that we are here concerned with a *traditional* sub-culture.   [2] See also pages 400 ff. and 410.

367

bad luck for you there are no children in the village. (The new-comer had a young family.) Happily this startling picture of rural depopulation was contradicted by statistics which showed that the village had a population of about five hundred with a normal complement of children. Yet this woman, who referred to 98 per cent of her fellow-villagers as 'nobody' . . . saw no contradiction in saying: 'I should not mind the socialists so much if they did not bring class into everything'.

Here we see cognitive poverty, attached as it often is to a traditional way of life, but this time in an upper-class setting. It is as intellectually and emotionally impoverishing here as it is lower in the social scale. This conversation displays all the narrowing features of the trait: the reduction of horizons, the implied contempt for other ways of life, the wilful refusal to share other people's experience.[1]

We may ask ourselves, after this, whether the qualities of enterprise and empire-building and psychological independence of which we have made so much, are perhaps concentrated in what are actually *deviant* members of the traditional upper middle class, being qualities which, either in themselves or be-cause inevitably associated with other traits, made it impossible for these people to live peaceably with their kin in the tradi-tional way of life and made them (at first in something like dis-grace) seek out situations in which they could live more con-genially. Is it an inability to get on with the tradition that sent district officers out to darkest Africa? To 'make good' in the colonies? Is there something in the modal upper-middle-class way of life—perhaps nothing more than the fact that it *is* tradi-tional—which keeps those at home cautious, unwilling to push things against opposition, self-satisfied, stolid, unimaginative, superior and blandly empiricist? Some fiction and some bio-graphy suggest that there is at least some truth in this view.[2]

A hostile critic in a book devoted to the excoriation of 'the establishment' argues thus:

They [the Victorians] knew what they wanted [in the Civil Service]. They knew what type of person and qualities they

[1] See pages 89–93.
[2] E.g. some novels of Evelyn Waugh's, Winifred Holtby's *Mandoa, Mandoa*, Jessica Mitford's *Hons and Rebels*.

wanted: absence of corruption and favouritism on the one hand, and reticence from bureaucratic pretensions on the other. The negative virtues of state administration, the virtues which make life safe and agreeable for the strongest of private interests at home and in the Empire, were to be cultivated to the utmost. It was an attitude of effortless superiority, combined with cultured scepticism, that was demanded from the Service (almost to the exclusion of others), and upon which that special mysterious art, Administrative Capacity, was said to depend. Positive knowledge and imagination, assertion of the social against the private interest, were obviously not looked for. The negative qualities were thought to be best attained by a judicious mixture of breeding, 'character-building' and a purposefully useless, somewhat dilettante, erudition which would keep 'dangerous thoughts' well away.[1]

The difference between the concept of 'character building' on the one hand and 'innate superiority' on the other, seems too small for most people to take account of it. This is the point of a passage from Simon Raven's furious 'Perish by the Sword' from the same collection of essays. The profession he has in mind is military and it is reasonable to suppose that the temptations of a hierarchy like the Civil Service are magnified a thousandfold in the Army.

The influence of the quasi-moral imperatives, our friends 'responsibility', etc., and the severe practical discipline based on these imperatives at Sandhurst, are the decisive factors [in creating the personality-type]. It all comes about this way. Boys chosen to be trained as officers are given no rest until they have absorbed certain moral influences 'which are essential to the character of an officer', and in themselves constitute a whole ethos. The transition from the imperative 'officers must have these qualities' to the general 'officers always do have these qualities' is easy. Then throw in the fact that these boys have always been set apart, both by their early education and in the Army, and it is equally easy to conclude that those so chosen must always, in a manner, have possessed these qualities and that training is merely designed to emphasize or bring them out. You have then passed, by two easy stages, from a state of affairs where certain theoretically

[1] T. Balogh, 'The apotheosis of the dilettante', in *The Establishment*, edited by Hugh Thomas (1959), Blond, London.

superior qualities are merely going to be taught, to a new conception whereby these very qualities are more or less conceded always to have existed in certain people—those chosen to become officers. And to this the insistence on 'pride as an officer' ('an officer never falls out', etc.) and you have completely deserted your original conception of officers as merely a highly trained professional body and have arrived at the notion of a moral *élite* and, what is worse, at a notion of a natural or born moral *élite*. And there we have it. The right of command is thus seen to be even more firmly based than the feudal right conferred by high birth on a land-owning class; for this modern right of command is supposedly conferred by birth on a *morally* distinguished class and, thus conferred, it is unquestionable by the average Englishman, the more so if he comes from those lower strata of the middle class which have always been so impressed by moral sanctions . . .

Once an officer is established, in his own view, as a member of a superior and order-giving class, he never loses his sense of superiority; but he can and often does lose all sense of the moral basis of this superiority and all the qualities which constitute this basis. He just becomes superior, as it were *in vacuo*. He becomes a 'gentleman' . . . Highly trained professionally and morally, he has forgotten his professional techniques and sloughed his sense of moral obligation: but he has retained an unassailable sense of his own superiority (for is it not innate?) and absolute right to give orders.

Balogh suggests that breeding, character and a cultured scepticism were thought by top people to be desirable qualities for a top Civil Servant. It is important to note that this idea persists, for it is the very antithesis of the professional approach to which reference was made earlier in this section. The anti-intellectual trend which is so deeply rooted in traditional English character here serves the function of excluding from the upper reaches of society those who have qualified themselves for the work but lack other characteristics which make for 'team-spirit'. Almost every day somewhere in print, on the wireless or television, someone expresses a variant of the idea that training for a job is a lower-class necessity while the upper class are born with 'leadership characteristics'.

This is almost bound to make for a dilettante approach. The very education whose other effects we have noted, is designed to develop, in Balogh's words, 'powers of dialectical argument only, rather than a knowledge of the present world and its problems. Anything smacking of vocational training and technical knowledge is severely discountenanced.'

Clements gives an indication of similar attitudes in the industrial sphere among those who have become managers in sales or commercial work. These are drawn more exclusively from the upper social grades than almost any others who were interviewed. They had mostly come from public schools: a rather smaller but still very substantial minority had attended grammar schools. Least of any of the various sides of industry had they been drawn from elementary schools. A quarter had degrees, few of which were in science. They showed a marked bias towards Oxford and Cambridge, only a minority having come from red-brick universities.

> Most of the commercial managers lack much technical knowledge, their work has been confined to one product, and they are not widely experienced in the methods of other organizations. They are not usually technical experts competent to advise customers on uses for their products, or their firms on what to make, or capable of judging what should be made. To a large extent they have been recruited because they are intelligent, able, educated and possess self-confidence and verbal facility. This may not be enough. Few of them, however, lament their technical deficiencies. Many of them would not admit their existence, whilst one spoke for most of the rest when he said that 'ignorance saves you from thinking that something is impossible'. Another claimed that there is 'no need to know how an article is made; you just need to have the right prices to sell it'. And he went on, 'technical language bluffs the customer for a little while, but he's not really interested'.[1]

> Although members of the British Administrative Class have often been praised for their incorruptibility [writes Kelsall], their willingness to subordinate personal interest to that of the Service, their loyalty to Ministers, their conscientiousness and industry, their tact, personal charm and literary facility, they have also

[1] These attitudes are also characteristic of a slightly lower social stratum, public school but not university, without specific management training, many of whom were encouraged to enter industry by family relations in business, a traditional middle middle stratum. An appreciable proportion of these 'special entrants' achieved top level. For instances, see pages 388-9 and 409.

been criticized for being cautious, for lack of drive and personal vitality, for having a negative attitude of mind, for smugness and complacency, for being out of touch with working-class problems and ignorant of recent advances in both the natural and the social sciences.[1]

These faults, as many of the critics have pointed out, are characteristic of those with a middle-class upbringing and a public-school education. So there is clearly a good side and a bad side to Spinley's generalization that 'if, in later life, the privileged young adult enters a situation in which he is subject to an authority which asserts rights and wrongs different from his own, it seems likely that he will resist such authority'. He is psychologically independent; he is psychologically impervious. He is liable to perpetuate in all circumstances the norms of his group in the cheerful confidence that they are the best. As Munro points out, he is liable to make a virtue of the very defects noted by Kelsall:

> The Treasury, to which many of the best entrants go, managed the finances of the State, it managed the servants of the State, and it sanctioned expenditure by the State. It itself did nothing 'constructive' and the result in my experience was that it never fully understood the nature of constructive activities . . . To advise the Minister is no doubt the highest function of the most senior Civil Servants. But from this the assumption tended to be made that the whole of the First Division should be recruited and trained with this end in view. The result was inevitable. Members of the Administrative Class were not expected to have the qualities of push-and-go or the organizing abilities necessary to drive any constructive undertaking through to success . . .
>
> Conscious of the great abilities which had brought them to the top of their profession, it was natural that they should regard themselves as having all the capacities required for such a career. Moreover, in the sphere in which they operated, it was abilities such as they possessed which were needed, not only in themselves but in those by whom they were surrounded. But the result was that, to the men whose views mattered most, brains and power of expression were the qualities that counted, while the practical energy that gets things done and, more important still, the power

[1] R. K. Kelsall (1955), *The Higher Civil Service*, Routledge and Kegan Paul, London.

to organize on practical lines, were regarded as qualities of a low order.

Many of the people of this traditional kind will by definition need to remain within their group to perform at their best. Inheritors of a great tradition, they are constructed by early socialization and later 'encapsulation in the group', to use a phrase of Bott's, to maintain and perpetuate the traditional pattern. But upper-middle-class socialization does not necessarily lead to this extreme; we shall see in the volume on child-rearing that a number of circumstances combine to create psychologically independent, enterprising personalities. The probabilities may be growing, however, that a man of this kind will go into business or a profession rather than into administration, if the picture drawn of the top Civil Servant in these last few pages is accurate. On the other hand, mobility is easier than it was. Some top professionals are enterprising non-traditional people who have made the grade to the upper middle class. Striving, earnest and competent people are likely to move up in the world and with luck will reach this occupational level, the Registrar-General's Class I. Analysing in terms of occupational level instead of sub-culture, we find that according to Nigel Walker, the typical Civil Servant at Administrative level is a man in his forties, *as often as not promoted* from the Executive or Clerical Grade, or from some other job inside or outside the Service. He is, in fact, not born into the establishment. Lewis and Maude take this mobility very seriously:

> The English middle classes had, and have, no frontiers; they were and are the recruiting ground of talent, the natural ladder of all who have the capacity for leadership in the widest meaning of the word. In the simile of Professor Burn, the social and economic structure of Britain has been like an escalator; some were higher than others, but all were moving slowly up and there was room for the agile to improve their relative as well as their absolute position.[1] The class structure knit society with order and cohesion, providing a graduated slope down which the standards of the highest might descend to the lowest, and providing the spur of ambition to urge the best from below into positions of responsibility and influence.

[1] Quoted in 'The English Middle Classes' from the *Quarterly Review*, 1946.

Aspects of Adult Life in England

Lewis and Maude show also a nice awareness of the ability of the middle class to absorb such an influx (a process made easier of course in so far as the group has in any case been a reference-group, with a way of life that was by definition attractive).

> The moment a man rose into them, influences were at work to civilize and change the recruit and fit him and his descendants for new purposes—for service to the community as a whole. A man who wanted social recognition was almost obliged to 'do good' with some part of his money, even though he did it hypocritically and with his tongue in his cheek. His children may have done it because it was the thing to do; yet the more thoughtful of them may have realized that, done or not, it was the *right* thing, necessary to the character of a gentleman and a Christian.

They continue—and the words they use are significant when later we see how early child-rearing techniques lay stress on these very characteristics:

> The English middle classes are what they are by virtue not of trade but of organization, not of property but of independence, not by virtue of power, but by government; not solely because they wanted to *have* but because of what they wanted to *be* . . .
> In all this it is possible to see a unifying principle at work; and a study of middle-class history should reveal it clearly. That principle is, in fact, the older tradition: the idea of hierarchy, and hence the idea that social progress was in part a process of *'becoming'*.[1]

---

[1] It is always interesting to note other writers' intuitions on the clusters of personality-traits which we are associating with social position. Here, for instance, one is reminded of Erikson's eight 'choice-points' of development. Erikson, primarily a psychotherapist, is concerned with what he conceives to be the ideal personality, which so often tends to be thought of as the middle-class personality with all the disadvantages removed. He lists, as problems which the developing child has to solve correctly if he is to arrive at happy adult life, (1) *trust* as opposed to basic mistrust. This is the kind of trait we dealt with in the text under the heading of confidence. (2) *autonomy* as opposed to shame and doubt. This item partly refers to psychological independence and partly to confidence. (3) *initiative* as opposed to guilt. This is partly our 'assumption of responsibility'. (4) *industry* as opposed to inferiority. (5) *identity* as opposed to role-diffusion which we shall discuss under individuality in another chapter (see pages 513–14 and 542–3). (6) *intimacy* as opposed to isolation. (7) *creativity* as opposed to stagnation. (8) *ego-integrity* as opposed to despair. (E. H. Erikson, *Childhood and Society*, Imago Publ. Co., London.)

Middle-Class Life

For the sake of variety and completeness, and possibly contrast, we may consider an extract from Lloyd Warner's *American Life* which gives a view of American top businessmen whose parents came from lower down in the social or economic scale. Lloyd Warner's source is Professor William Henry of the Committee on Human Development at the University of Chicago who 'in collaboration with several others, has examined the personalities and social worlds of several hundred successful and unsuccessful businessmen'. This examination took the form of interviewing and psychological testing.

We shall find here some resemblances to the sort of characteristics attributed to the professional man in the previous subsection and some resemblances to the kind of middle-class personalities which are considered below. The childhood origins of some of these traits will be discussed in the volume on socialization. No comment will be made in this sub-section, however, as very little is known of what might be English equivalents.

All the successful men have a common personality pattern, largely formed in childhood and adolescence, functioning in such a way that, when they join a corporation, they help re-create and continue the structure and values of this business organization. At the same time, as the years go by, they help select and train younger men of the same personality type as their own. The persistence of the business organization is maintained by their ability to continue sets of relations which are necessary for its existence when competing with other organizations like it.

The social role of the upward-mobile businessman, striving to succeed and to achieve a higher position than the one he has, is very similar to his personality structure. Although each successful businessman has certain unique characteristics of his own, he fits into the common personality-pattern of his type.

As would be expected, his achievement desires are very high.[1] He conceives of himself as a hard-working man who can only be happy when he is accomplishing something. We must precisely understand his conception of achievement, for this kind of upward-mobile, successful executive 'looks more to the sheer

[1] See also pages 604–11.

accomplishment of the work itself' than he does to the glory which may accrue when he achieves his end. The man who stresses the latter kind of achievement more often than not is unsuccessful.[1] The satisfaction of the successful man is in immediate accomplishment—immediate accomplishment that leads on to the next immediate accomplishment in a never ending series.

Such a personality has very high mobility drives. He feels the deep need of continuous upward movement, but he strives less for the upward movement than for the increased responsibility that comes with it, accompanied by the feeling of satisfaction he gains from completing a task and being prepared for the next one.[2] This kind of motivation is quite different from that of another group that looks rather similar. In this latter group there is the struggle for the social prestige gained by increased status. For its members, the first objective is the higher status rather than what it is that they do to get it. They tend to be less successful.

The upward-mobile executive's idea of authority is also of crucial importance in understanding him. He looks to his superiors for help and feels happier when involved in the controlling relationship that is established with them, for he believes he can consult with them on special problems and get special aid that he cannot receive from others.[3] Above all, he does not see a figure of authority as one that is destructive or likely to be harmful to himself. Those men who do view authority figures as destructive are likely to have difficulties in adjusting themselves to their superiors, and very often they are the ones who fail in the job.

The view which such men have of their own organizations and the world in which they live is exceedingly instructive . . . All such upward-mobile men who are successful in their business enterprises have a high ability to organize situations and understand the meaning and significance of what it is they have organized. They never see events as isolated and unconnected, but as inter-related, and they draw significance from the inter-relationships. In other words, they are constantly making decisions and judgements based on their organizing ability in a social structure which is ever changing and where new adaptations are forever necessary for the success of the person and the success of the enterprise. They have personalities capable of holding together the parts of a changing society—persistence and type of personality are inter-twined and parts of the same process.[4]

---

[1] See also pages 605–6. [2] See also pages 358 and 514.
[3] See also pages 366 and 404. [4] See also pages 521–4 and 621.

Middle-Class Life

It comes as no surprise that decisiveness is another personality trait of this type of man. It is not so much that he is the popular idea of the quick-thinking, fast-talking American businessman who makes a dozen decisions every second, but rather that he has the ability to form the necessary judgements and arrive at the necessary decisions among a variety of alternatives and not be harassed by making them. The changing social structure ordering the flow of a changing technology must have men with this characteristic to survive. The less successful businessmen find decisions difficult, and some of them become neurotically ill when, with a variety of alternatives, they are forced to make the decisions that constantly face those who occupy the higher levels of business enterprise.[1]

Another characteristic of successful businessmen is the great fear of failure; most of them harbour a rather pervasive feeling that they may not really succeed and be able to do the things they want to do. With the fear of failure acting as a whip, combined with their strong sense of self and the ability to initiate action, such men must always keep moving and must always see the immediate goal ahead . . .

Such men look to their superiors for identification—they tend to feel akin to them and to pattern their behaviour after them, and to do it more or less on a personal basis, whereas, with their inferiors, they tend to be more impersonal and more detached . . .

They have developed their lives in such a way that they feel they are on their own and that their emotional identifications with their parents have been dissolved. Literally and spiritually, they have left home. It must be stressed that the emotional severance of their relations with their parents does not mean that they do not carry on happy relations with them, nor does it mean that there is any resentment of them. Rather, they are emotionally autonomous and capable of making their own decisions and do not consciously or unconsciously refer their decisions back to their parents.

The unsuccessful man is not able to release himself from his ties to his parents, and, accordingly, he is overly dependent upon his superiors or resentful of them in the work situation. The successful, upward-mobile man tends to have a positive relation with his father; he does not feel a strong emotional tie with his mother. Men who have made these adjustments with their families of orientation can relate themselves loyally to the authority of their

---

[1] See also pages 396-7, 566 and 581.

own corporation and identify their own careers with the over-all goals of the organization. Essentially, the principal things they value—accumulation and achievement, self-initiation of action, individual autonomy, their never-ceasing activity, and the kinds of rewards they consider significant—as well as their constant fear of losing ground, are all basic characteristics of the upward-mobile, upper-middle-class American.[1]

EXECUTIVES: THE RATIONAL-LEGAL ATTITUDE

We come now to a middle range of middle-class occupations, and in particular to the kind of work for which people are needed who can be trusted to carry out, without constant supervision, the tasks which others have set them, the rightness of which they do not question. The tasks may be difficult and call for a good deal of skill, but they are routine in the sense that the way to set about them is known, and indeed often stipulated. In terms of Woodford, where people of this kind form the new top class, they will be professionals like bank-managers, accountants, surveyors and so on, rather than surgeons, architects, stockbrokers or barristers who can more easily choose what they will do and how they will do it. In Civil Service terms, they will be executives.

> Few people who do not have close and frequent dealings with them know much about the executives, the non-commissioned officers of the service—or are even aware of their existence as a separate class [writes Dunnill] . . . These people are not executives in the commercial or American or Army sense of the word. They are merely the middle section of the Civil Service pyramid, touching policy at one end and sometimes involved in quite menial tasks at the other . . . Some of them draw higher salaries and control more staff than do the junior members of the administrative and professional grades. Others, junior executive officers who have just entered the service, may well sit among the clerical officers, being trained by them and, for a number of years, doing jobs that are clerical or quasi-clerical in nature.

Before we consider them in more detail, it may be worth

[1] W. Lloyd Warner (1953), *American Life*, University of Chicago Press. For sociological (but not psychological) information on the equivalent English occupational group (but not sub-culture), see Anthony Sampson, op. cit., page 317.

while to be reminded again that in this occupational group are also those who will eventually find their way to the top—spiralists in mid-career.

It is at this level that those most closely approximating to the sociologists' stereotype of the bureaucrat may be found. Weber has furnished the classic description of this work-situation; later sociologists with greater psychological interests supply a commentary on the character-structure which makes this work-situation especially congenial to some people.[1] Summarizing Weber, the bureaucrat is appointed and performs his functions in accordance with the following principles:

1. He is personally free and subject to authority only with respect to his impersonal official obligations.
2. He is part of an organization with a clearly defined hierarchy of office.
3. Each office has a clearly defined sphere of competence in the legal sense.
4. The official is appointed, not elected. He is appointed on the basis of technical qualifications, sometimes as attested by diplomas.
5. He is paid a salary, with a right to a pension. He can make no profit out of his official position. The employing authority has the right to terminate his appointment only in specified circumstances, though the official is always free to resign.
6. The office is the sole paid occupation of the incumbent.
7. The office is a career. There is a system of promotion. Promotion depends on his superiors' judgement of his competence.
8. He is subject to strict and systematic discipline and control in the conduct of his office.

Robert Merton has matched the bureaucratic work-situation with an appropriate character-structure in a classic essay, part of which Miller and Swanson have summarized.

He will be cautious because he must work within the limitations and demands of an explicit set of rules of procedure if he is to succeed, he will be precise in performance because such precision rather than entrepreneurial flair is the basis of his promotion and tenure, unaggressive and impersonal because hostility and dealing

[1] Max Weber, *Theory of Economic and Social Organization*, translated into English in 1947 by T. Parsons and A. R. Henderson (publisher William Hodge & Co., London), being the first part of *Wirtschaft und Gesellschaft*, first published in 1922.

with people as unique special individual cases disturbs the intricate and pre-planned organizations of a large enterprise, rational because he must constantly attend to the reality presented by his work if he is to perform it with precision and caution'.[1]

Miller and Swanson add a contribution of their own. Large complex organizations must not only encourage such personal characteristics as these in their employees, but have also to create a moral community—a community of responsibility and loyalty—among them. They write of the 'security of belonging to a moral community in which the member has a personal stake and in which satisfactions come from participation in a common task as well as from the expert exercise of technical skills'.

The expert exercise of technical skills as a basis for community feeling, the pleasure in task-performance as it operates at its best, has been the subject of a number of previous discussions.[2] Each instance is marked by its own peculiarities. In the present circumstances, especial note must be taken of the carefully formulated rules of conduct, rules as rational as they are explicit, which have been marked as the characteristic of bureaucracy since the days of Weber. The authority of these rules derives from a number of mutually interdependent ideas upon which, it may be argued, this particular professional community is built.

One of these root ideas is that the bureaucracy exists only by virtue of a more ultimate authority, which is itself rational and can legitimately make the rules and expect obedience to them. The bureaucrat's sole function is to carry out the rules which the policy-making authority may only make because it derives the policy from principles acknowledged in the greater community. When the bureaucrat conforms to the rules and obeys his superior's instructions, he does so not because he owes him a personal loyalty, but because both owe allegiance to an impersonal order which all acknowledge. The moral community is given coherence by the allegiance of all to an abstract ideal. This is the strength behind the principle of hierarchy.

[1] R. Merton (1957), *Social Theory and Social Structure* (2nd ed.), Free Press, Glencoe, Ill.

D. R. Miller and G. E. Swanson (1959), *The Changing American Parent*, Wiley, New York.　　　　[2] See pages 97–100 and 358–9.

Middle-Class Life

A man's place in such a hierarchy is determined by the same conditions which define it as a rational and legitimate one: he is legitimately where he is by virtue of his ability, his rationality and his conformity to the rules. At each level the functions which can best be performed there are stated. In other words, the official has a specified sphere of competence: (*a*) a sphere of obligations to perform functions allotted to him as part of the systematic division of labour, (*b*) the necessary authority to carry out these functions (and no others), (*c*) the necessary means of compulsion. He must do whatever his office requires, but only what his office permits.

There are dangers to this kind of work-situation. Peter Blau made a study of administrative staff in American government and social welfare agencies which is worth considering here.[1] His starting point was a dictum he quoted from von Mises: 'Nobody can be at the same time a correct bureaucrat and an innovator. Progress is precisely that which the rules and regulations did not foresee. It is necessarily outside the field of bureaucratic activities.' Blau's first and most important finding flatly contradicts this idea. The bureaucrats of his investigation were not unwilling to reform or change or innovate. They did not sanctify rules of procedure. Sometimes they welcomed changes, sometimes they recommended them. One reason for this was their recognition that innovations might make the work easier—for instance, if certain changes were made in the way their office classified the occupations of the people they dealt with. On the other hand, they also advocated changes which would complicate their work. Blau considers that some found their incentive for recommending changes in their constant and direct contact with the people who were adversely affected by the anomaly they wanted removed. He also considered that, since much of the work was necessarily routine, some welcomed an occasional problem that put them on their mettle and required a new approach.

These findings are not surprising when viewed in the light of an earlier discussion. It will be remembered that according to Munro one of the reasons why Civil Servants work hard was that they wanted to do the job well. They were task-centred.

[1] P. Blau (1955), *The Dynamics of Bureaucracy*, University of Chicago Press.

They derived pleasure and prestige from the competent performance of their task. In the present context, the important point is that those administrators—a minority—who did not enjoy a change in technique or a new problem, were also less competent in other ways: they were in general less certain of their ability to manage. In short, the people who could cope welcomed changes; those whose work had got on top of them resented them. In so far as the organization is efficient the former—successful spiralists—will be promoted, the latter will stay at this level.

The connection between incompetence and rigid adherence to rules is well brought out by a distinction Gouldner draws between two forms of bureaucracy he calls punishment-centred and representative bureaucracy. In the latter, everybody knows what is necessary, agrees to the rules, keeps the rules because they appear to him to be only common sense and breaks the rules when common sense tells him to do that. Everyone is assumed to act as his work requires. The status-distinction between superior and inferior is as irrelevant here as it normally is in a task-centred group. In the punishment-centred bureaucracy, the rules are imposed by a status-superior who is insecure in his position (either for personality reasons, or because he is incompetent, or because he is new, or because his subordinates resist his authority even when he is task-related). He cannot trust others to act as the work requires. As a result, he tends to think of rules as requiring obedience rather than as principles underlying rational action.[1]

Gouldner cites a remarkable illustration of the punishment-centred attitude. In a factory was a deep pit, and because gases sometimes accumulated at the bottom, there was a rule that no man might go down the pit unless another was at the top to watch that he came to no harm. A foreman walking along noted from the position of a rope that a man had lowered himself into the pit, and there was no one at the top. This was therefore a breach of the rules. Instead of standing by the man to see that he was all right, the foreman went off to find an authority with power to reprimand the man who had broken the rules.

---

[1] A. Gouldner (1954), *Patterns of Industrial Bureaucracy*, Free Press, Glencoe, Ill. See also the discussion on pages 101 and 525-6, and Klein (1956), *The Study of Groups*, chaps. II and III.

Middle-Class Life

In this instance, Merton would say, the means had become the end, 'instrumental values had become terminal'. Although impersonality and strict adherence to the rules is only a means to securing a fair democracy, the danger is that these qualities become absolute values in the mind of the bureaucrat. 'Discipline, readily interpreted as conformance with regulations whatever the situation, is seen not as a measure designed for specific purposes, but becomes an immediate value in the life-organization of the bureaucrat.'[1]

Once this has happened, the personality is set against further change. Events not envisaged when the rules were drawn up (or not foreseen by parents in the process of socializing the child to fit into the work-situation they think he is likely to encounter) are resented instead of creatively used. Birmingham gossip still remembers the Local Councillor who was apparently aware of no absurdity when he retorted, to a complaint that there was overcrowding in a school, that the trouble was not that there were too few schools in the area, but that parents had had more children than had been expected.

The bureaucratic work-situation makes it easy for certain attitudes such as a liking for discipline and self-denial to become ends in themselves. In connection with this, a brief digression may be allowed. A set of traits relevant not only to this kind of work-situation, but also to a particular social position and attitude to child-rearing, has a tradition of sociological discussion behind it, under the general heading of 'the Protestant ethic'.

The Protestant ethic is more or less what popular speech calls 'puritanism'. It is another concept first outlined by Max Weber, who put forward the thesis that the conditions for the development of capitalist economies had obtained at various times in various places—China, Egypt, and so on—where capitalism nevertheless did not develop, because the attitudes that would allow people to take kindly to this form of economic life were absent.[2] With the Reformation, the emphasis on the

---

[1] Robert Merton, op. cit. These traits appear also in the group of clerical workers whose place in the bureaucratic hierarchy is below the executive level. In the next sub-sections the evidence merits continuation of this discussion.
[2] See pages 604-11.

individual's search for salvation created both an anxiety about his position in the scheme of things and a more individualistic, less communal approach to life. This led people to work harder and spend less time or money on sociable living.[1] The money saved in this way made it easier for capital to accumulate, and so on. This thesis has been subjected to much debate, but our concern here is not with its historical accuracy so much as with the intuition of social observers and commentators who were led to perceive certain frequently encountered clusters of personality traits as typifying certain cultural traditions.

The theory implicit in the psychologist's analysis of the Protestant ethic rests on a set of traits which seem peculiarly characteristic of the people in the social situation under discussion in this sub-section. One recent such list of traits will suffice to illustrate the sort of attitudes that are grouped together.[2]

Achievement and success	Freedom
Activity and work	External conformity
Moral orientation	Science and secular rationality
Humanitarian mores	Nationalism and patriotism
Efficiency and practicality	Democracy (i.e. majority rule
Material comfort	and procedure)
Equality (of opportunity rather	Individualism
than of condition)	

Discipline, a life ordered by rules, the strict control of impulse, hard work, the feeling that good behaviour entitles one to rewards, and a restriction of the demands made upon life, especially in adverse circumstances, are very congenial to a personality of this kind. Willmott and Young put it epigrammatically:

> It is always a *small* car they talk about (in Woodford), as though not even a puritan could object as long as it was not a *large* car.

[1] M. Weber (1904–5), *The Protestant Ethic and the Spirit of Capitalism*, Archiv für Sozialwissenschaft und Sozialpolitik, XX–XXI, translated by Talcott Parsons (1930) for Allen and Unwin, London. Cf. page 374 fn.

[2] Robin Williams, 'Value orientations in American society', in H. D. Stein and R. A. Cloward (1958), *Social Perspectives in Behaviour*. See also Kingsley Davis, 'Mental hygiene and the class structure', in P. Mullahy (1948), *A Study of Interpersonal Relations*, Hermitage Press, New York, further discussed in the volume on child-rearing, pages 609–10.

Middle-Class Life

And Dunnill, at greater length:

Certain attitudes run right through the executive hierarchy. They are for solidity and against brilliance. They distrust emotion and enthusiasm. They tend to be hard, cautious men and women of a type generally supposed to be more common in Yorkshire than in the South.

This professional scepticism and lack of fire is particularly pronounced in the older executives, but many of the younger and more junior members have imbibed a good deal of it. Anyone who has seen a group of young executives, supposedly the pick of the class, testing their wits against each other at Stoke D'Abernon [a centre where candidates for the Administrative Grade of the Civil Service were tested for various intellectual, personal and social qualities] or mingling with young graduates on training courses, will confirm that in general they are harder, safer, more solid, and less subtle or imaginative men than their contemporaries who have entered from a university. These heavy and careful traits do not make the executives, on the whole, the gayest of people.[1] They tend to have the qualities one finds useful but chilling in an actuary or an accountant.

Walker's findings on the character of the Chief or Senior Executive Officer seem remarkably similar to Dunnill's impression. The sample shows him at his most typical: in his fifties, having come up from the Clerical Grade below, with a long career behind him. His efficiency rating is high: his work is well thought of. He does not feel—as those at some other levels do—that the work is below his capacities. But he tends to find it less interesting than do the men in the Administrative Grade. His enjoyment of his work—though greater than that of some others below him—is only moderate. He trusts his subordinates but he does not particularly want to be friendly with them. He is not anxious for more democratic relations between the grades. He does not easily bring himself to complain about his work—in fact, he makes fewer complaints than any other grade about such aspects as variety or responsibility—but he is inclined to advise others against following a similar career. Relative to others, he feels that he is underpaid; this, we shall note later, may have an important bearing on his experience of social life.

[1] Cf. also cognitive poverty, discussed on pages 85–7 and 93–6.

385

Parallel to these, except in the matter of payment, may be the managers with technical qualifications, either in science or accountancy. High positions and financial rewards are the rule among them, though their career may have been on the slow side, and they do not, by and large, reach board level. Many of these qualified specialists come from homes Clements puts in the zone between the lower middle and the middle classes. Most have made their way through grammar schools and the scientific departments of the provincial universities. They are true spiralists. Though their lives in industry started comparatively late, they have changed firms rather more frequently than other managers. This illustrates the point that the possession of trained specialist knowledge is an aid rather than a hindrance to mobility. 'After all, accountants and engineers are required throughout industry and the basic principles of their crafts are applicable everywhere.'

> On the whole, those who read science at the university and whose careers have described this pattern were clearer in their minds as to what they wanted to do and what it would be like to do it, than many of the men who took up management traineeships (described later in this sub-section). At least, their wishes coincided a great deal more closely with the types of jobs that the world wants done in the greatest number, so they were the more easily able, especially in recent years, to get something like the job they wanted . . . Many were quite clear from the outset that they wanted a post in mechanical, electrical or chemical engineering, or in industrial chemistry or physics. Industry was their natural objective, where they could hope to pursue a career by building upon the specialist knowledge they had acquired during their training . . .
> The view is encountered in industry that qualified men of this kind are excellent in their places, in the accountant's office, or in the laboratory, but that their value in management is diminished by too narrow a view of the organization's activities as a whole, engendered by their highly specialized training. Their work, too, it is said, involves entirely factual matters capable of yielding clear and precise answers after the application of well-tried procedures; this incapacitates them from dealing effectively with management problems, which are hard to define, whose treatment can seldom be simple, and whose consequences may be obscure. In the words

of one technologist, 'a scientist cannot take expedient decisions, as the board must, for it cannot decide merely on facts'. And yet in some ways these specialists have the widest experience of all. While it is no more usual for them than for other managers to have changed their type of work, at least when they do so it is at a pretty high level, and they bring to the new job a really thorough knowledge of their previous work. It is a switch that can be of the most fruitful kind.

In theory, and at best, a man's position in an organization's hierarchy depends on his competent performance, and his whole outlook is geared to competence and pride in work well done.

Much depends no doubt on the degree of enthusiasm with which the Civil Servant approaches his work [writes Dunnill]. A person who devotes himself to the service of the State knows that he is inevitably sacrificing certain marginal opportunities. He will not grow rich and, even if the risk of utter poverty is absent, to sacrifice such a chance of wealth has a discouraging effect on the spirit of the energetic person. To be really efficient, the public servant must, therefore, believe in his life's work with almost religious devotion.

Often, however, we have the impression of a rather joyless, rather unemphatic sort of existence.[1]

Outside the office, the older executives—substantial and generally respected citizens who fit snugly into the middle-most middle classes—are inclined to hold themselves rather more aloof from political discussion and from social activities of a markedly intellectual character, than the more junior grades. Gardening and golf are popular pastimes. Those who have got on are often inclined, being self-made men, to be ambitious for their children;[2] and in many of their homes one senses a situation similar to that found among immigrants to the United States, whose children are often ungraciously aware of the cultural limitations of their parents. Steadiness and respectability are words that spring to the lips when one thinks of them; and sometimes it is only when one meets a wife, married in youth and left behind by the husband, that one appreciates how far he has come in an official lifetime.

Were they born this way? Some were. Mark Abrams analysed

---

[1] See pages 558-60 and 576-80 in the volume on child-rearing.
[2] See pages 602-4 in the volume on child-rearing.

the results of a survey of nearly a thousand Cambridge under-graduates. Though 17 per cent were choosing a career in business management or advertising, only half that number would have done so if other professions—notably teaching, writing or social work—had been equally remunerative. Ana-lysing the replies of this reluctant group, Abrams concludes:

> Their leisure activities suggest that they have comparatively little taste for individualistic competition, and less than average liking for the responsibilities of leadership and organization. When they take part in group activities they show a preference for anonymous and passive roles. They find information more satisfy-ing than ideas, and entertainment more attractive than con-troversy . . . Business might regret ever having recruited them.[1]

Clements gives a graphic description of the drift into industry of the manager without technical or scientific training.

> The circumstances attending the entry of these men into in-dustrial employment hardly suggests that many were impelled by a strong sense of vocation. Some non-graduates on leaving school went first into a law or commercial firm, reacted violently against that, and persuaded their fathers to use influence or contacts to introduce them into management training schemes in industry. Others drifted into their careers on the advice of their fathers with few positive ideas of their own except that they were incapable of taking up the Law or the Church. Many of those coming down from the universities were similarly vague, though a fairly large minority, especially those trained in science or technology, in-tended from the outset to make their careers in industry . . .
>
> One or two who were up at the universities about the time of the first World War fancied becoming parsons, or soldiers, or horse-breeders. More recent generations have thought rather in terms of joining the Civil or Colonial Services, and a few of teaching. One or two contemplated academic life, or probation work, architec-ture, accountancy, or actuarial jobs. These dreams faded under various influences. Failure in the Civil Service examinations or poor results in the law course were obvious inducements to look elsewhere. Crises of conscience or a mere waning of interest explain the abandonment of the idea of taking Holy Orders.

[1] Mark Abrams (1916), 'Business aspirants from Universities', *The Manager*, September issue. Quoted by Anthony Sampson.

War and its upheavals, the responsibilities of marriage and children, had their effects. Old ambitions were seen to require hard work, long preparation, to be uncertain of attainment, and to offer what now seemed but meagre rewards. Even if the attractions of security and a large salary were not poignantly felt, views changed under the influence of war, growing maturity, and greater familiarity with other possibilities. The most recent generation possibly has experienced fewer of these changes of feeling and frustrations, for the post-war boom and business propaganda may have made the idea of an industrial career more familiar and acceptable.

These were men who had been recruited by the firm and submitted to management training schemes. The great majority came from the higher social ranks and had been educated at public schools, then at Oxford or Cambridge, mainly in 'Arts' subjects. These men tended to stay in the same firm for their life-time, about half reaching top management positions.

Munro has described the task-situation which suits such people.

Young men, when they enter the Administrative Class, have to learn that the first necessity is to be accurate on all matters of fact and on the issues involved in any matter . . . 'If the Civil Servant makes a mistake, the Minister may have to stand at that box and eat humble pie.' . . .

If he failed to put up any constructive suggestion or express any definite view, no one would take any particular account of that. As a result, a diffident young man . . . would refrain from doing so as a matter of policy, *in case* he might by doing so reveal that there was some aspect of the matter which he had not grasped or some fact which he had overlooked. Such a state of affairs, therefore, tended to prevent him from taking a definite line even when he felt like doing so.

To assess the long-term effect of this is not quite simple. My own view is that it did not make much difference to the effectiveness of the men at the very top, for these were men who had had the buoyancy and self-confidence to break through the prevailing atmosphere and begin to express themselves fully and freely at a comparatively early stage . . . But some it stunted altogether . . . They were men who could write an excellent précis, but when one looked for a final conclusion, it was missing.

Some were brought up for this, but others were adversely affected by their life in the office.

> At the bottom end [writes Dunnill] are the junior executive officers. They may be young men and women straight from the sixth form of a grammar school who have entered the service by way of a fairly stiff examination. They may equally be older people, promoted, possibly during the war, from the clerical grades . . . In steadiness and attention to detail these may have much to teach their younger colleagues, but they are seldom notable for their grasp or self-confidence.

At a somewhat higher level, the Registrar-General's figures provide the statistics:

> Among administrative and other higher officers of the Civil Service in socio-economic group 3, the high proportion of those aged 20-24 with terminal education age 20 and over (69 per cent) compared with 27 per cent of those aged 25 and over reflects the fact that the older age group contained a large number who had attained such positions by promotion, while the younger section contained a large proportion of entrants at graduate level. (Such a situation differed from that found for physicians and surgeons where entry into an occupation is by qualification and not by promotion and whose terminal education age-distribution remained constant between the two age groups. In general, in occupational group 3, the typical terminal education age was high but the actual distribution depended on the system of training.)[1]

For those who are anxious to get on, there are strong pressures to develop a 'bureaucratic personality' even if their native trends in this direction are not very marked. If the system of promotion is wrongly applied, or wrongly perceived, even bright young entrants may react in ways which are not in the best interests of the organization. Gladden has analysed this whole complex very carefully.

> There is some truth in the view that, especially outside the Administrative Class, the Service tends to be apathetic and to lack enterprise. They find that bright ideas are dangerous, that they are expected to think in accordance with a well-established

---

[1] Census, 1951, *General report*, 1958, p. 118.

pattern of thinking. If they have surplus energies, it is better to expend them in outside activities.

To these outside activities further reference will be made in the next sub-sections. There are less desirable reactions. Gladden writes of those who came into the Civil Service at a relatively low level and remained subordinate for the rest of their working-lives. A second socialization takes place: the personality reshapes in order to adjust to the conditions now encountered.

The newcomer soon discovers that he is a generalized staff unit, regarded as a human being only by those with whom he has daily contacts. As the chain of command lengthens into the higher reaches, often into other geographical situations, it loses its humanness and becomes part of the system to which he has become subjected . . . Only the strong-minded will retain any real freedom of spirit. The system may be designed to protect the weak against the strong, in fact it has the inevitable effect of encouraging the growth of a slave mentality and of placing a premium upon caution.

There are two kinds of slave. Those who are happy in the system and adopt the values of their masters, and those who develop the cunning exploitative subservience of the weak. Gladden describes the young hopeful's decline into an organization man (U.K. model).

He soon learns that he is a cog in a large machine, and not a very important cog at that. He is of course told that if he perseveres in mastering his job, merit will receive its just reward in good time, but what he discerns around him in the results of previous history does not inspire confidence, and if his personal view is not very perceptive, the grouses of his older colleagues will soon make him aware of the other side of the coin. He will discover that in the best of regulated services, opportunity rests in the lap of chance as everywhere else, and when he has become experienced enough to judge, he will see that the hierarchy around him is not arranged in accordance with any scale of competence that he can comprehend. He might even, were he a cunning fellow—and fortunately such are not usually attracted to Civil Service administration as a career—conclude that his best prospects could rest in his cultivating opportunities that operate outside the normal channels. It is a good thing to cultivate one's own garden; it is even better to cultivate one's chiefs.

He would soon learn that outspokenness, though invited by those at the top and welcomed as a part of official policy, is not usually received very warmly by his immediate superiors. Yesmanship is an immemorial characteristic of bureaucracy and the ability to determine which way the ultra-bureaucratic wind blows can be of incalculable advantage to the aspiring junior.

This kind of relationship to status-superiors is uncongenial even to the hard-headed, realistic, unimaginative executives of Dunnill's description. Instead, we tend to find the kind of ego-defence already noted in a previous chapter and thought by Barbu to be characteristic in many English situations.

There is no other community in which the individual resents vertical relations with others, and super and subordination in particular, with a greater intensity. A clerk, a servant, even a charlady, when taking up a new job, feel that their first concern is to find out what they are 'supposed to do'. Once this is achieved they have won their independence, for, later on, whenever someone asks for their services their first reaction is to make sure whether they are supposed to do this or not, and to act accordingly. Thus any individual avoids being dependent on others in the exercise of his job; he makes himself responsible to a kind of abstract authority which consists of certain rules and requirements established by agreement or by tradition, and which define 'what he is supposed to do'.[1]

Weber made much of the importance of technical training for the bureaucrat, and of the examination system which determines his promotion in the hierarchy. But this must be considered with reservations. In the English Civil Service, promotion within a grade is not by examination but depends on reports submitted by superiors. Gladden lists the qualities on which superiors are asked to comment, and here again we see the pressure to become a 'bureaucrat'.

Knowledge of branch and department, personality and force of character, judgement, power of taking responsibility, accuracy, address and tact, power of supervising staff, zeal, ability to express himself clearly in writing and orally, official conduct.

Gladden comments on the absence of certain other desir-

---

[1] See page 202.

able qualities such as mental powers, speed of work, adaptability.[1]

Secondly, Weber's analysis is not directly applicable to the English situation because of that distrust of the intellectual and rational already noted on page 370 and which finds its expression in the Civil Service by means of promotion interviews and other schemes such as Stoke D'Abernon which test, among other qualities, the extent to which a man will 'fit in' the work-group. Such imponderable qualities of character, which are considered of great importance to a man's competence, are much less easily examined.[2] So, although formal examinations do limit entry into each of the major Civil Service grades, promotion within each grade, and promotion in the great industrial bureaucracies, often depends as much on the reports of superiors, who are more individual and fallible than examinations are normally admitted to be.

The rejection of patronage [thus Munro] and the search for defeating favouritism have decreased in every direction the scope for arbitrary decision and have rendered it virtually impossible to make any decision which favours an individual against the rest of his colleagues. Thus in a so-called merit system it becomes less and less easy for those in positions of responsibility to recognize merit. The decision is so masked as to appear to emanate impartially as a part of the daily routine of the department.

The chances of promotion are of very great importance in sorting out types of reaction to working in a bureaucratic organization. The personality type with which we are here mainly concerned is geared to hard work and the expectation of achievement. The younger people will expect to rise to the top, even into the Administrative Grade if they are competent. But older people near the top are reaching the ceiling of their capacity for promotion. Inevitably some do not attain the positions

[1] In fairness, it should be added that a later form was being discussed at that time which included under the heading of 'character and personality', such other desiderata as responsibility, relations with colleagues, contacts with public; under the heading 'capacity': penetration, constructive power, judgement; under the heading 'performance of duties': output, quality, expression on paper, oral expression, figurework, management of subordinates, organization of work.

[2] The discussion on whether entry at eleven into a Grammar School should be purely by intelligence tests and tests of intellectual performance bears this out very nicely. See also the discussions on pages 317, 361-3, 617 and 626-9.

to which they consider themselves entitled. The manager who comes into industry via a traineeship may find himself in a similar situation. About half of these did very well for themselves. But partly because of the promotion-policies of the firms, partly for other reasons, others were left behind.

Some firms using this [traineeship] system of recruitment extensively have many middle management and relatively few very top management posts. Consequently, after rapid promotion to management level in some small department, they have tended to remain there for many years and several older ones in the sample have become impatient and disgruntled, and compare invidiously the ability and rewards of directors with their own. It was said that there is a 'tendency to be left in cold storage by the directors and used as required, and one is not stretched to full capacity—there is a period of stagnation till the top layer dies off'. It is true that earnings are high, but long years of narrow specialization seem to be poor for morale and poor preparation for top management.

To sum up the distinctions made so far, we may say first of all that there are executives to whom hierarchy, a devotion to the task and conformity with the rules in a moral community are temperamentally congenial: 'natural bureaucrats'. Among the successful there will be those who, regardless of education or family background, have come to the top by competence in their work or by a hard-headed and unsentimental determination to use at all costs the opportunities which come their way.[1] Among the less successful will be those whose hard work, education or family made them feel entitled to success but who, for reasons they do not clearly understand, are left behind in the race for promotion and who see others, no more worthy in their eyes, overtake them. They are then apt to display a set of characteristics which we shall describe in the next sub-section as 'relative deprivation': they feel that an injustice has been done them.

THE CONCEPT OF RELATIVE DEPRIVATION

The term 'relative deprivation' was coined by Merton who argued, from evidence provided by studies of the American

[1] In contrast, Spinley's ex-Public School pupil 'wants success, but not success at all costs'. See pages 364 and 625.

soldier, that envy and dislike are more often to be found where opportunities for promotion are plentiful than where they are few.[1] In the latter case, the soldier is more likely to think of the opportunities as 'fairly distributed' and to be content with his own position. The reason seemed to Merton to be that when, in a social group, only a small number of people can move up, there is only a small number to which those who remain behind can compare themselves unfavourably. Circumstances which allow a great deal of social mobility therefore create hazards not only for those who move, but also for those whose position is not improving at the rate they desire.

Where many move up, and thus many feel they are being left behind, we get what Mills has called a status-panic. Basic to the status-panic is the concern for appearance. Mills quotes Veblen.

'Under modern conditions the struggle for existence has to a very appreciable degree been transformed into a struggle to keep up appearances.' But self-respectability is not the same as self-respect, and in so far as the stress is on appearance, there is an estrangement from the real self. When people are alienated in this way from their own real wishes and from enjoyment of their work because they feel that their present position is only temporary and that their real and soon-to-be-achieved position is higher up the scale, they become pre-occupied with matters of status. The minute gradations of rank at work, which are characteristic of the office worker, instead of being thought of as indicative of differences in skill, are then thought of as symbolic of status, and all the trimmings which convey these differences—the type of carpet, the type of chair—supremely important.[2]

It is here that we may place one of the roots of that competitive consumption to which reference was made in the sub-section on Woodford, but in Britain, at least, the evidence suggests that this behaviour is as characteristic of the socially static who find themselves relatively deprived, as of those who are moving up in the world, whom Veblen and Mills had in mind.

Relative deprivation, as we shall think of it, is therefore not

[1] R. Merton, op. cit.
[2] C. Wright Mills (1951), *White Collar*, Oxford University Press. See also pages 248–51.

simply a characteristic of some bureaucratic situations; it is a particular experience in a changing social structure. Given such changes, their effect can be studied at any occupational level: executive, clerical, or manual. We have an interest in it because evidence is accumulating on the effects of such an experience on parental behaviour, and hence on the next generation.

Our evidence comes from a very detailed study of the relationships between American social conditions and psychiatric illness, published in two volumes, *Social Class and Mental Illness* (1958) by A. B. Hollingshead and F. C. Redlich, and *Family and Class Dynamics in Mental Illness* (1959) by J. K. Myers and B. H. Roberts. The former involved the enumeration of all individuals in psychiatric treatment on December 1, 1950, and the selection and interview of a 5 per cent sample of the population of New Haven, Connecticut. The second reports on an intensive study of fifty cases of psychiatric illness with particular reference to their social and family situation.

The group of especial interest to us consists of a sample of neurotic patients of the middle middle class. In the sample, one quarter of the heads of households owned their business. The rest were employed, half of them in various administrative or clerical pursuits, half more or less equally in semi-professional, technical, supervisory or skilled manual work. Included are local government officials, civil servants, managers of chain stores, bank-clerks, photographers, draughtsmen. Their social and economic situation as it has a bearing on their feelings and attitudes is described in the following way:

> Salaried administrative employees tend to identify with the executive hierarchy rather than with the clerical workers or plant supervisors. They dislike unions, are unorganized and have few associations or spokesmen to protect their interests. They are respected by clerical and blue-collar workers but not viewed as equals by the small businessmen. The major bulwarks to an administrative worker's self-esteem and prestige are his right to wear a business suit while working, his authority over clerical employees, his desk and his place in the office, and his hope of climbing the executive ladder. The hope of advancement is a motivating factor among young men, but the middle-aged look back at the time when they dreamt of 'moving up'.

Supervisory personnel in the plant, key employees in the production process, are marginal men in so far as they are neither management nor labour. They are identified by administrative and clerical workers with labour, but they do not have independent unions to speak for them. They have little protection in labour struggles because they are largely an adjunct of management. Off the job they tend to be treated as factory workers by professional workers and businessmen. They usually tend to identify with management and its desires . . .

The labour market for the types of occupation represented is relatively stable, and employees feel secure in their jobs. They pay a high price for this security as there is little opportunity for advancement with respect to either salary or achievement . . . Most of these people held their positions during the prolonged depression of the thirties, but worked for relatively low salaries. Since then, their incomes have not risen fast enough to keep up with the rise in the cost of living. These people feel the pressure of prices on their paychecks, and there is a widespread feeling that they have lost ground financially . . . The small businessman does not feel the pressure of prices, but he knows that business is shifting to the chain stores.

Myers and Roberts attribute to these families an unusual conjugal relationship, in that the wife is seen to be the dominant partner in the marriage. It is perfectly possible that this family-constellation can appear at different social levels. The position of the mother who feels she is hard done by—relatively deprived —because she feels she has married beneath herself, or because her husband has not fulfilled her social aspirations, is discussed also in English sociological literature, though on the whole related to a social level lower than that at which Myers and Roberts saw the phenomenon. Although strict comparisons are not possible between social groups in somewhat similar positions in different cultures, the economic situation described by them is at least analogous to that of some discussed in these pages— the relatively deprived executives and clerks: people who could not keep up with others who started from the same mark in the race for promotion, or who saw others overtake them in spite of their own conscientious performance. The discussion will therefore be continued both in the next sub-section and in the final one, where we shall be concerned with the borderline between manual and non-manual work. Some implications of this family-constellation are to be considered in the volume on child-rearing, where the topic of dominant mothers and their effect on the children's personality is an important one.

(1) *The relatively deprived*

We have met them before [writes Dunnill], in works of fiction, in newspapers, at the cinema: the clerks, the typists, punched-card operators and Post Office sorters who, with many other similar people, comprise the base of our pyramid. These are the rank and file, from whose numbers come the tea-drinking typists who giggle their way through British films; the little men with sandwich lunches, who turn out to have murdered their wives in the short stories in evening papers; the people in the food offices who gave ridiculous answers to gentlemen who used to write to *The Times* about it; the chaps with cobwebs on their desk and tea at their elbow, much beloved of cartoonists; the traditionally talkative young ladies in the Post Office.

We have met them in real life too . . . There are so many of them, in proportion to the executives and administrators higher up the pyramid . . . that it is from them that all but the most cautious or expert of us derive our first impressions of the Civil Service. We shall see that they do not make the policies, frame the regulations or write the instructions. But it is they, almost invariably, who carry them out in detail and it is they who generally make the first impact on the public.

The difficulties of identifying the social class of these people has already been touched on in the early pages of this chapter. Fortunately or unfortunately, we have little information on any but the clerical workers and it is to these that the discussion will be confined.

It seems that this section of the population has been more affected than most by changes in the social structure.

The most noticeable index of change is to be found in the numerical increase [writes Lockwood]. In 1851, clerks formed less than one per cent of the total labour force . . . Since then there has been a great increase in the ratio of non-manual to manual workers in industry, concomitant with the increase in the size of offices and with the proliferation of 'non-productive' functions in commerce, finance, distribution and government . . . Scientific management initiated office mechanization; and office mechanization in its turn promoted further the recording of new types of data. Industrial concentration and amalgamation, born of joint stock enterprise, led to the concentration and rationalization of office work and staffs. And the vastly enhanced functions of government in an industrial milieu called for increasingly more efficient administration.

By 1951, rather more than one in every ten workers worked in an office. The other significant fact is that more than half of them were women. By the mid-twentieth century, writes Lockwood, to be precise we should no longer speak of the 'black-coated' but rather of the 'white-bloused' worker. In due course these girls marry and have children whose upbringing is affected by their mother's experience in ways to which we must refer below.

	Clerks as percentage of total labour force	*Female clerks as percentage of total number of clerks*
1851	0·8	0·1
1901	4·0	13·4
1951	10·5	59·6

The increased proportion of people in this occupation means that many more sons than fathers are clerks. Some of these sons have come up in the world, from manual working-class homes. We are therefore bound to find in this occupational group, even more than elsewhere, a distinction between traditional and non-traditional ways of life. For reasons which will become clear, we shall argue that the traditional black-coated worker is likely to feel that life has disappointed him. He has seen women catch up with him, younger people catch up with him, manual workers catch up with him. This is how the psychological state of 'relative deprivation' comes about. The non-traditional, on the other hand, is likely to feel that he is doing well for himself. These 'relatively privileged' are to be discussed in the next sub-section. The chapter ends with a consideration of the manual worker who feels that he belongs to the middle class and who may in fact be brother or father or in-law to the relatively privileged clerk.

Aspects of Adult Life in England

If we take a historical perspective, the concept of relative deprivation applies most strikingly to the older clerk, who comes from that section of society which by past tradition has supplied the bulk of clerical workers and which feels itself to be unmistakably middle class. Lockwood quotes a rather pathetic evaluation of the changed position of the bank-clerk, a group which may be considered to have experienced the most striking decline:

> Before the second World War, he enjoyed a middle-class style of life. Among the conventional necessities of his existence were included not only the sartorial and housing standards of the suburban salariat but also frequently private education for his children and perhaps even a motor car. In social status he ranked himself fairly high. As one bank-clerk saw it: 'The strata of society appear to me to be like this: First of all you have the country squire, with whom the vicar consorts, and the lawyer when it is necessary. Then you get the doctor . . . and just after him the bank-clerk, who may, on special occasions, hob-nob at church bazaars and on the village greens.' . . .

> Generations before this, in mid-nineteenth century, the black coat of the clerk symbolized his middle-class status. The broadcloth he wore was, however, only one mark of his distinction from the working-class man. Running deeper than this sartorial claim to status was the social gulf between the manual worker and the rest.[1] Working with one's hands was associated with other attributes—lack of authority, illiteracy, lowly social origin, insecurity of livelihood—which together spelt social depreciation. The dominant values underlying differences in social worth were those of the entrepreneurial and professional middle classes. The most widely influential criteria of prestige therefore were those which expressed the occupational achievement of the individual.

> The education required for the job, the rewards and responsibilities it offered, the fact that it was clean and non-manual, and therefore 'respectable', gradually established themselves as key determinants of a person's social standing over a wide range of society. But [Lockwood continues] with the institution of compulsory elementary education in the last decades of the nineteenth century, every literate person became a potential clerk, thus breaking the hitherto monopolistic position of the black-coated worker.

[1] See also Zweig, quoted on page 305.

Middle-Class Life

The increase in the number of clerks is partly accounted for by the influx of clerks from a working-class home. The clerk from a traditional black-coated background would find that more and more of his colleagues in the office held quite different values and he would feel much as people in middle-class residential neighbourhoods feel when there is an influx of manual workers: that he was going 'down in the world'.

In the place of residence, there are analogous stresses.

Objective differences in Woodford are slighter than they have ever been in the past. Not only have incomes come closer together, but people in different classes also spend their money on the same kinds of things, on cars, on refrigerators, on washing machines. The two classes live in the same kind of district, often in the same kind of houses, and have much the same kind of hopes for their children. One can see what Hoggart meant when he talked about 'our emerging classnessness'.

And yet these are only the outward and visible signs of class. Inside people's minds, the boundaries of class are still closely drawn. Classlessness is not emerging there. On the contrary, the nearer the classes are drawn by the objective facts of income, style of life and housing, the more are middle-class people liable to pull them apart by exaggerating the differences subjectively regarded. In Woodford this has been done with such success that to a very large extent social relationships are confined to one side or another of the dividing line in the mind.[1]

Not surprisingly, Willmott and Young found that the bitterest attacks on the way of life of the working classes seemed to come from people who were close to the boundary between working and middle class, whose own job had dropped in status or financial reward, or whose own future was insecure. They cite the commercial traveller whose trade was declining; the clerk who said 'I'd like to think I'm in the middle class but I suppose I'm in the working class. I know the fitters at our place take home more than I do. But look what they spend it on'; the works manager who complained that the working class don't know how to spend their money: 'They waste money on fridges, washing machines, T.V.s and cars'; the teacher who said, 'I suppose before the war I'd be middle class. Teachers had a high

[1] See also pages 418–25.

social standing then, but now professional people are the lowest. At least that's in money. Actually, we're a pretty high class.' In the matter of rising incomes, it is clear that the clerical worker is getting left behind. Lockwood cites statistics comparing him with the manual worker. Between 1946 and 1956, the median salaries of most adult clerks in commerce and industry increased by between 40 and 60 per cent. Industrial earnings for adult men doubled in that time. Again, it is the older clerks, with a middle-class background, who would find this especially hard to take, for they would compare themselves not only with the manual workers, but also with the younger clerks, many of whom would moreover have come from working-class homes, who now benefit from wage-increases which came to them early and not late in life. Lockwood adds that although they are normally paid at a higher rate than manual workers, the clerks' weekly income is often smaller because they have no opportunity of adding to their earnings by working overtime. In another way too, they may have less to show for the money, their pattern of savings and expenditure being different.

There is a good deal of truth in these considerations. All the same, the frequency and the bitterness with which these matters are often discussed may be more characteristic of the *attitude* than of the *facts* of relative deprivation. In 1957 the difference between the average weekly incomes of middle-class and working-class informants in Woodford was still striking: £19 12s. 0d. for the thirteen middle-class men, £10 14s. 0½d. for the twenty-four working-class men.[1]

> The attitude of the middle classes towards the future is much what the attitude of the individual middle-class breadwinner always is: an amalgam of dread and confidence. Dread of losing his security; refusal to believe that what happens to others could ever happen to him. Middle-class opinion similarly views the progressive impoverishment of the middle classes with deep misgiving, yet cannot believe that the class which contains both the brains and the leaders of the nation can be wholly destroyed. Both feelings arise from valid experiences.

The valid experiences Lewis and Maude have in mind here

[1] The figures are of personal incomes for single men, joint incomes of conjugal pairs.

are historical and socio-economic. (We may note in passing their own characteristic traditional belief that the events of the past are a fair guide to the future.) A social psychologist looks also for other roots of such beliefs: the amalgam of dread and confidence may have been compounded in the experiences of childhood and parental behaviour, and to this we must return in the volume on child-rearing. It is relevant to note here, however, that the secure element in such an amalgam may derive from an affectionate and stable home, while the uncertainty derives from the absence of the rewards which parents had confidently promised to those who practised such virtues as thrift, unobtrusiveness, good manners and application.[1] We cannot leave the passage without pointing out also the characteristic upper-middle-class divorce between brains and gifts of leadership, suggested here by the way Lewis and Maude express themselves.[2]

In so far as success has not followed behaviour which was confidently believed to lead to success, there is uncertainty. Because the causes of failure are difficult to identify, one reaction to the experience of failure may be a greater concentration on particular qualities required in the work. In unfortunate circumstances, what may become stressed is the liking for discipline and conformity which is required for contentment in a bureaucratic setting. If everyone did 'what they are supposed to do', as Barbu put it, everyone would receive his just reward.

The possibility exists that a man who has lived a good life as defined by his parents before the first World War, with emphasis on the Victorian virtues, finding himself less successful than he had been led to expect, will react by insisting on more discipline, better leadership guidance, greater conformity. Necessary organizational values transform themselves from 'instrumental' to 'terminal'.

Walker provides an interesting illustration of the way such sentiments about conformity and discipline express themselves in the office. He asked one of his samples of Clerical Officers what made for a really good Executive Officer. The answers display a liking for fairness in the sense of conformity to the rules

---

[1] See also pages 198, 383 and 534–5.
[2] See also pages 369–71 and 393.

Aspects of Adult Life in England

which is in marked contrast to another kind of fairness which takes individual differences of circumstance into account.[1]

The almost invariable answer was 'Well, he must know the [C.O.'s] job. He must be fair—not have favourites—but firm.' The Executive Officer had, in their eyes, to exercise his authority in two chief ways. First, he had to prevent time-wasting on the job. This might take the form of unnecessary talking or, occasionally, of some more boisterous activity among the younger males. The good E.O. apparently was the one who knew just how much latitude to give: he allowed them some diversion during the short mid-morning break for tea, and perhaps at the end of the day when they were well up to schedule and nobody needed to be helped out. But if he allowed it at other times he lost the respect of the other C.O.s and perhaps also of the offender himself. The other main point where firmness was needed was in time-keeping. The morning started at 8.15 and the E.O. had a book in which each C.O. had to sign on arrival. He was supposed to remove it at 8.20 so that anyone who came in later would earn a black mark and would eventually receive a reprimand. Some E.O.s were humanely slow in removing the book, but this did not seem to earn them any real favour with the conscientious majority . . .

. . . There were cases in which C.O.s spoke of some past E.O. who had been 'very strict indeed', yet they almost always added 'but very fair'. It was clear that strictness in itself, so long as it was not accompanied by favouritism or unpredictability, and as long as the C.O.s had some latitude, was not resented.

The love of discipline, of rules, of doing what you are supposed to do, was thought by Gorer to reside particularly in the section of the population to which the present occupational group belongs. 'The most marked characteristic of the lower middle class is the extent to which they welcome and approve the authority of the contemporary state. They are the most enthusiastic admirers of the police . . . the more resolute opponents of "fiddling", the most eager in their belief that laws should be obeyed under any circumstances, that it is always unfair to try to get more than others.' 'Quite a number of the fathers in this stratum, particularly the middle-aged and elderly, would grant chief authority to the teacher (that is, to another authority).'

[1] See pages 475–6, 479 and 524–6.

404

Gorer also found that the children tended to be subjected to discipline within a typically authoritarian setting: the father was thought to be entitled to punish the child *because he was the boss*; the question of child discipline was seen as connected with the nature of authority rather than, say, with the development of the child, or with the importance of affection, or with what the offence might have been. The following quotations all come from lower-middle-class informants.

'The father should be head of his household and therefore settle serious things.'

'One usually gets punished by "the boss", and, begging Mum's pardon, Father is the boss of the house.'

'A child should for his own sake have to answer to one authority —and by the very nature of that authority, it ought very properly to be the child's father.'

We have indicated in a number of places, however, that this tradition is changing. Other evidence will be presented in the volume on child-rearing to suggest that when the man is regarded by his wife as unsuccessful in his career, he is a good deal less assertive of his authoritative position.

In other families it may be the mother who is responsible for the ultra-strict joyless super-ego dominance. In Lockwood's sample of black-coated and white-bloused workers, over one-third of the girls from working-class homes married men from a middle-class background.[1] Strictly speaking, such a girl would be 'relatively privileged', and the way she learns about middle-class ways is discussed in the sub-section below. But psychologically she may feel 'relatively deprived'. Myers and Roberts, in the course of the investigation into the relation between mental illness and social background to which reference was made on page 396, found a very interesting phenomenon in this connection. The women in their sample of Class III patients tended to marry older men who were already established in

[1] Working-class girls who marry up in this way may be a rather select group. According to Scott, Illsley and Thomson, the more intelligent daughters of manual workers tend to go in for office work and then to marry men in white-collar jobs. They also tend to have a better education, a superior physique and better health, a lower rate of premature births, still-births and infant-deaths than their less mobile sisters. (Quoted by M. Lipset and R. Bendix, 1955, *Social Mobility in Industrial Society*. Heinemann, London.)

jobs with higher incomes and more security than the younger men had yet achieved. They did not consider men of their own age with similar social backgrounds attractive marriage-partners. But soon after marriage they would realize that the husbands they had married were now near the peak of their careers and not likely to progress much farther. Their apparent success had been due to their greater age and experience, not to their higher social status. Myers and Roberts hazard the guess that, having been affected in their marriage-choice by considerations of mobility, and having been frustrated in their ambitions, they are more likely than other women to transfer their drive to the next generation, and become pushing, demanding mothers (and often devaluing their husbands, relegating them to an unimportant place in the household).

The black-coated clerks may be divided in the same way as those at the executive level: a group of younger people and an older, rather more limited, rather grimmer set. Lockwood found that the older clerks in his sample came more often from a higher social level. Yet he also found that the younger group (aged 18–29 in 1949) was somewhat more drawn from a grammar-school population than his average was. But one would expect the people from a higher social background to have the better education. Lockwood explains these apparent contradictions by the hypothesis (the precise evidence is not available) that those in the older age-groups with the better education had moved out of routine clerical work more often than the others. This is indeed likely, for in the sub-section on Executive Officers it was noted that Walker found many of them to have moved up from the Clerical Grade.[1] So one section of this occupational group consists of people many of whom have been disappointed in their career while others overtook them. Relative to the latter, they feel deprived. Meanwhile they may be working in the same office as young people from a different social background.

This situation may clarify some of the contradictions Walker found at this level, taken as one statistical category and not sub-divided. In so far as it includes the ambitious, his informants in this category were more critical of the promotion-

[1] See also page 385.

system than their seniors were. In so far as they came from a group which in the past lived on low incomes, they expressed less dissatisfaction with the pay—a handful even considered that they were overpaid: a characteristic attitude towards clerks among manual workers. Presumably in accordance with social background and the socialization that goes with it, many regarded inter-level relations in the Civil Service as not democratic enough, while many others thought the discipline too easy-going.

Other attitudes show similar contradictions in this group. The office seems uniformly to be regarded as dull, for instance, though we shall see that this dullness is not always characteristic of the Clerical Officer himself. 'The atmosphere of the lower ranges of the Civil Service is doggedly unintellectual [writes Dunnill]. There is a descent from the atmosphere of school, a kind of heavy indifference and a confirmed scepticism.' He does not feel it inappropriate to quote from another writer, who certainly was not describing the English Civil Service.

> The world is abandoned and the gates close upon the recruit, as private possessions of the body and the mind are systematically destroyed; the will is thrown away; the subject is in a condition as abject as that of St. Ignatius in rags at Montserrat; only after abasement can obedience become an instinct and the old man give place to the new man, the required automaton, fulfilled in corporate pride and corporate wholeness. That is the ultimate reward; in the interim, he sinks restfully and unresponsibly into the dull, kind, corrupt world of the closed community.

That this description is not altogether unjustified is confirmed by Walker, whose sample of Clerical Officers were more conscious than any other grade of the lack of variety and responsibility. These did not value to any great extent the status or interest of their work. Nearly three-quarters of them considered their jobs to be a little or more than a little below their capacities, in spite of the fact that the efficiency ratings recorded for them by their superiors tended to be low rather than high, relative to the ratings of Civil Servants in other grades. One is given an impression of people who did what they felt to be not very useful, not very important work of which they had no reason to be proud, who felt they were capable of better things.

The passage from Dunnill stresses the dullness and evenness of the clerk's life. Gladden presents a very different aspect.

In the Whitley Councils and other committees which enable the staff to make some contribution to Civil Service management, the clerical grades seldom have any difficulty in making their voice heard. This is partly because there are very many of them, but partly, too, because they display a certain directness and militancy that is not always present in their superiors. In the higher grades there are usually several people present at any meeting who are only too capable of seeing two sides to every question. The junior grades have in general less time for sophisticated arguments. They usually know what they want, or some of them do, and they set out to get it.

Dunnill himself, two pages after the reference to the dull kind corrupt world of the closed community, takes a new breath.

We have looked at these people, so far, as officials. It remains to enquire whether they lead more vivid lives outside the office and whether it can be fairly said of the average junior Civil Servant that 'when he sits in place, he is another man'. Surprisingly often, one gets the impression that he is. Many a submissive creature, sitting obediently at her desk from day to day, will be found on closer investigation to be nursing some hidden talent. Unremarkable members of the minor and manipulative grades will turn out to be local councillors or Justices of the Peace. The evening schools and literary institutes of London attract very large numbers of Civil Service typists and clerical officers pursuing, at advanced levels, subjects that would surprise and perhaps scandalize their superiors. And the occasional exhibitions of handicrafts and the plays put on by various Government offices suggest that the lower orders of the service display much greater originality and enterprise outside the office than they are allowed to show at their daily work. The more personal experience one has of individual officers, the more this general impression is reinforced. One is led to the conclusion that in its vast lower depths the service wastes an unconscionable amount of talent. It is notoriously difficult to check impressions of this kind . . . But the story of the indifferent clerk who is found to be a person of some importance in his private world outside the office is repeated so often in so many different forms, that few people who know the lower grades of the service intimately or who have worked in them

Middle-Class Life

can doubt that in many cases the official duties scarcely scratch the surface of the available talent.

Lack of evidence must make us very cautious here, but tentatively it might be permissible to guess that, at the time of Gladden's writing—in the early nineteen-fifties—it was not the older clerks who displayed these characteristics which would normally be correlated with traits which make for promotion to the next grade. By contrast, in what was then a younger group we might find a relatively large number of upper-working-class and lower-middle-class clerks of good intelligence and the kind of upbringing that makes for energetic action, handicapped by relatively inferior schooling (during the war and in the immediate post-war years) and indeed under-privileged in all that makes for a cultivated background.

This impression is strengthened by Clements' account of the managers who rose almost 'from the bottom', a quarter from manual working-class homes, a quarter from middle-class and the other half from lower-middle-class homes. They entered the firms at junior clerical level and typically rose to management—on the works and production side rather than commercial or sales—more slowly than the others in Clements' sample, tending to remain at lower management level.

Due in part to the low level at which they entered industry, and in part to the nature of the jobs they first took up, they have benefited less from on-the-job training courses than many other managers have. The importance to them of part-time studies, however, stands out. Practically all took them for several years. The intensity of their studies is shown by the remarkably high proportion (forty per cent) who have obtained 'professional' qualifications. They were sufficiently educated to feel capable of undertaking these courses and to persist with them, and, in the absence of other advantages, had strong incentives to secure some such qualification. Except for the initial advantage of (usually) grammar school education and a decent home background, these really are self-made men.

They may carry their handicap throughout their career.

The top jobs are often occupied by men of higher social origin, ex-public schoolboys, graduates and men who have come up by the crown-prince, qualified-specialist and special-entrant routes.

The lower jobs have often been recruited from men who have made their way up from the bottom, from elementary schools, and who originated from working- and lower-middle-class homes. These men fill the many junior management posts and find it difficult to get the better jobs. These, in any case, are not so well-paid as superior jobs are, say, in office or commercial management, which, however, are even harder to get. The salary difference between the two sections is quite large, and those in the better jobs become managers much quicker than those in lower management.

The sense of relative deprivation may be strong in them.

In discussing assets and obstacles, some older men recognize that they were fortunate in getting into industry and on to the ladder before the competition of better educated men became more serious. It appears to others that the recruitment of university or professionally qualified men was an obstacle to their own advance even in the early 1930s, and more believe that they have now reached the level where the lack of qualifications or of higher education begins to tell against them. Where this lack is most often admitted to be a handicap, even by the most confident, is in applying to other firms for jobs.[1] . . . Many anticipate further promotion only if their firm or department grows, of which some are quite hopeful. Not all are convinced that the graduate is superior at his job, for many feel that their practical experience is of greater value, and others that they possess such qualities as 'force' and 'drive' or 'quick wits and low cunning' in greater measure than university graduates, and to that extent are better managers . . . Tales are told of being short-listed, from many applicants, with another man, who, however, 'had university education and got the job'.

Very similar attitudes, including the persistence in evening education, are encountered among those who came from working-class homes and whose schooling ended before they were fifteen. Although their social origin might classify them among those who came to be relatively privileged, their experience of the blockage in promotion—the fact that their reference-group is management and not the parental home—places them also among the relatively deprived.

[1] This is another light on the dictum of an old stager quoted by Clements, who said that 'the biggest grousers are those who stay the longest'.

Middle-Class Life

(2) *The relatively privileged*

We come now to those who do not have a family tradition of white collars. The great change in social structure, of which the increase in the number of clerks is one indication, has also meant a relative decrease in the number of manual workers. The sons of manual workers may go into clerical work.

Sample of Woodford informants	Informants' fathers were	
	Non-manual	Manual
	%	%
Non-manual	80	47
Manual	20	53

Lockwood's sample of over 200 male clerks shows a similar trend.[1]

6 per cent came from professional homes
36 per cent from lower professional, small business, office workers', salesmen's or shop assistants' homes
17 per cent from foremen's homes
30 per cent from the homes of skilled men
12 per cent from the homes of non-skilled men.

These sons are presumably distinguished by an upbringing and a personality which makes the opportunities for social mobility more possible and more palatable to them than to others. At the same time, they must also have traits in common with their manual cousins and brothers.

To these common traits may be attributed the 'directness and militancy of the clerical workers at Whitley meetings' which Gladden noticed and to which reference was made in the previous sub-section. This directness and militancy may be seen as one aspect of a rather tough-minded, hard-headed approach to other people, contrasting with the rather fearful subordination of some other clerical workers and some junior executive officers, contrasting also with the 'charming' technique of the higher Civil Servant and his other upper-middle-class counterparts, and finally, contrasting also with the manual worker's more typical reaction, for though the latter may share the lack of inhibition about expressing aggressive feelings, he often has

[1] From D. Glass (1954), *Social Mobility in Britain*, chap. IV.

not the verbal skill to fight a case tenaciously and convincingly on rational grounds.

If we compare the work-situation of the clerical worker with that of the manual worker, we see that it is in a number of ways less 'tough'. The clerk is more fortunate, for instance, in the extent to which his life is ordered by a more liberal routine than a machine allows. The pace at which he works is determined by impersonal office-routine and his own inner compulsions, less often by a machine. Lockwood describes the alternatives in the following terms:

> First, there are those machines which facilitate part of some complicated work, such as for instance the calculator used by a cashier. The machine is not used full-time: it is an ancillary device which takes over the mental drudgery involved in routine addition, subtraction, multiplication and division. Second, there are those machines which are not used continuously, but where the operator really directs them after having thought out certain details of the performance. Typing is a good example of this kind of work; the typist is usually specialized in relation to the machine, but the work involves discretion, and the tempo of the work is her own. Thirdly, there are those machines which are merely supplemented by the operator, the latter becoming really a cog in the machine. It is really in this third type of operation that the clerk is reduced to the status of a machine-minder, which for Marx and Veblen was the distinguishing characteristic of modern factory labour. The number of office machines which subordinate the work of the clerk to the tempo of the machine . . . is extremely small.

The clerk's experience of authority is also less 'tough' than that of the manual worker. He is less likely to be regarded as a 'hand', as potentially recalcitrant material.

> There is no radical break between management and the clerks corresponding to that between the 'office' and the 'works'. The clerk co-operates with management and supervisors in a day-to-day routine and is not simply directed by them. For a hundred years the manuals of office procedure have suggested that you do not get the best out of your clerks by ordering them about bluntly. At every point, the working contact between manager and supervisor, between supervisor and clerk, introduces a personal and continuous element into office organization and obviates the

harsh, impersonal and purely instrumental character of the command which industrial sociologists are beginning to single out as an important source of latent hostility on the part of the factory worker.

In a footnote, Lockwood amplifies this contention of his in a manner which strikingly recalls and contrasts with the relationship one of Zweig's informants postulated between toughness in the home and toughness in the work-situation.[1]

The peculiar role of the foreman, like that of the non-commissioned officer, often requires the incumbent to transmit orders to subordinates without fully understanding the reason behind the command. This leads to the execution of the order in a spirit of undue harshness (e.g. violent swearing) as a reaction to his own lack of comprehension and conviction, and thus alienates those working under him, not simply in a personal sense, but also as the visible representative of 'them up there'.[2]

Because of the work he does, and for other reasons, the first-generation clerk may be more conscious of his difference from his father than of his resemblance to him. He may feel, as Lockwood puts it, that in background, working conditions, proximity to authority and opportunity of social mobility, he can claim a higher social status than most manual workers. But the ambiguity of his occupational prestige shows: 'in terms of productive contribution, income, skill, masculinity and group loyalty, he may be accorded a lower social status, especially by the manual workers themselves'. Zweig's interviews led him to the same conclusions.

The black-coated worker, who works partly with his hands and partly with his brain, an office worker of lower rank who is paid a weekly wage, regards himself and is treated as belonging to the working class, but with a difference. Many manual workers, and certainly most craftsmen, look down upon the office worker. 'An office worker can earn five to six pounds a week, and I can earn twice as much,' said a craftsman to me, 'and as the work of a black-coated man has mostly to do with figures, it is most deadening to the mind and spirit.' And strangely enough, most clerical

[1] See pages 182 fn., 292–3 and 298.
[2] Cf. Gouldner's identification of 'punishment-centred' authority, referred to on page 382.

workers seemed to think the same. I came across some marginal cases where former clerical workers took up manual work and professed to like it more. 'Office work,' they said, 'was more monotonous and mentally tiring.'

Sometimes parents explained to Zweig that their sons were not strong enough to take up manual work and were therefore compelled to do office work, which had no prospects, was deadening and badly paid. But the deprecation of white-collar work is not only a question of such considerations as these. Lockwood points out that, as late as 1947, Thomas found that clerical workers ranked only above unskilled workers in terms of occupational training received. And he quotes from an article 'What is a clerk?' in *The Clerk* (1945):

> No authoritative body has ever bothered to put down in black and white what qualifications should entitle a person to call himself a clerk . . . The present low standard of qualification among clerks is a handicap to the Union by lowering respect for the craft among employers and workers alike . . . With better qualifications and grading will come greater craft consciousness.[1]

A parent of the traditional status-assenting kind, who has no ambitions for the social advancement of his family in the next generation, who has himself undergone a lengthy apprenticeship and is now in a highly skilled, highly paid manual occupation, is unlikely to be impressed by his son's achievement in clerking merely by virtue of the extra year he had at school. And in a previous sub-section reasons were given why the boy himself, coming into an office with low morale, may lack the feeling of self-respect and personal value which good performance of the task gives to the craftsman or the professional.[2]

So, what with the atmosphere in the office and the absence of respect from fathers and contemporaries who regard him as less skilled, less strong, less manly than themselves, the young clerk may for a while be in an unhappy position. In the past, young men may have reacted to this by a more tenacious insistence on what they perceived to be middle-class characteristics; it is possible that jeans, jazz and coffee-bars repre-

---

[1] Cf. pages 98–9 and 354.
[2] See also the quotation from Hoggart on page 580 in the volume on child-rearing.

sent, among many other things, a newer and more relaxed reaction to the dilemma. There may therefore be a difference between younger and older clerks, reflected in their reactions to relative deprivation. Girls, on the other hand, will suffer less from this, since middle-class tender-mindedness does not reflect on their sexual adequacy as it tends to do in the case of the man.

The white-bloused clerical worker is therefore in a position to act as a channel by means of which middle-class values directly affect the next generation. We then get the phenomenon of status-dissent. Some implications of this are to be discussed at greater length in the next sub-section and in the volume on child-rearing, but now is the appropriate point to look at the work-situation which enables her to do this.

One consequence of the small tightly knit work-groups [in the office as Lockwood describes it] is that the management of clerical work is not carried out with the same kind of impersonal discipline that is a common feature of factory organization; on the contrary it tends to be performed in a social context which must of necessity be fairly intimate in all but the very largest offices. The division of labour not only splinters the work-force among departments and through occupational differentiation, but also brings clerical staff into relatively close and enduring relations of co-operation with managers and supervisors . . . The supervisor or manager of an office is normally an older man and his assistants younger women; and whether the ensuing relationship is a paternal, a petty tyrannical or a sexually exploitative one, it is essentially personal.

There is here an opportunity to contact and take over selected aspects of middle-class culture. With more interaction, a greater liking and a wider communality of norms is to be expected.[1]

If the first-generation white-collar worker had a mother like this, of a status-dissenting kind, married to a manual worker, taking an interest in his education, encouraging his ambitions and interacting more with him, he is less likely to have the more extreme forms of tough masculine sex-identification which cast such a pall over the intelligence of many bright boys in working-class homes. The sharing of life-experiences with the mother is

[1] See pages 420–5 for a lengthier discussion.

also likely to be encouraged by the fact that he will come home from school at an hour when the other men of the family have not yet returned from work. He has more time with her, for longer.[1]

The relatively privileged clerical worker is by definition for a time on the border of the class division between manual and non-manual.

> Everything in his environment contrives to strengthen his attachment to the sentiments and way of life of the classes above him [writes Lockwood]. His economic position made him forward-looking, striving and individualistic. His working-life brings him into close contact with members of the middle class and from them he borrows the prestige which surrounds authority. The family from which he originated was middle class, if not in substance, at least in spirit. The basic skill of literacy which he possessed set him apart from the working man and gave him a foothold on the lowest rung of the middle-class ladder. All in all, the pull of the middle-class world was too strong for him to evade. In any case, he was a willing captive.

We must therefore look briefly at some differences between the way of life of the traditional status-assenting manual worker's family and the clerical worker's family, differences of which the 'relatively privileged' are likely to be particularly conscious. Lockwood summarizes the evidence on savings and other aspects of financial security, on house-ownership, on family size, educational aspirations and class identification. The figures refer, of course, to the whole occupational group, those who feel deprived as well as the more privileged.[2]

(*a*) The 'mean liquid assets' of clerks and salesworkers amounted to £190, as opposed to £150 for skilled manual workers and £134 for unskilled. As regards superannuation, the position of the office workers was also still noticeably different from that of the ordinary wage-earner. A 1952 survey quoted by Lockwood found that four out of five firms provided superannuation schemes for their male clerical staff. As regards

---

[1] See Hoggart (pages 244 ff. in the Pelican edition) on how this feels, subjectively experienced, and pages 492-4 and 512 ff. of the present work for further discussion,
[2] Statistics on house-ownership and savings come from H. F. Lydall (1955), *British Incomes and Savings*, Oxford University Press.

unemployment, figures since 1930 show that clerks suffer much less from this kind of occupational insecurity than do manual workers, the figures being five as opposed to twelve per cent. Lockwood adds, however, that less communal provision was made for the former.

(*b*) 34 per cent of the households headed by clerks and sales-workers live in homes they own, as contrasted with 23 per cent where the head is a skilled manual worker, 15 per cent where the head was unskilled.

(*c*) Lockwood refers to a preliminary investigation conducted by the Population Investigation Committee of the London School of Economics, which seems to indicate that male clerks tend to marry later than manual workers. He comments that

> a relatively small family and a strong desire for the educational success of one's children have been the hall-marks of middle-class status since the closing decades of the nineteenth century. Taken together they represent a concern with social mobility through individual achievement and a conscious discounting of the present against the future.[1]

(*d*) Where educational aspirations are concerned, the clerical worker ranks considerably higher on this index of middle-class identification than the skilled manual worker. Of a sample of clerks who were asked if they would send their children to a private school if they failed to get into a grammar school, 26 per cent replied in the affirmative as contrasted to 7 per cent skilled manual workers.[2] 59 per cent of clerks wanted university or professional education for their children as compared with 23 per cent of skilled manual workers. (They were even more decided in these ambitions than professional parents, only 45 per cent of whom expressed this desire.)[3]

(*e*) Deriving his arguments from a number of studies, which have since been confirmed, Lockwood comes to the conclusion that the majority of office workers are predisposed to identify their position as middle class, though there is a substantial

---

[1] See also pages 442–3, 503 and 586 in the volume on child-rearing.

[2] F. M. Martin, 'An inquiry into parents' preferences in secondary education', being chap. VII of D. Glass, ed. (1954), *Social Mobility in Britain*.

[3] Ministry of Education (1954), *Early Leaving*. A report of the Central Advisory Council for Education. See also pages 601–4.

number claiming working-class status, especially among the lower grades. This (often younger) minority seems to range from two-fifths to a quarter. Lockwood also quotes evidence that those who see themselves as middle class tend to magnify the distance which separates them from the working class. They see the typical working man as a navvy, a dustman, a road sweeper, rather than as the skilled man who might too awkwardly resemble their fathers.[1]

In the course of his discussion of the black-coated worker's marginal position, Lockwood argues that the frequent accusations of 'snobbishness' levelled at the clerk were founded on an exaggerated assertion of his middle-classness. Because he was insecure socially, he sought to maximize the social distance between himself and the class immediately below him. (The lack of comparative material kept Lockwood, like so many other writers, in ignorance of the widespread English fascination with social stratification and the widespread fear of contamination by an inferior group—each investigator seems to have felt that it was a peculiarity of the stratum he studied.)

> The black-coated worker's impulse was to orient himself to the middle class, and this very act of identification produced reactions from the working class that reinforced his attachment to the former and his alienation from the latter.

This is in line with the idea discussed in the chapter on changing aspects of working-class life, that class antagonisms are at their most acute where consumption-patterns most closely resemble one another.[2] In the previous sub-section also we had occasion to quote the disapproving remarks made by middle-class Woodford people about the spending habits of the working class. Yet many of these middle-class people were distinguishable from manual workers not by family origin but only by present occupation. They were reacting against a life they had left behind.

In other areas of life, also, this background may lead to

[1] John Bonham (1954), *The Middle Class Vote*, Faber and Faber, London. Also Lockwood's own work on file at the British Institute of Public Opinion.
F. M. Martin, 'Some subjective aspects of social status', in Glass, op. cit. Mark Benney *et al.* (1956), *How People Vote*, Routledge and Kegan Paul, London.
[2] See pages 266-9 and Dagenham, page 113.

Middle-Class Life

contemptuous attitudes. In the course of an investigation not primarily concerned with the social class of the teacher, Himmelweit and her associates found that in some ways the teachers were prejudiced against some boys.[1] Having asked the teachers who were the five most popular boys in the class, and having found that significantly greater numbers of middle-class boys were mentioned by the teachers, they also gave a sociometric test to the boys themselves. They thereupon found that the boys were not affected by class considerations in the same way as the teachers: the five boys who were in fact most popular with other boys were no more likely to come from the middle classes than could be accounted for by chance.

They looked further at the teachers' attitudes and found that those who had come from working-class families had a distinct tendency to opine that the wrong kind of boy was being allowed into grammar schools nowadays; this in spite of the fact that they themselves had been 'the wrong kind of boy' in earlier days. These teachers tended also to be in general more authoritarian in outlook.

> Grammar schools can exert a great—if well-meant or even unconscious—pressure to remove their working-class pupils from attachment to their homes and neighbourhoods; they tend to seek to attach them to middle-class values . . . A substantial proportion [of the teachers] not only reject their working-class background but reject it with scorn, and adhere grimly to their new middle-class attitudes.[2]

These last, we are told, are 'rigidly orthodox . . . (and) . . . wish to preserve a hierarchical society'. They sometimes explain their rejection of working-class life by an unpleasant meritocratic rationalization, arguing that those who remain in the working class nowadays *deserve* to do so, that they are 'those who lack abilities' and have been left behind because they were not good enough to get on. (About half of the sample have become teachers themselves; and so the process continues.)

[1] H. Himmelweit *et al.* (1955), 'Socio-economic background and personality', *Internat. Soc. Sc. Bulletin*, VII.
[2] A review in *The Observer*, Feb. 11, 1962, by Richard Hoggart, of B. Jackson and D. Marsden. *Education and the Working Class* (1962), Routledge and Kegan Paul, London. Himmelweit also has some relevant findings on this, further discussed on pages 569.

These are the accents of marginality. Yet they may be, or even already may have been, a transitional phenomenon. It is now undoubtedly already a little misleading to speak of the middle-class way of life in this connection. What has come about bears only about as much resemblance to the traditional upper-middle-class way of life as it does to the traditional working-class culture. The product is in fact that of a well-to-do working class of a non-traditional kind. Lockwood himself sees this and speaks of the 'growing haziness of the frontier of working and middle class', attributing it to the increase in skilled manual as well as of routine non-manual occupations.

> To be sure [he continues], the social centres of gravity of the two classes are today still located in the professional and lesser skilled manual occupations. It is here that the external manifestations of the social differences that go to make up a status order in society are most clearly marked. Differences in speech, dress, age of marriage, family size, interest in education, provision for the future, political outlook, respectability and so on. But in between these two poles the differences are quantitative rather than qualitative.

There is evidence to suggest that economic and social forces have produced such changes in working-class life that some manual workers have acquired middle-class aspirations. To these we now turn.

THE MIDDLE-CLASS MANUAL WORKER

The white collar is ceasing to be the easily identified distinguishing mark of the middle-class man. Not only have many clerks of middle-class origin suffered a relative reduction in their standard of living, not only have many clerks come from manual working-class families and made changes in their manner of life accordingly, but manual workers themselves are also adopting a middle-class way of life. The beginnings of this process were perceptible in the chapter on the status-dissenting working class.

Lockwood found that clerks of working-class origin tended to marry girls from middle-class homes. There is evidence that, in America at least, this will have effects on the next generation.

Middle-Class Life

Many parents who push children towards social mobility are members of mixed-class marriages . . . A lower-middle-class woman who marries a man from the upper part of the working class usually begins to try and recoup her original class status either by reforming and elevating her husband's behaviour to meet lower-middle-class standards or by seeking to train and propel her children towards the status she once had.[1]

Jackson and Marsden investigated the social background of working-class children who had completed a grammar school education. They found that in their eighty-eight cases, there were twenty families in which at least one parent had also been to a grammar school.

There were twice as many instances in which this was the mother rather than the father. In these homes the child had been born into an atmosphere of educational excitement and ambition; ambition which had been thwarted in the parents and now pressed intensely on the growing boy or girl.

Floud, Halsey and Martin provide evidence that parents' attitudes do, in favourable circumstances, make a difference to the child's acceptance into a grammar school, and hence to their ultimate position in the class-structure. To increase our confidence in our speculations about the function of mothers in mixed-class marriages, we may note that they also found that the mothers of working-class children who had gained entry into a grammar school had before their marriage often followed an occupation which was superior to that of their husbands. As is to be expected more generally speaking, the parents of children who got into a grammar school were better educated than the parents of unsuccessful candidates. This was almost as true for the women as for the men.[2]

It has been suggested that over-conformity to middle-class values characterizes the working-class families who have high aspirations for their children. Himmelweit has reported a study

[1] Quoted by M. Lipset and R. Bendix (1959), *Social Mobility in Industrial Society* (Heinemann, London), from Allison Davis, 'Personality and social mobility', *The School Review* (1957), LXV. See also pages 397, 415-16, 581 and 583-4.
[2] J. Floud, A. H. Halsey and F. Martin (1956), *Education and Social Opportunity*, Heinemann, London. See also pages 322 and 550.

in which the values of four different sets of people were tested: secondary-modern-schoolboys and grammar-schoolboys from either working-class or middle-class homes.[1] It was expected that the most marked difference in values would be found between the two social classes. This would then confirm that the working-class grammar-schoolboys were acquiring new values by virtue of their schooling or their association with middle-class children. (To the matter of friendship we return on pages 503 and 600.) But this was not the case. These boys had parents who were quite clearly dissenting from their working-class status. In fact, they had a more middle-class set of values (as defined in the study, in terms of hard work and rational-legalist virtues generally) than any other group, more middle-class than the middle-class parents themselves. 'Far from coming from a home where the values conflicted with those taught at school, these boys tended to come from the homes of over-conformers to middle-class values.'[2] It may be that this enabled the boys to pass the eleven-plus examination into the grammar school in the first place.

Where do these values come from? They may have come from a mother with a middle-class background who has married a manual worker and is now determined to regain a middle-class position for her offspring. But if she herself has a working-class background, determined that her children shall get on, how does she know what is important and what is not important for acceptance in a higher social milieu? Perhaps from working in an office, though she may have left to get married half a dozen years ago.[3] In this she has an advantage over the mother for whom the mass media of communication are the only guide.[4]

The general rise in the standards of living, the increased educational opportunities, the availability of mass-produced goods and all the other changes which led to a break-up of tradition, have led to a good deal of confusion, in the sense that people think of their social class in different ways. This is true not only for the clerks of working-class origin who were discussed in the previous sub-section. Of Zweig's sample of over

[1] H. Himmelweit (1955), op. cit., page 419.   [2] See also pages 568–9.
[3] See also pages 399 and 415.   [4] See also page 597 fn.

three hundred men ranging from the supervisory to the non-skilled grade, two-thirds placed themselves in the working class.[1] About a sixth beat about the bush or could not place themselves, and another sixth placed themselves firmly in the middle class. If we consider the foremen separately, half of them placed themselves in the middle class, half in the working class. And although Willmott and Young reckoned their middle classes rather exclusively, not so the people they studied! Nearly half of their sample of manual workers said they considered themselves to be middle class. Indeed several said upper middle, and the bulk said middle middle.

The question Zweig had asked was: 'How do you place yourself, working class or middle class or otherwise?' In their answers, some showed an awareness that the class structure was collapsing at this level.[2]

> 'Classes are coming nearer—the top grades of the working class are middle class really', 'Working class and middle class are the same thing'. 'Actually I don't see any difference: I earn as much as a shop-keeper', 'There are no differences; I live in the same neighbourhood as my manager, have the same kind of house and have a car'.

Some made a distinction between being working class and being poor. They did not feel that they belonged to the bottom layer of society. 'I am working class but comfortably off.' Of others, Zweig sensed that though they called themselves working class, they did not in fact believe they were, but would have regarded it as an act of snobbery to place themselves elsewhere. Such people said: 'It would be snobbish if I said otherwise', or, 'I regard myself as working class, while others would take me for middle class', or, 'Although I have a house and a car, I am still working class'.

For these people, the meaning of social class had changed until it is almost the opposite of the classic Marxist definition. They reckoned social class not according to relationship to the means of production, but according to consumption. This suits the social psychologist very well, because above a certain level

---

[1] F. Zweig (1961), *The Worker in an Affluent Society*, Heinemann, London.
[2] See also the discussion in Dagenham, chap. IX, 'Affluence, status and class'.

of income, consumption patterns are very good indices of culture patterns. Willmott and Young provide evidence which is relevant here. The manual workers who thought of themselves as middle class were distinguishable from those who identified with the working class by virtue of their ownership of certain possessions which traditionally require middle-class saving and spending habits.

Percentage owning	Self-ascribed social status	
	middle class	working class
	%	%
House	56	36
Car	39	20
Telephone	38	20

Zweig notes a similar correlation in his study of the affluent worker. Out of the hundred men who did not put themselves in the working class, half owned a house, nearly half a car. Willmott and Young conclude that the social class to which people felt they belonged was associated very strongly with the way they spent their money.[1]

For many, social class depends not so much on occupation or income or education, not so much on the world of production as on the world of consumption.

House ownership and the residential area are, in affluent conditions, obvious criteria for class-identification. We may guess that it is because they lived in Woodford, a middle-class suburb, that so remarkably high a proportion of manual workers thought of themselves as belonging to the middle class. In Dagenham, a one-class estate with many rented houses, the proportion of middle-class manual workers was very much smaller, not least because they moved out and bought a house elsewhere. Zweig is very much alive to this connection. After noting that his manual workers often mentioned house property in their discussions of their own social class, he gives a variety of illustrative quotations.

'Your own house puts you up in class, doesn't it?' 'I live in a middle-class neighbourhood where everyone has his own house.'

[1] See also pages 251 and 330.

Middle-Class Life

'I try to get into the middle class; having my own house, that was a start.'

Often he is not satisfied with the neighbourhood when his standard goes up, so he moves out in order to 'give his children a better chance'. He becomes 'respectability-minded', one could say even snobbish; he belongs to a class of his own among the working men, finding himself, as he often says, on the border of the middle classes.

Two daughters from Dagenham, now living in semi-detached houses of their own in private suburbs, expressed their views like this:

'I certainly wouldn't live at Dagenham. Certainly not. It's perfectly awful. The class of people living there—without being snooty—they're a shocking class of people.'

'I don't like the place. It's not that we're snobs, but I find it a depressing place. After all, it's a slum clearance estate, isn't it?'[1]

'There's more scope for the children here. I'm not a snob by any means, but if you bring the children up with, shall we say, people with better income brackets, they tend to look for higher things in life.'[2]

With different spending habits and different neighbours go other new life-experiences and new perspectives.

House property [writes Zweig] also brings a man into contact with life insurance and banking. To start with, he often has to insure himself for life when engaging on a long-term mortgage. He usually gets a cheque book, since he has to pay rates, mortgage charges, insurance, and so on. He starts thinking about interest rates, local rates and local council affairs, he watches local developments in the movement of population in his neighbourhood. He wants respectable neighbours who keep their property in good order as that affects the value of his own.[3]

He adopts other middle-class habits. Of the manual workers in Woodford who call themselves middle class 52 per cent attend church, 42 per cent go to social clubs—higher percentages than the 36 per cent and 27 per cent respectively of manual workers who call themselves working class. A shop steward in Zweig's sample, having lived for two years in his own modern house, observed: 'In the previous house the front door was never

[1] See also pages 243-4. [2] Compare page 597. [3] See also page 239.

425

meant to be used; we had a settee across it. Everyone, including the postman, called at the back door. Now it is different. We've moved to the front.' Zweig comments that the move to the front has a deeper meaning. 'It stands for the shedding of the sense of inferiority of the old-fashioned workman.'

To buy a car or a house, to plan a holiday abroad, to take out life insurance, are not acts which depend simply on earning more money. The ability to save and to put up with present discomfort for the sake of a future gain is required, a gift attributed normally to the middle-class mentality, its absence being applauded or deplored in the working classes. This is now changing. Mr. Lloyd, who had arrived in the middle class and whose experience was quoted on page 328 in the sub-section on Woodford, provided one illustration of this change. Zweig quotes an electrician (N.B. a skilled man), married eighteen months and living in furnished rooms, whose statement comprises all the elements required for the identification of a high *achievement motive*.[1]

'We are saving about £10 a week to get a house of our own. My wife works as a telephonist. She would rather have the inconvenience of night-shifts to get what we want. If you have an object in front of you, you can do it easily. I want everything first class and put in the hours for it. As soon as we get £500 for a deposit we will buy a first-class house.'

In this case, as in Mr. Lloyd's, and as generally, the attitude of the wife is of foremost importance. She can encourage or discourage. For many men, marriage made the great difference. Zweig heard men say often: 'Since I married I take the job more seriously', or, 'I am a better time keeper', or, 'I am more careful about the job', or, 'I feel a sense of responsibility to the job'.

This is a newly evolving pattern. Zweig observed a difference between the young married men in their twenties and the older group which showed the former to be markedly ambitious and status-dissenting.

---

[1] 'Achievement motivation leads to the perception of performance in terms of standards of excellence, so that discrepancies from this frame of reference can produce positive and negative emotion.' For detailed discussion see pages 506 ff.

The whole group was doing very well, with their main effort directed towards getting a house and building up a home . . . About one third saved more than £4 a week . . . Most men in this group worked very hard, putting in long hours or applying for shifts . . . This group is more promotion-minded than any other group, often being encouraged in this by their wives. I heard such remarks as 'My wife encourages me to go as high as I can' . . . It is the most acquisitive or at least the most money-minded group.

Two trends may be discerned, each exemplifying an aspect of middle-class life, one attractive, one unattractive. The unattractive side is the money-minded, promotion-minded side, which Zweig considers to be peculiarly characteristic of the semi-skilled worker. The attractive side is the full blossoming into a professional attitude of what must have been, before the depressed pre-war days, the craftsman's pride in his work. Thus the Radby Report notes in connection with the better grade (IV and V) households that

generally speaking it may be said that the attitude of the men to their work is good. Work is not regarded merely as an evil, made necessary by the desire for 'beer money'. Work is a means to an end—that of building up a pleasant home—but it is also something about which to plan ahead to some extent. Some of the men had been apprenticed and had attended evening classes in order to learn more about their job . . . There may also be pride in the job . . . Two miners are keen First Aid men. They feel they are more useful employees at the pits because of this, and at the same time gain greater satisfaction from their work. Similarly, a skilled engineer was said by his wife to 'have worked his way up from being a garage-hand', whilst a policeman was studying for his Sergeants' Examination.

These feelings of self-confidence and of the value of effort are of course partly the result of the changed circumstances which validate them. Zweig notes that many more men are now satisfied with their work and working conditions than was the case before the war. 'I enjoy my work now, but if you had asked me the same question before the war, I would have said definitely not' and 'In my life I had jobs to endure, believe me. It was different in those days.' But Zweig is also aware that while such circumstances affect attitudes, they do not determine them.

Aspects of Adult Life in England

There is a basic diversity in attitudes to work between skilled and semi-skilled workers. The former mostly took an interest in the work itself. The nature, tone and intensity of their interest differed very greatly from that of semi-skilled men. They would say: 'I was always interested in metals', 'I like fiddling with machines, you can always learn something new', 'I like making things'. The skilled man has a trade which he follows no matter which firm he is working for; the semi-skilled man looks for a job whose nature often changes from one firm to another. The skilled man often said, 'If I had my time over again, I would do the same' [indicating that he regarded himself as fulfilling his vocation, as fully competent within his field]. The skilled man showed a longer service record than the semi-skilled. The majority of them disliked piece-work, regarding it as conducive to scamped work, while the semi-skilled on the whole preferred it. They disliked nightwork much more than the semi-skilled, regarding it as not conducive to a good piece of work.

Among these men Zweig also notes the connection between respect for skill and lack of formal leadership which were commented upon in the discussions on Ashton and on the professional man.[1]

In one department in a steel-works, with a complex division of labour, I asked, 'Who is your leader?' This was answered differently by men on the same job. One would say: 'The blower who is actually in control of the process', another might say, if he were a vesselman: 'The first vesselman', or if he were a pitman: 'The first pitman'. Still others might say: 'The foreman', or 'the shift manager'. . . . Authority, as far as the men are concerned, is actually split between the blower, the foreman and the shift manager, even if one disregards the Union delegate who would have a great deal to say if something unexpected happened or a change were required.

Clearly, therefore, we have come a long way since 1948, when the two-class model was still appropriate enough to allow so perceptive an observer as Zweig to write:

The most striking difference in the mentality of both classes comes out in regard to saving and the betterment of conditions. A working-class man does not save as a rule; when he saves, he

[1] See pages 98 and 358-9.

428

saves with a definite purpose which is in the near future . . . But he does not believe that he can better his position by saving, or by any individual effort. We have to remember that a working man rarely, if at all, goes higher in the social ladder. A lorry-driver of twenty-one would earn £6 and so would a lorry-driver of forty or fifty . . . There is practically no promotion in the manual jobs. The worker relies primarily on organization, and protection of the community. His trade union and the community should give him protection against ill-health, accident, unemployment, or old age, and the contributions he pays he regards as a sufficient saving effort. The money he gets is for living—i.e. for housekeeping and for his pleasures. On the contrary, a middle-class man thinks first of all of the betterment of his condition by his own individual efforts, and he does not rely on organization at all. All the time he is thinking how he can climb up the ladder of social achievement, while the working man is content to stay put as he is.

As Zweig himself recognized later, we now know that in this borderland between middle class and manual work there are working men 'thinking all the time how they can climb up the ladder' and traditional middle-class men who want 'only to stay put'. Raymond Williams also, who in another mood castigated what he called 'the ladder version of society' which he attributed to the middle classes and to those who move away from the working-class tradition, showed a finer insight when he wrote:

> A culture, while it is being lived, is always in part unknown, in part unrealized. The making of a community is always an exploration, for consciousness cannot precede creation and there is no formula for unknown experience. A good community, a living culture, will, because of this, not only make room for but actively encourage all and any who can contribute to the advance in consciousness which is the common need. We need to consider every attachment, every value, with our whole attention; for we do not know the future, we can never be certain of what may enrich it; we can only, now, listen to and consider whatever may be offered and take up what we can . . .
>
> Thus, in the working-class movement, while the clenched fist is a necessary symbol, the clenching ought never to be such that the hand cannot open and the fingers extend, to discover and give a shape to the newly forming reality.[1]

[1] R. Williams (1958), *Culture and Society*, Chatto and Windus, London. Cf. the quotation cited on pages 279–80.

Appendix

SOCIOLOGICAL CATEGORIES FOR SOCIAL DIFFERENCES

OUR interest lies mainly in those aspects of social stratification which have a bearing on the formation of characteristic personality-traits. But because sociologists concerned with different aspects of stratification have made available a variety of social class categorizations and because the evidence we have used comes from various sources, various criteria of classification must be set out, however cursorily.

The simplest is the **Registrar-General's** classification of census-data into five social classes:

	Percentage of working and retired men in Britain (*1951 Census*)	Percentage of working and retired men in Woodford and Wanstead (*1951 Census*)	Percentage of working and retired men in Woodford sample	Percentage of men in the Banbury sample
I. Professional	3	8	16	2
II. Intermediate	15	29	31	14
III. Skilled	53	50	43	55
IV. Partly skilled	16	7	5	20
V. Unskilled	13	6	5	10

This grouping [one authority comments] leaves much to be desired. It is based on the allocation to social classes of broad occupational groups, within which there are bound to be people of different levels of skill and earning widely different incomes. Classes I and II are relatively homogeneous, though they contain a number of anomalies. Teachers, for example, are placed in Class II, away from the bulk of the professions, and so are actors, actresses and other artists; musicians are even relegated to Class III, as, incidentally, are the small band of men and women classed as cricketers, footballers, golfers and so on. Class II is

430

not defined by its title, but over half of it is made up of lesser professional, administrative and managerial occupations, the remainder being farmers, shopkeepers and small employers. In fact, the greater part of what we call the lower middle class is in Class II, the remainder being in Class III. The size and heterogeneity of the latter class is the main defect of the census classification, since it contains over half of occupied and retired males, and has within it vast numbers of skilled manual workers—perhaps 70 per cent of the total in Class III are so described—as well as shop assistants, clerks, typists, foremen, supervisors, and so on.[1]

A slightly more informative picture for our purpose is provided by the Registrar-General's other census classification: into socio-economic groups.

Socio-economic group	Percentage of occupied and retired males in 1951
Agricultural	
1. Farmers	2
2. Agricultural workers	5
Non-Agricultural	
I. Non-manual	
3. Higher administrative, professional and managerial (including large employers)	3
4. Intermediate administrative, professional and managerial (including teachers and salaried staff)	9
5. Shopkeepers and other small employers	4
6. Clerical workers	5
7. Shop assistants	3
8. Personal service	2
II. Manual	
9. Foremen	4
10. Skilled workers	36
11. Semi-skilled workers	11
12. Unskilled workers	13
III. Others	
13. Armed Forces (other ranks)	3

[1] D. Caradog Jones, A. Carr Saunders, C. A. Moser (1958 edn.), *A Survey of Social Conditions in England and Wales*, Clarendon Press, Oxford.

Appendix

The only exact correspondence between this and the previous scheme is between Class I and group 3. Elsewhere the allocation to groups cuts across social class. This second table is of particular interest because of the way the traditional two-class model is (assumed to be) still perfectly representative of the rural situation. Group 13 is interesting for the same reason. Officers are presumably gentlemen and belong elsewhere on the scale.

The Hall/Jones scale used by Glass and his collaborators distinguishes seven classes.[1]

1. Professional and High Administrative
2. Managerial and Executive
3. Inspectional, Supervisory and other Non-manual, Higher Grade
4. Inspectional, Supervisory and other Non-manual, Lower Grade
5. Skilled Manual and routine Grades of Non-manual
6. Semi-skilled Manual
7. Unskilled Manual

The four top categories are of especial interest for the study of the middle classes. They are described by Moser and Hall in the following way:

> Category 1 includes all occupations calling for highly specialized experience and frequently the possession of a degree or comparable professional qualification necessitating a long period of education and training. Category 2 includes those responsible for initiating and/or implementing policy, e.g. personnel manager, headmaster (elementary school), while those in category 3 have no such responsibility but may have some degree of authority over others, e.g. police inspector, assistant teacher (elementary school). In category 4, authority over others is restricted, but the nature of the job itself involves a measure of responsibility, e.g. costing clerk, relieving officer.

Lockwood allows for seven categories among the middle class alone:

[1] C. A. Moser and J. R. Hall, 'The social grading of occupations', in D. Glass (ed.) (1954), *Social Mobility in Britain*, Routledge and Kegan Paul, London; also J. Hall and D. Caradog Jones (1950), 'The social grading of occupations', *Brit. J. Sociol.*, I.

Sociological Categories for Social Differences

1. Professional occupations, owners of large businesses (employing more than fifty persons), middle and higher management, officers in the armed forces.
2. Lower professions, such as teachers, nurses, qualified technicians.
3. Self-employed persons with small businesses, including farmers, also lesser management in shops, offices, etc.
4. Office workers, clerks, shorthand-typists, book-keepers, secretaries, cost clerks, wages clerks, etc.
5. Salesmen and commercial travellers.
6. Shop assistants.
7. Foremen, lower inspectional and supervisory workers in industry, N.C.O.s in the armed forces, policemen, etc.[1]

Cole is even more liberal in the number of sub-groupings he allows in the middle class, though curiously illiberal in the people about whose middle-class affiliation he has doubts.[2]

(*a*) The main body of heads of private businesses, or of active partners or directors in businesses, except the greatest, concerned with manufacture or wholesale trading, or with other commercial or financial occupations.

(*b*) The main body of salaried administrators, managers, technicians and accountants in similar types of business, including businesses publicly or co-operatively owned; and the higher salaried officers of a wide range of institutions and societies, from political parties and Trade Unions or Trade Associations to philanthropic, educational and cultural bodies.

(*c*) The members of the principal recognized professions, whether salaried or working as consultants and remunerated by professional fees, including medical men, lawyers, ministers of religion, officers of the armed services, the upper ranges of the teaching profession, and the upper and middle ranges of the artistic professions.

(*d*) The higher and middle grades of the Civil Service, the Local Government Service and of other public or semi-public administrative services; and the corresponding grades of 'voluntary' social service employees.

(*e*) The big and middle shopkeepers, garage keepers, hotel keepers, and also the analogous groups of employed managers,

---

[1] D. Lockwood (1958), *The Black-Coated Worker*, Allen and Unwin, London.
[2] G. D. H. Cole (1950), 'The conception of the middle classes', *Brit. J. Sociol.*, I.

433

accountants and other officers employed by joint stock companies operating in these fields.

(*f*) The large and middle farmers, and with them the relatively small numbers of managerial salaried workers employed on big farms.

(*g*) The unoccupied rentiers, living on unearned incomes, except the largest and some of the smallest—the latter a group composed mainly of retired persons, widows, poor relations of wealthy families, reduced members of the aristocracy, and other very heterogeneous minor groups.

(*h*) Full-time students who have embarked on higher education at a university or comparable level, but have not completed their education, including students drawn from working-class households.

(*i*) More doubtfully, the main body of clerks, typists and other non-manual workers whose work falls below the managerial or recognized professional level.

(*j*) Still more doubtfully, the members of certain lesser professions, such as nursing, the lower ranges of school teaching, and the less recognized social service occupations.

(*k*) Most doubtfully of all, the main body of shop assistants, warehouse workers, postal workers other than clerks, and minor institutional officials.

(*l*) Just possibly, persons belonging to the lower supervisory grades in industry, transport and other types of business, but falling below the managerial grades.

Cole's list is nearer present realities at least in this, that he makes little pretence of following a hierarchical pattern among those whom he places without reservation in the middle class. But the difficulties of hierarchical ranking are not explicitly stated, perhaps only because he is engaged not in an empirical investigation, but in a general survey of literature.

What happens when one does attempt to construct a realistic image of social structure from a more psychological point of view, i.e. in terms of the attitudes and conscious experience of actual people living actually in a town, has been frankly and sensibly stated in the course of Mrs. Stacey's discussions of the problems she encountered in her study of Banbury.[1]

The class structure revealed by the evidence collected was in

[1] M. Stacey (1961), *Tradition and Change*, Oxford University Press.

Sociological Categories for Social Differences

many ways different from what had been expected: the impossibility, for example, of placing everybody, even broadly, in one class system had not been suspected at the outset. Statistical data, measuring objective status characteristics, were collected on the assumption of a unitary system. Consequently only partial measurement of the groups finally identified and described was possible. The authors preferred, however, to describe groups which have been seen to exist rather than to classify people on an objective characteristic, thus apparently identifying and measuring a group, although it has not been observed in operation.

For Product Safety Concerns and Information please contact our EU
representative GPSR@taylorandfrancis.com
Taylor & Francis Verlag GmbH, Kaufingerstraße 24, 80331 München, Germany

www.ingramcontent.com/pod-product-compliance
Lightning Source LLC
Chambersburg PA
CBHW050556270326
41926CB00012B/2084

9 780415 605656